REVOLT AGAINST MODERNITY

American Political Thought
edited by Wilson Carey McWilliams
and Lance Banning

REVOLT AGAINST MODERNITY

Leo Strauss, Eric Voegelin, and the Search for a Postliberal Order

Ted V. McAllister

University Press of Kansas

© 1996 by the University Press of Kansas
All rights reserved

Published by the University Press of Kansas (Lawrence, Kansas
66049), which was organized by the Kansas Board of Regents and is
operated and funded by Emporia State University, Fort Hays State
University, Kansas State University, Pittsburg State University,
the University of Kansas, and Wichita State University

Library of Congress Cataloging-in-Publication Data

McAllister, Ted V.
    Revolt against modernity : Leo Strauss, Eric Voegelin, and the
search for a postliberal order / Ted V. McAllister.
        p.   cm.—(American political thought)
    Includes bibliographical references (p. 309) and index.
    ISBN 0-7006-0740-4 (hardcover)
    1. Conservatism—United States.   2. Liberalism—United States.
3. Strauss, Leo—Contributions in political science.   4. Voegelin,
Eric, 1901-   —Contributions in political science.   I. Title.
II. Series.
JC573.2.U6M36   1995
320.5′2′097309045—dc20   95-35016

British Library Cataloguing in Publication Data is available.

Printed in the United States of America

10 9 8 7 6 5 4 3 2 1

The paper used in this publication meets the minimum requirements
of the American National Standard for Permanence of Paper
for Printed Library Materials Z39.48–1984.

To my mentor and friend
Paul K. Conkin

CONTENTS

PREFACE

I began working on this book—then a dissertation—during the Bush administration. Ostensibly the nation had undergone a "conservative revolution" during the previous decade, and yet I was confused about what exactly made the times conservative or revolutionary. The key words of the political and ideological debate (words like conservation, liberal, community, rights) signified little, or too much. Politicians, pundits, scholars, virtually everyone relied heavily upon these words to mark groups and beliefs even as it became increasingly evident that few useful semantic conventions governed their usage. The most important words of our political life seemed worse than useless; they obfuscated rather than clarified.

Now, in the mid 1990s, the key words of our political lexicon seem even more divorced from the precise meanings that might allow us to understand one another. This book began, in part, as an attempt to understand better the political discourse of the last fifty years. More precisely, at least in terms of the original motivation for writing it, I attempt to define what it means to be a conservative in modern America. I largely ignore, therefore, the more popular usages that tend to go in so many directions as to make all efforts at generalization hopeless.

It would have made matters easier had I discovered that conservatism is an ideology, but I discovered that the intellectuals of the conservation "movement" reacted to modern and liberal changes (definitions pending) rather than pushing an agenda that would transform society. In their reaction (or because of their reaction) one can detect a persuasion or way of looking at the world that set them apart from liberals—including "right-wing liberals." It was here, at the level of basic attitudes toward the world, that I wanted to explore and chart. I thought as I began this study, as I do today, that any hope

of understanding the competing political views of our time depends
upon uncovering the basic philosophical commitments that, consciously or not, shape particular beliefs and political agendas. To understand conservatives and to categorize meaningfully individuals
and groups one must get beyond or behind the particular policy issues to uncover people's most basic commitments—their way of seeing the world.

To this end I endeavored to discover the intellectual heart of the
conservative movement, not its endless variety, but its irreducible
core. Since the conservative intellectual "movement" (that is, a
group of intellectuals who understand themselves to be working toward the same "conservative" ends) is largely a product of the post-
1945 era, I concentrated on the founders—those men whose books
helped energize and define the movement. I came to think of five
books as a sort of conservative Pentateuch: Richard Weaver's *Ideas
Have Consequences*, Leo Strauss's *Natural Right and History*, Eric
Voegelin's *New Science of Politics*, Russell Kirk's *The Conservative
Mind*, and Robert Nisbet's *The Quest for Community*. Many other
intellectuals participated in the evolution of the movement during
the 1950s (to say nothing of the decades since), but these five not
only penned perhaps the five most important books for the creation
of a self-conscious conservative movement but also represented the
most important divisions among conservative intellectuals.

The original project—which appeals even yet because of its
breadth and symmetry—proved too large. As I began working
through the beliefs and ideas of the five thinkers, I discovered that
the complexity of their thought (that which is all too often missed
in books and articles about these men) required an extraordinary
amount of space and that at the very least the project would require
two books. Rather than add yet another book that deals with conservative intellectuals in thumbnail sketches I decided to concentrate
on the two philosophers whose works are the most complex and the
most in need of explication—especially by a historian. My decision
to concentrate on the two least conservative of the intellectuals,
Strauss and Voegelin, was also a result of my belief that the long-
term development of the conservative intellectual movement depended (as it still does) upon a thorough philosophical defense of
conservative principles. Conservatism is a reactionary movement
that emerges only when cherished traditions, folkways, beliefs, and

norms appear threatened, but once constituted conservatism must penetrate to the philosophical issues in order to do battle with the powers of innovation. Intellectual conservatives may not be philosophers, but they do need philosophers.

In recasting my study to focus on Strauss and Voegelin I necessarily moved away from my original purpose, so this book is no longer about what I used to call the conservative imagination. It is instead about the critique of the modern world as articulated by two European emigrés. It is most difficult to think of them as American conservatives because they did not inherit the Anglo-American traditions so cherished by Russell Kirk and other traditionalists. Perhaps more to the point, neither Strauss nor Voegelin were able, in my judgment, to provide a thorough philosophical defense of the conservative principles embraced by the promoters of the movement. Still, a complete understanding of the source and nature of the problem necessarily precedes any meaningful attempt at defense. At this task Voegelin and Strauss proved nearly indispensable to the evolution of the movement.

This book is about two philosophers struggling to understand their times. For both men the point of departure was the modern age, against which they revolted. They understood liberalism to be part of modernity, albeit a part largely free from the perverse results of Nazism, communism, and even socialism. Nonetheless, because liberals share modern assumptions in common with other ideologues, Strauss and Voegelin were worried that fidelity to liberal principles would ultimately undermine liberal goals. Consequently they advocated a postliberal order—a society dedicated to basic liberal principles but fortified by a widespread belief that these principles reflect a normative order.

The flow of this book is from the general to the specific, from historical context to close textual analysis. In Chapter 1, I try to sketch out the essential "problem" that Strauss and Voegelin faced; provide key definitions to words like "conservative," "liberal," and "modern"; and supply a brief intellectual biography of each philosopher. In Chapter 2, I describe the American context of the 1950s in which these two German outsiders operated. More precisely, I explore the debate among the dominant intellectual class—liberals. Chapter 3 concerns Voegelin and Strauss as they initially confronted the cluster of problems that would dominate their careers. The context of this chapter is continental since for both men that remained their main intellectual inheritance. Thus Chapter 2 describes the issues Strauss and Voegelin faced in America while Chapter 3 explores the intellectual and philosophical context of their thinking when they came to America. Voegelin and Strauss saw American problems with European eyes.

Because the problems of modernity emerge, in the thinking of our two protagonists, as a rejection of political philosophy, this is where they began their critiques. Of course, their immediate problems required a historical inquiry into the root of the present difficulties. In Chapter 4, I examine the historical dimension of modernity—what is it and how did it emerge? Chapter 5 continues this historical analysis, but its focus is on the developing crisis of modern beliefs. The chapter ends with the problem of liberal democracy as a version of modernity. In Chapters 6 and 7, I explore the distinctive normative theories of Strauss and Voegelin, respectively. The progression of these chapters imitates the development of the thinkers. From resistance against their own times to a deeper analysis of the nature of the problem, both men struggled, finally, to articulate a postmodern and postliberal alternative. In Chapter 8, I seek to understand the relationship between these two philosophers and the American conservative movement.

I could write this book only because of the love and support that Dena Upton McAllister furnished from beginning to end. She is my wife, my friend, and (more often than she knows) my guide. As I entered a crucial phase of my writing Elisabeth entered the world—my world—full of demands. She diverted me, she charmed me, and because of her everything looks different. My parents, Vernon and Delores McAllister, have provided me with all a son could need or should want. Their undying support of me and my work bolsters me still.

I was blessed by generous financial help from numerous sources. I am especially thankful to the Woodrow Wilson Foundation for awarding me a Charlotte Newcombe Dissertation Fellowship (1992–1993). That full year of uninterrupted work was crucial to the successful completion of my dissertation. I am also grateful to the History Department at Vanderbilt, which awarded me the Sage Fellowship for 1991–1992, and during that same year the Graduate School supplied me with funds that allowed me to interview Russell

Kirk and to consult the Voegelin Papers at the Hoover Institution on War, Revolution, and Peace.

I spent an exhilarating four days in, of all places, Mecosta, Michigan. Russell and Annette Kirk welcomed me into their home and suffered several days of questions about the history of the conservative movement. They never tired of their persistent guest. While there, Dr. Kirk gave me complete access to his letters and all his papers. That peek into the constellation of conservative thinkers provided me with insights unattainable anywhere else.

Paul Carringella graciously gave me several hours of his time during my visit to the Hoover Institution, and those conversations about Voegelin helped clarify my thinking on a number of subjects. A large number of people have read parts or all of this book and supplied me with invaluable advice. Many participants in the Conkin Seminar labored through early drafts of chapters—I am especially grateful to Alexander Lian for his serious attention to the many flaws of my work. I also thank the members of my dissertation committee. Michael Bess provided me with well-placed and much-appreciated compliments to help the criticism go down more easily. George Graham, who knows me too well, saw through my feints of objective distance. Because he knew that my dissertation was freighted with deep moral and spiritual concerns, he suffered through more conversations than he ought. Lewis Perry taught me much about the sensibility of a good scholar. Such a gentle soul, he has tolerated my annoying idiosyncrasies while he cultivated my better side. I am more tolerant because of him; as a historian I am more understanding.

I am also thankful for the careful scrutiny of my manuscript provided by Jean Bethke Elshtain, J. David Hoeveler, Jr., Lance Banning, and Wilson Carey McWilliams.

The staff at the University Press of Kansas has been exceptional in every respect. I am especially thankful for the support and enthusiasm of Fred Woodward and Susan Schott. Sometimes, I think, Susan was more excited about my book than I.

Most of all, I must thank my mentor Paul K. Conkin. Although he allowed me to shape this particular work, he shaped the scholar who wrote it. To him this book is dedicated.

ABBREVIATIONS

AN   Eric Voegelin, *Anamnesis*
AR   Eric Voegelin, *Autobiographical Reflections*
CM   Leo Strauss, *The City and Man*
CW 12 Eric Voegelin, *Published Essays, 1966–1985*, vol. 12 of *The Collected Works of Eric Voegelin*
CW 28 Eric Voegelin, *What Is History? and Other Late Unpublished Writings*, vol. 28 of *The Collected Works of Eric Voegelin*
FER   Eric Voegelin, *From Enlightenment to Revolution*
LAM   Leo Strauss, *Liberalism Ancient and Modern*
NRH   Leo Strauss, *Natural Right and History*
NSP   Eric Voegelin, *The New Science of Politics*
OH 1   Eric Voegelin, *Israel and Revelation*, vol. 1 of *Order and History*
OH 3   Eric Voegelin, *Plato and Aristotle*, vol. 3 of *Order and History*
OH 4   Eric Voegelin, *The Ecumenic Age*, vol. 4 of *Order and History*
OH 5   Eric Voegelin, *In Search of Order*, vol. 5 of *Order and History*
OT   Leo Strauss, *On Tyranny*
PAW   Leo Strauss, *Persecution and the Art of Writing*
PL   Leo Strauss, *Philosophy and Law*
PP   Leo Strauss, *Political Philosophy: Six Essays by Leo Strauss*
RCPR   Leo Strauss, *The Rebirth of Classical Political Rationalism: An Introduction to the Thought of Leo Strauss*
SPPP   Leo Strauss, *Studies in Platonic Political Philosophy*
TM   Leo Strauss, *Thoughts on Machiavelli*
WPP   Leo Strauss, *What Is Political Philosophy?*

Prologue

Resting at the very heart of Western self-understanding is the paradoxical nature of human knowledge. In the paradigmatic account of this paradox the serpent appealed to Eve's lust for power. Only knowledge, he told her, separated the two humans from their creator. Godlike power, he continued, awaited an act of will since God had given her the means of her deification. Eve needed only to reject the authority of God, to act on her own authority, to lay claim to God's power. Knowledge, power, control—the eternal human dream.

Eve refused to accept on the authority of another the rules or the role that would govern her life. She preferred self-rule, and she believed that knowledge would supply her with the means to live free and independent. Eve was the first philosopher. But knowledge placed her and all humans in an alienated or naked state, exposing to her a realm of being she could only see dimly, a tantalizing if unclear image of human potential. Eve occupied a state somewhere between God and the animals, between eternity and finitude. Made in God's image, she possessed a spark of divinity, though she languished time-bound on earth, limited in perspective and knowledge while feeling the ceaseless attraction to be like God, to be with God. Stuck between God and animals she had reason to envy both—one secure in absolute knowledge, the other nestled in blissful ignorance. Eve could see the promised land from afar and felt, suddenly, homesick, a stranger in a strange land. This is the alienation born of human knowledge.

The lustful grasp for the knowledge that saves does not exhaust the range of human responses to the human condition. As mortals who feel somehow immortal, as moral creatures who are imprisoned in an unjust world, and as purposeful beings who rarely perceive clearly a grand teleology, however, humans cannot long live without challenging something, someone. Job responded to his capricious world with an admirable blend of courageous acceptance and well-placed demands for justice. The story of Job's tribulations begins with an unjust agreement between God and the deceiver to test Job's faithfulness. The suffering Job experiences as a result of this accord leaves him baffled, but his strong faith in God and His justice remains largely unchallenged. Job endures his fate because of his faith that in the end all things will work out for the best. But as the period of trial extends, even Job's endurance falters and his innate sense of justice forces him to call God to account. Despite the limitedness of Job's vision he came to believe that he was suffering unfairly and that were he to bring God before an impartial party he, not God, would win. Job's sense of justice was too powerful, too well conceived, for him to long endure injustice without reproaching God. Unlike Eve, Job did not seek to be like God or to gain greater power; he responded to his experiences with a demand that God conform to some normative standard of justice. In the end God spoke to Job, not about justice but about power. In the presence of the Almighty, the creator, Job could no longer maintain his sense of a normative ground ''beyond'' God. Justice is what God decides it is, and His designs are inscrutable. Job returned, because he had no real option, to his humanly trust of God. Job accepted his place in God's plan, but he did not understand it. He understood, however, the literal meaning of God's name: I SHALL BE WHAT I SHALL BE.

The story that follows emerges as part of the human struggle symbolized by Eve and Job. The perspective has altered somewhat, but the goals, motivations, and deep-down stupidity—to evoke Nietzsche—remain the same. If one understands the modern world to have its conception in a lust for power through knowledge, then in its old age modernity is the struggle for power without the presumption of something knowable. To ask an ontological or epistemological question is to expose oneself as naive or maladjusted.

Leo Strauss and Eric Voegelin, the subjects of this book, dared to ask the questions. No one would think them naive. But asking questions about the foundation of knowledge, or about the ground of being, or even about old-fashioned truth has been a sensible and even honorable profession for well over two thousand years. What made philosophy so unfashionable? I have no idea. But it might be worth pausing over the answers offered by Strauss and Voegelin as well as their struggle to escape the assumptions they thought had deadened the spirit of other moderns.

In odd ways I have been reminded continuously of Henry Adams as I have examined the work of these two Germans. Adams sought unity and order but refused to hide from the chaos and multiplicity of life—and not just modern life. Adams was stuck with the modern dilemmas, but he could not accept the modern answers. Strauss and Voegelin inherited the same dilemmas, but they struck out in the search for answers. To be more precise, they searched for other ways of seeing the world. Adams did the same when he examined the moral, intellectual, and spiritual furniture of the Middle Ages. He understood, but he could not accept. Adams seemed lost, not in a world of tidy natural laws, but in the grips of a nature as unpredictable and capricious as the Puritan God. Such a mysterious force, without any sense of order or purpose, becomes a new god directing the world of humans. Human destiny is bound in a realm of capricious force. Strauss and Voegelin were less deterministic in their understandings of the world and so had recourse to premodern thinkers as antidotes to modern provincialism. Whether they succeeded where Adams had failed—whether they found unity, purpose, and order—who knows?

I

Labels, Definitions, and Other Forms of Coercion

If you will not have God (and He is a jealous God) you should pay your respects to Hitler or Stalin.

T. S. Eliot

The modern world is disenchanted. The gods have gone, and with them mystery. One cannot help wondering how much the demystification of the cosmos represents the enduring human aspiration to become gods. Eve grasped the forbidden fruit because it represented the power of knowledge that could free humans from dependence upon God. Job, on the other hand, struggled to understand a God who violated the most basic human conceptions of fairness and justice. In their very different ways, both characters engaged in the most basic human struggle to find and accept one's role in the drama of existence. The stories of Eve and Job, though, have an increasingly hollow ring for moderns. Those characters played their parts in the context of a palpable god who walked among them, who spoke with them, and whose "existence" established the boundaries of their beliefs. They occupied a world in which almost every event played some role, spoke some message, had meaning in terms of purposes both human and divine. But in our world the questions raised by Job sound much like the little boy who, struggling with his Sunday school lesson, asks, Who made God? We made God, and we killed Him too. Nonetheless, as Job recognized—though he may not have accepted the idea fully—the bearings by which humans orient their lives come from the one or the many who have the power and the will to establish a normative order. If we toss aside Jehovah the burden of establishing order falls on slender human shoulders.

Like Eve, moderns believe in the redemptive power of knowledge. Mystery and uncertainty represent nothing more than the unexplored territory. In the physical realm knowledge empowers humans to manipulate and transform this world into a more comfortable home. Or, to put the matter another way, humans gain ever-increasing facility in using nature to satisfy human wants. In the social and political worlds, knowledge of behavior allows humans to achieve greater success in satisfying social desires. In both cases moderns understand these desires in terms of a world free from any contingency on divine being or any human responsibility to a normative order not of their creation. The will of the people has replaced the will of God.

The existential fallout from a cosmos purged of gods and spirits is not uniform. Although Western societies no longer sanction belief in any god or act self-consciously on behalf of a god or his principles, many people remain believers. Some live in a richly textured world in which the spiritual and the physical realms coexist. Others accept a more abstract god whose distance from this world makes him little more than an authority to whom they appeal when they near the dangerous nihilistic chasm they believe will swallow them the moment they jettison their abstract god. Still others live without any personal reference to a god. But while gods of various descriptions continue to live among us, they have little purchase on the intellectual life of our society. The same is true concerning our public or social life. In the West one is unaccustomed to hearing substantive discussions about the good or the end of a society or a government. More often than not some vague and widely held assumptions substitute for this discussion. The final authority, insofar as we can escape the elusive language of power, rests with the "people" in some sense of that abstraction. The collective desires of a body of people, as expressed through a pluralistic political structure, provide modern society with ends or goals.

These conditions of the modern West led to an intense antimodernism. The T. S. Eliot quotation at the beginning of this chapter expresses both the thrust of the cognitive claims of many antimodernists and their existential mood. Eliot wrote *The Idea of Christian Society* in 1939 after British Prime Minister Neville Chamberlain gave Hitler part of Czechoslovakia. Eliot experienced a "feeling of humiliation," not so much for the specific policy, but over the drift of a civilization in which this policy made sense—a civilizational decline in which he felt "deeply implicated and responsible." He concluded his book with this explanation of its existential source and motivation: "Was our society, which had always been so assured of its superiority and rectitude, so confident of its unexamined premisses, assembled round anything more permanent than a congeries of banks, insurance companies and industries, and had it any beliefs more essential than a belief in compound interest and the maintenance of dividends? Such thoughts as these formed the starting point, and must remain the excuse, for saying what I have to say." Another way of asking Eliot's primary question is, For what does Western civilization stand? Do Western societies have an "idea" that invests their existence with meaning or purpose? Because liberal democracies like Eliot's beloved England no longer stood for some defined normative order, they had not the stomach to stand up to Hitler. This is what Eliot meant when he said, "If you will not have God you should pay your respects to Hitler or Stalin."[1]

By the end of World War II the social, political, and intellectual deformity of Western thought known as Nazism had became evil incarnate. With Germany in ruins and Nazism vanquished, the entire struggle passed easily into popular history as the classic struggle between good and evil. For a whole range of thinkers, however, the "good war" had heightened their concern for political and moral conundrums once confined to the airy discussions of "intellectuals." For those thinkers equipped with the sensitive moral compass of a T. S. Eliot these conundrums represented nothing less than a challenge to Western civilization. The experiences of the first half of the twentieth century had the effect of presenting the long-standing crisis of the West as an especially urgent matter.

In the decades following the war diverse thinkers sought to understand something they called "modernity." The complicated lines of thought that wrapped around this concept linked this discussion with similar efforts reaching back to Kant. This present book focuses on two scholars, Leo Strauss and Eric Voegelin, who shared with Eliot the belief that modernity encompassed Nazism, communism, and liberalism. They detected family resemblances in these ideologies, and they labored to lay bare the modern core, the "genetic code" that linked the apparently good sister of liberalism to her violent brothers. In the reified discussion of modernity, the entire cluster of related ideologies belongs to a dysfunctional family. Resting at the existential core of the protagonists of this story was the fear that despite a stable liberal democracy, America might eventually pay its respects to a Hitler or a Stalin.

LABELS

If the malcontents of modernity diagnose a disease affecting the spiritual, intellectual, political, and social realms they must do so from an understanding of health. A critique of modernity entails some desired alternative. All the same, even the most thoughtful and articulate medical doctor would be hard pressed to define health. The same is true with social and spiritual life. Health emerges as a concept only in the context of a perceived disease. Although sickness does not define health, it certainly provides the occasion for thinking about the matter. As a concept, disease presupposes something normative (health); nonetheless, it should not surprise us that most critics focus upon the easier task of diagnosing the problem. Moreover, we ought to expect critics to find more commonality in their diagnosis than in their prescription.

So it was for Leo Strauss and Eric Voegelin. They did not fit into any easily identifiable camp, nor did they share a normative theory. Nonetheless, some label or tag helps locate them in a larger field of critics. They were conservative antimoderns. That is, their antimodernism pointed back toward something lost, a heritage worth recapturing. Unfortunately, the word "conservative" is no sooner uttered than a whole series of images—usually conflicting—shrouds our thinking. The biggest problem with the label is its generalized use in a schema that organizes beliefs in relation to one another on a two-dimensional field. The traditional linear construction of beliefs bounded by two poles has the distinct advantage of relating beliefs to one another in an unambiguous way. To think and speak in this sort of shorthand is not a structural requirement of language but a strategy designed to give one a sense of intellectual surefootedness. The intellectual terrain viewed from this perspective has no hills or dips, only a straight, narrow beam running from left to right. Constricting the intellectual topography to two dimensions brings any number of compatriots together as well as tossing an enormous range of others into a manageable number of camps. Unfortunately, this form of intellectual mapping conceals as much as it exposes, and perhaps for this reason we seem wedded to it.

In the case of Voegelin and Strauss the conservative label presents special problems. Numerous books on American conservatism draw Strauss and Voegelin into the conservative orbit, often without useful or careful qualifications. Voegelin was especially upset when the label was applied to him. In one particularly vigorous response Voegelin upbraided John East for his application of the conservative label to Voegelin's work. He wrote in a personal letter: "I have not spent the time of my life and done my work, in order to amuse and comfort American Conservatives. It is, of course, quite legitimate to write an essay about the reception my work has found among conservatives, but I am afraid a serious treatment of this subject would have to become a satire on the Conservatives." Voegelin wrote the letter in response to an essay that East later incorporated into his book *The American Conservative Movement.* Voegelin accused East, with cause, of taking scattered quotes out of context and pasting them together into a patchwork conservative cloth. "In order to make it complete," Voegelin continued, "you would have had to confront the actual content and purpose of my work, which has nothing to do with conservative predilections. . . . Why you have left the satire incomplete, I am sure, you will know best yourself. But as a basis for satirical purposes your study merits high praise, and I shall use it sometime." The correspondence with East, of which this was the most caustic letter, demonstrates the great frustration Voegelin experienced in the late 1970s after his work had been misunderstood by politically oriented conservatives for nearly three decades. Voegelin objected primarily to the way labels tended to flatten out his work and to the fact that East and others used his work to buttress a political persuasion he did not openly share.[2] Strauss, for his part, invited an appropriation of his work by those who misunderstood him.

Nonetheless, both men played important roles in the development of a conservative intellectual movement born in the 1950s that retains a pugnacious vitality appropriate to a minority—with the help of several well-financed institutions. The history of American conservative "intellectuals" (a label they abhor) is complicated by alliances of convenience, an ill-advised marriage between cultural conservatives and politically oriented classical liberals, and a popular

expansion of the meaning of the word "conservative." These confusions obscure the very significant differences between such porous
groups as traditionalist conservatives, neoconservatives, classical
liberals, numerous other hybrids, and an odd assortment of angry
men and women. All definitional boundaries seem arbitrary. Even
Russell Kirk, whom I take to be the best example of an American
conservative—in style and belief—found numerous affinities with
cultural critics on the left while supporting politicians on the right,
from Barry Goldwater to Ronald Reagan (even Patrick Buchanan).
Whatever the word may mean, I use it to describe a way of seeing the
world: a conservative imagination that contrasts sharply with modern, instrumentalist, ways of thinking.

The model for my own definition is what people often call "traditional conservatism." Strauss and Voegelin were not fully conservatives in this sense, especially considering the reverence conservatives have for the Anglo-American tradition. Rather, in their case,
"conservative" modifies antimodernism—it helps locate their version of antimodernism. Nonetheless, an etymological exploration of
the word "conservative" should help suggest something about the
direction of their thinking. By moving from the most generalized attitude to a reasonably rigid set of beliefs (an ideal type), the conservative label may help explain the sense in which Strauss and Voegelin moved into the conservative movement without becoming a part
of it.

All conservatives reject modernity (which is understood in many
different ways) while at the same time wishing to preserve "Western
civilization." It is this yearning to preserve what appears terribly
threatened that makes them conservatives. But since both of the
terms "modern" and "Western civilization" require lengthy expla-
nations, I should outline those views more specifically. What would
an ideal conservative believe? I began this section with the metaphor
of health and disease applied to social and political life because such
language assumes a belief in some normative order or an authoritative standard to which humans are responsible. For this reason one
characteristic of most conservatives is a chronic concern for order, or
the search for order, or the experience of order.

Since an order transcending human control must be accessible in
some measure for it to be of any use to humans, we may accept as a
postulate of conservatives that they believe humans can "know"

something about the order that embraces their lives. Consequently, they reject the "modern" restriction of knowledge to the "objective" knowledge obtained through the methods of the physical sciences. More comprehensively, conservatives reject the subject/object dualism that fostered the division of human experiences into the privileged and reliable experiences of the senses (the objective realm) and the suspect and private nonsensual experiences (the realm of the subjective). In contrast to the sterile intellectual universe created by Descartes, in which humans are abstractly separated from the objects of their knowledge and little remains that might constitute knowledge except physical objects and their relationships as well as tautologies, conservatives embrace a participatory theory of knowledge. Accordingly, humans participate in a reality not of their making, a reality with several strata that humans may understand by examining their participation in being. It is meaningless to refer to "objective knowledge," since the only knowledge available to humans comes from inside. Humans are part of that which they seek to know.

With regard to philosophical matters, antimodern conservatives operate within the traditional categories of ontology, epistemology, and anthropology, all three of which have been challenged by recent philosophical moves. Rich variety characterizes conservative philosophical thought, but conservatives share the goal of recapturing what they believe to be essential philosophical questions or problems—the very questions that certain versions of "modernity" have eclipsed by emphasizing the scientifically knowable. Consequently, conservatives characteristically take a "classical" turn, emphasizing the objectives if not always the conclusions of ancient Hellenic philosophy. They seek to return Western thought to the perennial questions that have slipped slowly out of the philosophical horizon, though they remain very real issues in the political and social realms. I will explore the substance of these questions throughout this book.

Related to clearly and traditionally philosophical matters are the "conservative" social and political principles that emerge from the conservative construction of the normative order and of human nature. These two constituents of reality remain constants in an otherwise perpetually changing political and social order. Consequently, conservatives believe in no paradigmatic human political and social structure, only flexible and general principles learned through centuries of human experience, reason, and, for some, revelation. The most important principles are: one, the social need for a myth or a "meta-narrative" to invest a society with a communal sense of purpose and meaning; two, the need to provide members of a society with a sense of community, belonging, rootedness; three, the social need for competing nodes of authority (like state, church, family, guild, union, village) as the context for the development of personal identity as well as a protection against the aggrandizement of power by a single authority; four, a recognition of the fundamentally hierarchical nature of existence and the social need for hierarchy; and five, the prescriptive roles of tradition, habit, and prejudice as protection from abstract innovation. Recognition of these conditions comes from an apperception of the normative order and from a reading of human nature. One common characteristic of these principles is their nonabstract character. Conservatives begin their thinking with the social character of humans (in contrast to an abstracted human in the state of nature) and work through the ways societies have most effectively met human needs. Even the individual as a human personality emerges as a product of a social environment—without society, there are no humans.

Do any conservatives fit this ideal type? Many come very close—Russell Kirk and Robert Nisbet come to mind. Eric Voegelin and Leo Strauss clearly differ from the ideal type in important ways. Strauss's emphasis upon "nature," at first glance, appears to undermine any order resting upon habit and prescription. However, Strauss's teachings concerning "nature" as a standard serve a conservative function of undermining historicist or relativist arguments against a normative order. His motivations were nothing if not "conservative," and it is no wonder his most popular book, and the book most embraced and plundered by conservatives, focused upon the problem of natural right in the modern world. The case of Leo Strauss is instructive because his early reception by conservatives—many like Kirk later rejected him—points to an inherent tension in conservative thought. Conservatives affirm a normative order while holding human traditions in high esteem. They affirm an authoritative order that transcends human control while emphasizing that the limits of human knowledge necessitate a reliance upon developing methods of adapting to the changing world (tradition, habit, prejudice).

The labeling game can go on forever. What is amazing, however, is how well Voegelin and the teaching of Strauss fit the model. No doubt in the 1950s their books influenced a generation of conservatives. Later disaffection seems to have more to do with religious differences than anything else. Yet the basic structure of their positions retains an essentially conservative cast—at least their philosophical assumptions closely resemble those of traditionalist conservatives. Without question, self-conscious conservatives have found and continue to find much that is instructive in the works of both men. If Strauss and Voegelin did not join the conservative movement, they received honorary memberships—or should I say they were drafted into it? At the very least, both philosophers shared with self-professed conservatives a rejection of modernity. More than that, the philosophical critique of the modern world offered by conservatives since the mid 1950s rests primarily upon the work of Strauss and Voegelin.

THE MEANINGS OF MODERNITY

The word "modern" means more and more these days. Unfortunately, more is less when applied to the currency of a word, as the range of possible meanings expands so far that the word cries out for adjectives. To make matters less clear, scholars increasingly employ the even more elusive words "premodern" and "postmodern" as though they marked some unambiguous cognitive territory familiar to all their listeners and readers. Nonetheless, these confusions should not cloud the fact that thinkers have for some time thought in terms of a historical category called "modern" that separates the present from earlier ages like the ancient era and the medieval era. A consciousness of historical periodization and of distinct differences separating the present era from those that came before is itself a modern notion, and therefore is bound up in any useful definition of the word. More important for our present concern, this consciousness of difference tends to make people reflect about the novelties of their own age and its internal and even subterranean logic.

This self-reflection on the very philosophical or perhaps even mythical foundations of one's civilization has grown steadily since Kant. The nineteenth and twentieth centuries have witnessed a proliferating concern about modernity primarily because of the fear that "it" will eventually implode after "reason" has emptied its moral and metaphysical core of meaning. The numerous but related concerns about this possibility may be called "the crisis of modernity." To understand the various meanings that people have given to this crisis, we must stipulate that modernity has a project or goal. One is hard pressed to provide clear temporal boundaries to this process, but the developing confidence of the thinkers of the so-called Enlightenment in the human capacity to know and in due course to control the reality in which humans participate will serve as the modern project (this assumption seems to be nearly universal among those who speak of a crisis of modernity). Ever since the Renaissance, a growing faith in the power of human knowledge has propelled an extensive intellectual examination of almost all beliefs. At first these activities did not threaten ancient assumptions, but the hegemony of the Christian construction of reality did not long remain unchallenged in a skeptical age. By the eighteenth century, a wide range of intellectuals considered themselves free thinkers. They no longer labored under irrational beliefs enjoined on orthodox Christians. Yet even as Voltaire, Paine, and Jefferson challenged the peculiarly Christian doctrines, they assumed and therefore defended the Semitic cosmology that lay beneath. God remained largely unchallenged and undoubted.

Enlightenment confidence rested upon faith in human reason to unlock mysteries long shrouded by superstition. God's great creation would someday give up its secrets, and humans would possess unimagined control. The skepticism that in part cleared the intellectual space for the Enlightenment also cast into doubt the very instrument that was to usher in a new age of human knowledge and control. David Hume, for instance, challenged orthodox beliefs in causation by calling into question the necessary connection between facts. How can we "know" that A caused B just by noting that B followed A? Kant salvaged faith in human reason by restricting the realm of rational inquiry to phenomena. He saved reason by eliminating metaphysics from its orbit (understanding metaphysics in a very broad way). The rich and confusing debate that followed stretched to many fields of inquiry but returned always to the questions, What and how can we know? Kant saved reason at an awful cost.

To this crisis of rationality we must add the related phenomenon of a crisis of faith. As faith in "science" grew, concern abounded over the more clearly human problems of meaning, morality, and metaphysics. For an increasing number of intellectuals in the nineteenth century, religion became a matter of private belief about imponderables. Without the sanction of reason how could one speak of "knowledge" about God, morality, or transcendental teleologies? The matter grew more precarious as various evolutionary theories challenged the very Semitic cosmology that was so central to Western self-understanding. Whereas earlier challenges to religion had focused upon particular Christian doctrines, evolution went to the heart of the Semitic cosmology of God and creation by accounting for life in all its variety and plenitude. Belief in God became obsolete.

These challenges to past verities spawned numerous attempts to regain certainty. But so long as these efforts progressed using modern notions of rationality, the area about which humans could speak with confidence would grow very small. Certainty achieved at the cost of a self-imposed silence concerning the most important human issues hardly seemed satisfactory. In the late nineteenth century, a group of philosophers of what James Kloppenberg called the "via media" began to seek a way to live with the contingency and uncertainty of the modern world.[3] Knowledge became a human tool for making our way in the world. Rejecting more appeals to some transcendental norm, or to any form of ontology, these philosophers made the operable words of human society like "good," "just," "right," and even "knowledge" into contingent and historical artifacts. They recognized the need to address the social and political matters of meaning, purpose, and value, but they did not accept the older forms of dealing with these concerns. Human matters were now purely human matters.

These constructions of modernity as a philosophical problem developed alongside other concerns. Modernity also meant revolution (best expressed by the French Revolution) as a means to re-create utterly human social and political life. Some people used the word in reference to large and impersonal processes like industrialization, urbanization, bureaucratization, and collectivization. Critics of modernity often attributed these processes to the Enlightenment attempt to use reason to control every aspect of human life, an attempt that bore great if bitter fruit in the scientific revolutions that followed. The relationship between humans and nature—or at least human attitudes about this relationship—have changed, making nature the servant of human needs.

With regard to the more purely philosophical debates, Voegelin and Strauss rejected root and branch the "modern" categories perpetuated since Descartes. Much like the philosophers of the via media, both men accepted a more holistic understanding of human experience. However, they extended their analysis to a normative center. All humans experience what Voegelin called a "primordial community of being" structured by four identifiable constituents: "God and man, world and society."[4] The universality of this structure provides an ahistorical construction of human reality, though any understanding of its structure is historical. As an actor or participant in being, humans have the task of making sense of their individual and collective lives "in terms of ends divine and human." Antimodern conservatives believe that the philosophical investigation of the human experience of reality is a science and that we can claim "knowledge" about our experience of God just as we can claim "knowledge" about our experience of the "world." In all cases our knowledge is incomplete and open to revision, but the structure we examine is unchanged so long as we remain human.

This understanding of the crisis of modernity places the emphasis upon constricting the horizon of investigation—the limiting of "science" to phenomena. Because conservatives believe that humans belong to an order not of their making, they understand the paradigmatic human pursuit to be a search for attunement to this order. Because modernity developed through a restriction that eclipsed the normative order, conservatives saw modern attempts at order as destined to create unprecedented social and existential disorder. This "egophanic revolt," as Voegelin labeled it, led to revolutions, rational planning, and more generally to increasingly collective attempts to ameliorate human problems. The rationalization and collectivization of human energies, first by capitalists and then by states, created an ugly industrial and urban landscape, a polluted earth, a mass society, a homogenized culture, and, paradoxically, a deep sense of homelessness in a world entirely under human control. These are the fruits of a society driven by a mania to control and master, a society no longer chastened by a belief in a creator who has given into human hands the husbandry of his creation.

Because the dangers of modernity served as the common ingredient in the thinking of Strauss and Voegelin, the biographical sketches that follow trace the evolution of their critiques. These critiques, of course, are investigated much more thoroughly in later chapters, but the contrast that follows exposes the broad outline of the themes that dominate this book.

ERIC VOEGELIN

If philosophers were judged on the incomprehensibility of their work, Voegelin could be compared with the likes of Hegel. Voegelin's philosophical explorations taxed language to bear the weighty content of his insight. He could advance only as far as his language would allow him. Impasses forced Voegelin to seek new words, not simply to convey his thought, but as tools to pursue a line of inquiry. Voegelin's linguistic tools are precise, and for that reason they are not always clear to others. His neologisms express something no other words convey and therefore tax the reader to understand his always precise meanings. Voegelin wrote to understand, a sort of vehicle for his philosophical journey. The vast written record of this journey (both published and unpublished) is rich, but only to the person willing to labor over virtually every word and to engage earnestly in the same journey.

For Voegelin, modernity is the age of ideology, and by ideology he meant a closed intellectual system in which human knowledge serves as a means of achieving earthly felicity. This intellectual closure is not restricted to identifiable ideologues but to varying degrees affects the entire culture of the West. Voegelin's reflections on Hitler help clarify the philosopher's meaning: "The phenomenon of Hitler is not exhausted by his person. His success must be understood in the context of an intellectually or morally ruined society in which personalities who otherwise would be grotesque, marginal figures can come to public power because they superbly represent the people who admire them."[5] Voegelin's indictment rests with the German people rather than Hitler; German society had so decayed that Hitler could become the spiritual representative of the people.

Born in the first year of the twentieth century (1901), Voegelin's life spanned a number of ideological clashes. He grew up in Germany and Austria, where he received a classical education in a *Realgymnasium*, which emphasized language (he studied Latin, English, and Italian), physics, and mathematics. Because of the excitement generated by the Russian Revolution, Voegelin used his time before entering university to read *Das Kapital*. "Being a complete innocent in such matters," Voegelin reflected many years later, "I was of course convinced by what I read, and I must say that from August of 1919, to about December of that year I was a Marxist. By Christmas the matter had worn off," with the assistance of university classes in economic theory.[6] Voegelin flirted with an ideology only this one time, he proclaimed, but the problem it posed in his world became central to his work.

When Voegelin matriculated at the University of Vienna in 1919 to pursue a doctorate in political science *(Doctor rerum politicarum)*, he entered perhaps the most intellectually energized atmosphere in Europe. In economics, "the Austrian school" begun by Eugen Boehm-Bawberk continued into the second and third generation, including the young Ludwig von Mises (and, as a student, Fredrick von Hayek). In physics there was Moritz Schlick (and his Vienna Circle); in law, Hans Kelsen; and similar luminaries in psychology, art, and philosophy. Perhaps more important for Voegelin's intellectual development were the very talented students and young professors who pursued their high-octane discussions in various non-or semiformal ways. Voegelin tells of one group of which he was a member *(Geistkreis*, spiritual or intellectual circle) that met once a month to listen to and then "tear to pieces" a paper presented by a member of the group. Voegelin presented more papers than any other member and rather enjoyed the fierce but amicable game they played. And he played the game very well. One friend characterized Voegelin as having a "fiendish erudition and the ability to take off vertically from any question whatever, to disappear within minutes in the theoretical ionosphere, leaving a trail of recondite references behind."[7] Voegelin worked on his doctorate, which he received in 1922, under the direction of Hans Kelsen, a neo-Kantian professor of law who drafted the Austrian Constitution (1920), and Othmar Spann, a romanticist much influenced by German idealism. Voegelin tried to puzzle through the competing philosophic schools vying for attention in central Europe and was influenced early on by his professor Hans Kelsen, whose Pure Theory of Law had made him famous. Kelsen operated within the neo-Kantian categories worked out by Hermann Cohen of Marburg. The problem for Voegelin with this form of neo-Kantianism was its restrictive method, which "determined the field of science by the method used in its exploration."[8] In Kelsen's case political theory *(Staatslehre)* became the theory of law *(Rechtslehre)*, making everything beyond the scope of the theory of law outside the realm of political theory.

Another important early influence was Max Weber, perhaps the most imposing intellectual figure in Germany and Austria at the time. Reading Weber reinforced Voegelin's animus for ideology. Weber did offer a useful distinction between ethics of intention and ethics of responsibility. Ideologues are blinded by their heady goals and do not consider the immediate effects of their actions, which they hope will usher in the desired future. Voegelin emphasized that "no excuse for the evil consequences of moralistic action could be found in the morality or nobility of one's intentions. A moralistic end does not justify immorality of action."[9] In other areas, however, Voegelin found Weber's work problematic. In an attempt to make social science a science, Weber restricted the role of the scientist to an exploration of cause and effect. Like Kelsen's neo-Kantianism, this restriction amounted to the method dictating the subject, a sort of reductionism (which became legion among various positivists) that Voegelin found most unsatisfying. He wanted the realm of science to be much broader and applied to all areas of human experience. He wanted the questions scientists ask to be more important.

During the mid 1920s, Voegelin studied in the United States as a Laura Spellman Rockefeller Fellow. "These two years in America," he wrote, "brought the great break in my intellectual development."[10] During his first year he studied at Columbia University, taking classes from, among others, John Dewey. Through Dewey, Voegelin came into contact with the English common sense tradition, which sent him working back to Thomas Reid and Sir William Hamilton.[11] Even during this first year, America's rich philosophical heritage inoculated him against "the methodological environment" of central Europe. During his second year in the United States he divided his time between Harvard, where he was influenced by Alfred North Whitehead (a visiting professor from England), and Wisconsin, where he studied with John R. Commons. One other intellectual influence of these years was the works of George Santayana. From all these experiences Voegelin wrote the book *On the Form of the American Mind* (1928). He had left Vienna a provincial; he returned a cosmopolitan. After his American sojourn, the raging debates that had once been so important to him left him cold.

Voegelin returned to Vienna (1929), after an additional year in France, to take a position as lecturer at the University of Vienna (later, associate professor). Already the environment was much changed, with increasing ideological strife and National Socialism's growing influence in Germany and Austria. Voegelin began working on subjects related to National Socialism such as examining race doctrines, especially the biological theories that supported them. He produced three books— *Race and State, The Race Idea in Intellectual History,* and *Political Religions*—each of which undermined Nazi theories. Because of the political climate these books had short lives, the second book was removed from circulation by its Berlin publisher in 1933, the same year it came into print. These books would still play a very important role in Voegelin's life, especially when the Nazis came goose-stepping into Vienna in 1938. Voegelin's work on the race myth and his well-known dislike for ideologies in general, and National Socialism in particular, made him a target for the Gestapo. He escaped to Zurich the same day his wife confronted a Gestapo agent at their door. Both Voegelin and his wife made their way to the United States, leaving behind most of their possessions, though he secured his library.

Once in the United States, Voegelin bounced around, moving from Harvard to Bennington College to the University of Alabama, until he finally settled at Louisiana State University in 1942. He began working on a massive project bearing the title, "The History of Political Ideas," but in 1945, after having written over four-thousand typed pages, Voegelin came to the conclusion that the study was theoretically flawed.[12] "It dawned on me that the conception of a history of ideas was an ideological deformation of reality. There were no ideas unless there were symbols of immediate experience. Moreover, one could not handle under the title 'ideas' an Egyptian Coronation ritual."[13] Ideas are secondary constructions that depend upon experience.

Voegelin did not first understand how he should proceed, and he dropped the project.[14] He began afresh in 1951 when he delivered the Walgreen Lectures in Chicago, published later under the title, *The New Science of Politics: An Introduction* (1952). Really a sort of prolegomenon to his magisterial series *Order and History,* this book performed two related services. In it, Voegelin examined the contemporary state of political science and how it had sunk to this point, and he attempted a restoration of premodern political theory. The work served both as a declension story and as an introduction to a "new science of politics" that is rather old. It was, on the whole, an arrogantly written book. Voegelin dismissed without so much as an argument whole schools of thought while casting his own work as more "scientific." This assurance of his own position lasted his entire career, but he also displayed great courage in rejecting some parts of his earlier work when he discovered that they were flawed.

For the rest of his life Voegelin worked on what amounts to a history of consciousness. Especially important works, which stand like signposts marking his intellectual journey, are the five volumes of *Order and History* (volumes 1–3 were printed in 1956–1957, volume 4 in 1974, and volume 5 in 1987); *Science, Politics, and Gnosticism* (German edition in 1959 and the English edition in 1968); and especially *Anamnesis* (German edition in 1966, a somewhat altered edition in English in 1978). These works represent Voegelin's attempt to overcome the theoretical problems he had detected while writing "The History of Political Ideas" in the 1940s. No brief summary of this body of literature is possible, but I will discuss this phase of Voegelin's work at greater length later.

In 1958, after the first three volumes of *Order and History* had been published, Voegelin left Louisiana State to become the director of the Institute for Political Science and a professor at the University of Munich, where he stayed until 1969. In that year he became the Henry Salvatori Distinguished Scholar at the Hoover Institution on War, Revolution, and Peace at Stanford University. In 1974 he retired, but he continued to live in the San Francisco Bay area, still teaching and lecturing, until his death in 1985.

In Voegelin's copious works one finds numerous pages about "modernity" and the conditions for its emergence. His clearest and simplest, though not especially thorough, account appears in *The New Science of Politics*. To put the matter briefly, modernity is a gnostic revolt against reality. Voegelin chose the word "gnostic" because it refers to claims about esoteric knowledge, knowledge that saves, but the problem is that most people associate the word with the infamous group of early Christians who were known as Gnostics. Voegelin, however, intended no such specific reference. Gnosticism, in the Voegelinian sense, is a belief in the power of knowledge to transform reality, to create earthly perfection. It refers, moreover, to an existential core that has three primary components: one, a strong sense of alienation, a feeling that some essential part of one's humanity is unfulfilled; two, a revolt against the conditions that create alienation; and three, a belief that human knowledge is sufficient to overcome these conditions, that humans have the power to transform themselves, or both.

Every society requires a symbolic expression of reality to give meaning to its existence—and to the existence of its members. These symbolic expressions emerge from human experience and subsist until a "leap in being" provides a deeper understanding of reality, through the medium of a single person. All symbolic expressions are inadequate because they emerge from human participation within the reality they wish to understand. Therefore, pressures springing from human experience demonstrate the uncertainty of human understanding, spawning the perpetual dream of grasping the whole of reality with the certainty of a god, a creator. Given the anxiety of human life, torn between the material world and the pneumatic pull from a palpable spiritual source, the greatest temptation is to believe in a symbolic expression of a deformed but fully intelligible reality. Modernity is just such a deformation.

The Christian order, articulated best by St. Augustine, had radically separated the mundane (earthly) from the divine (a result Voegelin called de-divinized) by emphasizing the eternal destiny of humans. Gone were the polytheistic societies in which the divine and the mundane commingled in the world. The Christian order separated the mundane from the divine, which secured the sense of human limitation while promising perfection in another world. Modernity, as Voegelin meant it, is the process by which the world is re-divinized and the uncertainty of faith (as expressed in Hebrews 11:1) is replaced with the certainty of ideology.

Joachim of Flora, in the twelfth century, began the gnostic revolt by creating the "aggregate of symbols which govern the self-interpretation of modern political society to this day."[15] Joachim developed a new conception of history around a trinitarian eschatology, in which history is divided into three stages or periods, each represented by a member of the Trinity. Each age is progressively more spiritual than the previous and the third, scheduled to begin in 1260, "would bring the perfect spiritual life." This tripartite progressive view of history became a standard way for ideologues to view historical reality, which culminated with the third and perfect period. Unlike Augustine's sharp separation of the mundane and the divine, this view of history has the divine working in history to produce some utopian end time (later, the divine collapses into the human). History has a meaning that the seer (prophet) can understand. There would be many seers.

This sort of gnostic symbolism proved very attractive since it resolved the tension necessarily associated with faith (it not only explained history but gave an inevitability to it). "Gnosticism," as Voegelin used the word, represented an attempt to alter the inevitable human perspective, from participant in a whole not of one's making (seeing from the inside) to observer and participant, having access to some Archimedean point. Ideologies require this assumed perspective because they suppose a closed system about which they have knowledge. Gnosticism is a closing of the soul and the construction of an alternative reality, "a counterexistential dream world."[16]

The process that began with Joachim culminated in twentieth-century totalitarianism. "The immanentization of the Christian eschaton made it possible to endow society in its natural existence with a meaning which Christianity denied to it. And totalitarianism of our time must be understood as journey's end of the Gnostic search for a civil society."[17] Voegelin's construction of "modern" history turns on the importance of the new symbolization that Joachim created; few scholars have given so obscure a figure such a central place in the drama of history. The distance between this medieval monk and Hitler is vast and filled with numerous figures who, infected with a belief in the saving power of knowledge, have played their roles in the deadening story of modernity. According to Voegelin's account, each of these thinkers, in very different ways, believed that he had obtained the knowledge necessary to transform this earthly world of woe into a paradise. Those dispossessed of utopian imagery nonetheless projected a progressive future fueled by human knowledge and control over the environment. Of all the gnostic paths the most enduring is "science." Modern science is a visible tool of "progressive" change, and ever since the nineteenth century, "science" has been the primary repository of human knowledge and faith. The church, with its uncertainties, could not challenge "science," which offered people increased control over their lives. The dream of supreme knowledge and control works in the modern era to seduce people into believing in an ideology in the same way the serpent seduced Eve.

Gnosticism, Voegelin admitted, unleashed phenomenal creative

energy. The attempt to remake the world "produced the truly mag-
nificent spectacle of western progressive society"—but the price of
such a spectacle was high.

> The death of the spirit is the price of progress. Nietzsche revealed
> this mystery of the Western apocalypse when he announced that
> God was dead and that He had been murdered. This Gnostic mur-
> der is constantly committed by the men who sacrifice God to civi-
> lization. The more fervently all human energies are thrown into
> the great enterprise of salvation through world-immanent action,
> the farther the human beings who engage in this enterprise move
> away from the life of the spirit. And since the life of the spirit is the
> source of order in man and society, the very success of a Gnostic
> civilization is the cause of its decline.[18]

"The order of history emerges out of the history of order," Voegelin
wrote at the beginning of *Order and History.* In its historical dimension,
human existence exhibits an intelligible structure. Humans have always
tried to understand the reality of which they form a part and to orient
themselves to their conception of the whole. The history of order is the
history of human societies symbolically expressing their experiences of
order. Even though those symbolic expressions differ with regard to their
grasp of separate structures in reality, they each express the same reality.
Attempts to deform that reality, to ignore one's experience of reality, is
an attempt to escape the tension that is necessarily part of any honest
approach to the human condition. But reality remains constant, and the
structure of a humanly fabricated reality can only bend so far before it
breaks. One senses while reading Voegelin's work that he believed the
ideological worlds were about to collapse under the pressure of reality.
The struggle for a new symbolization of order was beginning, and he expected that, like Moses and Plato, he was contributing to a further differentiation of reality and a more adequate symbolic order.

LEO STRAUSS

No thinker was more oriented to "the crisis of the West" than Leo
Strauss. One may see his entire career as a project with two parts: exposing the "modern project" and recovering classical philosophy. Such
an enormous effort resists attempts at quick summary, made the more

difficult by the elusive methods for which Strauss is infamous. Strauss strove to teach the teachable how to read, which is to say how to read the works of great philosophers. One must read Strauss the way he read the greats. In his method lies part of his answer to the modern problem. This is all very cryptic. His methods differ profoundly from his contemporary political philosophers, and his messages are ''guarded by seven seals.'' To understand his teachings requires patience and a bracketing of traditional ''modern'' categories. Strauss's work is internally coherent, but one must learn the rules by which Strauss operated. We can begin to understand the development of these rules, this private language, by tracing Strauss's intellectual development.

Two facts about Strauss's birth in 1899 would prove very important in shaping his intellectual perspective. He was born Jewish and German, and the conjunction of these two facts with the cultural, intellectual, and political upheaval of the first half of the twentieth century placed Strauss in a rich, complex, and lively cultural and intellectual universe and a political context that challenged him to examine the assumptions that dominated his universe in light of especially compelling and personal questions and problems. From his first book, published in 1930, to his final posthumous work (published in 1989, sixteen years after his death), one can trace an ongoing engagement with a single problem—the problem of modernity, a symbol for the congeries of problems he faced as an intellectual in the highly charged environment of Weimar and Nazi Germany. More precisely, modernity meant the rejection of the method and goals of classical political philosophy. Strauss's method of addressing—if not always answering—the problem(s) was to engage in a conversation with the most important and interesting philosophers of the tradition that had handed him this conundrum. To understand Strauss requires that one understand the tradition he inherited and the conventional interpretation of the seminal figures of that tradition. No short cuts; Strauss's work is too elliptical for that.

Strauss was raised an orthodox Jew in Kirchhain, Hessen, in south-central Germany, a rural area north of Frankfurt. He was educated at the Gymnasium Philippinum in Marburg and graduated from there in 1917. After World War I, in which he served in the German army, Strauss studied philosophy at several schools, including the University of Hamburg where he earned his Ph.D. under the direction of Ernst Cassirer. Strauss continued his education after his doctorate (which he took at the age of twenty-two) by studying and doing research at schools across Germany, including Freiburg where he had brief contact with Husserl and Heidegger. In most German universities philosophical debate was highly charged and erudite. No single school of thought predominated, but common to most was a sense of uncertainty, with roots stretching back as least as far as Kant. But the uncertainty of the twentieth century appeared more ominous because it had spread from the cloistered ranks of philosophers to a larger portion of the population, though in popularized or vulgarized form. The experiences of World War I and the chaos that followed further heightened the anxiety many thinkers were experiencing. Strauss's commitments in this debate are not clear, though he seems to have held, and in some respects retained, neo-Kantian views. More important, he was much influenced by Husserl's phenomenology and his attempt at a new ontology.

In 1925, Strauss accepted a position at the Academy of Jewish Research (Akademie für Wissenschaft das Judentums) in Berlin. His research there led to his first book and the first expression of his life-long problem. The book was *Die Religionskritik Spinozas als Grundlage seiner Bibelwissenschaft* (first published in 1930; published in English in 1965 with the title *Spinoza's Critique of Religion*); his life-long problem: "The theologico-political problem has remained *the* theme of my studies." As Strauss's student Allan Bloom correctly noted, Strauss's early work on Jewish thought, of which the book on Spinoza was the first fruit, was influenced by his concern for "the Jewish problem." Should Jews try to assimilate, or should they try to establish a separate Jewish state? Strauss seemed unwilling to embrace either option. Bloom wrote: "Strauss, while accepting the Zionist view of assimilation, wondered whether a strictly political and secular response to the Jewish situation in Europe was sufficient and whether a Jewish state that rejected the faith in the Biblical revelation would have any meaning."[19] His belief in the inevitable conflict between philosophy and revelation exacerbated this theologico-political[20] problem. Depending upon incompatible assumptions, these two ways of looking at the world could never be made compatible—although their tension is the genius of Western civilization. What relationship should religious orthodoxy have to the political order? If, as Strauss assumed, the life of intransigent inquiry (the life of the philosopher) and the life of faith were ultimately incompatible, and if the political order depended upon a minimum orthodoxy to provide it with purposes and moral beliefs, what becomes of a society in which citizens cling to revelation while accepting philosophical assumptions not clearly compatible with orthodox religion?

To help understand such issues, Strauss turned to the famous Jewish philosopher whose work helped undermine faith in revelation, Spinoza. Although Strauss found that Spinoza examined religious issues with the methods and assumptions of philosophy (and thus found an acceptance of the literal teachings of the Torah intellectually untenable), Strauss emphasized the different assumptions grounding the two positions, insulating each from an examination based on the methods of the other. Only by accepting the assumptions of philosophy can one find persuasive a critique of revelation on those grounds.

Wishing to understand the attempt by some people to reconcile philosophy and revelation, Strauss turned to the medieval Jewish philosopher Maimonides. Reading Maimonides was unlike reading Spinoza and other modern philosophers. Spinoza sought to expose the fallacies underlying religious belief in an effort to ground human understanding on a more secure epistemological base. He wrote, consequently, with the rigor and precision appropriate to the philosopher. Maimonides, by contrast, wrote without the driving clarity of Spinoza, leaving the careful reader confused. A superficial reading of Maimonides' work leaves a very clear impression that he was reconciling faith and reason—or at least attempting such a reconciliation. However, Strauss came to believe that Maimonides was up to much more, that he had no intention of reconciling the incompatible but wanted to make philosophy appear to the nonphilosopher as an ally to faith. Someone attending carefully to Maimonides' text stumbles over innumerable small things—contradictions or highly ambiguous phrases or shifts in the meanings of words according to context. Maimonides placed these stumbling blocks in the text, Strauss argued, to arrest the attention of the careful reader. Strauss had discovered a way of writing that presents two messages: the politically useful message and the true message. Strauss decided that if he wanted to understand Maimonides—as Maimonides understood himself— he would have to learn a new way of reading.

These philosophical "discoveries" developed slowly and in a political context that heightened their significance. The Weimar regime posed problems for Strauss well before the rise of Hitler. This first "liberal democracy" in Germany's history arose during a period of moral, religious, and epistemological decay. The malaise extended from a wide-spread naive relativism among the general public to a radical historicism among intellectuals who understood knowledge to be a social construction, contextualized thought bound to a specific time and, to a lesser degree, place. For Strauss, such beliefs result in political suicide, since this way of thinking excludes from the realm of the knowable the most important political questions concerning the good, the just. They lead, he argued, to nihilism, at least insofar as political matters are involved. The state in which citizens accept these limitations is no longer bound by any conception of the good. Power alone remains.

In 1931 Strauss received a Rockefeller Foundation fellowship that supported him while he did research in France and England. After this research grant ended in 1933, Strauss elected not to return to a Germany, which had been transformed in the interim into the Third Reich, but remained in England to complete his book, *The Political Philosophy of Hobbes: Its Basis and Its Genesis* (1936). Like his book on Spinoza, this examination of Hobbes's thought proceeds conventionally and does not yet incorporate Strauss's developing ideas about esoteric writing. In due course, he made his way to the United States (1937) where he was affiliated first with Columbia University and then the new School for Social Research in New York City, where he remained until 1948.

Strauss made few references to the Nazi regime or its deeds, but the holocaust profoundly affected him. He understood, to simplify a good bit, Nazism to be the fruit of modernity. Heidegger's Nazi affiliation only exposed more graphically the pernicious drift of modern thought, and for Strauss, Heidegger symbolized modern nihilism. But the thinking that had made Hitler possible had not gone away. The philosophical, political, and theological developments of the past several centuries were unaffected by the Nazi defeat, so Strauss's call for a recovery of ancient wisdom was no academic or sterile intellectual exercise. For Strauss, the fate of the West rested on the outcome of his attempt to recover political philosophy.

In 1949 Strauss moved to the University of Chicago (where he later became the Robert Maynard Hutchins Distinguished Service Professor), and it was there that he made his name in the United States and cultivated a number of students who, over the years, have demonstrated amazing admiration for and loyalty to their mentor. They and their students evolved into an identifiable, though fractious "school" in the political science profession. Strauss's tenure at the University of

Chicago represents his richest period of scholarship. Beginning with
On Tyranny (actually published a year before his move to Chicago), the
characteristic Strauss style, method, and message began to emerge.
Two quotes from the introduction of *On Tyranny* help demonstrate the
important message and the method of Strauss's work.[21]

> Socratic rhetoric is emphatically just. It is animated by the spirit
> of social responsibility. It is based on the premise that there is a
> disproportion between the intransigent quest for truth and the re-
> quirements of society, or that not all truths are always harmless.
> Society will always try to tyrannize thought. Socratic rhetoric is
> the classic means for ever again frustrating the attempt.[22]

> In explaining writings like the *Hiero*, one has to engage in long-
> winded and sometimes repetitious considerations which can arrest
> attention only if one sees the purpose, and it is necessary that this
> purpose should reveal itself in its proper place, which cannot be at
> the beginning. If one wants to establish the precise meaning of a
> subtle hint, one must proceed in a way which comes dangerously
> close to the loathsome business of explaining a joke.[23]

By this point in his career Strauss had adopted Maimonides' methods by stressing the different needs of philosophers (those engaged in
an intransigent quest for truth) and society. This division of the
needs of the few from the many became central to Strauss's thought.
Although society needs beliefs, the philosopher brings every opinion
into question. These incompatible needs require that one must accommodate the other. The few must bow to the needs of the many.
Politically wise philosophers choose to do so because they will not
long survive in a society whose citizens hold strongly to their beliefs. Moreover, if these socially useful beliefs begin to decay the society will crumble, leaving disorder (and philosophers, like everyone
else, desire order). Therefore, in order to pursue their quest, which
usually includes teaching the few with sufficient spiritual stamina
to be philosophers, they must present themselves to the society as
good citizens, faithful to the religious beliefs that ground the political and social order. In their writings, consequently, they must
present their message in such a manner as to conceal from the many
their true teaching while leaving sufficient evidence for the careful

reader to uncover the esoteric message. The second quotation above indicates not only Strauss's conviction that ancient philosophers so wrote but that one must read him in the same manner.[24]

With the publication of *Natural Right and History* in 1950, Strauss emerged as a major influence in political theory. This book proved especially influential for conservatives because of its full frontal assault on modernity as well as its defense of ancient categories so dear to conservative hearts. The book's simplicity cloaks a rich teaching, and only introductory observations are possible here. The title presents the essential dualism. Natural right developed in Greek philosophy as a result of the discovery of nature. By assuming that all things have a nature, some unchangeable characteristics that define them as a class, it is possible to consider what is right by nature, i.e., what conforms to nature (a very different meaning than the phrase "natural right" has today). For a human to live well he must live according to his nature, and since the defining characteristic of humans is their reason, naturally humans should live a contemplative life. In political terms natural right refers to proper governing, with the constituent parts of the polis performing their proper roles (roles for which nature has given them ability). It follows, then, that political philosophy is the attempt to discover the nature of the polis. This is not a simple normative claim with an ought, for to discover the nature of something and the consequences of acting in violation of that nature does not enjoin one to conform to that nature.

Strauss traced in *Natural Right and History* the alteration that early modern philosophers had made in the natural right tradition until, finally, the entire concept of nature had dissolved as a useful assumption. In response, modern philosophers replaced nature with History, a developmental view of life that emphasizes change rather than unchanging and defining characteristics. In Strauss's work, History often stands for historicism, the most advanced form of relativism. In modern thinking, philosophy no longer is possible because philosophy is the quest to know nature, or the eternal. According to Strauss, for moderns nothing is unchanging except change.

Strauss's primary critique of modernism is contained in *Natural Right and History*, though he had much to add in his numerous books that followed. At the end of his career—by which time he had moved to St. Johns College in Maryland where he was Scott Buchanan Distinguished Scholar in residence—he focused entirely upon the classical texts, especially Plato's work. He had well established the failure and the flaws of modernity, and now wished to engage in a fuller examination of classical philosophy, not in order to imitate it but to recapture the innocence of those beginning discoveries.[25]

This short intellectual biography highlights the basic assumptions Strauss associated with "modernity," but a more synthetic account of his mature thought should provide the necessary rudiments for later sections where I take up the highly controversial specifics. No brief overview could possibly include an adequate commentary on the profundity of Strauss's views.

Strauss often wrote of the modern "project." The implication of this language is that modernity is characterized by goals that suggest a conscious break with classical understanding. The makers of modernity, therefore, took their bearings from the premodern tradition they rejected. The first such break came from Machiavelli. The tradition against which Machiavelli consciously revolted was characterized by certain beliefs and goals. First, political philosophy is the quest for the best political order, the order "most conducive to the practice of virtue" and in which each person gets his due and occupies his rightful place according to his nature. Second, chance is necessary for the establishment of the best political order because it requires the very unlikely circumstances when philosophers possess or greatly influence political power. And third, nature dictates the proper limits on humans—they cannot overcome their nature. Machiavelli subverted these beliefs and goals by rejecting nature—that is, a nonhuman standard that provides the model for human aspiration. In this way he lowered the goals of political philosophy and of human society. Machiavelli began with humans as he found them rather than as they should be and thought that leaders should seek to take care of basic human needs rather than their highest aspirations. Machiavelli also dismissed the role of chance (fortuna). Humans make their own chances. In some restricted sense leaders have full control of their destinies, and so long as they devote their energies to human desires instead of "the good," then leaders can achieve a stable political order. Machiavelli reduced the scope of political philosophy from the quest for the good or the natural to a technical problem of achieving a political order best suited to satisfy human desires.

Machiavelli's revolt produced changes in two areas of human thought. By rejecting nature as a standard or ideal, the word changed meaning as

did the science meant to study it. Nature became something to understand, to manipulate, to conform to human needs (rather than humans
conforming to nature). Such an understanding of nature produced a science focused upon using nature to remove physical limitations. After
Machiavelli, a teleological understanding of nature grew increasingly
precarious, and from Bacon and other Enlightenment thinkers to the
natural and social sciences of the twentieth century, the revolution begun by Machiavelli ended with a frenzied attempt to control nature. The
second change Machiavelli inspired occurred in political philosophy.
His primary heir, Thomas Hobbes, elevated the lowest of human ends—
self-preservation—to the highest political goal. In the process, natural
right became individual right, first a right of self-preservation and then
rights as members of a state to relief from some burdens. This stream of
thought, leading through John Locke, became the source of liberal democracy, which, springing from the earliest manifestation of modern
thought, would prove far less vulnerable to the self-destructive tendencies of later modern political systems.

A second "wave" of modernity, more radical than the first, had its
beginnings in the thought of Rousseau. Unlike those in the first wave,
in which techniques of satisfying basic human demands in the context
of self-interested individuals became the focus, Rousseau sought to
achieve a transformation of human nature. In the state of nature humans were "subhuman" and have acquired their measure of humanity
through the historical process. Human development springs, not from
reason, but from will—the general will, "a will inherent and immanent in properly constituted society takes the place of transcendent
natural law."[26] Rousseau linked humanity with historical development
rather than with nature and reason. His ideas would find a more complete development through Kant and Hegel and would provide the
source for the second modern form of government, communism.

The third and most radical wave of modernity Strauss associated
with Nietzsche and Heidegger. Nietzsche also rejected nature and
timeless standards in favor of historical development, but unlike Rousseau or Hegel, Nietzsche believed this development had no reason to it,
no teleology, no progress. Nietzsche saw the nihilism in the universe,
leaving only power and the will to power. The historicism of this third
wave did not allow for knowledge of eternal relations, there being nothing about which one might have knowledge—except the knowledge of
this state of affairs. This denial of standards makes intellectually un-

tenable any ardent defense of moral ideals (though some people, like Max Weber, tried). The true crisis of modernity, then, is the inability to affirm or believe in anything or any goal or ideal. Heidegger, for instance, could find no moral grounds upon which to condemn Hitler. To Strauss, Heidegger's amorality was an obscene abdication of responsibility, exposing a failure of nerve in the greatest philosopher of the century. No matter the brilliance of Heidegger as a philosopher, he failed utterly as a political philosopher, which is to say as a politically responsible philosopher.

Strauss argued that the practical consequences of this radical historicism was Nazism. But modernity did not crumble in 1945. It remains in the liberal democracies. He was unclear about the relative importance of this virus, since liberal democracies appear to have sufficient ''premodern'' influences to protect them. Still, the danger is great and the stakes high. A healthy political philosophy, one grounded on nature rather than history, would provide the best intellectual bulwark against modernity. If Strauss may be said to have had a political goal, it was to reorient political philosophy in the West.

The modern crisis was the focal point for Strauss's work rather than his point of departure. This summary provides the basic public outline of the story he had to tell, but the twists of interpretation and the turns of Strauss's own esoteric message must wait for later chapters. Here we have Strauss the political philosopher; Strauss the philosopher remains as yet partially hidden.

Strauss's and Voegelin's critiques of modernity matured in the context of the unprecedented prosperity of postwar America. Why? Had not the war, a titanic struggle between ideologies, destroyed the most dangerous form of modernity? Perhaps their critiques make sense as versions of anticommunism. Both philosophers were undeniably anticommunists, but their critiques focused upon liberals and the kind of society they were creating in the United States and the West. The political stability and economic prosperity of postwar America hid, they believed, a deeper angst and a fear that the center would not hold. America would take a course similar to the totalitarian states if it could not shore up its moral center. Liberal democracy in the United States required, they believed, a reinvigorated idea or purpose.

2
Liberal America and Its Discontents

Strauss and Voegelin participated in the huge migration of scholars from the Continent to America before and during World War II. No one has yet adequately measured the impact of these thinkers on American intellectual life. Probably no one can.[1] In science, one can point to numerous emigrés who participated in the celebrated breakthroughs during and following World War II, but even here one can only indicate their most obvious, and by no means most fundamental, influence. Who can calculate the effect of having so many talented scientists in one nation? How were American scientists changed, challenged, and improved by this intellectual cross-pollenation? The problems are multiplied when one discusses the nonscientists. For every celebrated figure like Hannah Arendt, numerous scholars of great repute in Europe lived in obscurity in the United States. Eminent scholars taught wherever they could find a job, and of course, many of them had no jobs because language and cultural barriers proved too daunting. They could not adapt. Those who could, especially the younger ones, often started in positions of low rank and prestige, and many of them did not teach at elite schools until near the end of their careers. At almost every level, then, American colleges and universities gained the services of talented Europeans who brought to their new environment erudition and fresh perspectives.

Even the young emigrés, however, tended to remain intellectually tethered to the continental tradition. Few of them grappled with William James or John Dewey—or even the luminaries of the English tradition—as they did with, say, Kant, Hegel, Nietzsche, Husserl, and Heidegger. Moreover, the traumatic experiences in Europe, especially since 1914, had shaped their outlook in ways Americans could hardly imagine. These transplants, then, tended to examine the liberal, democratic America in which they lived against a background of continental thought and through eyes that had witnessed two world wars and visions of genocide.

Americans were not untouched by these events, to say the least. World War II especially created an environment in which many had to reevaluate their most basic assumptions about the directions of modern society. The sheer scale of the war, and consequently of the human cost, shocked those who retained some sense of human progress, and the war's fury frightened those who had long believed in the fallen nature of the species. The ferocity of the war, symbolized not only by kamikazes but also by Hiroshima, made modern existence appear fragile before the spectacle of humans possessing such awesome power. Moreover, the graphic revelations of Germany's methodical genocide forced many intellectuals to grapple with the most difficult conundrum of them all, How could it have happened? Auschwitz and Dachau were not products of Hitler's mind alone; they were products of a nation of people no more monstrous than any other. If the pictures sent back to the United States of concentration camps caused most Americans to curse Hitler, they caused many intellectuals to doubt their own society—to question the future of civilization.

The Holocaust functions as a dividing line in our understanding of human history. The pictures of concentration camps populated by emaciated figures whose blank eyes betrayed their loss of humanity elicited shocked silence or even embarrassed giggles among the Americans as they watched the newsreels in movie houses because they had no frame of reference for such an experience, no way to label these images.[2] These observers belonged to the pre-Holocaust world in which such a deed was unimaginable—unthinkable. Once the unthinkable has become real, the world can never look the same. Whatever prescriptions once prevented such behavior have now been breached, and one can never again feel secure. Some people sought solace by blaming such a terrible event on Hitler, that "madman." But even if one so personifies the horror one is left with the millions of people—presumably not mad—who participated in or otherwise silently acquiesced to the mass slaughter.[3] The Holocaust was a legal operation (therefore technically not murder) of a legitimate state that used the most rational means available to accomplish its objectives.

World War II, the "good war," offers lessons not easily understood. It was not a war against totalitarianism (after all, Stalin was an ally). It was not a war in which either side observed the traditional code of conduct normally befitting a proper war.[4] Moreover, the war itself, along with the character of the enemy, raised questions about the very direction of modern thought. If one dismisses Nazism as an aberration from the "normal" course of Western development, then one may easily dismiss the war. But if, as many observers did, one sees Nazism as an understandable product of (i.e., it is explainable in terms of) the preceding century or so of intellectual development, then the course of Western civilization is problematic.

This chapter is about the reevaluation of American liberal ideals and assumptions in the fifteen or so years after 1945. Most of the characters in the story are Americans, to be sure, but although it is impossible to tell how much, the European emigrés did influence the debate and heighten its significance. Clearly, Hannah Arendt helped shape the discussion in obvious ways. In some cases American scholars noted how they were influenced by one or more of these refugees, and others, like Reinhold Niebuhr, were always oriented toward the Continent. However, one senses that the most powerful influence existed at a level far beneath the surface. These emigrés simply recast many of the old questions without knowing they were doing so and without their American colleagues fully realizing it. Perhaps it is America's benevolent fate to have the perils of modernity come in the form of victims rather than tyrants. Or, to put the matter another way, European tyrants presented Americans with problems not easily ignored.

THE PROBLEM OF TOTALITARIANISM

Totalitarianism arises as an intellectual problem if the differences between Nazism and communism appear cosmetic rather than philosophical. The hatred between the Nazis and the communists, some people concluded, sprang, not from fundamentally antithetical ideologies, but from the competition of two gangs seeking control of the same turf. The two, then, represent an equal threat to liberal ideals. Indeed, they may share with liberalism the same intellectual roots. A preoccupation with totalitarianism inspired insightful (sometimes imaginative) examinations into the nature of the phenomenon, influential polemics against the threatening regimes, and not inconsequential concerns for the health of liberal ideals, thought by most intellectuals to be the only real modern alternative to the fascist madness. If the significance of the problem caused scholars to blur the very real distinctions between totalitarian regimes, this flaw does not diminish the theoretical penetration into the problem achieved by these scholars and it exposes a preoccupation that helps explain the times.

People dispossessed of their illusions rarely tolerate with equanimity those who remain true believers. Illusions shattered often beget an ardent skepticism and a "realist" posture. During the decade following the Ribbentrop-Molotov pact, numerous American Communists and fellow travelers became doubters and even strident opponents of their old comrades. They were disillusioned. James Burnham's journey from Trotskyism, with which he identified in the thirties, to his association with the *National Review* mirrors the development of several others.[5] More important, many of the once faithful believed that Burnham had exposed the Communist lie, and the lies of all such statist utopian schemes.

Who better to puncture the illusions of utopia than Niccolò Machiavelli? In his study of the political thought of "Machiavellians" (i.e., Gaetano Mosca, Georges Sorel, Robert Michels, and Vilfredo Pareto),[6] Burnham argued that the expressed goals of all ideologies warred against the political nature of humans. "Majority rule," "classless society," and even "democracy" are fictions. A small elite rules every society. Even if one class emerges to power in a country in which it formerly possessed no institutional control, the leaders of that class become the real brokers of power. In Western democracies the expansion of voting privileges allows people to participate in the selection of their leaders, but they do not rule themselves. Given that a small elite always rules, and that without checks to their power they seek to gain more power and control, freedom is best maximized by providing substantial and varied checks on power—ruling elites checking other ruling elites.

To forget these hardheaded truths concerning power and ruling elites is tantamount to giving up any hope of achieving any worthy political goal (e.g., an expansion of freedom). American Communists, filled with illusions about a classless society, had sacrificed their ability to see things clearly. How else, Burnham asked, can one explain the enormous gulf separating Communist words from actions? "Without a stutter," Burnham wrote,

> the Kremlin thunders against the anti-democratic acts of Hitler, Franco, Chiang Kai-shek . . . while it maintains at home the most anti-democratic regime in world history. Aggression and annexation are denounced in the midst of soviet aggression and annexations. . . . The most totalitarian state that exists and that has ever existed not only claims to be, but is everywhere accepted as—the world leader in the struggle against totalitarianism.[7]

Burnham critiqued, not Stalin, but communism—which is to say one form, very much like any other, of totalitarianism. Burnham presented Stalin as the heir of Lenin; Stalin fulfilled the revolution. Defining Soviet communism with regard to its actions rather than its stated principles, Burnham found the aggrandizement of power, the institution of terror as a weapon of the state, and the effective use of lies to be extensions of Lenin's policies. Stalin simply eliminated, with brilliant effectiveness, alternate sources of power, as any realist would expect of someone in that position. Communism, therefore, was nothing more than an ideology employed by the governing elite to maintain and expand power. All totalitarian regimes require some ideology—a set of dreams and lies—to expand and protect power. One cannot understand totalitarianism by resorting to stated principles, for the answer lies elsewhere, in the deeper structures that allowed for its development. Karl Marx never really ceased to influence James Burnham.

The threat to freedom seemed even more ominous when Fredrick von Hayek, an Austrian economist at the London School of Economics, published *The Road to Serfdom*. Writing during World War II (the book was published in the United States in 1944), Hayek's emphasis upon the Nazis extended quite easily to the Soviet Union (he said so in later editions) and even to the "creeping socialism" of the United States. The frightening aspect about Hayek's argument was his claim that the real danger comes from human efforts to direct society toward higher ideals. In the name of freedom reformers attempted to construct a more just world through the mechanism of a greatly strengthened central power. Well-intentioned socialists laid the foundations of Nazism, because centralized power, with leaders bent upon social planning, is incompatible with freedom, argued Hayek. Perhaps most ominous, at least to readers during the waning years of the war, was the claim that the United States had already embarked on the same path taken by the Germans. The central planning of the New Deal ("creeping socialism") would lead to a similar destruction of freedoms if the United States did not abandon the utopian goals of socialism.

The powerful and centralized state threatened human freedoms. Grand goals and the best of intentions did not mitigate the threat; indeed, insofar as people became deluded by impractical expectations so that they were willing to embark upon radical reforms aimed at instituting some felicitous future, these good intentions made the state more dangerous. No matter why power once invested in other institutions (formally or by tradition) devolves to the central government, that power may be used capriciously in the future. This theme, elaborated in different ways by both Burnham and Hayek, reinforced the growing suspicion of the dangerous direction of modern thought.

George Orwell's *1984* expressed the growing disaffection of intellectuals with modern life. Orwell presented the power of a future state so ubiquitous that it controls the interior lives of its citizens, their thoughts as well as their actions. Totalitarianism becomes so complete that no real social arrangements exist, just the state and the undifferentiated atoms who (or should I say "that") work and live for the interest of the state. Not only has individualism been destroyed in *1984*, but so also the very context that makes the growth of individuals possible. Society, along with its rich tapestry of arrangements, duties, attachments, traditions, and customs, has been swept away by the state, leaving individuals politically and existentially naked.

In the summer of 1950, in what seemed a peaceful lull in the otherwise violent twentieth century, Hannah Arendt sat down to write the preface to *The Origins of Totalitarianism*. In the process she exposed her feeling of powerlessness, of anxiety bred from a life without the stabilizing influence of dependable political and social institutions. In the first paragraph of the preface she wrote of the destruction of the "old world order"; of violence, chaos, and decay;

of "hopelessness on an unprecedented scale"; and of "rootlessness to an unprecedented depth." Arendt presented an image of a civilization in the process of self-destruction and of unimaginable existential rootlessness for the survivors of such a civilization. *Origins* is not a happy book; it charts no course out of the troubled waters. Arendt cannot say with Hayek that the threat to civilization will cease when states relinquish their power over the economic and social freedoms of the people. Nor can she limit her analysis to exposing the dangers of utopian thinking and the need to recognize the necessary role of elites in government, as Burnham does. More than any analysis before hers, Arendt's book is about a spiritual disease— the pathology of a civilization.

No one was better placed to examine this disease than Arendt. A student of Heidegger and exceptionally well versed concerning the continental philosophers of modernity, Arendt came of age in the flowering of Weimar. She knew the intellectual instability of a postwar Germany, and she saw how easily a liberal society bowed to Hitler and his Nazi ideology. A Jew, Arendt fled to Paris and then, when the Germans moved against France, to New York. A refugee in a strange land with an unfamiliar language, Arendt understood the sense of homelessness that became a helpful metaphor for her in understanding the chaos of the twentieth century. Her work centered upon the problems of this violent and chaotic age, and out of her work and anxiety came *The Origins of Totalitarianism*.

Despotism, tyranny, and dictatorship are categories of government that are well known in the human experience. Totalitarianism emerged as an entirely novel system, essentially unlike any pre-twentieth-century categories, bringing with it altogether alien values. Depending upon some identifiable relationship between experiences of a society and its political structure, Arendt sought to expose the conditions that allow an unprecedented political structure to develop and summarily sweep away the existing political, social, legal, and economic institutions.[8]

Totalitarian ideology occupied the space created by the collapse of the bourgeois capitalist system. With a unique blend of passion and scholarship, Arendt traced the effects of imperialism and World War I on the existing system, making race a defining construct and creating an ever-increasing number of homeless, rootless people who stood outside the protection of a state. The growing number of

people who felt isolated and lonely, who were shut out from participating in the social and political institutions of their state or the
state in which they lived, made possible the appeal of totalitarian
ideology. The problems, aggravated by World War I and the Treaty of
Versailles, of minorities in newly created nation-states and of displaced and eventually stateless people pointed to the very real limitations of natural rights, so long a foundation of liberal society. Humans ostensibly possess natural rights as a condition of their
humanity, but in the difficult world of stateless people living in a nation without the rights granted to citizens (and not having claim to
citizenship anywhere), the abstractions of natural rights seemed
meaningless without the concrete protection of a state. Outside of
that protection, the lonely and homeless people—from all classes—
became superfluous to the state.

As the philosophical foundations of liberal ideals crumbled in the
social, economic, and ethnic chaos of post-Versailles Europe, dissat-
isfaction with existing authority and institutions grew apace. The
old Christian bourgeois morality decayed, in part because the system of which it formed a part (liberalism manifested in capitalism
and nation-states) was exhausting its historical capital. In Arendt's
analysis, influenced substantially by Marx, Europe could not sustain
capitalism in its nineteenth-century manifestation because it carried the seeds of its own destruction. The imperialist move by capitalist nations delayed the inevitable by finding a new means of using
its superfluous capital and labor in markets not yet saturated. Whatever peace and temporary security such a course brought also created
the necessary conditions for the obscenities of the 1930s and 1940s.
The details with regard to the effects of imperialism are complicated
and highly debatable, but Arendt credits imperialism with creating
race as a defining characteristic and, in part at least, leading to the
cataclysm of World War I. The war and the treaty that followed
spawned grievances not quickly forgotten and an unholy collection
of new nation-states, each a cauldron of ethnic groups with long-
standing rivalries.

In these years filled with petty wars, displaced people, economic
devastation, and brewing hatred spawned from a sense of betrayal,
the old verities that had preserved nineteenth-century civilization
lay in ruins. In Germany, Russia, and elsewhere a growing percent-
age of the citizens found themselves shut out from meaningful par-

ticipation in the economic and political life of their nation. These citizens, much like the stateless people, constituted what Arendt called a mass—an undifferentiated group with no real allegiances or ties, not even to class. The masses, lonely and despondent, proved susceptible to ideological constructions of reality that explained their condition. Mobilized by the logic of ideology—which, once accepted, renders one immune from counterevidence—the masses identified existing authority and institutions, along with the morality of the establishment, as the source of problems. By drawing the masses into the compelling, if circular, logic of an ideology, a few leaders can transform the masses into a powerful political force.

Once in power, a totalitarian regime is loosed from traditional moral restraints. It maintains its power through violence and terror, but violence and terror directed at no one in particular. Unlike classical tyranny, in which violence served to disable politically a particular person or group, a totalitarian government employs terror against its own population as a means of paralyzing every individual and thereby removing all potential internal sources of dissention. In such a *de*-moralized state, equipped with an ideology that explains the world and promises the masses that they participate in a glorious, world-historic movement, the people are capable of virtually any obscenity—including genocide and participation in their own destruction.

Arendt's brilliant historical account penetrates to the moral problem better than any attempt before or since. Her book is nonetheless flawed. She too easily conflated Communist Russia and Nazi Germany, and her description of totalitarianism has proved too rigid or static to account for the development of communism in the Soviet Union, for instance. Moreover, her argument that the assimilation of Jews into society—i.e., intellectual, political, and economic institutions—placed them in the unenviable position of being identified with the crumbling and hated establishment is not without its problems. Nonetheless, *Origins* provides the most damning critique to date of the modern world. In 1951, with the memory of the world's most destructive war still fresh and with the Soviet Union, having secured Eastern Europe, now possessing "the bomb," Arendt's book sounded to some people as much a prophecy as a history. For a great many people the war between liberal ideals (or "democracy") and communism loomed as the most important threat to Western civilization. Far more perplexing to those who were keen to look at history as the playing out of competing ideas—sometimes with absurd consistency—was the concern that liberal ideals always self-destructed.

AMERICA AND THE LIBERAL TRADITION

The burden of precision is too heavy for people who wish to describe an American character (or even for those who accept as a meaningful construct some less-bold overarching description of their society and its traditions). For American intellectuals in the 1950s no more accepted or less defined label persisted than "liberalism." America was and always had been liberal. That such a label was meaningful to those who used it one cannot doubt. They used the label with confidence, without concern that by using it they might be misunderstood. Still, to the historian, such words defy clear, precise definition. Rather than aiding in its definition the very ubiquity of a word may make its meaning more elusive.

In the broad context of the modern West, "liberalism" represents constitutional rule, pluralism (expressed most obviously in competing political parties), and a legal structure predicated upon some concept of individual natural rights (e.g., Rights of Man, Bill of Rights). Within the setting of recent European politics, then, liberalism has been a broad category that stands in contrast to socialism, to the various totalitarian ideologies, and to the ancien régime with its monarchical structure and legally privileged classes. Understood in this context the American experience appears distinctively liberal—that is, at least since 1776 no real alternative to liberalism has existed. Nonetheless, liberalism defined this broadly allows for enormous internal variety, and when applied to the history and circumstances of one nation, the word requires a more precise definition. Semantic consistency is possible only in the abstract world of the thinker; historically, the meaning people have given to the word has changed constantly, often with most confusing consequences. Still, one can account for—and defend—the long-standing appropriation of this word.

Liberalism is etymologically related to liberty. At least some liberals have always dedicated themselves to expanding individual liberty. They have assumed that individuals are endowed with the natural rights of life, liberty, and property (and such other rights as are convenient). Inalienable human rights (natural rights) provide the foundation for all liberal theorizing about politics. Society and state are both products of individuals; useful conventions justified only insofar as they serve the interests of those who created them.[9]

The question begged by this construction is where or from whom do these rights come? In the case of the United States a strong Christian tradition has long provided a nearly universally accepted theological answer to this question. Rights come from God. But self-evident truths to one group of people, who rest in the metaphysical comfort of a Christian inheritance, appear suddenly dubious to others who live without such security. Increasingly, liberals have had to defend rights on more pragmatic (even utilitarian) grounds or to depend heavily upon the fragile language of self-evident truths ("human rights") without theological underpinnings.[10]

In a second assumption related to the first (that the individual is the basis of government), some liberals emphasize the secular nature and goals of government. They reject all claims grounded on the assumption that government is natural and with it the claim that specific groups (classes) are "naturally" suited to rule. Rather than having a metaphysical sanction or teleology, government serves as a useful means to achieve conventional goals. For liberals those ends are secular and deal with the protection of individual rights and liberties and, in a related goal, of securing a peaceful environment.

These foundations, more or less present in every manifestation of liberalism, allow considerable latitude for people with widely differing political agendas (i.e., public policy) to camp in the same philosophical tent. Clearly, modern liberal ideas developed initially among people who had a suspicious eye fixed on the encroaching power of government. Liberty meant "liberty from," the freedom to pursue individual choices with a minimum of governmental interference. Economic freedoms rest at the heart of this concept of liberty. However one may understand liberty, in many ways and in due course many self-designated liberals began to emphasize the need to establish a fair environment for individualism to flourish (in economic and other areas).[11] To this end liberals have argued that liberty from government is meaningless if the individual has no opportunity to succeed. Given this understanding, liberals can justify the use of government to level the playing field. In so doing they do not violate their principles by expanding the scope of government. Rather, they make government a more useful instrument in securing the basic rights of each individual.[12]

This flexibility with regard to individual liberties or rights, for the protection of which government exists, creates tensions. Increasingly since 1929 (and even before) the people who have embraced selective socialist means to achieve their liberal goals have accepted the mantle of liberalism. Correspondingly, those who have resisted socialist measures and who tend to emphasize liberty from government involvement (especially in economic affairs) have accepted the conservative label (after all, they consider themselves the conservators of a "pure" liberalism). Both groups—or ends of the spectrum—emphasize the primacy of individuals and conceive of government as the protector of their natural rights. Both think of government as a profoundly useful institution created by humans to help accomplish human ends.

This muddy outline is perhaps not muddy enough. The space for profound differences remains vast and facilitates a most voluble discourse. For those who surveyed the tradition in light of World War II other more subtle trends proved worrisome. Two tendencies—apparently in tension—particularly vexed many liberals. First, some liberals largely dismissed moral and ethical questions from political discourse, or at least they thought they had. Second, a significant number of liberals co-joined progress and liberalism. Whether playing down the negative side of human nature or denying that humans have an essential nature, such liberals believed that the more humans free themselves from corrupting institutions or from debilitating environmental circumstances the more individual and social ills would fade. Many emphasized the role of education in creating a population endowed with sufficient knowledge and wisdom to improve, through democratic means, themselves and society (the second tendency suggests a moral objective that wars against the first). Looking back from this side of two cataclysmic wars and all their concomitant horrors, neither emphasis appeared healthy. For a great many self-conscious liberals the 1950s were not so much a time of gloating as of critical reassessment of the very foundations of their beliefs.

Among the cacophony of voices critical of liberalism an especially strident wail came from those who had lost faith in instrumental reason. Liberals had always placed their faith in the human capacity to make calculated choices toward desired ends as the best means of promoting happiness. Freed from the irrational restrictions of traditions and superstition, humans could choose goals consistent with experience and consistent with such goals both in individual pursuits and, through democratic means, as a "collective." What use was this rationality in Weimar? What calculations justified Hiroshima? To what kind of American society had such rationality led? In the twentieth century, when the reason of liberalism emerged without its metaphysical object, reason became merely instrumental. So defined, liberalism was assaulted from all sides. From the old left and from conservatives came an attack on the failure of liberals to focus upon ends, upon the proper object of government and society. From the emerging new left, much influenced by French existential philosophy, came the rejection of the rationality of means to any end.

For the bohemian crowd—especially the beatniks in San Francisco—the settled middle-class world stifled creativity and smothered the individual in layers of organizations, bureaucracies, corporations, and other "rational" structures of American society. The irony is that these critics faulted liberals for creating a conformist society. Indeed, in their attempt to liberate the individual, past liberals had justified and perpetuated a political and economic system that required a mobilized population capable of producing the economic surplus necessary to make material progress possible. Although a full examination of this phenomenon would come from conservatives, the beatniks rejected the goal-orientation of liberal society, emphasizing process instead. Their poems and novels end without closure, and their best works exhibit a restless energy reflecting their breathless lives filled with movement but no telos. Chemical epiphanies and powerful orgasms seemed goals enough for the moment. Instinct, will, passion, these things drove the beatniks. Whether in "The White Negro," in which Norman Mailer glorified the black hipster who lived authentically, outside the rules that guide the behavior of most people, or in the person of James Dean, who lived, played, and died as the Nietzschean rebel seeking no end other than life itself, the protagonist always rejected the settled and rational goals of liberal society. It was enough to be "on the road," one need not care where the road led.

The absurdity of life, at least life viewed from the perspective of human reason, became a dominant theme among many of the period's most profound and influential writers. Ernest Hemingway's last great novel, *The Old Man and the Sea*, testifies to the futility of human goals within the context of a meaningless universe. The works of playwrights Eugene O'Neill and Tennessee Williams emphasize the ambiguity of life, the frailty of existence, and the internal illusions that work to cloak the horrible reality. In religion, Paul Tillich, an influential German theologian who settled at the Union Theological Seminary in New York after losing his position in Germany when the Nazis came to power, sought God in the deepest regions of human despair and anxiety. The unparalleled events of this century posed problems for which reason can offer no answer. God is not found in human tautologies or in knowledge sanctioned by science but in faith—and faith emerges from the unfathomability of human experience.

These critiques more often than not were very generalized and took a form not easily integrated into the liberal debate. Far more important was the extensive reflection of liberals on their own tradition. Here, as before, the criticism and the praise reflected the expansiveness of the label "liberalism." Still, their remarks contain very few adjectives or qualifiers. One does not find the people who wrote about this topic directing their comments to stream X or stream Y of liberalism. They wrote as if the word referred to a clear and unambiguous concept. This analytical failure suggested an intellectual universe so widely accepted and comfortable that no one felt the need to define it more precisely.

The criticism from within reflected well a certain temper: a fidelity to such liberal goals as liberty and tolerance balanced with some concept of social justice[13]—but without many settled convictions about means and with an eye to historic ironies, to efforts that beget unanticipated results. One such unanticipated consequence—though Tocqueville anticipated it—was the creative stupor of American liberals, or a society in which liberal ideals become articles of faith. Lionel Trilling chose the hopeful rather than descriptive title for his 1950 collection of essays, *The Liberal Imagination*. Trilling, an erudite literature professor at Columbia University who influenced both the beatniks and later the neoconservatives, surveyed the imaginative terrain of liberals and found a desert. The paradox: liberalism was the only substantive tradition in America and liberals possessed all the seats of power, but the great literary works came from a decidedly nonliberal cadre—Eliot, Faulkner, Pound, and Yeats. Liberalism lacked imagination; without an antagonist it had become intellectually flabby. "It is not conducive to the real strength of liberalism," wrote Trilling, "that it should occupy the intellectual field alone."[14] But since he saw no respectable antagonist developing who might challenge and thus sharpen a lumbering liberalism, he proposed to revive it from within. Liberals had to be more critical of their own "movement."

One senses in Trilling's work a discomfiture with modern culture, a sad and pessimistic posture influenced by Freud, frightened by Marx, and inspired by Matthew Arnold. But if Arnold was sanguine, Trilling could excuse him because he had not lived to see the full development of the masses who became the instruments of Stalin and Hitler and who were developing in the United States a vulgar, conformist culture. Living on this side of World War II (and the events of the three decades prior to the war), Trilling saw danger everywhere. It lurked even in the American middle class, the class most identified with liberalism and the class with which Trilling himself most identified. The "mass of educated people"—the middle-class professionals like lawyers, bankers, doctors, and professors—were succumbing to philistinism. They grew ever more suspicious of the arts since artists fly on wings of imagination rather than walk the sturdy ground of reality. This tendency (which Trilling called "stalinism") alienated the creative world of literature and the arts from the world of politics.[15] But, as he made clear in his famous preface to *The Liberal Imagination*, literature can enrich *or* debase the political and social world. A poverty of imagination in the arts inevitably impoverishes politics as the relationship between "high culture" and politics is symbiotic. Trilling explained the matter this way, in part a paraphrase of Charles Peguy: "Everything begins in sentiment and assumption and finds its issue in political action and institutions. The converse is also true: just as sentiments become ideas, ideas eventually establish themselves as sentiments."[16]

Somehow in this symbiotic relationship liberalism had become dull, bland, and unimaginative in politics and in the arts. Trilling placed himself in the company of John S. Mill when he described the objective of his book and the conditions in which he wrote it. Like Mill, who found the search for happiness (Trilling calls this an emotion) had decayed into a deadening rationality, Trilling wanted to bring back to liberalism the complexity of human life, its "variousness and possibility." For instance, the charm of a poem is that its insight is captured in the special form of poetry. Such insight, trapped by the poetic form (and otherwise inaccessible), does not translate easily into political or social action. Trilling urged that these insights nonetheless inform (as "sentiments") the "ideas" of political and social life. He wrote persuasively of the conditions that encouraged liberals to abandon these sentiments:

> So far as liberalism is active and positive, so far, that is, as it moves toward organization, it tends to select the emotions and qualities that are most susceptible of organization. As it carries out its active and positive ends it unconsciously limits its view of the world to what it can deal with, and it unconsciously tends to develop theories and principles, particularly in relation to the nature of the human mind, that justify its limitation. Its characteristic paradox appears again, and in another form, for in the very interests of its great primal act of imagination by which it establishes its essence and existence—in the interests, that is, of its vision of a general enlargement and freedom and rational direction of human life—it drifts toward a denial of emotions and the imagination.[17]

Whether or not liberalism leads to philistinism, Trilling was only the most articulate of a great number of liberals who lamented the course of American social and cultural life. If Americans had emerged from the war years with their liberty intact (i.e., sharp restrictions on governmental intervention in private affairs and governmental protection of defined rights) and the prosperity necessary to make the most of that liberty, intellectuals began to question the way most people enjoyed their liberty. Liberal intellectuals had fought for freedom and prosperity, not for a mass culture with its mind-numbing television, its material acquisitiveness, its look-alike houses, and its act-alike people. Unfortunately, the "common man" remained common. The hope of so many that universal education would elevate the citizenry appeared premature or even illusory in the 1950s. Throughout that decade, liberal intellectuals filled the pages of journals like *Partisan Review* and *Commentary* (then a liberal organ) with laments about the political apathy and the aesthetic poverty of the American middle class.

Liberals were victims of their own success. Their immediate goal of maintaining a large measure of freedom from governmental institutions (and much earlier from other restrictive institutions) while employing the government to level the playing field a bit had met with a large measure of success (racial inequality was still not an important issue for liberals). However, from the perspective of many liberal intellectuals, their accomplishments had not led to the kind of society they wanted. Americans were not using their liberty and prosperity wisely or humanely.

Did this homogenized America spring into existence because of postwar prosperity, mass media, and suburbs? Liberal and conservative critics alike relied heavily upon these developments to help account for the bland America, but what if America had always been so bland? The Harvard historian Louis Hartz confirmed this fear in his influential book *The Liberal Tradition in America*. Like Trilling and most other intellectuals, Hartz affirmed that America had a hegemonic liberal tradition. According to Hartz, American "liberalism" was exceptional, institutionally and psychologically unlike European versions. The new world meant new conditions. Europeans came to this new world with European ideas but without European conditions. Unhinged from the conditions that created it, "Lockian liberalism"—a term that has more often confused than illuminated—took root in an American soil free of the acid of feudalism. Americans were, as Hartz put it, "born equal." Hartz packed a great deal into such phrases (this one borrowed from Tocqueville). On one level Hartz referred to the social and political freedoms that immigrants found in America, which allowed for social and political developments free from class and other privileges. On another level, Hartz contrasted the American experience, *born* equal, with the European experience, *made* equal. European liberalism emerged out of struggle against feudalism, and that struggle, like all struggles, carried a cost that Americans never had to pay. From the beginning white American experiences differed so substantially from European experiences as to make the struggle of Europeans, who suffered from a social and political revolution, virtually unintelligible to the blessed Americans.

Hartz traced the rather peculiar shape and development (or lack of development) of American liberal ideals. Born without the pains of social revolution or even the resistance of substantial antiliberal forces, the United States bounded its politics within the confines of liberalism. No real classes—as Europeans understood them—existed whereby substantially differing agendas might create turmoil. Without regard to social or economic status, Americans accepted the values of individual liberty and private property. Moreover, the fantastic material success of American capitalism (aided by an enormous wealth of natural resources) meant that this liberal consensus experienced no serious competition (unlike Europe where class struggle and severely restricted opportunities spawned a socialist movement). This hegemony continued even through the threat of the 1930s depression. Even under such dire conditions Americans chose "liberal" reforms without so much as a serious glance at communism. The America Hartz described is so trapped by an "irrational liberalism" that it neither sees alternatives for itself nor understands (or even tries to understand) the different circumstances and experiences of Europe.

In Hartz's book the key categories were imprecise, the language almost private, and the historical record plundered. Its brilliance lay in Hartz's ability to weave together historical conditions and the role of ideas along with a cosmopolitan perspective into a passionate critique of American provincialism and naiveté. The unique American liberalism about which Hartz was so critical offers no credible model for others to follow; meanwhile, Americans—self-satisfied and comfortable—knew precious little about Europe or the rest of the world. A dangerous ignorance this since the cold war made American isolationism obsolete. Hartz used his book to prod Americans out of their irrational myopia, to push them into "leaving adolescence." Near the end of the book, as he surveyed the United States and its cold war responsibility, he wrote that "what is at stake is nothing less than a new level of consciousness, a transcending of irrational Lockianism, in which an understanding of self and an understanding of others go hand in hand."[18] If the United States had an inferiority complex, Louis Hartz served as its spokesman.

In the 1950s most liberals were cold warriors. Their ranks swollen with disillusioned Communist Party members—many in transit to the right—liberals learned from recent experiences the dangers of totalitarian regimes. Perhaps the most influential thinker in this regard was Reinhold Niebuhr. A prominent Protestant theologian who had spent his early career as a Christian Marxist, Niebuhr emerged as the leading proponent of neo-orthodoxy. From his doctrine of original sin (the cornerstone of neo-orthodoxy), Niebuhr came to see the enormous gap between human aspirations and human accomplishments. The most laudable human goals fail because they do not account for human sin. Therefore, power dedicated to noble ends will decay into tyranny unless some opposing power checks it. Sounding much like James Burnham, Niebuhr emphasized the danger of a Soviet Union left to pursue its aims unchecked.

In Niebuhr's 1952 book *The Irony of American History*, he exposed the complexities and ambiguities of American liberalism. Soviet communism presented a profound threat to freedom because it was guided by sentimental and simplistic assumptions about human nature and the path to paradise. But these same tendencies, Niebuhr argued, lay embedded in liberalism. "The liberal world," wrote Niebuhr, "which opposes this monstrous evil is filled ironically with milder forms of the same pretension. Fortunately they have not resulted in the same evils, partly because we have not invested our ostensible 'innocents' with inordinate power."[19] The "milder forms" of which Niebuhr wrote are the assumptions that regard human nature as plastic and the naive belief that education or changes in environment can mold a happy and guileless person. Niebuhr prescribed a strong dose of realism for liberals so that they might never forget the human potential for evil and the foolishness of trying to change the human condition. "If only we could fully understand that the evils against which we contend are frequently the fruit of illusions similar to our own."[20]

Niebuhr insisted urgently that both liberalism and totalitarianism (Niebuhr wrote specifically of the Soviet Union) traced their intellectual heritage to the same poisonous source. Liberals castigating communism might assault its materialistic creed but remain blind to the inherent and dangerous materialism of liberalism. Liberals strike moralistic poses easily, but they pursue ends in such a way as to make ambiguous their moralisms. The liberal emphasis upon "the dignity of man" presents a number of conundrums for people who have a "naturalistic" bias. The claims of human dignity suggest some spiritual or nonmaterial worth, but liberal goals, Niebuhr argued, are reduced to materialistic conceptions. Niebuhr called liberals back to the fuller, messier, and confounding vision of humans that he found in the Christian religion. Human sinfulness and human dignity, human aspirations and transcendent ends, material yearnings and spiritual yearnings, all of these antinomies played out in gruesome and glorious detail in the drama of human history remind one of the tension that sustains human life.

The criticism by liberals of the American liberal tradition took many forms and referred to many different Americas. Listening to these critics one might think that Americans, dominated by this tradition, were unimaginative, narrow, provincial, and self-satisfied yet given to fantasies about idealized futures based upon naive assumptions regarding human nature and human potential. In part, this critical reflection arose out of the experiences of European societies in this century and because of the move of the United States to center stage in world politics. How might the United States avoid the mistakes of European liberalism? To a large number of scholars and intellectuals this question made little sense, as they felt the uniqueness of the American experience precluded any real danger of such mistakes. The point worth remembering, these intellectuals insisted, was that the United States had avoided the difficulties of Europe. Consequently, the peculiar system (although system it is not) that grew on American soil is worth celebrating and not regretting.

Americans have always celebrated American institutions and habits. America represented—in reality and in myth—a new beginning in which conditions and opportunities allowed immigrating Europeans to adapt their institutions (including eliminating superfluous institutions, creating new ones, and radically altering others) to the changing needs of the nation. By the 1950s historians and other scholars had become enamored with American exceptionalism, and a whole new discipline emerged from this adoration: American Studies. Although these scholars were not uncritical, they did express a pride in the "pragmatic" American method of governing the country as well as the singularly nondogmatic character of the people. The peace, prosperity, vigor, and commonsense of America contrasted sharply with European strife, ideological clashes, class friction, and world wars.

The flood of scholars in search of America's secrets to prosperity and stability testifies to a general approval of the status quo in the United States by a number of intellectuals. But even for these celebrants the issue was often complicated and ambiguous. Consider Arthur Schlesinger's 1949 book *The Vital Center*. At mid century America looked as if it were the beacon of freedom in the world and perhaps its last great hope to secure peace, prosperity, and freedom. Schlesinger affirmed this picture. "I am certain," he wrote near the end of the foreward, "that history has equipped modern American liberalism with the ideas and the knowledge to construct a society where men will be both free and happy." His next sentence is very instructive. "Whether we have the moral vigor to do the job depends on ourselves." Schlesinger warned against an American liberalism unchanged by the lessons of this century. "The soviet experience, on top of the rise of fascism, reminded my generation rather forcibly that man was, indeed, imperfect, and that the corruptions of power could unleash great evil in the world. We discovered a new dimension of experience—the dimension of anxiety, guilt and corruption."[21] Much like Niebuhr—though perhaps with more faith in liberal ideals and institutions—Schlesinger urged his fellow liberals to shed their illusions of human perfectibility in favor of a recognition of the irreversible limitations placed on all human designs.

A similar though more puzzling example is Daniel Boorstin. The University of Chicago historian—and later, librarian of Congress— eludes all attempts at labeling. His ability to tell a good story, complete with quirky details that in his capable hands take on profound significance, makes Boorstin's histories exciting, controversial, and very popular. In his *Genius of American Politics* (1953), Boorstin argued that Americans have never been attracted to broad ideological constructions of reality; they take their bearings from their practical experiences. With no propensity to engage in metaphysical madness, Americans have gone about their social and political lives making practical choices in concrete circumstances without resorting to ideology. Boorstin told the story of such an anti-ideological character in his popular trilogy, *The Americans*.

In the midst of writing that three-volume history, which praises the American nontheoretical nature, Boorstin wrote *The Image: A Guide to Pseudo Events in America* (1961), a mordant critique of the American fascination with images rather than with reality. Americans are victims of their success. They have so successfully tamed nature and turned its power to their purposes that Americans entertain excessive expectations, wanting more than nature and reality can provide. As a consequence they create events—pseudo-events. Newspapers and the electronic media no longer simply report events, they get behind the story or otherwise manufacture a news event. Americans do not travel anymore; they go abroad as tourists seeking the comfort of familiar surroundings provided by international (and interchangeable) hotels, each with the requisite splash of manufactured local color, all in an effort to guarantee that their preconceptions get rewarded. Heroes are manufactured, and an entirely new category of fame has developed: celebrity, ''a person who is known for his well-knowness.'' Boorstin's analysis exposed an increasingly bored people seeking diversion and comfort. Such people, who accept rapidly shifting fashion and trends and who work to conform themselves to the newest images, present a frightening prospect for a democracy operating on this side of Nazi Germany.

One is apt, I think, when writing about such a diverse group of intellectuals to think that this intellectual atmosphere, charged as it was with such profound anxieties and doubts, defined an age. The intellectual universe I describe in this chapter was tiny and in some important respects very different from the host society in which it operated. Although it is true that one could trace these same fears, anxieties, frustrations, and even hopes in a great many other sectors of society, they nonetheless characterize only intellectuals—and by no means all of them. Without a doubt the large, white middle class—from whose ranks most of the intellectuals came—remained mostly undisturbed by the conundrums of modern life. The war was over, and they had won. Hitler was dead, the Nazi concentration camps had been liberated, old enemies had been transformed into allies, and democracy and prosperity prevailed over what seemed like half the world. Communism threatened most Americans, and the arms race attending the cold war created anxiety among all segments of society, but, despite all the hoopla about red scares and bomb shelters, most Americans successfully suppressed their fears and involved themselves in McCarthyism only insofar as it presented more of that peculiar entertainment found in idiosyncratic American politics. Moreover, one gets the strong sense that Americans enjoyed their nice, boring, look-alike suburban houses and all the values one associates with them and their occupants. If their recreation failed to stimulate they nonetheless enjoyed themselves. Why not rock around the clock or spend half an hour with the Ricardos on television? If the small world of intellectuals found fault with these diversions—and they did—the vast majority of Americans did not share their sentiments. Although no simple bifurcation between intellectuals and nonintellectuals helps one understand the period, one cannot overlook the growing concern of intellectuals for the tastes and behavior of a democratic population.

LIBERALISM AND THE MODERN WORLD

The questions that emerged with such urgency at mid century continued and perhaps altered an ongoing critical engagement with the various meanings hidden behind the word "liberalism." In almost every respect the doubts, fears, and ambiguities expressed by the postwar generation of intellectuals and scholars about liberal ideals mirrored those intellectuals had wrestled with two generations earlier. This continuity must not, however, overshadow the very real differences of tone and of emphasis that the evolving historical conditions forced on this tradition. After 1945—and perhaps as early as 1933—the concerns took on a new significance, and the conditions that shook the faith of liberals bred, in others, a rejection of liberal ideals.

Well before the twentieth century all of the various intellectual, technological, and even demographic developments that one might associate with the word "modern" served as corrosive agents acting on the stabilizing verities, prejudices, and habits of Europeans and Americans. Technological innovation outdated certain ways of making a living and, hence, ways of living. The related phenomenon of urbanization created new political and social problems that tended to vitiate a truly individualistic liberalism as expressed by the dominant nineteenth-century liberals. Perhaps equally important as these complicated changes—and no doubt subtly related to them—human knowledge was undergoing profound shifts that unsettled the very foundations of all types of liberalism. This intellectual earthquake—though its shock waves moved slowly and unevenly across the American intellectual landscape—forced many liberals to abandon their crumbled foundations.

Evolution, in its many theoretical forms, is especially useful in discussing the changing intellectual environment of the late nineteenth and early twentieth centuries. Taken in its broadest context, evolution undermined the theological and eventually the ontological supports of nineteenth-century liberalism. In its wake the universe lost its mysterious aura as did humans, whose essence no longer reflected the imprint of God but rather a changing, experimenting, "becoming" creature. Dislodged from their theological cradle, liberals could no longer think of human claims to knowledge as possessing any divine sanction. Increasingly, intellectuals emphasized the fundamentally contingent nature of human knowledge and the need to experiment in order to adjust better to changing conditions.

The dark side of this move is that liberals now lacked the support of a specific and an unquestionable moral and divine sanction. Humans were cast adrift with no one to navigate for them and with only themselves to posit an appropriate destination. The bright side is that these intellectuals recognized the profound—if sometimes frightening—truth of human freedom; the world had now opened up as the locus of limitless possibility. Moreover, armed with this understanding, humans can better apply themselves to searching for better ways of living, i.e., ways of living that are more satisfying to humans and that better reflect their modern, secular perspective. In light of their evolutionary past, humans ought to look forward to greater freedom (especially over the constraints of nature) and happiness.

These intellectual changes, coupled with the social, economic, and political developments of this period helped mark a watershed in the meanings given to the word "liberalism." Most nineteenth-century liberals emphasized the autonomous individual and the absolute rights of individuals, rights that were not subject to repeal by any earthly power. Indeed, these rights or liberties, in the context of the nineteenth century, were philosophical bulwarks against majoritarian rule as much as they had been bulwarks against the oligarchical rule of the previous century. For a variety of complex reasons, late in the nineteenth century liberals shifted their emphasis from natural rights to positive rights, from the autonomous individual to the social creature. As a result, the liberal label became increasingly identified with democracy and with the procedural means of adjusting and adapting to ever-changing conditions.[22]

From the beginning these shifts created doubts amid optimism. To the degree that the United States had always been a democracy it had also been a democracy chastened by prescription and prejudice, operating always within more or less identifiable moral, epistemological, and ontological boundaries. These new liberals (or "progressives," as they sometimes called themselves) had to find an operating principle that functioned to direct the democratic process. The methods used by the natural and physical scientists suggested a way of experimenting, adjusting, and learning without the comfort and limitations of religious or metaphysical certainty. But to get the people who compose a democracy to behave like scientists with regard to political, social, and economic decisions would not prove easy. After all, just because liberal intellectuals had stepped into an open-ended and uncertain universe did not mean that many people had followed them. Concern for the problems of a democracy preoccupied liberal intellectuals, and it was not always entirely clear what grounds a liberal might use to criticize a democratic decision. Still, education, they thought, was the key to any hope for a future desirable to liberal intellectuals. In a democracy education is the primary means of realizing social restructuring by teaching children to solve problems and to experiment with new answers without the certitude of old metaphysical crutches. Education ought not, then, focus on bodies of knowledge—which are provisional—but on developing the scientific means of acquiring answers relevant to life's problems.

During the first fifty years of the twentieth century the concerns about the drift of modern liberalism grew as historical shock followed historical shock. The development of Walter Lippmann's thought best illustrates this evolution and helps to explain the altered tone and sense of urgency that followed victory in 1945. Following his college career at Harvard, where he earned the respect of such luminaries as William James and George Santayana, Lippmann embarked on an amazingly successful career as journalist and public philosopher. Although he was influenced by socialist thought—especially the thought of Graham Wallas—Lippmann emerged as a bright light in the progressive-liberal constellation. His long career as a public intellectual began before World War I and ended with his death in the 1970s, and his works reflect his evolving thought in light of the devastating developments of the the first half of the twentieth century.

In 1914 Lippmann published his influential book *Drift and Mastery* in which he presented a vision or a purpose to replace the old traditions and moralisms that he had so devastated in his first book, *Preface to Politics* (1913). Together the two books exposed the danger and the promise that the new freedom presented. The old ways of thinking and behaving simply did not work anymore, and American politics must adjust to the profound changes taking place in society. The United States was no longer dominated by villages and towns with their agricultural cycles and their attunement to permanent things. Cities and large firms vastly complicated human life, making it impossible to behave according to old traditions. The United States needed a way of organizing and governing the activities of its citizens that took into account constant change and motion. Government would even have to regulate the ever-growing industries that individual citizens could no longer monitor. How could a consumer make a rational choice about canned food or even fresh meat sold at the grocery store? Who could keep up with the safety measures taken by the various railroads? These functions, once capably performed by the consumers, now required expert and centralized guidance. Religion and traditional beliefs also suffered in the modern era; the clerics, from the perspective of intellectuals, were now superfluous, and their message ill-attuned to modern exigencies.

Lippmann's great concern was that the destruction of prejudice, habit, and religious beliefs would leave behind chaos: "In liberal thought there is chaos, for it lacks the foundations of certainty." In *Drift and Mastery* he attempted to fill the vacuum by articulating a vision, a task for American society: "The kind of vision which will be fruitful to democratic life is one that is made out of latent promise in the actual world. There is a future contained in the trust and the union, the new status of women, and the moral texture of democracy. It is a future that can in a measure be foreseen and bent somewhat to our hopes. A knowledge of it gives sanction to our efforts, a part in a larger career, and an invaluable sense of our direction."[23] The new freedom may outstrip the capacity of the people to use it. Lippmann always warned about this possibility, but his optimism about the future eclipsed this concern. Science (Lippmann thought of democracy as science applied to politics) offered a means of searching for new answers that helped remove or distance people from old prejudices. As David Hollinger remarked in an essay about *Drift and Mastery*, for Lippmann the "intersubjectivity of science might not fully 'wipe out the older cleavages' of race and nationality, but it could provide the 'common discipline,' the 'bridging passion' needed to unite civilization and to inspire the energies of diverse individuals."[24] By trading ancient traditions for scientific hypotheses people would lose their emphasis upon differences and discover their common goals.

During and after World War I, Lippmann reassessed his faith in democracy and came to think that his hope for a nation of scientists was illusory. Most people lacked the education or ability to forget their irrational impulses, much less work through the vast quantity of images and information to make rational choices. The crudest caricatured images influenced people more than the most rigorous and carefully rendered argument. Lippmann expressed these new doubts with regard to the people who compose a democracy in his book *Public Opinion* (1922).

Lippmann had assumed in *Drift and Mastery* that the new conditions of the complex world would force people to move beyond a localized and provincial perspective. He thought that people would recognize the interdependence so characteristic of the evolving age and, with this enhanced perspective, make more rational political choices. By the 1920s, Lippmann had concluded that the complexity of the world far outdistanced anyone's ability to comprehend it. To master such complexity is impossible, and to expect voters with widely differing abilities, interests, and perspectives to master the world beyond their immediate experience is delusory.

Democratic theory, Lippmann argued, rested on two erroneous and contradictory assumptions. First, democrats have focused unduly on process, on self-determination, believing that a citizenry will choose wisely because of some "innate goodwill." Second, democrats argued that each person making choices consistent with one's own self-interest would work for the good of the entire republic. Lippmann emphasized the need to examine interests greater than self-determination and to focus on the ends of government rather than on the means. Furthermore, the good society cannot arise from a democratic process if voters are educated to vote according to their self-interest without regard to larger social interests.

In *Public Opinion*, Lippmann faced squarely the profound difficulties of a democracy, though without providing compelling answers. This book exposed his doubts (perhaps without Lippmann's knowing it) that modern problems are soluble by methods born of modern beliefs. Somehow, he averred, a democracy must become less tied to the provincial worlds of its constituents. Not every person, he admitted, can or should become informed about complicated political and social matters, for their lives are often filled enough with the daily demands of their very small worlds. Somehow, nonetheless, a cosmopolitan understanding of the wider world must inform the democratic process—must inform decisions made by the people involved in the process. Formal education, the increased function of experts, and the improvement of journalism (as well as a more sophisticated response to newspapers by the reading public) form part of the improvements Lippmann suggested for an improved democracy. But these and other suggestions only exposed further Lippmann's frustration with the inability of a democratic nation to gain the mastery he had expected a few years before.

By the time *The Good Society* was published in 1937, the world seemed more adrift and the future more frightening. This book begins with an honest retrospective by Lippmann of his own evolving thought. How idealistic those earlier books seemed to him in 1937. From this new perspective—a perspective that now included not only World War I and the Russian Revolution but the rise to power of Mussolini and Hitler—Lippmann attempted a more thorough examination of modernity and its problems. The book possesses two fundamental parts: an examination of totalitarianism and an examination of contemporary liberalism. These are not two separate arguments collected between the same covers; rather, Lippmann argued in *The Good Society* that contemporary liberalism (especially as manifested in the New Deal) and European collectivism share common goals and lead to the same outcomes.

Although the partisans who are now fighting for the mastery of the modern world wear shirts of different colors, their weapons are drawn from the same armory, their doctrines are variations of the same themes, and they go forth to battle singing the same tune with slightly different words. Their weapons are the coercive direction of the life and labor of mankind. Their doctrine is that disorder and misery can be overcome only by more and more compulsory organization. Their promise is that through the power of the state men can be made happy.[25]

Other people in the late 1930s emphasized the differences separating communism, fascism, and liberalism, but Lippmann noted their genetic links. Many commentators found the connection between Hitler's regime and Roosevelt's New Deal preposterous, yet a decade later many intellectuals would be tracing the same links.

The Good Society is a complex, subtle, and often subtly contradictory book that still breeds controversy about the precise substance of its many arguments. But away from the fascinating detailed arguments, the focus is unmistakable. Lippmann argued against the contemporary axiom that greater power in the hands of government officials further ameliorates human problems. Lippmann argued, not for a rejection of liberalism, but for its rehabilitation. According to Lippmann, liberal ideals—at least the ideals of Adam Smith—emerged as the revolutionary political theory compatible with the changing economic structure, more precisely, the evolution of a division of labor. This change made anachronistic old self-sufficient economic entities (e.g., villages) and forced interdependence. The laissez-faire economics that emerged helped make this new economic structure work more effectively for society. The entire process had the effect, in its early development, of liberating people and giving them more options. Unfortunately, Lippmann argued, liberals took the free market to be somehow natural, which made them reluctant to tamper with it even as changes in society made these economic theories incompatible with the good of the society. This reluctance derailed liberals in the nineteenth century from their goals of expanding the realm of freedom and restricting the level of authoritarian coercion. Through several changes bred of obvious social need, liberals made radical changes, forgetting the economic theories of laissez-faire and adopting new forms of coercion as ways of achieving justice.

Avoiding these excesses, Lippmann presented a free market (a rather elusive concept at best), but a free market adapted to evolving social and economic conditions, as central to a liberal society in which productivity and freedom rest on ever-increasing interdependence and freedom of choice. No person or agency could possibly organize the needs of an industrial society. Moreover, Lippmann argued, borrowing from Fredrick von Hayek, a directed society leads to increasing authoritarianism. It was the peculiar role of liberals, thought Lippmann, to lead society away from authoritarian control. In a very revealing segment of *The Good Society*, where Lippmann explained his own intellectual development on these questions, he offered an alternative to contemporary liberalism.

> I saw then that historic liberalism was the necessary philosophy of the industrial revolution. Then I could see why it was that the progress of liberty has accompanied the division of labor, and finally I realized that the specific achievements of liberals were founded upon the supremacy of a common law replacing the dominion of men over men. I began to realize that this has been the guiding principle of the struggle against the arbitrariness of men and their masters; that the history of constitutionalism is the effort to transform the coercive authority of the state so that it shall be employed to protect and disarm, not to magnify by privileges or repress by discrimination, productive energy and voluntary association of individuals. After that it was clear that the division of labor, democracy, and the method of the common law are organically related and must stand or fall together, because they are different aspects of the same way of life.[26]

In many respects the liberalism for which Lippmann agitated in *The Good Society* reflected a Burkean insight. He was disillusioned with the necessarily limited perspective of the average voter (and the voter's gullibility), but he also found the increase in the power of a bureaucratic elite (experts) suicidal for liberty. He, like Burke, argued that the species is wiser than the individual and that tradition ought to be a guide and a restraint. Above all, Lippmann urged that the developing positive law be shaped with a view to "natural law," or the ancient tradition of seeking answers that transcend competing perspectives. Only by governance of laws—rather than people—can members of a modern democracy hope to expand the realm of liberty.

Lippmann vented his growing antimodern impulse most forcibly in his 1955 book *The Public Philosophy*. Western liberal democracies suffered from a profound disorder—a sickness unto death—that resulted "not from the machinations of our enemies and from the adversities of the human condition but from within ourselves."[27] Hitler and Stalin represent the future of the West unless strong treatments arrest the disease and return the West to health. Only self-examination can save liberal democracies. The problem lies within, not without.

The United States suffered from an excess of democracy. The public good is not served by a government servile to the passions of the masses who have not the training, time, or predilection to study the large questions. Lippmann argued that these conditions developed in the United States by the triumph of "Jacobinism," a word Lippmann employed to stand for a series of beliefs that, since Andrew Jackson, have served as a steady acid to the liberal democracy of the founding fathers. Jacobinism is the belief that "natural man" is good and that the evils of this life spring from traditions and customs that hamper the free exercise of human passions. Jacobins believe, moreover, that a heaven on earth is possible by freeing people from institutional hindrance. For Lippmann, who operated with a more traditional anthropology (human nature), the destruction of the accoutrements of civilization leads, not to a felicitous future, but to a Hobbesian war of everyone against everyone and of the rise of totalitarian regimes that harness the uncivilized (i.e., unchecked) passions of the masses.

This modern faith in the perfectible natural human has meant a continuous expansion of voting privileges to give more people control over their destiny and the destruction of the power or influence of traditional institutions and beliefs, because the unhampered (i.e., natural) mind of the individual is superior to the mind of one clouded with superstitions. Slowly, the important doctrines of democracy transformed into Jacobin equivalents. "The people," a symbol representing the genuine interests of the community, became a symbol for the majority of autonomous, equal citizens. Lippmann argued that this deformed democratic ethic was nominalist, never able to see beneath the surface, and unequipped to begin an examination of the public good.

Lippmann urged a return to "public philosophy," by which he meant the traditional discourse of the good to which all societies ought to aim. Lippmann warned against a society losing its ability to engage in public discourse about goods or goals. When a society relegates morals to the inner sanctum of private choice it has no means of maintaining itself. No society can long last without a purpose to give it meaning and a series of beliefs about proper public ends. To this end, Lippmann argued for a return to "natural law." One may debate endlessly about the meaning Lippmann invested in "natural law," but at the very least he meant for it to represent the continual human attempt to locate and encode in positive law the objectives and truths that transcend the welter of human perspectives. Natural law represents a common criterion by which to judge the shifting political life.

The loss of a public philosophy (natural law) is the result of the Jacobin revolution. Lippmann defined moderns as people who possess no binding principles, no beliefs held in common about what constitutes the good society. They are set adrift from the verities of the ancient order and without a public discourse capable of helping to establish new verities. Without the support of sanctioned beliefs most people cannot withstand the freedom, they fall easy prey to dictators who provide them what they lack.

Lippmann wrote *The Public Philosophy* under the dominating motif of the "crisis of the West." He called for a restoration, a return to the tradition of an ongoing discourse about public ends and public morals. Lippmann's intellectual journey from *Preface to Politics* to *The Public Philosophy* illustrates the deepening problems of liberal democracy in the West. He began with the sanguine expectations of youth, exultant over the new freedom that came with release from the beliefs, habits, and traditions of the past. Although he recognized that such freedom entailed not a little anxiety, he fully expected that the people of a free and democratic nation would embrace new social and political goals which they would discover through experimentation. His early books were fully modern, down to the names he invoked. The experiences subsequent to 1914 shook his faith in democracy as it had evolved in the United States. The intellectual freedom he had praised, had brought moral conundrums he had not anticipated. By mid century Lippmann was conversing more with ancient Greeks and Romans than with moderns like Freud. He wished to recapture the evolving tradition he had so joyously cast off years before.

The education of Walter Lippmann illuminates the ongoing conversation among many intellectuals in Europe and the United States about the direction of modern thought, of which liberalism was the dominant stream. To many of the people who rejected modernity, liberalism appeared directionless and morally empty. According to conservative antimoderns, liberals confused pleasure with happiness and thereby sought to maximize the former without regard to spiritual, moral, and aesthetic qualities one apprehends only through the eyes of imagination. Without those eyes, the material world appears as everything—the sum total of existence. It possesses no intrinsic moral sanctions, and it is governed by a rough law of power. For liberals, these truths, no matter how they are covered with humanitarian impulses, lurk beneath the surface like a snarling nihilist behemoth—threatening, ever threatening. The nihilist logic of modern liberalism, conservatives averred, was now exposed. The alternatives from which humans could choose—in their starkest manifestations—were totalitarianism or a civilized order guided by the higher imagination. Most conservatives fought, or thought they fought, an intellectual battle to save the West from liberalism a la totalitarianism.

3
From Philosophy
to Positivism

Turning and turning in the widening gyre
The falcon cannot hear the falconer;
Things fall apart; the center cannot hold;
Mere anarchy is loosed upon the world
W. B. Yeats

Henry Adams worshiped the dynamo but yearned for the Virgin. The tension between cherished traditions, beliefs, and ideals and the promise of a brighter future built with the help of new knowledge traps every American generation. Change, or the prospect of certain kinds of change, cannot help but engender excitement over new possibilities chastened by the fear that the old ways will be lost. New ways of living rest on the graves of older, often-cherished forms. The election of 1828, for instance, presented the nation with new possibilities and new fears. Did not the later populists propose change in order to protect a threatened way of life? The Southern Agrarians fought a losing battle to stop the changes transforming the American South. In one sense or another, all of these people fought against changes we associate with modernity; the United States has always had a vigorous antimodern impulse. Conservatives in the mid twentieth century continued a version of this impulse, reaching back to John Adams and developing through Henry Adams, the New Humanists, and Southern Agrarians. Yet they were also greatly influenced by Europeans who placed the American experience in a larger context. As participants in a larger Western culture, some Americans wondered if Europeans had not seen the future—or at least a potential future. And so the conservative critique of American liberal ideals and institutions advanced as part of the more European-rooted critique of modernity. The philosophical debates that occupied Continental thinkers during the nineteenth and early twentieth centuries did much to form the temper of the antimodernism that emerged in the United States in this era.

If life in Hobbes's England was nasty, brutish, and short, life for the first European generation born to the twentieth century was uncertain, irrational, and violent—above all, violent. The catalogue of atrocities of this era is as familiar as it is long, but though not distant in time, these events are not particularly fresh in the imaginations of the people who will shape the twenty-first century. The intellectual uncertainties of this earlier generation afflict the current generation like a thorn in the side, but as with most chronic difficulties one finds ways of ignoring or cloaking it, of seeking distractions that hide intellectual realities. Perhaps the enormous human cost of the recent past robs many of us of our courage, maybe even our concern, but in central Europe during the early decades of this most bloody century, young and agile minds felt the attraction of the intense self-conscious doubting, questioning, and searching that made the half century prior to World War II so intellectually rich, so heady and exciting.

The towering figures of Nietzsche, Weber, Marx, Husserl, and behind them the more imposing figures of Kant and Hegel dominated the intellectual landscape into which Leo Strauss and Eric Voegelin were born. These major figures formed the primary landmarks of their intellectual horizons, providing the initial boundaries and orientation of their thought. Eventually both Strauss and Voegelin sought to expand their horizons, to see over those mountains, but they could do so only by surmounting the heights that restricted their vision. In ways not always evident, much of Strauss's and Voegelin's work reads like one side of a discussion with their intellectual ancestors. Neither man really left his intellectual home, for their challenges were always to understand and reply to the work of the dominating thinkers they had confronted in their youth.

This philosophical context was clearly post-Enlightenment. In contrast to the optimistic project of Enlightenment thinkers to cast the light of reason into the dark corners of human experience, the philosophers of the nineteenth century (1790–1920) labored to salvage reason and to secure some epistemological territory. As the ontological base of the Enlightenment project crumbled—that is, the assumptions about God, creation, and above all cosmic purpose—post-Enlightenment thinkers struggled to supply new and sturdier verities and to dispel the anxiety of uncertainty by regaining certitude or by learning to live in an open-ended universe. The crisis of modernity, which dates at least as far back as Kant's *Critique of Pure Reason* (1781), inspired many attempts to save modernity by securing an epistemological ground. The modern project would no longer rest upon a discredited Semitic cosmology but upon the methods of science. The great metaphysical questions would fade away like the unreal phantoms of a dream. In the end, some people believed they could salvage the Promethean goal of employing knowledge to master human destiny. To others, the epistemological ground consisted of shifting sand. These thinkers gave up on the modern project and sought ways to accommodate themselves to this new and uncertain environment. The philosophical conversation from Kant to Husserl was complex, with the various interlocutors struggling with the same essential problems—the problems that most challenged Voegelin and Strauss.

The intellectual environment in the 1920s, when Strauss and Voegelin became philosophically aware, had the distinct smell of decay as modernity moved into senescence.[1] As the two men began their careers in the sort of nether world below philosophy called social science, the residual project of decaying modernity struck each as a hollow, deracinated enterprise. Although philosophers still went about their work, intellectual life in Europe and the United States became increasingly the province of social scientists. With metaphysics in disrepute, the modern project of accumulating knowledge and control fell to those who employed the most respected methods (science) in search of knowledge in those areas of human life still believed by most people to be knowable (the physical and, perhaps, the social world). In the hands of mere practitioners (to catch the spirit of Strauss's and Voegelin's complaint), the subtle and rich tensions that the thinkers of late modernity tried so hard to understand and resolve were reduced to simplistic methods and unquestioned assumptions, all wrapped in the prestigious garb of science.

Strauss, and to a lesser degree Voegelin, derided the self-contradictory and sophistic thinking that dominated contemporary scholarship. They labeled this trend "positivism," a catch-all word to indicate a blind attachment to the methods of the physical sciences, a naive belief in the "value-free" nature of the social scientific enterprise, and the often-subterranean belief in progress (but the essence of the word is the *tendency* to allow a privileged method of inquiry to define the scope of the knowable and thus to limit the scope of inquiry). The broadside against positivism damaged Voegelin and Strauss as much as their target, which is so elusive that one wonders at times if they were not attacking abstractions. Who were these social scientific positivists? For the most part we know them only by the label. Presumably numerous enough to pose a threat to clear thinking, few individual positivists warranted specific mention by Strauss or Voegelin. Positivists were the largely unreflective heirs to a tired philosophical tradition reaching back to the Enlightenment, a tradition that eventually dispensed with philosophy altogether.

To dismiss as sloppy Voegelin's and Strauss's critique of positivists, to ask for names and specifics, or to play ceaseless word games in search of a semantic particularity is to miss their point entirely. Indeed, they mischaracterize their largely bloodless opponents on numerous occasions. The point, however, is that they understood the issue in the context of a complex construction of contemporary Western thought and therefore characterized a tendency expressive of the "idea" of modern Western thought. In large part the social scientists to whom they pointed were not self-conscious positivists but simply loyal practitioners of their guild. For Voegelin and Strauss, the problem lay, not so much with the individual scientists—who often conceived of their work as a distinct and separate part of their lives—but with the logic immanent in the guild. The canons of the profession, in other words, were infected by the largely outdated beliefs of the modern project.

The critiques Voegelin and Strauss launched against positivists become intelligible when we understand the typically German emphasis they placed on theory, which they contrasted to empiricism. Their analysis slipped naturally, then, to the hard theoretical core that anchored social science, even if few or none of the practitioners thought about or recognized that core. Strauss was especially keen to expose the nihilist heart beating beneath the benign exterior. Thus Voegelin and Strauss could examine a cluster of beliefs and assumptions, reify them into positivism, and have "it" thinking and acting. Even if positivists were innocent of the theoretical core of their scholarly labors, the trajectory, the consequences of their work, would nonetheless be unchanged by their ignorance.

Other factors help account for the reaction of these two philosophers to the dominance of social science (of an allegedly positivistic persuasion) in intellectual circles. The circumstances of their intellectual environment forced Strauss and Voegelin to grapple with positivism early in their careers. After the positivistic moment in mid and late nineteenth century Germany, the general trend among Germanic philosophers had been an attempt to overcome the deadening logic of positivism (and here I refer to a philosophical school bearing the label) without recourse to the now-discredited metaphysics. Weber was an especially important figure in the attempt to sail between the Scylla of positivism and the Charybdis of the still-pervasive idealism. Despite the general trend, numerous and competing philosophical camps occupied the intellectual field.

The university training and early intellectual influences of both thinkers help us understand their later responses to positivistic social science. Voegelin's academic career was especially unusual in that he took his doctorate under the direction of Hans Kelsen and Othmar Spann, two mentors with apparently incompatible philosophies. Kelsen became famous for his Pure Theory of Law, and during his career in Austria and the United States he became noteworthy as the purest of legal positivists. Spann, on the other hand, was very much in the idealist, universalist tradition that had dominated much of German intellectual life during the nineteenth century. Voegelin worked more closely with Kelsen and developed an enduring respect for his work. He especially respected Kelsen's precision and analytical rigor, which he tried to imitate in his own scholarly pursuits. But to whatever degree Voegelin might have been a positivist in the early and mid 1920s, he decisively rejected the "theoretical" implications of positivism. In many interesting ways Voegelin's intellectual style demonstrated the persistent influences of his two very different mentors. Voegelin always appreciated and very much required for his own work the careful analytical work of social scientists. Their careful distinctions and qualifications became his; even few legal scholars, he believed, surpassed the erudition and rigor of Kelsen. But all of this work merely contributed to Voegelin's much more sweeping analysis that one can only call metaphysical. Voegelin was a grand theoretician blessed with the analytical rigor of a positivist.

Strauss, like Voegelin, became very familiar with the various versions of positivism during his university education. His doctoral director was Ernst Cassirer, the famous neo-Kantian who himself struggled to find some accommodation with positivism. Although one detects an enduring debt to Strauss's neo-Kantian training, he found Cassirer's attempt to form a new modern system of philosophy evasive. Cassirer had "*silently* dropped" ethics and therefore "had not *faced* the problem,"[2] so the overly positivistic Cassirer influenced Strauss less than "the most outstanding German philosopher" of the time, Edmund Husserl.[3] Husserl's attempt to save philosophy by returning to the life-world (prescientific world) of humans is a pervasive Straussian theme and the primary position from which he denounced the positivists. Nonetheless, the great Husserl, however important, ranks behind his student, Martin Heidegger, as an influence on Strauss. Strauss's fifty-year career may be reduced to a struggle with the problems Heidegger presented to this Jewish philosopher. Strauss's deep admiration for and hatred of Heidegger lie behind every significant thing he wrote, and almost every reference Strauss made to Heidegger displays the tension. In one revealing comment—really an aside—in a brief letter to Alexandre Kojeve, Strauss wrote: "Have you seen Heidegger's *Holzwege?* Most interesting, much that is outstanding and on the whole *bad:* the most extreme historicism."[4] To understand Heidegger's influence on the young Strauss it is worth quoting an unusually revealing passage:

> I remember the impression [Heidegger] made on me when I heard him first as a young Ph.D., in 1922. Up to that time I had been particularly impressed as many of my contemporaries in Germany were, by Max Weber: by his intransigent devotion to intellectual honesty, by his passionate devotion to the idea of science—a devotion that was combined with a profound uneasiness regarding the meaning of science. On my way north from Freiburg, where Heidegger then taught, I saw, in Frankfurt-am-Main, Franz Rosenzweig . . . and I told him of Heidegger. I said to him that in comparison with Heidegger, Weber appeared to me as an "orphan child" in regard to precision and probing and competence. I had never seen before such seriousness, profundity, and concentration in the interpretation of philosophic texts. I had heard Heidegger's interpretation of certain sections

in Aristotle, and some time later I heard Werner Jaeger in Berlin interpret the same texts. Charity compels me to limit my comparison to the remark that there was no comparison. Gradually the breadth of the revolution of thought which Heidegger was preparing dawned upon me and my generation. We saw with our own eyes that there had been no such phenomenon in the world since Hegel. He succeeded in a very short time in dethroning the established schools of philosophy in Germany.[5]

The deep psychological—even spiritual—involvement of Strauss with the problems and personalities of modernity makes him the greatest conservative critic of modernity, his work springing from some hidden personal dialectic. As a consequence Strauss's analysis becomes rich and textured, with layers of meaning often hiding others. Voegelin proceeded, by contrast, in a much more traditional manner, so I will use his analysis to open the matter of positivism before attempting to understand Strauss.

Voegelin thought of his scholarship as contributing to a burgeoning new age of philosophical pursuit. Modernity was largely a spent enterprise for intellectual luminaries, though it had left behind a theoretical (philosophical) wasteland. From this intellectual disorder the search for order was well under way. William James, Max Weber, Henri Bergson, to name a few, had begun the restoration of a science of order; Voegelin and his generation were building on their foundations. Voegelin cast his work, therefore, in a generally optimistic mode, and for this reason he did not devote an extraordinary amount of space (in terms of his published materials) to examining the contemporary manifestations of a nearly dead modern project. Still, his first American book—the work that gave this obscure Louisiana State professor exposure—was a declaration of a "new science of politics." The title (The New Science of Politics) played on several themes, the most important being Voegelin's rejection of positivistic social science in favor of a "new" science that would deal more comprehensively with human experience. Positivism was the proximate cause for the book as the author sought to "retheorize" political science.

Voegelin never diminished the value of positivist scholarship. Done well, the restrictive methods employed by positivists can isolate and illuminate important areas of human experience, but Voege-

lin meant something more sweeping, more pernicious by his use of
the label in this book. Because positivists had accepted as an axiom
"that only propositions concerning facts of the phenomenal world
[are] 'objective,' while judgments concerning the right order of the
soul and society [are] 'subjective,' " they have restricted the range of
permissible questions.[6] Political scientists may ask questions to
which the methods of the physical sciences can provide reliable and
persuasive answers—but it is these questions alone that the positivist will allow the political scientist to consider. The issues were two
for Voegelin: one, that positivists allow their method to define the
subject and, two, and very closely related, that the most important
political and social questions get tossed aside because a crucial component of human experience is effectively devalued as "subjective."[7]
One must remember that Voegelin did not direct his critique solely
at self-conscious positivists but also to the pervasive positivism (albeit in a decayed form) in social science. He advocated, by contrast,
a more empirical science that followed more closely human experience no matter how elusive or how difficult to understand.

This appeal struck an especially important chord at mid century.
In a time of great ideological strife and with World War II (an ideological war) just over, Voegelin insisted that political scientists must
pursue the truly important and most basic political questions concerning justice, freedom, order—the most value-laden issues. In orderly times with no important ideological clashes, relativism (for
Voegelin a logical result of positivism) might be an excusable luxury,
especially for academics. But in the most ideological and violent
century in human history, it appeared to be a luxury moderns could
ill-afford.

The New Science of Politics, and especially the introduction
where this discussion occurs, is strangely axiomatic. Much of what
Voegelin said took the form of assertion rather than argument, so
one must place this introduction in the context of his larger project.
The book invited misinterpretations. Even Hans Kelsen, Voegelin's
old mentor, wrote a lengthy response that he sent to Voegelin.[8] In
this fascinating document (fascinating because of the close attention he paid to the book, the defensive tone, and the psychological
dynamic), Kelsen defended positivism. He noted what anyone
should note, that Voegelin's use of the label was hopelessly loose and
vague. Voegelin wished to look beyond the rather narrow band of

scholars called positivists to identify the larger trends at work in the West of which the positivists represented the logical conclusion. As a result, as Kelsen noted, Voegelin defined this group by virtue of a shared negative. Kelsen put it this way: "The decisive trend in his fight against positivism can be only the reaction against the anti-metaphysical attitude prevailing in modern social philosophy and science."

The accuracy of Kelsen's characterization depends upon the meaning he gave to "metaphysical," and Kelsen provided plenty of clues. He meant any appeal outside those accepted by the methods of positivism, especially theology. Voegelin did not write a theological response to positivism; instead, he appealed to the philosophical "sciences" of anthropology and ontology. This would always be the point of tension for Voegelin (and other conservatives) and his philosophical opponents—do these disciplines supply socially and politically useful "knowledge?"

The late modern turn away from anthropology and ontology, Voegelin thought, represented a failure of modern methods to address the most important human questions: What does it mean to be human? What is one's place in the totality of reality? When the delimited methods of inquiry could uncover no subject behind these traditional philosophical categories, moderns denied the legitimacy of the existential tensions that had produced the quest. This position places us very near the heart of Voegelin's critique and exposes the unbridgeable chasm separating his understanding and Kelsen's. The privileging of certain methods meant that one must ignore or cast aside larger regions of human experience as "meaningless" or "subjective."[9] The objectifying (abstracting) of reality artificially externalized "it" from consciousness, making intelligible only those areas amenable to objectification. The distortion of human participation in reality (and it is a mistake to allow the spatial imagery of "in reality" to distort the truth of the participant being a coordinate of reality) into a false object/subject dualism sharply delimited the knowable region to the realm of science. As a consequence, the whole was lost as a subject for theoretical examination and this eclipsed "pregiven" perceptions of reality in favor of an ideological system.[10]

But how could this contraction of reality take place? Voegelin sought to answer this question by contextualizing the work of scientists and by exploring the social and intellectual environment that shaped both the political and scientific world. Positivism, from this larger perspective, represented a resilient strain of a more generalized intellectual virus called scientism. The social success of ideologies like communism and National Socialism shared with positivism a similar spiritual deficiency and a common intellectual history reaching back to the sixteenth century. Thus, this combination of spiritual disorder and particular historical circumstances dictated the actual shape of the ideological revolt. By examining his argument concerning the development of scientism we understand better the peculiar danger of positivism (as the carrier of the scientistic virus most evident in liberal democracies), and we can adumbrate the structure of Voegelin's argument about modernity.

Voegelin's essay "The Origins of Scientism," which appeared in 1948, clarified the issue. The date is important because it places this essay in the crucial years when Voegelin was working through the problem (and definition) of modernity.[11] Already, in his *History of Political Ideas*, Voegelin had focused on the sixteenth century as a crucial period.[12] Equally important, Voegelin had begun to deepen his understanding of the experiential source of all ideas. Throughout the forties, but especially in the next decade, Voegelin looked behind (or underneath) the ideational structure of a thinker or an age to the experience of reality that engendered ideas.[13] In this focused essay these themes played a central role.

Scientism is the closure to all nonphenomenal reality. Voegelin operated with an unclear dualism (though one with resonances going back to Plato) of the phenomenal realm and the realm of substance. The latter involved the underlying ground of being and stands for the realm of essences—the real rather than the merely existent. Scientism, as a theoretical issue, meant the treating of philosophical and spiritual matters (what today we might call human matters concerning social life) with the methods appropriate to the natural and physical sciences. But the more important historical question concerns the social effectiveness of this scientism. Why did it become paradigmatic in terms of epistemology and in defining proper human aspirations and social goals? Because Voegelin understood these shifts to be the results of an "antispiritual revolt," he had to find the answer in the human soul.

Two related existential ingredients have crucial roles in the story

Voegelin had to tell. One was the growing need or desire for certainty in the sixteenth and seventeenth centuries. These were bloody years in Europe with violence on all scales spawned by the dissolution of the catholic church and the hardened doctrinal disputes that followed. Also, the new intellectual horizons opened by the rebirth of classical philosophy gave thinkers new and persuasive models of social and political order. These conditions created a great desire for certainty—a way to supersede doctrinal disputes and to find the truth capable of ordering European social and intellectual life. The search for certain truth was invested with a special importance as the means of preventing chaos. A society besieged by conflicting truths lacked the stamina required for an order grounded on faith. The uncertainty of faith gave way to apodictic knowledge—the only foundation sturdy enough to sustain order, or so moderns believed. The second existential ingredient was the hubristic grasp at power inspired by the technological success of the sciences. As the mysteries of the phenomenal realm gave way to human intervention and control, humans dreamed of godlike mastery.

To isolate the existential source in this historical process Voegelin focused on Newton's assumption of absolute space. The particulars of this fascinating story cannot detain us here, but the importance of this story rested with Newton's rejection of relative space and motion on religious grounds. His metaphysics could not tolerate a physics that included relative space and motion. Because Newton's scientific claims became paradigmatic, subsequent scientists accepted his scientific arguments without recourse to the religious motivations for the claims. Consequently, "the well-intentioned theory of absolute space resulted in precisely the disorder it had intended to avert."[14]

But Newton the scientist did not occupy the intellectual field alone; Leibniz the philosopher addressed Newton's theories directly in his well-known correspondence with Newton's ally, Samuel Clarke. Leibniz attacked the theory upon grounds later developed by Kant and Einstein, and Voegelin emphasized that Leibniz, assessing the matter as a philosopher, anticipated the relativity theory that was widely embraced in the twentieth century. However, in scientific and social terms Leibniz lost. In response to Leibniz's argument, Clarke wrote that he did not understand. "This complaint," wrote Voegelin, "carries us beyond the theoretical discussion into

the human situation. The complaint was sincere: Clarke and Newton did not understand. As far as physicists are concerned, this
ended the debate for the next century and a half." Leibniz understood that phenomena cannot be isolated and made into simple objects that have properties. The properties of any objects "must be
conceived as part of a field of phenomenal relations."[15] The social
authority of Newton, however, protected his deficient understanding
of space and motion from the theoretical analysis of a philosopher.
The unacceptability of relativity—the threat, that is, it presented to
the goal of certainty—meant that scientists would operate according
to an untenable "cosmology" (as Voegelin labeled it). Even though
the philosopher in this story won a "theoretical victory," the social
victory went to the closed soul of the scientist.

The changes technology made in the ways humans lived reinforced the social effectiveness of "mathematizing science." Power
and wealth became interrelated with science, and Voegelin emphasized the "interaction between science and environmental
changes." The success and prestige of scientists encouraged the in-
vestment in more science (i.e., scientific investigation), which in
turn increased the success and prestige of scientists who took on the
role of high priests and whose machinations produced magical transformations. The utilitarian rationality of science was transplanted to
the political and social process. Even though all societies, Voegelin
emphasized, engage in utilitarian calculation, the growing prestige
and authority of science made this virtue predominant (and effectively eclipsed from view any values reached by other means). By the
nineteenth century this process had led to "the belief that the dominion of man over man would ultimately be replaced by the dominion of man over nature, and that the government of man would be replaced by the administration of things."[16] In this era humans could
dream of a transformed world. By applying to the human realm the
methods employed so successfully in the phenomenal realm, moderns believed they could gain mastery over social and political affairs—even human nature.

The results of this belief in scientific magic are socially debilitating. The belief that "human existence can be oriented in an absolute
sense through the truth of science" leaves society ignorant about the
most important issues of human existence (substantial rather than
phenomenal matters), and the social institutions that once shaped

personalities toward substantial order do not survive in this environment. A social order so structured "creates an environment that favors the social success of the deficient human types"—creating
"spiritual eunuchism."[17] The biologizing of humans by making
them objects of the natural sciences meant the loss of the human as
"the spiritually creative center of society and history."[18]

In this pessimistic essay Voegelin despaired about the future—
"the insane have succeeded in locking the sane into the asylum."[19]
Scientism had become so pervasive that by the mid nineteenth century it dominated intellectual circles, and by the twentieth century
it had demonstrated its resonance with the masses in Russia and
Germany. The desire for certainty and control so overwhelmed
people's experience of reality that they accepted the deformed reality
of an ideology—and did monstrous things to fulfill the dream.

Voegelin's pessimism had largely evaporated a few years later
when he published *The New Science of Politics* (the title itself suggests a new beginning). The effects of scientism had not disappeared
suddenly, as Americans by and large still believed that technological
advancement harbingered real (substantial) progress—that the answer to the limits of science was more science (including a more rigorous application of scientific methods to social and political matters). Nonetheless, Voegelin found reason to hope. Positivism—the
most obvious manifestation of scientism in the United States—no
longer dominated intellectual circles. What is unclear is whether a
new science of substance could prove socially effective in such an
environment. This was the very live question that directed or
spurred Voegelin's work during the following decade.

For Leo Strauss positivism was one of two primary intellectual disorders that motivated his own philosophical investigations. In virtually every work he had something to say about positivists and their
more radical heirs, historicists. By drawing attention to these dominating intellectual trends, Strauss's works became alternatives to or
bulwarks against these modern conceits. A careful examination of
all of Strauss's comments on positivism exposes numerous evasions,
a few apparent contradictions (does positivism lead to conformism
and philistinism or nihilism?), and a plethora of exaggeration.[20] One
senses from reading Strauss that he found positivists threatening or
dangerous because they (sometimes unconsciously) undermine beliefs necessary for political and social order. But to go no further

than this cynical reading trivializes what for Strauss (much like Voegelin) was a matter of grave importance. With Strauss the larger issue, of which positivism formed a part, concerned nothing less than the fate of Western civilization.

To understand Strauss's assault on the positivists one must recall that for Strauss, positivism cleared the intellectual space (much like a bulldozer clears a stand of trees) for a widespread and morally incapacitating nihilism. Whereas Voegelin believed that positivism represented the dying gasp of modernity, Strauss thought of it as the penultimate stage leading to historicism—or "existentialism," a term he used to suggest, among other things, an inward turning to the individual soul because no socially constructed meanings or purposes have any more purchase, a final and complete relativism. An extensive examination of this argument must be put aside until later, but we need to understand Strauss's views of the state of contemporary intellectual life. His concise and largely straightforward essay "Social Science and Humanism" (first published in 1956) supplies the essential components of his diagnosis.

Strauss's point of departure on the subject of political science (and the social sciences in general) was the unfitness of the "scientific spirit" for examining political and social matters. Often employing important but elusive terms like "commonsense" and "civic art," Strauss pointed to the real, value-laden world people experience, especially in their capacity as citizens or as social creatures. Science "is characterized by detachment and by the forcefulness which stems from simplicity or simplification."[21] These characteristics are alien to politics and to the social world more generally. The scientist wants to take the rich, confusing, prerational life-world (to borrow from Husserl) experienced by ordinary people as a whole and divide it into digestible segments—parts of the whole that one can examine detached from the larger fabric which gives them meaning. The scientist hopes to understand the whole of the political and social order by understanding its parts. But, while the scientist holds out the hope of understanding the entire order by putting the abstracted parts back together, the "scientific spirit" works against any such reconstruction. Strauss wrote: "The sovereign rule of specialization means that the reconstruction cannot even be attempted. . . . The whole as primarily known is an object of common sense, but it is the essence of the scientific spirit, at least as this spirit shows itself within the social sciences, to be distrustful of common sense or even to discard it altogether."[22] By "commonsense" Strauss meant the world as we experience it nonabstractly—the prescientific experience of the world. The scientist can only deal with this experience by dividing it into parts and dealing abstractly with them. These parts, as they take shape (since they did not exist as parts before the scientist created them), have relevance only for the scientists—the citizen has no use for them. Strauss identified the striking difference of relevance in this way:

> The scientific social scientist is concerned with regularities of behavior; the citizen is concerned with good government. The relevances for the citizen are values, values believed in and cherished, nay, values which are experienced as real qualities of real things: of man, of actions and thoughts, of institutions, of measures. But the scientific social scientist draws a sharp line between values and facts: he regards himself as unable to pass any value judgment.[23]

The foregoing characterization deals with a social science set loose entirely from the world of commonsense. For reasons not entirely clear, Strauss navigated around the word "positivism" in this essay and chose instead to write about the "scientific spirit." Strauss was, in fact, careful here to largely avoid code words and to employ labels carefully. Nonetheless, his argument was essentially the same in this essay as in the broadsides against positivism that he sprinkled liberally throughout his works. In reconstructing Strauss's more hard-hitting critiques, two issues stand out as paramount. First, the dichotomy between facts and values, which Strauss took to be the heart of the social scientific method, robbed positivistic social science of the crucial means of understanding the political and social world—a world constituted on values rather than facts. Second, these methods, in the hands of lesser practitioners (in contrast to Weber, for instance) engendered an unthinking relativism. Scientists who perform their labors in fealty to the god of a value-free science become unreflective about the assumptions that undergird their enterprise even as they begin to dismiss as unimportant phenomena not amenable to their method. Strauss came dangerously close on several occasions to claiming, incorrectly, that the ethical neutrality of the scientific method entailed a philosophical relativism. However, his point was somewhat more complicated.

"The habit of looking at social or human phenomena without making value judgments," Strauss wrote, "has a corroding influence on any preferences. The more serious we are as social scientists, the more completely we develop within ourselves a state of indifference to any goal, or aimlessness and drifting, a state which may be called nihilism."[24] For Strauss the positivistic core of social science ("scientific spirit") created several unavoidable (though not logically entailed) conditions. The emphasis upon complete neutrality concerning ultimate values spilled over into the thinking of the scientist qua citizen. This, of course, is a difficult case to make. Even Strauss argued that despite their dedication to truth as their only value, all the social scientists he had ever met were unqualified democrats (and usually not reflective about democracy).[25] However, Strauss's point of emphasis was their unthinking acceptance of their values, and a generalized belief among scientists that they posited their own values. These were subjective choices and therefore indefensible. Strauss assumed that social scientists found the traditional discourse concerning moral and political matters illegitimate, and to the degree that these beliefs gained currency, therefore, the very elements natural to political and social order were undermined. All hope for social and political stability rests upon a widespread belief in a moral or metaphysical core, beliefs one gains through "commonsense" or a prescientific apperception of the whole. Science applied uncritically to human affairs undermines commonsense, or the very characteristics necessary to the society under investigation.

In "Social Science and Humanism," however, Strauss held out a role for social science so long as the scientist's bearings are taken from commonsense (the world as lived, not abstracted) and that individuals, in their capacity as scientists, be "ruled by the legitimate queen of social sciences . . . ethics."[26] Strauss packed more into this assertion than I have room to discuss, but the most obvious meaning is the inherent valuative nature of human life. A science of human things must, above all else, involve the human quality of evaluating, creating hierarchies, and deciding upon the good. On almost all matters and on nearly all things, humans place a value. In a broader context, Strauss meant that social scientists seek to understand human things, therefore they must understand "the human knowledge of what constitutes humanity, or, rather, of what makes man complete or whole, so that he is truly human.''[27]

Strauss called scientists to the philosophical pursuit of defining the human—the universal qualities that provide the grounds for talking about the species. He called them to do even more, to examine the human in terms of the whole. This demand requires that scientists account for humans in terms of ends or purposes, which is to say their place in an order not of their construction. Social science, then, ''cannot be based on modern science, although it may judiciously use, in a strictly subordinate fashion, both methods and results of modern science. Social science must rather be taken to contribute to the true universal science into which modern science will have to be integrated eventually.''[28] In other words, Strauss argued for a social science of the sort practiced by Aristotle and Plato— social science properly used becomes philosophy.

We learn halfway through the essay that Strauss found social science in its modern manifestation a meaningless exercise. The social scientific objective of understanding human society requires controlling methods (as opposed to subordinate methods) unlike those of the physical sciences. In an especially clear summary Strauss wrote:

> To treat social science in a humanistic spirit [i.e., to transform social science into philosophy] means to return from the abstractions or constructs of scientistic social science to social reality, to look at social phenomena primarily in the perspective of the citizen and the statesman, and then in the perspective of the citizen of the world, in the twofold meaning of ''world'': the whole human race and the all-embracing whole.[29]

The positivism of social science formed one extreme position that threatened a proper understanding of human social and political life. The other extreme, historicism, which Strauss took to be the logical modern answer to conundrums created by positivism,[30] he explored in the second part of the essay (see Chapter 5 for a discussion of this subject). What is important for the present is that Strauss, like Voegelin, found insufferable an intellectual environment dominated by social science.

The ''historicists,'' who became for Strauss the greatest expressions of modernity (albeit modernity in the throes of self-destruction), were reacting to the same positivistic environment that spurred Voegelin and Strauss to revolt against modernity. One is even prone to think that for Strauss, historicism and an antimodernism of the sort practiced by Voegelin and Strauss were the only real alternatives for the modern world. At any rate, the historicist's answer to the positivists was to accept the final logic of modernity, to look deeply into the abyss and to leap, gleefully or mournfully, into its bottomless reaches. If they took this act to be the manly acceptance of truth, Strauss took it to be a nihilist rejection of responsibility. If Strauss had any hope for a recovery of order he, and to a lesser degree Voegelin, had to understand modernity—"its" character and its constitution. Because this diagnosis, this search for the fatal intellectual gene, was so essential to the process of recovery we must better understand Strauss and Voegelin's construction of the problem. Then, and only then, will the deep involvement Strauss had with the problem of historicism, or with Voegelin's more generalized though less-acute concern for the present age, become clear. Eventually, of course, the problems of modernity must relate to those people who live in stable democracies.

4
The Nature of Modernity

MACHIAVELLI THE CHIRON

Few writers as blunt as Niccolò Machiavelli have spawned so rich a debate over their teaching. Should one understand him as an Italian patriot devoted to reviving the glory of Rome or as an ardent republican? Was he a pagan who considered Christianity an effeminate religion that sapped the creative energy of the Italian people? Did his patriotism so overwhelm him that he advocated immoral methods to achieve the "good" of a strong and united Italy? Was he the first "scientific" political thinker and hence the founder of political science? To these general interpretive questions concerning his teaching one must add other questions that deal with the intertextual structure of his corpus and how that structure may relate to his audience. How important is the *Prince* in identifying Machiavelli's teaching? What is the relationship between the *Prince* and the *Discourses*? Should one read the former in the context of the latter? To what degree ought one take into account the identified audience in making a judgment as to the messages of these two works and their relationship to Machiavelli's genuine thought? How do these manifestly "political" works relate to his works of fiction and history?

Leo Strauss's examination of "modern" philosophers began with Machiavelli. Strauss saw in Machiavelli's teaching the origin of modernity, and in his exegesis of Machiavelli, one glimpses the difference between classical philosophy and modern philosophy with a clarity unmatched from any other vantage point. Here one witnesses the mature thinking of Strauss as he moved from a sense of disorder to a search for order (the classical solution) to his accounting for the fateful shift. Strauss's examination of the first modern came only after the categories modern and classical had developed some precision in his mind. Only after he understood what modernity meant could he find its origin. Also, the nature of Strauss's work on Machiavelli provides an excellent entrée to Strauss's famed hermeneutic.

Strauss's most penetrating study of any modern thinker bears the modest title *Thoughts on Machiavelli*. Rarely has a title promised so little, and a book delivered so much. Read it once and get lost in the confusing levels of analysis, the shifting from Machiavellian texts to the works of Livy and other historians. Read it twice and witness its architectonic genius, its subtly crafted structure, its logical steps. Read it a third time with the care of a detective, following the carefully placed clues, identifying the many blind alleys, and putting the pieces together into a single, unified picture. Just do not read it a fourth time, when the sly and systematic Machiavelli that Strauss constructed begins to look too sturdy beside the untidy and intellectually disheveled Machiavelli one remembers reading. Nonetheless, a careful reader notes the loving care with which Strauss engaged the thought of this "fallen angel."[1] Machiavelli did not serve as a foil for Strauss's larger story. Indeed, his fidelity to Machiavelli's texts and the genuine respect Strauss displayed for Machiavelli's greatness make this book a remarkable engagement between two philosophers.[2] I do not mean to suggest anything about the veracity of Strauss's interpretation, just that his study of Machiavelli displays a special care, dedication, and a strange sort of beauty.

Strauss's text is compelling and elusive because of his famous and controversial claim that great philosophers write in such a way as to present an exoteric exterior protecting an esoteric core. In other words, there are two messages: one for the superficial reader who reads to confirm his conventional beliefs, another for the careful "young" reader who dedicates his life to the intransigent search for truth. Great philosophers serve both readers, protecting the political order, which is grounded on conventional beliefs, while "teaching" untold generations the politically dangerous truths that undermine beliefs. If one accepts Strauss's contention that great philosophers write esoterically because their teachings threaten the political order and thereby their own safety, then Strauss's own career poses some very perplexing problems. In the first place, if Strauss believed that philosophers write in this fashion and that such a political deception is necessary or desirable, then his discussion of esoteric writing along with his careful exegesis of the great philosopher's texts make him an evil man unless he, too, presented his teaching within an esoteric structure that is inaccessible to the superficial reader. Not only has he called to the reader's attention the fact that philosophers hide dangerous truths from the rest of us, but he has taken great pains to expose the very teachings that most threaten our political order. Moreover, one might be excused for asking that even if Strauss were correct in a general way, does not Machiavelli offer a strange example of a philosopher who wrote in such a fashion as to cloak his true teaching? Ought one not be surprised that Strauss applied this principle even to the first modern whose works do not appear at first glance to be hiding anything?

Still more perplexing is the problem these conditions pose for interpreting Strauss's own works. Despite his exposure of esoteric writing in others, might his "modern" style be the protective coating for his own teaching? Since he often and clearly expressed his agreement with the "classical" assumption that a philosopher's relationship to the contemporary political and social order is always precarious, one must assume he wrote esoterically. Nonetheless, one wonders what persecution Strauss faced in such a liberal and tolerant society. For a Jew who came of age during the Weimar regime in Germany, a liberal political order might not appear especially stable. Although Strauss emphasized that persecution comes in many forms, the political and intellectual climate does not explain his evasiveness. Two other factors played more important roles in his decision. First, philosophers have an obligation to prevent widespread skepticism, which is inimical to political society. Second, philosophers should protect people who are unsuited for the skeptical life of philosophy from having their beliefs undermined while providing the means for the natural philosophers to learn.[3] I believe this last reason for writing esoterically influenced Strauss the most. Philosophers are not just born, they are trained, and hiding one's message through sophisticated textual clues forces the reader to think through matters with much greater care and to challenge all the assertions made in the book. Reading a book of philosophy should resemble a discussion.

No matter the reasons, Strauss's method of writing complicates matters considerably, and this complication provides ample opportunity for sloppy or hostile scholars to read virtually any message into Strauss's works. Some scholars unmask Strauss by using his esotericism as a shield to ward off competing interpretations as though writing esoterically effectively hides one's real teaching from everyone. The difficulties facing one who seeks to unravel this Straussian web present special dangers, but they do not preclude understanding. An extended discussion of these matters is impractical in this book, but *Thoughts on Machiavelli* provides an entrée to Strauss's special hermeneutic. One learns through an examination of this book not only his method but its fruit, and one clarifies much about Strauss's critique of modernity along the way.

The problems with interpreting Strauss fade away, however, if Strauss did not think of himself as a philosopher. A historian of philosophy has no teaching to hide, and Strauss made numerous claims to this more humble role. But since he argued that only a philosopher can understand fully, i.e., understand the thinker as he understood himself, then Strauss would be a purveyor of vulgar doctrines if he did not consider himself a philosopher. Given his own understanding of the position required for someone to speak on a subject, he must have considered himself a philosopher capable of understanding those about whom he wrote. One ought, moreover, apply to Strauss his comments about the Arabic philosopher Farabi: "Farabi avails himself then of the specific immunity of the commentator or of the historian of order to speak his mind concerning grave matters in his 'historical' works, rather than in the works in which he speaks in his own name."[4]

But one need not resort to that sort of evidence alone to support the claim that Strauss considered himself a philosopher and his commentaries as means of teaching. In his study of Machiavelli, for instance, Strauss articulated the theme that governed his entire philosophical career and expresses the substance of both his critique of modernity and his attempt to recover the classical tradition. "Our critical study of Machiavelli's teaching can ultimately have no other purpose than to contribute towards the recovery of the permanent problems."[5] Moderns since Machiavelli have lost sight of the permanent problems, the insoluble connections and conflicts between faith and reason, political life and the philosophical life, theory and practice. By exposing the changes Machiavelli made in the goals of philosophy—that is, the goals of philosophers qua philosophers—Strauss recovered the original enterprise. Reading *Thoughts on Ma-*

chiavelli requires that one grapple with two philosophers, or rather the use one makes of the works of another.

Since both Strauss's commentary on Machiavelli's work and Strauss's own teaching are bound up in his hermeneutic, one has to begin with the art of writing esoterically and the meaning Strauss invested in that activity. Strauss's critics, and some of his followers, think of his method as a sort of decoder that one might use inflexibly. This idea puts one in mind of spies who write notes with invisible ink, or in code, to communicate with other spies. Perhaps a more accurate image is of a cryptic map uncovered by a young treasure hunter who is thus confronted with at least two exciting prospects: the joy of deciphering the map and the expectation of enormous treasure. This second image, however, is different in important respects from the first. A spy needs an instrument; a chemical to expose the ink or the code to decipher the message. In other words, this image represents the critical assessment of Strauss's reading, that it is a magical code, a sort of hermeneutical chemical that exposes the message written between the lines (and "between the lines" is exactly where Strauss said one finds the message). The second image better reflects Strauss's method. A cryptic map does not come with a code book but with curious clues that one must puzzle through. One will almost assuredly not unravel the mystery with the first try, and one will find that solving a puzzle one way only leaves the relationship with other symbols on the map more problematic. One tries again, and again, each time eliminating some answers while seeking new ways to make sense of the relationships on the map. The excitement of the discovery, of finding some great treasure that has been hidden away for years and protected by countless snares, gives Strauss's hermeneutic its power and is also the source of the most hostile criticism of him and his followers. The Straussians form a rather snobbish and closed cadre, the critics contend. They believe they have discovered what everyone else has missed; they think they are the real philosophers and that those who read the great books without seeing the hidden message expose themselves as being nonphilosophers (by "nature" incapable of being philosophers), unworthy as intellectual partners. If this critique does justice in describing some of Strauss's followers, it considerably distorts Strauss's own attitude toward the community of scholars in which he participated.

In theory, the method of following the clues left behind by the great philosophers will take the discoverer down different paths. In theory, Strauss's method is very particularized, adapting to the widely varying ways of communicating a hidden message. In practice, the philosophers Strauss studied followed very similar strategies. Machiavelli, though his message may have been very different, taught in the same manner as Plato. Yet one might expect this similarity since Strauss assumed that superficial readers read one way and careful readers another. Certain clues should always alert the one and pass by the other. These clues, Strauss argued, appear on the "surface," and the careful reader of a book written by a great thinker (an essential qualification) ought to account for everything in the work. An interpreter of a great book has not the freedom to omit problematic passages or to seek hidden meanings without accounting for textual contradictions to those teachings. In other words, Strauss demanded a rigorous empiricism with regard to texts. "Reading between the lines" means that one finds one's answer on the "surface." "There is no surer protection against the understanding of anything than taking for granted or otherwise despising the obvious and the surface. The problem inherent in the surface of things, and only in the surface of things, is the heart of things."[6] The writer leaves all the clues in the open, on the surface, and writes nothing without a purpose. The key to understanding then lies, not just on the surface, but in the "problem inherent in the surface of things." One has no justification for thinking that a writer wishes to communicate two different messages if one fails to detect a "problem" in the surface of the text.[7]

By problems Strauss meant anomalies; places in the text that strike one as odd or out of character with the general flow of the argument. They act as stumbling blocks, forcing the careful reader to stop and discover why one stumbles at that point. Machiavelli arrested Strauss's attention with his discussion of manifest blunders in the *Discourses* (bk. 3, chap. 48), making the universal claim that for every error an enemy makes "there will always be a fraud beneath it." After offering this universal rule, Machiavelli presented an example that undermined its universality: that enemies may make obvious blunders because of some weakness on their part, whether panic or cowardice. Why did Machiavelli choose an example that undermined his universal claim? According to Strauss:

"What is important is the fact that Machiavelli, in the act of speaking of manifest blunders, himself commits a manifest blunder. He does what, as he says, enemies sometimes do. His action ceases to be absurd if he himself is an enemy, a clever enemy." The example that contradicts the rule—which was the central example among many—supplies a clue to understanding Machiavelli's work. But this finding does not solve all the problems or give one access to the fullness of his teaching, for it is but one clue. Once one recalls that Machiavelli advocated "new modes and orders," then his odd example—his blunder in the context of the discussion about the meaning of blunders—informs the reader of an important strategy of criticizing the old modes and orders (as well as advocating the new).[8]

Contradictions, whether in the form of small "blunders" or more obvious self-contradictions, provide the richest single source for hints concerning an author's intention. Machiavelli's works are full of incompatible statements, but how does one decide which of two contradictory statements to believe? Few general rules dictate an answer. If one assumes that the author knew the contradictions existed, then the act must have been purposeful. The interpreter must follow the logic of the particular case, and Strauss's works overflow with these exercises. Nonetheless, because the author assumes the necessity of concealing his message, the interpreter must assume that strong statements repeating or affirming common and popular beliefs must be ironic if they are contradicted by more or less oblique statements.[9] In its simplest form the construction looks like $a = b - a \neq b$. In many cases an author will offer views with much greater indirection, such as $a = b - b = c - [a = c] - a \neq c - [a \neq b]$, with the brackets signifying arguments not specifically made but entailed in the argument. In such a construction one must assume that the author meant to communicate that "a" does not equal "b."[10] These two examples only begin to suggest the numerous ways a writer might contradict himself without appearing to do so.

Strauss detected a pattern in Machiavelli's work. Machiavelli presented his message in stages by supplying "first statements," which represented acceptable positions, followed by "second statements of a different character," and according to the assumption one makes about the relationship of the two stages the message will vary. "If one does not realize the difference of 'purpose' between 'first statements' and 'second statements,' one may read the 'second statements' in light of the 'first statements' and thus blunt the edges of his teaching." Machiavelli will appear quite conventional if one makes this mistake and thereby fail to "grasp the magnitude or enormity of Machiavelli's enterprise."[11]

The best way to read a great book is to learn from the author how one ought to read it, and one clue is to examine the way the author reads the works of other thinkers. Because Machiavelli's *Discourses* is a commentary on the books of Livy, Strauss had access to Machiavelli's method of reading others and found that Machiavelli argued from the silence of Livy as well as from his explicit statements. Concerning the common assumption that money is the sinews of war, Machiavelli, relying upon the authority of Livy, noted that when discussing this subject Livy remained silent regarding money. Machiavelli argued that Livy taught through his silence, and as Strauss put the matter regarding Machiavelli's strategy: "If a wise man is silent about a fact that is commonly held to be important for the subject he discusses, he gives us to understand that the fact is unimportant. The silence of a wise man is always meaningful."[12] If Machiavelli used this method when explaining the work of another, Strauss assumed that the same technique applied to Machiavelli's own works. To understand how much Strauss relied upon this method of reading Machiavelli, a lengthy quote is necessary.

> In the *Prince* he fails to mention the conscience, the common good, the distinction between kings and tyrants, and heaven. We are reluctant to say that he forgot to mention these things, or that he did not mention them because there was no need to mention them since their importance is a matter of course or known to the meanest capacities. For if this reasoning is sound, why did he mention them in the *Discourses?* We suggest that he failed to mention them in the *Prince* because he regarded them unimportant in the context of the *Prince.* There are, however, certain subjects which he fails to mention, not only in the *Prince* but in the *Discourses* as well, whereas he does mention them in his other works. He does not in either book mention the distinction between this world and the next, or between this life and the next; while he frequently mentions God or gods, he never mentions the devil; while he frequently mentions heaven and once paradise, he never mentions hell; above all, he never

mentions the soul. He suggests by this silence that these subjects are unimportant for politics. But since each of the two
books contains everything he knows, he suggests by this silence
that these subjects are unimportant simply, or that the common
opinion according to which these subjects are most important,
is wrong. . . . He expresses his disapproval of common opinion
most effectively by silence.[13]

The argument from silence assumes a rather large place in
Strauss's overall strategy of interpreting Machiavelli (justified by the
example of Machiavelli's interpretive strategy applied to Livy). Silence on matters generally considered integral to the subject under
examination (in this case the political order), especially in a book in
which the author claims to have written everything he knows about
the subject, led Strauss to believe that Machiavelli taught by his silence that conventional beliefs were untrue.

Strauss dutifully attended to Machiavelli's arguments concerning
Livy's texts. What examples from Livy's books did he choose? What
significance do those choices have? How accurately did Machiavelli
characterize Livy's arguments? Strauss found a pattern of misuse of
Livy that could not have been accidental, and Strauss also found
other strategies of encoding a secret message in such things as di-
gressions and ambiguous terms, especially virtue.[14]

The most notorious and controversial Straussian method was his
numerology. Strauss counted just about everything: books, chapters,
paragraphs. Operating on the assumption that superficial readers pay
greater attention at the beginning and the end, Strauss expected to
find the most controversial teachings at the center of a book (or,
sometimes, at the center of chapters or a series of chapters that compose a section). If a book contained thirteen chapters, for instance,
Strauss presumed that chapter seven contained the most important
clues to the purpose of the book.[15] This idea is only the beginning of
his fascination with numbers. One especially challengeable exercise
in numerology exposes the lengths to which Strauss went.

The *Prince* consists of 26 chapters. Twenty-six is the numerical
value of the letters of the sacred name of God in Hebrew, of the
Tetragrammaton. But did Machiavelli know this? I do not know.
Twenty-six equals 2 times 13. Thirteen is now and for quite

sometime has been considered an unlucky number, but in former times it was also and even primarily considered a lucky number. So "twice 13" might mean both good luck and bad luck, and hence altogether: luck, *fortuna*.[16]

That exercise represents only a portion of Strauss's analysis of the number twenty-six in both the *Discourses* and the *Prince*, but it is sufficient to expose what most critics find as Straussian excess. It remains to be emphasized that the most important part of Strauss's interest in this subject was his constant attempt to locate the "center" of an argument. A careful reader of Strauss's works diligently counts paragraphs.[17]

This hermeneutic and the many assumptions that go with it play so central a role in the thinking and teaching of Leo Strauss that no meaningful discussion about his beliefs is possible without some understanding of this matter. The significance of his reading for esoteric messages extends well beyond his intriguing and usually profound interpretations of the great books to the complexities of reading and interpreting Strauss himself and even to the heart of his revolt against modernity. But this subject, like so much with Strauss, must wait until we better understand the details of his project.

With an overview of Strauss's theory of esoteric writing and his methods of reading a book, we are better prepared to examine his critique of Machiavelli. The reader learns that Strauss intended to transcend the particular topic in order to recover the origins of modernity, and any extended study of one of Strauss's books requires an examination of the way he structured or organized his argument. Strauss divided *Thoughts on Machiavelli* into five parts, consisting of an Introduction and four chapters. The Introduction informs the reader that Strauss intended to revive an old-fashioned understanding of Machiavelli as a teacher of "evil," and the reader also learns that he had a purpose that transcended the particular topic: Strauss intended to recover the "permanent problems."

The relationship between these two objectives emerges out of a complicated dialectic. Chapter 1, "The Twofold Character of Machiavelli's Teaching," establishes the esoteric nature of Machiavelli's works. In Chapters 2 and 3, Strauss did much of his textual spadework on Machiavelli's *Prince* and the *Discourses*, respectively. In the final and longest chapter, "Machiavelli's Teaching," Strauss brought together his discoveries from all of Machiavelli's works—but especially from his two political works—to establish Machiavelli's political and philosophical goals, i.e., his teaching. Excluding the Introduction, Strauss's book develops from an argument regarding Machiavelli's method, through a textual analysis of the two central books, to the final unmasking of the real Machiavelli. Despite Strauss's admission in the Introduction that he had come to a well-established and therefore not surprising interpretation of his subject, the book bears a strong resemblance to a mystery story with clues emerging slowly from painstaking work, some of which turn out to be misleading until placed in a larger context, until finally the reader comes to discover Machiavelli's true identity. One should not be surprised if by the end of the story one learns that Strauss's introductory characterizations of his conclusions are misleading.

The damnable characteristic about Machiavelli, from Strauss's point of view, was the newness of his teaching. Machiavelli broke from the great tradition of philosophers, and this break led to a new constellation of beliefs about control of humans over nature, and hence their own destiny; about the proper goals and objectives of political society; and about the philosophical pursuit (or a change in belief regarding the highest human aspiration). Strauss warned the reader that the very success of Machiavelli's teaching, the degree to which moderns have accepted his teachings as truistic, makes moderns unable to see the master for the innovator he was. Machiavelli so corrupted moderns that to them his work has lost the vivid color of a creative if demonic genius—they see only pallor and no evil. Looking back with the provincialism of the nineteenth and twentieth centuries, readers have lost the "surprise" of Machiavelli. Strauss examined Machiavelli from the perspective of the premodern so that his creativity in the context of his inherited biblical and classical heritage would show more clearly.[18] This context includes Machiavelli's intellectual and political horizon, both of which shaped what he taught and the method of his instruction.

Strauss characterized Machiavelli as a "fallen angel," referring to the heritage he perverted. He mastered the classics. He knew well the tradition against which he rebelled. He took the evil doctrines advocated long before ("as old as political society itself") through the medium of characters, like Plato's Thrasymachus, and advocated them in his own name.[19] From the very start the reader gets mixed signals. Was Machiavelli's evil his "open" advocacy of the beliefs hidden by those Strauss admired, like Plato? If so, then why would Machiavelli write in such a manner as to hide his real message? Or should the reader assume that the classical philosophers not only did not advocate "Machiavellian" beliefs but expressed those beliefs through characters for the purpose of disproving them? Machiavelli advocated those once discredited beliefs and sought to persuade others (though not everyone). Strauss's book, and his larger assault on modernity, makes sense only if he believed that Machiavelli had changed classical teaching.[20]

In the first chapter Strauss sought to establish that Machiavelli wrote in such a way as to present different messages to two audiences. Beyond discussing the various methods Machiavelli employed to convey his two messages, Strauss argued for the basic unity and agreement between the two books. They do not differ with regard to subject matter but present the same teaching from two points of view. The twofold character of his teaching, therefore, does not refer to contrasting teachings in the two works but to a twofoldness in each book. Each book speaks to the old and the young reader, each hearing a different message. The reader learns that Machiavelli aimed the real teaching at the young (a point that will be discussed in greater detail later).

In Chapter 2, Strauss pointed out that the revolutionary part of the *Prince* is not Machiavelli's particular advice but his claims to universal truth. The work, Strauss argued, has the characteristics of a tract for the times and of a treatise concerning truth for all times. Since Machiavelli addressed the work to a particular prince the reader might not note that Machiavelli's real audience was not the prince (or not just the prince) but an indefinite multitude, the young.[21] He sought to begin a complete revolution[22] through the young—a revolution that entailed "new modes and orders," which resulted from a revolution in one's understanding of right and wrong. Italy needed liberation, not from barbarians, but from "a bad tradition," by which Machiavelli meant a Christian tradition (or at least a certain kind of Christian tradition). Brought up with the Christian religion, the young of Italy had become "too confident of human goodness, if not of the goodness of creation, and hence too gentle and effeminate."[23] A revolution of such proportions requires a complete turning over of beliefs (new modes and orders) and a founder for the new order. The times required a new Moses, one of Machiavelli's favorite historical examples.

The precise content of Machiavelli's revolutionary message remains unclear in this chapter, though Strauss exposed most of the important themes in their nascent form. Especially important are the relative roles of *fortuna* and virtue and of the common good and self-interest, as well as the relative importance of patriotism in explaining Machiavelli's advice. The issue of *fortuna* and virtue is especially complicated because it involves Machiavelli's confusing statements about religion. In Machiavelli's *Prince*, Strauss found that chance plays some role in human life but also that leaders must learn to control *fortuna* and must never depend upon her. Unlike the *Discourses*, Machiavelli avoided mentioning "the common good" in the *Prince* until Chapter 26, in which he justified his immoral policies on the grounds of a moral goal. Once Strauss exposed Machiavelli's language of the common good as a cover for his arguments concerning the nature of political and social life, Machiavelli's patriotism appeared similarly feigned, or at least secondary. "The core of his being," wrote Strauss, "was his thought about men, about the conditions of man and about human affairs." Machiavelli's goals extended well beyond the moment or the particular to the creation of new modes and orders.

Strauss intimated in this same chapter that Machiavelli thought himself a founder. The *Prince* was about foundings and the requirements for a leader to establish a new political society. The "center" of the book, Strauss argued, is Chapter 19 (which is the center of what Strauss called the third division),[24] in which Machiavelli exposed the truth about founders who acted most unjustly and ruthlessly to accomplish their tasks. The civil and political order is grounded upon injustice, and since one can hope for justice only within the context of an established political order, justice depends upon prior acts of injustice.

Strauss's discussion of the *Prince* ended with two problems that he would not resolve until the final chapter: one, how did Machiavelli account for the victory of Christianity in view of his belief regarding its effeminate character? and two, if all unarmed prophets fail, what was he but an unarmed prophet? The subsequent chapter addresses, in rich detail, the arguments made in the *Discourses*.

Strauss identified the purpose of this chapter in paragraph thirty-seven (out of fifty-nine). Having already established in an earlier chapter that all founders are frauds—which is to say they found their society upon a fraud—Strauss noted that Machiavelli believed it acceptable for some writers to expose this fraud, "under certain conditions. . . . To reveal those conditions may be said to be the chief purpose of our chapter."[25] An odd purpose, perhaps, but it leads to one very important question: To what end or purpose did Machiavelli write?

Machiavelli developed a contrast between "modern" (by which he meant Christian) and "ancient." Playing upon the existing prejudice in favor of antiquity—especially concerning Rome—Machiavelli encouraged his readers to accept the authority and superiority of ancient modes and orders to modern Christian examples. The pagan Romans appeared strong, well-armed, and focused upon glory; Christianity encourages weakness and denigrates glory in favor of some future felicity. Having discredited modern and Christian modes and orders by contrasting them with ancient examples, he then exposed Roman modes and orders as being similarly defective. Ancient examples lost their charm and authority. The success of Rome and other ancient examples depended upon chance *(fortuna)*. The Romans "discovered their modes and orders absent-mindedly or by accident," and just as moderns accept the vicissitudes of this life, so also were the ancients limited by fate. One who accepted the teachings of Plato and Aristotle would expect that such is necessarily the case, because the good society, to the degree humans can realize it, depends upon circumstances beyond human control. Machiavelli understood the classical teaching and rejected it. "Machiavelli," wrote Strauss, "achieves for the first time the anatomy of the Roman republic, and thus understands thoroughly the virtues and the vices of the republic. Therefore he can teach his readers how a polity similar to the Roman and better than the Roman can be deliberately constructed." The Machiavelli of *Thoughts on Machiavelli* presented a new normative order based upon human conditions and possibilities.[26]

Near the middle of the Chapter 3 (paragraph thirty-two out of fifty-nine), Strauss made the odd claim that the central theme of the *Discourses* is an analysis of the Bible.[27] To make sense of this interpretation the reader must remember three things. First, Machiavelli wrote with two audiences in mind—the old and the young. Second, for the prime audience (the young) he wished to expose the fallacy of the existing and all past orders, and third, Machiavelli was but an unarmed prophet. Since the modern order is Christian, Machiavelli must appear to accept current religious and moral beliefs while undermining their legitimacy.[28] In the final chapter Strauss examined in great detail Machiavelli's rejection of Christianity and all religions. For the present the relevant fact is that Machiavelli sought to disabuse his youthful audience of beliefs that clouded their reasoning and made them intellectually compliant to authority. In a passage both clear and confusing Strauss emphasized Machiavelli's audience and agenda as well as the results of his teaching.

> Machiavelli addresses his passionate and muted call to the young—to men whose prudence has not enfeebled their youthful vigor of mind, quickness, militancy, impetuosity and audacity. Reason and youth and modernity rise up against authority, old age, and antiquity. In studying the *Discourses* we become the witnesses, and we cannot help becoming the moved witnesses, of the birth of that greatest of all youth movements: modern philosophy, a phenomenon which we know through seeing, as distinguished from reading, only in its decay, its state of depravation and its dotage.[29]

The first two sentences identify the reasons for Machiavelli's choice of audience as well as the scope of the break Machiavelli's teaching initiated. Some youths might be saved from blind acceptance of authority and learn to employ reason, and these pupils, however distant in time, become Machiavelli's soldiers. The unarmed prophet became a founder—and like all founders he resorted to fraud to hide the true basis of the new order.[30] In the confusing second part of the quote Strauss gave Machiavelli his due as a founder.

The purpose of Strauss's chapter on the *Discourses*, one should remember, is to understand the conditions under which a writer (as opposed to a prince) might reveal the fraud upon which all society rests. The imperatives under which Machiavelli operated, Strauss argued, were the manifest failings of the contemporary modes and orders and the truth he had discovered about the nature of all order. Strauss intimated that a genuine concern for the common good motivated Machiavelli to initiate a new order based upon reason. "Machiavelli therefore needs readers who are discerning enough to understand not only the new modes and orders but their ultimate ground as well. He needs readers who could act as mediators between him and the people by becoming princes."[31] Machiavelli exposed the fraud so that others would realize the intimate relationship between good and evil, justice and injustice, and thereby understand the need to use evil means prudently to accomplish the common good. Machiavelli claimed a new knowledge that allowed humans control over their destiny by conquering *fortuna.*[32]

The final chapter of Strauss's book is the most important. "Machiavelli's Teaching" refers to his universalizing philosophy (which Strauss identified as the revolutionary part of his work) in contrast to particular advice. The long chapter comes in two equal parts: the first deals with Machiavelli's teaching regarding religion; the second, his teaching about morality. Thus one is reminded of the Introduction where Strauss contended that "Machiavelli's teaching is immoral and irreligious."[33]

Of all of Strauss's brilliant and imaginative textual analysis of Machiavelli, the most intriguing and debatable is his reconstruction of the Florentine's religious beliefs. No other subject requires that Strauss rest so much of his argument upon Machiavelli's silence. Similarly, Strauss's position requires that Machiavelli shift the meaning of key words two or even three times. In other words, if Machiavelli actually hid his teaching, then we must assume from the evidence that his views concerning religion in general and Christianity in particular he deemed in special need of protective cover. Strauss followed the trail of Machiavelli's elusive beliefs concerning religion from the particular, Christianity, to the most general—*fortuna*, chance, providence.

Machiavelli's praise of pagan religions have led some scholars (including Eric Voegelin) to insist that Machiavelli was a neopagan, but Strauss characterized his views as neither Christian nor pagan but Averroist.[34] Christianity interested Machiavelli because of its capacity as a political force. Because Christianity lowered esteem for this world and for glory while accepting humility and abjectness as highest goods—attitudes that demonstrate "contempt for things human"—Machiavelli considered Christianity inferior to pagan religions.[35] Nonetheless, his was a Christian society and, he had to operate in such a way as to not appear excessively heterodox.[36] For this reason he taught in silence, leaving unsaid what logically should be part of a given discussion and thereby demonstrating his disagreement with conventional views.[37] But he expects the young readers whom he has trained to read to "read the Bible 'judiciously'; he limits himself to giving a few indications."[38] Strauss emphasized the example of the exodus from Egypt led by Moses. The judicious reader should catch the willingness of a people, led by a great leader, to leave enslavement and conquer their own land. Moses viewed from this perspective possessed the same defining characteristics of other founders like Cyrus and Romulus.[39]

Christianity, which like all religion is of human origin, became powerful because of circumstance. At a time when Rome's corruption made it weak and morally powerless, "the severe morality preached and practiced by the early Christians created respect and awe especially in those subjects of the Roman empire who equally lacked political power. By demanding humility, Christianity appealed to the humble and gave them strength." The young reader learned not to respect Christianity, because its force came about as a result of circumstances rather than special virtues in its teaching or because it represented God. Machiavelli insisted that no correspondence connects success and justice. The only correspondence demonstrated by empirical evidence—the historical record—is between success and prudence. Here, near the center of Strauss's discussion of Machiavelli's views concerning religion, Machiavelli emphasized the insignificance of God or gods in human affairs, placing human virtues as the determining factor in human success. In this case virtue represents the prudent use of both justice and injustice, the only means of successfully operating a state. Machiavelli reduced God to a symbol for chance that favors neither the just nor the unjust, leaving the world open for the wise to employ their knowledge of worldly matters to gain control over their destiny.[40]

When Machiavelli reduced God to a symbol equivalent to *fortuna* or chance, he emphasized the role chance plays in human affairs. *Fortuna* appears in Machiavelli's work as a woman to be controlled, a foe to be conquered, but Strauss emphasized that in Machiavelli's most extensive analysis of *fortuna* the word takes on a meaning that designates the comprehensive order rather than a willing being. Consequently, Strauss suggested that *fortuna* and nature, while perhaps not identical, become nearly so in Machiavelli's thinking. As the mysterious comprehensive order, one must always deal with and react to *fortuna*. One never conquers her, but the wise man knows her real character, and this knowledge gives him his special dignity and independence. More important, the conflation Strauss found in Machiavelli's use of words like "chance" and "nature" identifies an altogether new understanding of nature. He "has abandoned the teleological understanding of nature and natural necessity for the alternative understanding. He speaks very frequently of 'accidents' but never of 'substances.'" According to Strauss, then, Machiavelli not only loosed human behavior from the coercive dictates of a god or gods but undermined the classical belief in the teleology of nature, replacing both with a world in which humans must live with "chance understood as a non-teleological necessity which leaves room for choice and prudence and therefore for chance understood as the cause of simply unforeseeable accidents."[41]

Machiavelli's new modes and orders threatened not only Christianity but also classical political philosophy,[42] and Strauss's attention turned to the latter tradition as his analysis moved from religion to morality. Since the classical science of political philosophy "took its bearings by how one ought to live or what one ought to do," classical thinkers worked from paradigms rather than from what is. By contrast, Machiavelli spurned principalities or republics that "exist only in speech" in favor of concrete lessons he could draw from empirical evidence about how people live (Machiavelli devalued theory). In this sense Machiavelli reduced the goal of political philosophy from the goals posited from nature, as understood by Plato and Aristotle, to the goals a reasonable man could expect to achieve given the "nature" of humans discerned from examples of human behavior. Machiavelli argued from particular knowledge to general or theoretical knowledge, thus supplying a normative order attainable by humans.[43]

Operating from a nonteleological cosmology, Machiavelli redefined virtue to fit an open-ended universe. No longer relative to a fixed moral compass, virtue represents a prudent course one selects to achieve desired ends. In contrast to the Aristotelian construction of virtue as the mean between two excesses, Machiavelli posited a mean between virtue and vice as they are understood conventionally. "Unqualified virtue and unqualified vice are faulty extremes.

The true way is the way which imitates nature. But nature is variable, and not stable like virtue. The true way consists therefore in the alteration between virtue and vice."[44] The true way consists of knowing when to use cruelty (and other useful vices) and when to act in full accord with conventional canons of goodness and justice. Founders must rely heavily on vice to instill fear, which serves to make people "good," and since founders operate outside a stable social and political structure, which normally provides the necessary means of making people good (laws, punishment, i.e., "justice"), they must act as tyrants to establish the requisite terror. This is vice used prudently. The leader(s) of a well-established political society with highly structured codes of behavior must lean more heavily toward "virtue." In the end Machiavelli dissolved the difference between tyrants and well-run republics since both operate because terror forces selfish people to act in the interest of the "common good," which Machiavelli understood to mean collective selfishness.

Even the self-interest of tyrants is salutary because they experience an attraction to glory, especially immortal glory. Tyrants blessed with "virtue" (i.e., the prudent use of vice and virtue) seek the glory reserved for effective rulers (the highest glory goes to founders). Such tyrants strike a desirable balance (in the context of the common good understood as collective selfishness) between immediate satisfaction of pleasure—which unchecked would make them imprudent—and the pursuit of immortal glory that comes from leading a state well. In acting selfishly the tyrant behaves the same way all humans do. If one understands selfishness to be coequal with evil, then humans are naturally bad. Consequently, "the only natural good is the private good. Since this is so, it is absurd to call men bad with a view to the fact that they are selfish."[45]

Beyond the private good, Machiavelli found it useless to discuss good in any unqualified sense. The common good, which serves the private good of the citizens (though not all of the citizens), requires knowledge about humans (i.e., knowledge about how they are rather than how they ought to be). The person who acquires this knowledge holds the key to the greatest achievement of the common good and in this sense may be understood as a virtuous and good person. Machiavelli, driven by his desire for immortal glory, considered himself the greatest of founders because he knew the truth about human political and social affairs and so was not a captive of chance in the same way as other founders. Since Strauss credited Machiavelli with inaugurating modernity (new modes and orders), he agreed that Machiavelli was a great founder. We have now the answer to one of the puzzling questions Strauss raised: How could Machiavelli expect to succeed as an unarmed prophet? As a teacher of the truth about human affairs, he established "new modes and orders" through the young readers who learned from him. He secured his glory as the founder, in a way similar to Jesus. The crucial difference lies in Machiavelli's claim to have found a way to free humans from the control of *fortuna*—and so Machiavelli's glory outshone all others.

The modernity of Strauss's Machiavelli emerges on two uneven fronts: Machiavelli's assaults on religion and on classical philosophy. Movement on both fronts tends toward the same objective, the contraction of the political horizon. Machiavelli would unhinge the political and social order from any suprapolitical context that once shaped and directed earthly concerns. The most disturbing and dangerous front from Strauss's perspective was the threat Machiavelli's teaching posed to the classical philosophical tradition reaching back to Plato. This tradition posited fixed ends (nature) for humans and assumed the more humble position that the good political order depended upon chance, not virtue in the sense that Machiavelli used the word. Moreover, the ancients presumed a natural rift separating the political order from the philosophers. Philosophers must seek an accommodation with the dominant political order, but they must never give up their higher pursuit of truth, which makes them the best of people (the most excellent relative to their natural end, i.e, the "idea" of humans). They must never allow their philosophy to become politicized.

"Machiavelli's philosophizing," wrote Strauss, "remains on the whole within the limits set by the city qua closed to philosophy. Accepting the ends of the *demos* as beyond appeal, he seeks for the best means conducive to those ends." Philosophy under this paradigm (which includes "science") loses its autonomy and its special dignity as the unencumbered search for excellence and truth. In its new shape science (i.e., philosophy) works on behalf of the political order, unquestioningly serving its ends. Since this new model of human nature unleashes humans from fixed ends, science serves to reshape human nature according to desires expressed through the political order. The lowering of human aspirations from the excellences of nature has the paradoxical effect of making gods of humans who posit their own goals and goods. The transformation Strauss explained in this fashion: "The brain which can transform the political matter soon learns to think of the transformation of every matter of the conquest of nature. The charm of competence bewitches completely first a few great men and then whole nations and indeed as it were the whole human race."[46]

The connections Strauss made between Machiavelli and the moderns who swallowed him whole emerge with rarely matched Straussian clarity in the concluding pages of *Thoughts on Machiavelli*. Humans moved out of a universe of necessity into a realm of godlike freedom, with their desires positing ends and their evolving science employed in the discovery or creation of means appropriate to those ends. In due course Hitler posited the ends, ratified by the support of the German population, and science and philosophy supplied the means. What was "the final solution" but a rational method of achieving a political goal? I go well beyond the claims made by Strauss in this book, but only to anticipate the larger flow of his argument as expressed in the totality of his work. Nonetheless, in the context of his commentary on Machiavelli, the careful reader discovers a message that goes beyond or deeper than (though is not incompatible with) Strauss's closing comments.

The matter of the substance of Strauss's teaching requires a lengthy textual analysis extending not only into *Thoughts on Machiavelli* but through the works of Machiavelli, Livy, and a host of authors with whom Strauss dealt in the footnotes. The careful reader can nonetheless harbor few doubts that Strauss placed stumbling blocks designed to force the reader to ask questions about the author's intention and meaning. One cannot help noting the odd and elliptical sentences, the lengthy diversions, and the unique combination of subjects. A few examples relevant to our larger inquiry will suffice.

One is hard pressed to account for Strauss's glaring cases of imprecision. In other contexts he wrote about historicism, positivism, and other isms with only the barest hint as to the content of these words. Other scholars similarly employ broad labels as though definitions are unnecessary. However, few thinkers of Strauss's ability, much less those possessing his concern for the meanings of words, write so glibly. Reading *Thoughts on Machiavelli* requires constant attention to the subtle and shifting meanings of words like virtue, vice, God, *fortuna*, chance. By contrast, Strauss wrote of the "classical tradition" as though political philosophy was dormant between Plato and Machiavelli. The complexity and enormous heterogeneity of philosophy in the West before Machiavelli makes Strauss's constant and simplistic use of a premodern paradigm absurd. In this case one cannot dismiss the issue on the grounds of Strauss's ignorance or his sloppiness, for he knew full well the violence he was doing to the tradition. Consequently, Strauss's characterization of Machiavelli's teaching as new and shocking takes on a more problematic character. In the Introduction, we recall, Strauss referred to Machiavelli as a "fallen angel," meaning that Machiavelli perverted the classical tradition and therefore in some sense was derivative. More to the point, Strauss stated that Machiavelli's "opinions" were not only not new but as "old as political society itself." Strauss resolved this problem (i.e., the newness of opinions as old as society) by emphasizing that Machiavelli expressed these views in his own name rather than through the use of characters.[47] The unsatisfying nature of this explanation leads one to wonder how wide is the chasm that separates Machiavelli from the tradition he ostensibly rejected.

I suspect that Strauss employed the classical-modern dualism in such striking relief for pedagogical reasons and that he found in Machiavelli much greater ambiguity as well as much more confluence with important classical thinkers. Whatever verdict might emerge from a study of this question, one cannot doubt that much of Strauss's concern revolved around the growing inability of more recent moderns to read and understand the great philosophers. The importance of this characterization for understanding Strauss's intentions becomes evident in a very interesting paragraph at the very center of the final and most important chapter (paragraph forty-three out eighty-five). After exploring Machiavelli's teachings with regard to religion and before turning to the issue of morality, Strauss offered a lengthy observation about the string of thinkers subsequent to Machiavelli and the difficulty of understanding them because of the contemporary ideological climate. Concerning Machiavelli and his successors Strauss wrote: "We no longer understand that in spite of great disagreements among those thinkers, they were united by the fact that they all fought one and the same power—the kingdom of darkness, as Hobbes called it; that fight was more important to them than any merely political issue."[48]

Strauss emphasized the modern loss of understanding, which reminds one of the primary sin Machiavelli committed, the sin of constricting the horizon. As heirs of that constricted horizon, contemporary moderns have not the proper perspective to understand what Machiavelli knew. Machiavelli could not have been a modern in the same sense that Strauss's contemporaries were, because he had before him the full horizon that he had inherited from the great tradition.[49] Strauss introduced a new factor near the end of paragraph forty-three: "The conditions of political thought were radically changed by the French Revolution. To begin with, we cannot help reading earlier thinkers in the light afforded by the changed condition or the novel situation of political thought."[50] Hence, the French Revolution produced a historical watershed, one that, as he continued to argue, created a philosophical parochialism that made understanding pre-nineteenth-century thinkers much more difficult. This blade cut two ways for Strauss. On the one hand, modern parochialism blinds thinkers to the genetic link connecting Machiavelli with those who followed him. They follow in his footsteps but do not know it. On the other hand, these thinkers cannot understand fully the thinkers who served as their intellectual ancestors because their own dependence upon Machiavelli prevents them from understanding him. Moderns may be Machiavellian more than disciples of Machiavelli.

The final words of Strauss's book remind the reader that for all the analytical rigor and textual care displayed in his commentary, it was more than a work on Machiavelli. "It would seem that the notion of the beneficence of nature or of the primacy of the Good must be restored by being rethought through a return to the fundamental experiences from which it is derived. For while 'philosophy must beware of wishing to be edifying,' it is of necessity edifying."[51] Strauss did not prepare the reader for the first of these sentences, but clearly Strauss believed with Husserl and Heidegger that moderns have lost access to "fundamental experiences." A fuller explication of this subject must wait, but in the second sentence the reader is reminded of the Introduction, in which Strauss announced that the larger purpose of his book was to recover the "permanent problems" that are coeval with philosophy. To grasp the content of Strauss's teaching one must understand his use of the word "problems" as well as comprehend the relationship between the science of permanent problems (philosophy) and political affairs.

Strauss's interest in problems emerged early in his book. In the Preface he thanked the Walgreen Foundation for the "opportunity to present my observations and reflections on the problem of Machiavelli,"[52] and in the Introduction he shifted to "Machiavelli's problem." Nowhere in his book, so far as I can tell, did Strauss ever clarify what he meant by Machiavelli's problem, an odd omission given that Strauss devoted this examination to answering this "problem" and considering that the larger philosophical goal justifying the enterprise was the recovery of permanent problems. One must work from oblique clues.

Strauss established the context for the discussion of Machiavelli's problem by referring to the United States, the only country "founded in explicit opposition to Machiavellian principles." To justify this claim Strauss drew upon the words of Thomas Paine, though not without qualification. Unlike European nations, which owe their foundings to evil doings and their maintenance to tyranny and conquest, the founders of the United States grounded the new nation, to quote Paine, upon "a moral theory, on a system of universal peace, on the indefeasible hereditary Rights of Man." By contrast, Strauss wrote, "contemporary tyranny has its roots in Machiavelli's thought." The next sentence provides an important clue: "At least to the extent that the American reality is inseparable from the American aspiration, one cannot understand Americanism without understanding Machiavellianism which is its opposite." The connection between reality and aspiration illuminates the difference between the United States and "contemporary tyranny." The meaning of the United States, or its idea, stands in sharp contrast to other nations. Machiavellians are not motivated or even responsive to aspirations that posit universal justice, a social, political, and individual good. These serve but to obfuscate the real issues about power and collective self-interest.[53]

Strauss then pointed out in the next paragraph that were Machiavelli to examine the United States, he would expose the dirty deeds behind American success. "He would not hesitate to suggest a mischievous interpretation of the Louisiana Purchase and of the fate of the Red Indians. He would conclude that facts like these are an additional proof for his contention that there cannot be a great and glorious society without the equivalent of the murder of Remus by his brother Romulus." But for Strauss the germane fact was, not that the United States failed to live up to its aspirations in its official dealings, but that Americans seek always to reaffirm the idea or ideals of their society against a backdrop of practical failure and disappointment. The relationship between political society, with its ever-shifting contingencies, and a society's ideals, only realized fully in speech, remains problematic. But a society with clear ideals reflects a continual attention to theory and therefore escapes the restrictions caused by substituting instrumental reason (e.g., method-driven science) for theoretical questions about the good and the just. In the United States, techne (technique or instrumental reason) had not entirely overtaken theory.

The contrast between Strauss's permanent problems and Machiavelli's problem (or the problem of Machiavelli) becomes reasonably clear. Machiavelli's problem was to define the matter in such a way as to eliminate the permanent tensions—his constriction of the horizon. The permanent problems concern the irremovable tensions between politics and philosophy, between practical matters and theory, between is and ought.[54] By placing philosophy in service to politics and by eliminating theory and the universal good from the political equation, Machiavelli solved a problem at the expense of ignorance concerning the highest excellence open to humans as individuals and as part of a political order. If the line of thinking inaugurated by Machiavelli made gods of humans because they could posit their own direction according to their own lights, it also made them animals because they lost sight of the noble, the excellent, the good.

In the midst of the many confusing arguments between moderns and ancients, we should recall that Strauss used the United States as the example of a non-Machiavellian order. The philosophical foundations of the United States were sufficiently premodern to maintain a tradition of justice and freedom, but in praise Strauss issued an ominous warning.

HEGEL AND THE EGOPHANIC REVOLT

Reading Hegel once provides few comforts but one important reward; the knowledge of having read Hegel—a prerequisite for joining

the ranks of serious pretenders. Reading Hegel, Voegelin, and Voegelin on Hegel means an end to comfort, but not to rewards. No one
reads Voegelin and Hegel in tandem to impress the pretenders. One
must sense an important existential issue resting at the heart of the
conversation to summon the will to work through the thousands of
pages of leaden prose. For people who seek to understand the Voegelinian use of "modernity," the effort rewards one with a characterization of modernity's paradigmatic man.

In the last section I discussed two court fools whose worldly advice, laced with irony, they spoke with a mixture of hearty laughs
and furtive smiles. Now we must grow serious and examine the work
of sober philosophers. Although the differences appear stark, both
Machiavelli and Hegel represent two stages of a process of reorienting humans away from older classical and Christian understandings
of reality to a modern view that allows for human mastery of their
human world and their fate. For Machiavelli, nature no longer served
as a paradigm defining human good but as something more akin to
putty or clay that humans might shape to fit their desires. Machiavelli revolted against the Platonic-Aristotelian model of political
philosophy, with its binding "nature." Hegel revolted against the
Christian reliance on a world-transcendent God by bringing God to
earth in the mode of becoming and as immanent in history—a history that only God and Hegel can comprehend. One can see already
the similarities in Strauss's and Voegelin's critiques of modern hubris.

Indeed, the attacks on modernity launched by these two philosophers display numerous similarities. On the descriptive level the
word expresses an unambiguous meaning accepted by both Strauss
and Voegelin: modernity is the quest to answer the problems and resolve the tensions once considered permanent or irresolvable. Moderns, one might say, are given to "final solutions." Problems once
considered structural become projects, and the limitedness that is so
integral to a definition of humans emerges in the modern era as a
temporary obstacle to overcome. In due course even God must be
murdered to make room for human creativity and power, but this descriptive consensus does not extend to the matter of causality. When
establishing the reasons or necessary conditions, or even primary
(paradigmatic) characters, of the modern revolt (against nature—
Strauss; or reality—Voegelin), the stories display sharply contrasting

understandings of the problem. Strauss constructed the problem as a purely philosophical matter. Machiavelli began a new science of philosophy in competition with the Platonic-Aristotelian science. From this root many ideological branches sprang, as did the final rejection of philosophy as a science.

For Voegelin modernity represented the most recent and most virulent manifestation of a recurrent spiritual disease (pneumapathology). The source or cause, consequently, was not ideational. Political ideas are crystallizations of experiences of order, and the ideas form a conceptual cover that protects their experiential sources. (Here I am discussing ideological constructions. The people who engage in a proper science of order produce symbols of their experience designed to express experiences that cannot be articulated on the conceptual level. These symbols are transparent to the experiences that engendered them.) A proper diagnosis requires that one penetrate to the spiritual source of a disorder. Voegelin did not mean, however, that all manifestations of spiritual disorder are in all important respects identical or even similar. Modernity developed in a historical context that gave it a unique—and uniquely dangerous—character. To understand Voegelin's use of the word "modernity" requires that one understand the generic qualities of a more or less ubiquitous disease and then relate the conditions that made these pathological qualities socially dominant.

Because Voegelin emphasized an underlying pathology to modern movements, it makes sense that he would find little hope for remedy in addressing the symptoms. Only by returning to the true science of order could people hope for renewal. This answer has its problems since one cannot expect the sick to heal themselves, because the very nature of their disease is a blindness to the disease. With Voegelin, hope rested, finally, with the emergence of a new Moses, or a new Plato, or a new Jesus. The "spirit" must select a carrier for its message. Voegelin could find some hope in noting that each of those spiritually gifted men emerged during periods of severe social disorder.

Order emerges out of resistance to disorder. In a context of resistance Plato produced the most penetrating analysis of this condition in reaction to the disordered souls of the sophists. As lovers of opinion rather than of wisdom, sophists had lost sight of the universal context of human existence. The philosopher, on the other hand, "is the man who lives in partnership with what is common to all men, that is, with the divine nous or reason that transcends them all. Through participation in what is common, men become a community. . . . The philosopher who orders his own life, as well as his relations to his fellow-men, by this experience of the common, is in fact every man who has achieved full actualization of his manhood.''[55] The sophist does not recognize this part of reality and must order life with ''the resources of empirical, immanent man, without recourse to transcendent orientation.''[56] The immanent becomes the encompassing reality, making humans rather than God the measure of things.

The sophist must create an order rather than attune to an existing order. This state of affairs requires imaginative constructions and an active resistance to those facts that challenge one's construction. The modern equivalent of the sophist is the intellectual, a label of opprobrium for conservatives. In one brief description Voegelin displayed the deformed thinking of an intellectual. Condorcet, the eighteenth-century French intellectual, inferred from available statistics that life expectancy would go up indefinitely on the grounds that acquired characteristics could be inherited. Condorcet's expectations of ''practical immortality'' were not inconsistent with the science of the day, yet this extrapolation from the evidence would be impossible for someone who participated fully in human reality. Voegelin's analysis:

We know that the speculation is ridiculous; but we know it only because we know about our human finiteness through experience of transcendence. If we do not accept the reality of the rhythm of life and death; if we do not experience death, as Socrates and Plato so strongly did, as an essential ordering, cathartic force within our lives; if we do not experience that without death life makes no sense; then the speculation of Condorcet is not ridiculous at all. And that is what makes this type of dreaming so dangerous. On the assumptions of the dreamer, we have no argument against him. If essential sectors of reality are declared to be non-existent, the dreamer is free to develop, with rigid logic[al] consistency, the most atrocious nonsense on the basis of his fragmentary reality.[57]

The example of a single intellectual's dreaming begins to open up the matter by identifying the restricted ontological horizon from which moderns operate. What is not as clear from this example is the experience that engenders ideologies. A felt tension and a profound anxiety, usually expressed as a sort of alienation, provided the experiential source for modernity. Yet Voegelin associated the discovery of the tension between divine and mundane with the great spiritual "leaps in being" of Moses, Plato, and Paul. Nonetheless, a sense of alienation depends first upon the differentiation of the poles of reality. Plato, for instance, emphasized the in-betweenness of human existence, but he did not attempt to resolve this inherent tension. Only the person whose spiritual stamina is insufficient to withstand the tension, and whose intellectual capacity is sufficient to understand it, is capable of producing a second reality. The spiritual disorder of modernity became possible, therefore, only after a spiritual advance.

Voegelin's historical account of this process is extensive, and only the broad outline of this story is possible here. The best starting place is the "ecumenic age," which extended from the rise of Persia to the fall of the Roman Empire. The historical events of this era (what Voegelin liked to call the pragmatic events, which has a resonance with Augustine's distinction between profane and sacred history) shook old conceptions of humanity and forced the adoption of new ones. An "ecume" is a multicivilizational empire created by conquest and maintained by military power. Empires are not societies, for their order is imposed rather than emerging from the existentially meaningful symbols of the divine cosmos. The older cosmological societies destroyed by the empires once understood themselves to be analogues to the cosmic order, or "cosmions," and the orderly cosmos that operated cyclically, according to the seasons, was inhabited by a pantheon of gods whose actions secured the ongoing existence of the society in a ceaseless pattern of life, death, and rebirth. A delicate economy secured the social order, with rituals and other rites marking the changes and preventing the always changing order from slipping into nothingness (rituals might be understood as measures to prevent change, to create stasis). The members of cosmological societies understood their lives individually and collectively to have meaning as a part of this enduring process in which the indices of divine and immanent blurred. Empires broke the cosmological symbolism by destroying the cyclical pattern and by placing ethnic societies in a political and social order that did not represent the experiences of reality that supply the meaningful symbols of that order.

The complex results that sprang from the new conditions of the ecumenic age are too rich to explore here, and I instead focus on the most important preconditions for the modern revolt against reality. Voegelin explored with brilliant insight the development of history as a mode of existence. The cyclical model of existence common to cosmological societies gave way to an understanding that humans live in history. Experiences that create a "before and after" realization force a "leap in being," a deeper understanding of the structure of reality. In this case the leap in being destroyed the symbolization of endless cycles by discovering the historical mode of human existence. Still, history was not yet conceived of as an object, a totality. One might speak of the history of something, but not of History as a knowable object about which one might make propositions regarding "its" meaning. The tremendous expansion of knowledge of other nations or other civilizations helped forge in this period a concept of universal humanity while calling into question the local gods. Humans form a single race or species and live under one God (the Christian tale of history that includes the Fall and redemption provides the best example of this universalizing process). During the ecumenic age the great universal religions arose, effectively eliminating the plentiful gods who had once cohabited the cosmos with humans. These religions (especially Christianity) stripped the heavens of their capricious and colorful gods. Although the cosmos no longer contained the gods, humans nonetheless recognized the divine source of their existence, that their lives are bounded by both the mundane and the divine. The Christian God represented the mysterious ground of existence beyond the cosmos.[58]

The unchangeable structure of human consciousness became increasingly differentiated during the ecumenic age, and the symbols that emerged from these new insights into human nature effectively expressed the tensions of human existence. Voegelin especially favored the Platonic word *metaxy*, meaning betweenness, to capture this truth. Humans live in the tension between an experienced divine pole and the pole of worldly or mundane life. Or, in other words, humans recognize that they occupy a plane of experiences that extends from the "pole" of worldly or sensual experiences to the "pole" of divine or numinous experiences. Voegelin and Plato expressed this betweenness in many ways (between the one and the many, the whole and the part, the timeless and the historical), each exposing elements in the unchangeable structure of human existence. Humans necessarily experience alienation because they feel the attraction of the divine, whole, timeless pole of existence while they live in the mundane, partial, and historical cosmos. Despite the pull toward the divine pole of our existence, human life is constituted in the tensional field between the two heuristically understood poles of existence. To ignore or attempt to eliminate one of the poles is a futile attempt to escape one's humanity.

All of these developments Voegelin understood to be important insights into the structure of the reality in which humans have their being. But these very insights—which were nothing more than the differentiation of the component parts of the experienced reality of the earlier cosmological societies—tended to accentuate the tensional nature of human existence, heightening the alienation experienced in the soul of the individual. Once one recognizes the tensional attraction toward transcending the very structure of existence (and this attraction toward transcendence is itself part of the structure of existence), the desire to escape earthly alienation becomes more powerful, and the threat to the balance of consciousness symbolized by the *metaxy* becomes more real. Christianity heightened the tension with a further differentiation and thus called for an extra measure of spiritual stamina. By highlighting earthly alienation and by introducing a heightened sense of chiliastic expectation, Christianity made this world less attractive. As the accent fell on humans as heirs or sons of God, the world seemed more of a prison from which one sought release.

The Christian religion altered human understanding in at least two very important respects. First, by emptying the cosmos of immanent divinity, Christians gave the world completely over to humans as their special domain. Second, Paul's vision of the resurrected led him to expect an imminent end of history with the early return of Jesus. Consequently, Paul was the first important figure in Western history to develop a philosophy of history in terms of identifying the meaning of history. He traced its beginning from Adam, and its imminent conclusion was to be Jesus's second coming (1 Cor.

15), which would lead to a transfiguration of all God's people. Paul introduced two related concepts into Western thought: history has a meaning with a clear and identifiable teleology and human alienation would soon end with the eschaton (or end times). Although Paul was wrong about Jesus's speedy return, he introduced an expectation of the eschaton (or the end of History) that has become a recurring theme in Western thought.[59] Moreover, once this world became the temporary home of alienated souls, the soul became unbalanced in two distinct ways. First, the emphasis upon the other world deemphasized human reality by denying the proper place of the world, and when this existential condition became secularized, alienation became a condition in need of immanent elimination. As the heavenly hereafter lost its appeal, in other words, humans sought to create a heaven on earth.

The expectations spawned by Paul (which he later deemphasized) but not fulfilled during his lifetime sent many people who followed him in search of the apodictic knowledge that Paul had claimed, and that need shifted Christianity as a historical movement off its existential foundation of faith. In an especially lucid passage, Voegelin indicated the meaning and importance of Christian faith and the difficulties it imposed upon the believer:

> Uncertainty is the very essence of Christianity. The feeling of security in a "world full of gods" is lost with the gods themselves; when the world is de-divinized, communication with the world-transcendent God is reduced to the tenuous bond of faith, in the sense of Heb. 11:1, as the substance of things hoped for and the proof of things unseen. . . . The bond is tenuous, indeed, and it may snap easily. The life of the soul in openness toward God, the waiting, the periods of aridity and dulness, guilt and despondency, contrition and repentance, forsakenness and hope against hope, the silent stirrings of love and grace, the very lightness of this fabric may prove too heavy a burden for men who lust for massively possessive experience.[60]

The anxiety caused by the uncertainty of faith leads people in search of knowledge (gnosis). The existential heart of the modern revolt is made up of this anxiety and the attempt to provide apodictic knowledge about those things humans can only see dimly. Thus, the great insight of Christianity about the world-transcendent God whom humans can know only through faith proved too heavy a burden for most people to bear.

From the beginning, the Christian church struggled to balance the expectations of transformation and the realizations of earthly existence. Augustine formulated the orthodox position with the greatest success, and he resolved the problem of history inspired by Paul's metastatic expectation by making the post-Resurrection era a time of waiting. The world, moreover, became the temporary home for the invisible church trapped in an irredeemable world, as Augustine balanced the apocalyptic expectations against an earthly existence that could not be perfected. But even Augustine's masterful construction could not eliminate the heightened sense of alienation, and numerous attempts to escape the taint of corrupted earth threatened to unbalance the Augustinian construction. However, the more dangerous manifestations of these experiences of alienation would take the form of earthly perfectionism as humans tried to turn the prison into a paradise.

For the earthly paradise to become real moderns had to replace Augustine's construction of history with one that allows for, or inherently requires, a transformed world. In the twelfth century Joachim of Flora created a speculative construction of history that would become paradigmatic for modern ideologues. History moves progressively through discrete stages or eras, and these eras, for Joachim, corresponded with the three persons of the Trinity.[61] The first stage of history was the age of the Father; the incarnation of Jesus inaugurated the second, more advanced age; and Joachim speculated that he was living at the cusp of the final age, the age of the Holy Spirit. History moved toward ever-greater godlikeness, or freedom, as God was slowly perfecting humans. Joachim had discovered the structure of this process.

Each age opened with three important figures, two precursors and the leader of the age (Abraham was the first spiritual leader, followed by Jesus). Based upon Joachim's calculations, he expected the leader of the third age to appear by 1260. This final age of spiritual maturity would be the age of the monk and be characterized by complete autonomy made possible by spiritual maturity. History had progressed from the law, to a mediated grace, to the anticipated autonomy of the third age. Belief in the evolving human was a necessary prerequisite for all such constructions of history, because only when a belief in human perfection becomes existentially viable can the past be shaped into progressive phases leading inexorably to the felicity of the near future. Moreover, only the person who believes himself to be sufficiently mature to occupy this final stage has the ability to recognize that history leads directly to himself as the paradigmatic last man.

Voegelin emphasized that Joachim constructed the "aggregate of symbols which govern the intellectualist interpretation of politics and history to this day."[62] These "symbols" are four in number. First, the three stages of history, with varying degrees of precision, became crucial components in the thought of Turgot, Comte, Hegel, Marx, and Hitler. Second, Joachim emphasized the spiritual leader, which also became part of the modern understanding of history. Third, the new age requires preparation in the form of prophets or precursors, and the ideologues themselves take on this role. The fourth symbol is the final freedom of the third realm in which all tensions will be absorbed and the sources of corruption eliminated. These four symbols form the primary ideological resources of the modern age, though various ideologues have placed different emphases on each.

Joachim replaced the mystery of existence with unquestioned knowledge about human destiny, and he resolved the tension between a fallen world and a transcendent paradise by making history the process through which humans reach their final destination in an immanent eschaton—a worldly paradise. Also important was the sense of living in the final moments of history. The profound and as yet unresolved alienation he and others experienced only sharpened their desire to bring about the final transformation.

From this obscure beginning, Voegelin emphasized the "immanentization" of the process of history. Later ideologues would create a history with no otherworldly eschaton, and they would even begin to equate human knowledge with the power necessary to bring the process of history to a desired but worldly conclusion. All of these developments issued from the logic of a sick soul confronted with knee-knocking uncertainty. When the world appears suddenly imbalanced and faith supplies only hope based upon an apperception of a normative order, people lacking spiritual guts will close their eyes and dream of a better reality. Closed to a world that does not fit their

expectations, these dreamers must live closed to reality, and one final need makes them especially dangerous. In order to validate their
dream reality, they must draw others (by persuasion or force) into the
dream by characterizing the world as being divided between the elect
and the enemy. The stakes are too high to tolerate the unenlightened. Of the many independent but existentially related lines of development, there is space here for a quick glance at only a few of the
more important ones.

Voegelin placed much of the burden for later ideological developments upon Calvin and his followers (even extending this indictment to all parts of the Reformation), which may help account for
Voegelin's appeal among Catholic scholars. In a letter to Leo Strauss,
Voegelin tried to explain his position.

> If we follow the logic of the problem (that is, immanentization)
> to its beginning, then I would see in orthodox Protestantism al-
> ready the start of immanentization. Calvin flirts with the prob-
> lem in the *Institutes*, where his concern for the *certitudo salutis*
> through the unequivocal "call" is quite clearly a Gnostic at-
> tempt to gain certitude of salvation, which is a bit more certain
> than orthodox *cognitio fidei*. Luther vacillates, but his hatred of
> the *fides caritate formata*, his wild efforts to take love out of
> faith, and to make deliberate knowledge into its substance,
> seems to me to lead in the same direction.[63]

Out of the messy history of the Reformation, Voegelin focused
upon the English Puritans as models of modern gnosticism (borrowing too heavily for his characterization from Richard Hooker, an An-
glican foe and a poor judge of Puritans). Calvin and the Puritans
sought a greater certainty of salvation, and in order to achieve this
psychological advantage, they had to doctrinalize the Bible. Since all
their claims would ultimately be tested against the biblical text,
they had to establish a standardized interpretation that brought ideological order to the rich work. Calvin accomplished this task with
his *Institutes*, which Voegelin likened to the *Encylopedie Francaise*
produced by the philosophes. Both works presented the believer with
the essential knowledge (or interpretation) for a proper life. Once the
Puritans viewed themselves as the chosen people of God (the elect),
possessing the only proper reading of God's word and certain knowl-

edge about their own salvation, they became God's agents on earth. Consequently, their knowledge, their discipline, in the words of Richard Hooker as cited by Voegelin, "must be received although the world by receiving it should be clean turned upside down; herein lieth the greatest danger of all."[64] The Puritan possession of spiritual knowledge necessitated a form of imperialism and dogmatism. Oddly, Voegelin tended to refute standard interpretations of texts by claiming that his reading had penetrated to the experiences that had engendered the story. Perhaps Voegelin and Calvin had more in common than either would recognize.

The Puritan episode took place in a historical field crowded with claims to certain knowledge. Voegelin detected a doctrinalization of the Bible in the Middle Ages, making the symbols of numinous experience, meant to be transparent to the experience, into concepts about which competing parties might argue, fight, even kill.[65] Even with the great Thomas Aquinas, Voegelin found the separation between natural reason and revelation to be a major step toward losing the experiences of the Bible, and thereby their truth. Even though a certain amount of concretizing is necessary to transmit the truths contained in the experiences to ever-larger and less educated populations, the reductionism of the late Middle Ages followed by the Reformation was a final capitulation to the gnostic spirit of reducing every sort of knowledge to "ideas." This hypostatization, especially concerning a text as rich as the Bible, leads to innumerable conflicts. In an environment in which certainty was prized above all else, and where the future paradise depended upon the promulgation of the right ideas, such ideological pluralism would naturally produce violence and disorder. The sixteenth century was nothing if not disordered.

For much of the modern age, thinkers have sought to find a common ground that would transcend the bloody differences of opinions. Descartes's attempt was only one of a number of such struggles to find a new ordering truth, and at first all such efforts were Christian. Descartes and Newton, for instance, both sought to confirm their faith through immanent reason. In due course the Christian objective would disappear, but not the faith that immanent reason was the compass that would lead humans to the new promised land.

Thomas Hobbes, according to Voegelin, was one of the last great Christian philosophers. "Hobbes's intention," wrote Voegelin, was to establish "Christianity (understood as identical in substance with the law of nature) as an English *theologia civilis.*"[66] Hobbes argued, for all his Christian faith, from natural science, which supplied, he thought, the foundations of civil thought. Reason drawn from natural science provided no *summum bonum* around which to organize a society (at least not modern society with its competing factions). Instead of a greatest good, Hobbes introduced the *summum malum*, the fear of death, as the controlling factor. By changing the orientation from the greatest good to the greatest fear, Hobbes had performed an "ontological reduction," meaning that he had lowered the controlling element from the human spirit attuned to the transcendental order to a crude self-interest (eventually this ontological reduction would culminate in the sexual drives of Freudian thought). Moreover, Hobbes made order a product of agreement (contract) rather than a common bond. "The binding force of specific agreement," Voegelin argued, "derives from the ontological pre-existent common bond: one cannot derive the common bond from agreement. . . . It is the typical doxa of an immanentist intellectual who, since he has no experience of the transcendental sources of order, must let the phenomenon of order originate in actions of individuals who want to avoid the disadvantages of disorder."[67] Voegelin reminded the reader that these developments issued from diseased souls.

Nonetheless, the contract theory of Hobbes appears quite distant from Marx's proletarian revolution or Hitler's Third Reich. The transformation took place in the eighteenth century—the century of Enlightenment—and by the nineteenth century, with Hegel, Comte, Marx, and others, the full fury of modern thinking was unleashed as ideological plans for world transformation. Much like the back edge of a hurricane, the twentieth century would absorb the full blow of this ideological madness. The historical connections that tie these phenomena together run beneath the ideational constructs. John Hallowell aptly stated the thrust of Voegelin's argument: "What many regard as the political crisis of our times is shown to be a deeply rooted spiritual crisis that challenges the very substance of our humanity."[68]

Voegelin published a portion of his *History of Political Ideas* under the title *From Enlightenment to Revolution*, his most extensive analysis of the spiritual roots of modernity. A rough chronology structures the book, leading from the mild and tolerant Voltaire to Karl Marx's "intellectual swindle" (from Enlightenment to revolution). A necessary precondition for this transformation was the slow attenuation of Christianity as the source of social and political order. By Voltaire's time Christianity had already divided into warring camps, each dedicated to some doctrinal reading of the Bible. The richly textured stories of the Bible had lost their luminosity, and the images and myths had become objectified, severing the symbol from the experience of truth and thereby cutting the power of the Bible to order the individual soul. Although many of the forms and habits of Christianity maintained some hold upon thinkers, even these residual and salutary effects of Christianity would fade.

For Voltaire, much like Newton, whom he much admired and imitated, the symbols of Christian life had grown opaque. He did not abandon the symbols completely, but submitted them "to rational simplification, psychological interpretation and utilitarian justification."[69] The transformation was nonetheless decisive. The overarching drama of salvation that had structured Christians' understanding of themselves in relation to the whole no longer had meaning because he had rationalized away the spiritual dimension. As a consequence Voltaire inverted Christianity and history, making the former a part of the latter rather than history serving as the temporal dimension of the Christian tale. Still, Voltaire retained the Christian emphasis upon history as a universal and meaningful process, only now the meaning was purely "intramundane."

Once Voltaire had divested history of its transcendental dimension he had the profoundly difficult task of constructing a meaningful course out of the empirical evidence—by then swollen with new information about Eastern civilizations. The skein of meanings running through history frustrates any honest attempt to declare the meaning (singular and universal) of history (singular) when the only reference is the phenomenal realm. Voltaire stepped around this difficulty by declaring a meaning and then constructing the historical evidence to support it (moving from the present to the past). Yet even as Voltaire changed the frame of reference to the mundane realm, Voegelin insisted that he did not jettison religion: Voltaire's history "serves as the expression of a new intraworldly religiousness."[70]

The historicizing of Christianity was only part of the emerging new religion. Because the Christian experience of faith and knowledge had disappeared (at the level of socially relevant experiences), and with it the force of order, Enlightenment thinkers turned to the most effective sort of knowledge—scientific knowledge. The new standard for knowledge made the personal god of Christianity untenable but allowed room for the distant god of deism. "The existence of God is the object of an hypothesis with a high degree of probability," wrote Voegelin,[71] but a hypothetical god creates problems in terms of deciding the good. Voltaire's new worldly religion required that ethics—social and personal—be defined according to immanent reason (in contrast to the Platonic nous). Whereas the Platonic-Christian notions of ethics sprang from the well-ordered soul, Voltaire could not make sense of virtue in a personal sense but only in relation to "that which is useful to society."[72]

A restricted ontological horizon means that social utility will take on a materialistic or even an animalistic cast. Voegelin saw great significance in this early form of utilitarianism. All of the evils of the Reign of Terror, the gulag, and Dachau seemed bound up in the ontological reduction of the Enlightenment.[73] He wrote that the "identification of the good with the socially useful foreshadows the compulsory goodness of the social planner as well as the idea of revolutionary justice, with its assumption that right is what serves the proletariat, the nation or the chosen race."[74] Social utility is reduced to the material needs and comforts that science has proved so capable of supplying. So defined, the good places an exaggerated emphasis upon technological advancement—a characteristic common to all the ideologies: Marxism, National Socialism, and liberal progressivism.

The relative harmlessness of Voltaire, who never claimed the special, final knowledge of a Comte or Marx, camouflaged the damage he inflicted on Western civilization. He not only helped introduce (and here Voegelin discussed Voltaire as much as an example as for his creativity or direct influence) the new worldly religion of social utility that destroyed the Christian transcendental orientation and the Christian anthropology or view of human nature, but he created a style of thinking that encouraged irresponsibility. A willingness to speak on any subject whether he was grounded in the subject or not (the forerunner of the pundit), a superficiality protected by an air of authority, a sophomoric delight in detracting from the thought of

better minds, a belief that "irresponsibility of thought is synony-
mous with freedom of thought"—in all these ways Voltaire "has
done more than anybody else to make the darkness of enlightened
reason descend on the Western world."[75]

The eclipse of the transcendent pole of human experience (the
process of immanentization) served, as we have seen throughout this
section, as Voegelin's point of departure for understanding modern
ideologies. The new, limited perspective requires new forms of social
and political order like the one developed by Hobbes. Few Enlightenment thinkers would equal the careful and subtle arguments made
by Hobbes, rendering their answers to the problem increasingly
questionable on a theoretical or philosophical level. John Locke, for
instance, served as the target of some of Voegelin's harshest criticism. Much like Voltaire, Locke's "habits of philosophizing" did
more damage than his arguments, and Locke's penchant for exposing
to criticism some philosophical position without penetrating to the
issue resting beneath the particular argument especially galled
Voegelin. Moreover, Locke tended to argue against abstractions,
pressing some argument to its absurd conclusion, though he names
no person who makes that argument.[76] This "style of speculation"
resulted in a theoretical desert that allowed others—even encouraged
them—to concoct the most noxious claims out of their perverted
but fecund imaginations. Helvetius was one such character who occupied this philosophical wasteland, drew suspect conclusions from
the thought of Locke, and created a speculative order.

Voegelin characterized Helvetius as standing between Locke and
Bentham, and with Helvetius, the process of salvation became fully
secularized. He constructed his perfectionist dream upon an anthropology that empties humans of moral force: humans are neither
good nor bad. Humans have drives, the most powerful being the desire for power, which Helvetius understood to be a function of an
even more basic desire for pleasure (Helvetius failed to solve some
logical difficulties concerning the relationship between pleasure and
power). Human nature so displayed exposes to the scientist the
means to a virtuous society; virtue and a moral society become possible because human nature has supplied the means that a legislator
can use to create harmony. Order, happiness, and virtue are imposed
by the giver of the immanent equivalent of grace, "the analyst-legis-
lator."

Because this view makes the disordered soul normative, order becomes "intimately connected with the . . . instrumentalization of man. Man is no longer an entity that has its existential center within itself; he has become a mechanism of pleasure, pain and passions which can be harnessed by another man, the 'legislator,' for purposes of his own. . . . Only when the spiritual center of man through which man is open to the transcendental *realissimum*, is destroyed can the disorderly aggregate of passions be used as an instrument by the legislator."[77] Once the transformation into the closed horizon of immanentist reason is complete and education becomes the shaping of the socially useful member, the spiritual source of order is all but lost—the transcendental ground of existence hidden behind a second reality.

Voegelin emphasized that this dream calls, not for the abolition of religious life, but the transfer of religious symbols into an immanent religion. The political religions, as Voegelin called them, become the primary replacement for Christianity in the modern world. They externalize the personal journey of the individual soul. Salvation is no longer personal and individual but social or even tribal. By the nineteenth century the spiritual state of the West had so deteriorated that the spiritually deficient (who were becoming increasingly powerful in a de-Christianized civilization) had only two real choices: they could embrace a relativism, or they could claim to have saving knowledge that will usher in paradise. Voegelin traced the second of these options through the ideological madness of the twentieth century. Strauss focused upon the threat of relativism.

The philosophical climate of the nineteenth century meant that people seeking escape from the spiritual deformation of the age had little support or means of influence. They were largely trapped by the immanentist language of their time and by the general reduction of all thought to ideas. The socially effective intellectuals of the nineteenth century were those who discovered the meaning of history and offered themselves as prophets, or even as saviors. They constructed an intellectual iron curtain around this world and mustered immanent reason as the defense of and instrument for the transformation of humans and human society. The enlightened dreams of intellectuals culminated in an unprecedented orgy of power with visions of human potential hitched to revolutionary passion. A revolutionary intellectual cannot afford doubt nor suffer those who stand in the way of the fulfillment of human potential. Communication ceases, and the curtain joins on the far side, trapping all those inside.

We have made our way to the age of egophanic revolt—the age of Comte, Hegel, French philosophes, and Marx. Voegelin argued that the human attempt to transform the world and human nature reached its most obsessive and libidinous depths in the nineteenth century, and perhaps with Comte the fusion of the Enlightenment dreams reached its greatest synthesis. With him the religiousness of ideological thought had been thoroughly de-Christianized and the locus of human potential had centered most unquestionably in the political realm. Comte joined together the prestige of science with the need for a new ordering principle, and his positivistic sociology would replace the worn-out superstitions of Christianity as the new religion and guide toward perfection. Along with Condorcet, the vision had grown to universal proportions. The entire human race became a single tribe.

Voegelin stressed the religiousness of Comte's system. God was dead, but divinity was not exhausted. The experience of divine reality had simply been absorbed into the closed mundane system, divinizing the human species: "Man" will save himself. The earth has become the tribal habitat for "mankind." The phenomenal world, once so mysterious and dangerous, was fast giving up its secrets, and the total domination of humans over their home appeared a tantalizing prospect. Total power intoxicated Comte.

The worship of human power and dignity had already become a part of concrete human affairs during the French Revolution. The transformation of humans (i.e., human nature) that Enlightenment figures had thought of as a process of education leading to enlightened nations (or even world tribe) no longer satisfied people who lusted for a new world order. Revolution, Voegelin further argued, became the means rather than the result of change. Remove the corrupting institutions and state of affairs, and the intellectuals would midwife the birth of a new human—chaste and good and, above all, malleable. This shift in emphasis to revolution as the means of transformation was expected most strongly by Karl Marx.

The pressure felt by other intellectuals to articulate the objective, the paradise, was all but absent in Marx. In an elusive way the end of history was freedom. But freedom to do what? The great emphasis

Marx placed upon the abolition of private property emphasizes his reluctance to examine the final objective of revolution, since the stipulated goal must be understood as leading to some greater goal. Marx's shift later in his career to the practical preparation of revolution absolved him of the duty to articulate the objective. "The immenseness of the preparatory work in the realm of necessity," Voegelin wrote concerning Marx, "completely overshadowed the eschatological experience which had motivated the revolutionary vision as well as the ultimate purpose of the revolution, that is the realization of the realm of freedom."[78] The greater emphasis upon revolution meant the attenuation of Marx's vision, leaving the field open for those who came after to take up Marx's revolutionary fervor and its theoretical justification without having to share his vision of freedom.

The triumph of the will to power made the elusive but real realm of substance too elusive for intellectuals. They sought to narrow human existence to that which they could control, to reduce humans to self-interest, economic interest, sexual drives, or some other manageable and calculable characteristic. Voegelin emphasized that the spiritual heart of modernity was the nexus of power, control, and immanentization. But the true depth of the spiritual disease was represented by one of the age's most brilliant thinkers, as Hegel's system far surpassed all others with regard to its theoretical penetration and philosophical acumen. Because Hegel did not escape the desire to collapse divinity into himself, and to lead all of history to his own revelation, he represented the paradigmatic modern for Voegelin. This status came to Hegel because his spiritual disease was so advanced that even his extensive philosophical knowledge and his brilliance as a philosopher could not keep him from deicide. The will to power overwhelmed or hid the tensional nature of human existence, and Hegel sought to resolve the tensions, which is to say, he sought to transcend the human condition.

My examination of Hegel will center on Voegelin's lengthy essay "On Hegel: A Study in Sorcery." The use of sorcery in the title introduces the magical component of modernity. All mature expressions of modern eschatology, Voegelin believed, include an intellectual sleight of hand. Moreover, gnostics expect to achieve a transformed humanity through magic. Voegelin became more convinced during the latter part of his life that a belief in the magical ability ("metastasis'' was Voegelin's word) to change reality animated all gnostic thinkers, especially those who emphasized revolution. A sorcerer or a magician is a fraud or a swindler; such people perform tricks, not magic.[79] One might think of Hegel as a magician and Voegelin as the one who revealed his tricks.[80]

Despite Hegel's sorcery, Voegelin considered him a profound thinker. Indeed, his very brilliance makes him of special interest in explaining the modern phenomenon. Voegelin must explain how so superior a thinker could deform reality, and early in the essay he characterized Hegel as a divided self, a tortured soul. Hegel, wrote Voegelin, ''is a sensitive philosopher and spiritualist, a noetically and pneumatically competent critic of the age, an intellectual force of the first rank, and yet, he cannot quite gain the stature of his true self as a man under God. From the darkness of this existential deficiency, then, rises the *libido dominandi* and forces him into the imaginative construction of a false self as the messias of the new age.'' Hegel the angel and Hegel the demon, locked in the same soul, fight for supremacy. Voegelin considered Hegel to be an effective critic of his age—even more, to have fully realized the disorder of his time. Hegel's inability to ''achieve the truth of his own existence'' transmogrified his efforts to solve the disorder into a further example of the disorder.[81]

The deficiency of Hegel's soul might best be understood as the inability to live in the *metaxy* (''betweenness''). The anxiety of existence so overwhelmed him that he had to resolve the antinomies that constitute human existence, which is to say that he sought an end to human alienation. But since no person can step out of reality—no human can choose to become a god, or in any way alter his nature—Hegel must ''eclipse'' reality and construct a ''second reality.'' His brilliant and grand scheme to resolve the antinomies of reality through an inherent logic in being gave Hegel his new reality. But the depth of Hegel's spiritual disease required more of him than philosophy. ''Hence, in order to accommodate a *libido dominandi* that cannot be fulfilled by a philosopher's existence, philosophy must be dressed up as 'religion.' '' Voegelin believed that Hegel considered himself the new Christ, the locus of a spiritual energy that inaugurates a new age. Hegel did transform philosophy into something new. In the age of Hegel, the philosopher would no longer limit himself to the search for wisdom (which is the chastened search of the one who recognizes human limitation) but would search for truth. Hegel's pursuit was further blessed with the "new symbol 'science' which began, in the wake of Newton, to acquire its peculiar modern magic."[82]

Voegelin's reading of Hegel takes a far more radical tone than most. He rejected or sometimes just dismissed as too vague the characterizations of Hegel as an Enlightenment philosopher, or a Christian (Protestant) philosopher, or a conservative philosopher. Voegelin accepted Hegel's own designation as the philosopher of the French Revolution,[83] and even though the meaning of the label is elusive, it does mark Hegel as a revolutionary. One must always keep in mind Voegelin's characterization of Hegel as a soul lusting for power. The existential imperative controlled the shape of Hegel's work, and in some way Hegel had to make his philosophy an integral part of the evolving process of history. The famous example of Hegel's watching Napoleon as he passed through Hegel's town becomes the occasion for intense jealousy when viewed from Voegelin's portrayal of Hegel's psychology.[84] To understand Voegelin's interpretation of Hegel we should examine a key passage from Hegel and Voegelin's reading of it.

> Every single man is but a blind link in the chain of absolute necessity by which the world builds itself forth *(sich fortbildet).* The single man can elevate himself to dominance *(Herrschaft)* over an appreciable length of this chain only if he knows the direction in which the great necessity wants to move and if he learns from this knowledge to pronounce the magic words *(die Zauberworte)* that will evoke its shape *(Gestalt).* [85]

Voegelin placed great significance on this quotation, for it reveals Hegel's "resentment" as well as providing the key insight into "modern existence." Voegelin emphasized the utter inconsequential nature of humans, what Voegelin called a "blind particle." From this state of essential nothingness, the individual human (the single person) provides himself with knowledge—the blind particle gives itself sight. More obvious, and very much a part of Voegelin's larger characterization of modernity, was Hegel's emphasis upon what one might call "redemptive knowledge." If the single man can learn the direction of necessity, he "can elevate himself to dominance"—

knowledge and dominance—the source and the objective of modernity. Finally, one notes the reference to "magic words" that will evoke the shape of the great necessity. Voegelin wrote: "The imaginative project of history falls in its place in the pattern of modern existence as the conjurer's instrument of power."[86]

Hegel's spiritual condition served as the focal point of Voegelin's analysis because it exposed the motivation for the "system." Textual analysis of Hegel's *Phenomenology* is conspicuously scant in Voegelin's scholarly corpus; indeed, he developed most of his conclusions about the purpose behind Hegel's work from other works. Nonetheless, having called Hegel a sorcerer, Voegelin had to expose his tricks, and a few examples will help us understand what Voegelin meant. He labeled Hegel's philosophy of history a "system," which suggests a kind of internal and circular logic. Once inside—that is, once one accepts the premises—one is trapped. Part of the trick for Hegel was to employ standard symbols and invest them with new meanings. More important to Hegel's game was a circularity of language. After describing a paragraph from the *Phenomenology* Voegelin characterized it this way:

> Though the paragraph begins with the Incarnation of God in Christ and ends with self-consciousness that operates its own transfiguration, by writing the *Phaenomenologie*, Hegel has talked, with the appearance of perfect innocence, about nothing but the *Wesen*, that is *Geist*, about the *Geist* that is *Selbstbewusstsein*, and about the *Selbtbewusstsein* that is the *Wesen* of the *Geist*. The game is rigged; you can't win once you let yourself be sucked into accepting Hegel's language.[87]

Hegel took the precaution of protecting himself by affirming Christian orthodoxy and even employing doctrinal language in his works. But these moves do not change the self-deification that Voegelin found logically entailed in Hegel's philosophy. The progressive development of Consciousness—which Hegel equated with absolute reality—that forms the core of Hegel's story leads to Consciousness as absolute knowledge. The final transformation that culminates in the fully realized Consciousness is the development from religion (inaugurated by Jesus) to philosophy. This final age (the third age) is the age of Hegel. Hegel has replaced Jesus by bringing the fullest revelation; once again spirit and flesh have become one.

The strange coupling of Paul and Hegel in the same chapter of Voegelin's *The Ecumenic Age* now makes some sense. Both Paul's vision of the resurrected and Hegel's philosophy of history express the same experience of "the movement of reality beyond its structure."[88] The erotic pull toward the divine pole of existence is a permanent part of human existence, but it is a part that one experiences as seeking to transcend this structure. This is the source of human alienation. Plato understood the movement toward transcending reality as being a constituent part of reality and recognized that all of these moves take place in the *metaxy*, which is the tensional field between God and man, the divine and the mundane, the One and the many. The fact that a quality of that field is the erotic desire to transcend this very structure does not mean that humans can escape the *metaxy*. Paul introduced the anticipation of transfiguration (resurrection), which would be the end of history and human fulfillment in the presence of God. Paul expected God to transform humans outside of history into something other than humans. This expectation became a part of the Western self-understanding, which in time developed from an expectation of God's transforming humans outside of history to the transformation of humans by humans in history. Hegel's system was the product of the same experience known by Paul but with the added ingredients of a diseased soul bent on domination, and a brilliant mind able to perform magic with words.

The second reality created by Hegel or other ideologues becomes a replacement for the *metaxy*. But the *metaxy* does not cease to characterize human existence because humans will it away. Because the second reality sprang, not from reality, but from the speculative mind of a megalomaniac, it will produce constant tensions caused by its ill-fit to the human experiences on which it is superimposed. No conditions poses greater danger to human society than an ideological failure. The diseased souls who accept any second reality can no longer see an alternative and will become most violent in their efforts to realize the final paradise promised by some ideological deformation of reality. Only a return to the balanced consciousness and an acceptance of the reality of the *metaxy* can deliver us from the violence and disorder of modernity.

5
The Crisis of Modernity

THE END OF MODERNITY

The common denominator of the two preceding chapters is the emphasis Voegelin and Strauss placed upon the emerging belief that humans could control their destiny and transform the world. Only when the world became plastic, and humans alienated, could this belief and aspiration become possible. Whether one places the emphasis upon a cosmos purged of gods or on the transformation of nature from a normative order into a physical realm ripe for human manipulation, the modern world becomes the location of human-directed transformation. Humans, meanwhile, go through a radical redefinition. They become alienated but come to believe they can ameliorate this condition. Knowledge, the fulcrum upon which this complex of ideas rests, seems able to transform humans and, in turn, the world. Knowledge brings power, and an empowered human is a creator—we are back to Eve. The creator-human will try to make right what is wrong, will try to transform the malleable world into a proper home, and will try to end forever the anxiety of alienation. Because knowledge played so central a role in this process, moderns had to make especially sharp epistemological judgments. Only that about which they could be certain would they call knowledge. The certainty of their knowledge created great confidence that they were entering a new and luminous age, but even with a plastic world and the human power to mold it, the question of ends remained problematic. By whose lights should humans construct their new world? Do they operate in a world grounded in any transhuman standard? If humans find themselves possessed with Promethean power, do they have wisdom concerning ends?

The modern project of creating a new world and a new ''man'' depended upon and facilitated a belief in the saving power of human knowledge. As God grew more distant and traditions took on the taint of superstitions—emerging as they did out of the dark past of unenlightened human experience—knowledge became the only acceptable guide to human action. When God withdrew, the empirical sciences expanded. New and workable ways of understanding the physical world reinforced faith in human knowledge until nothing seemed beyond the human ken. "Reason" was the symbol for this human capacity. In all things—in ethics, politics, cosmology—"reason" became the true and reliable guide. The corresponding devaluation of habits, customs, and traditions opened a new space for ever more radical change. A new theodicy pitted the rising power of "reason," ahistorical and abstract theorizing, and universalism against the waning evil forces of an unenlightened past: religion (superstition), tradition, and local particularity. So long as belief in this certainty remained intact, modernity would be immune from any real challenge.

But knowledge was a secondary or facilitory goal; it was freedom (power, creativity, will) that rested at the heart of the Enlightenment project. In subtle but important respects these two goals worked at cross-purposes. The search for truth—so central to Western and Christian self-identity—supposed something beyond human control (e.g., nature). Strauss detected this tension in Machiavelli, who turned nature into a technical problem. Voegelin emphasized the willful heart that sought freedom through knowledge. The differences between the two are matters of emphasis. Nonetheless, Strauss more accurately emphasized the power of the triumph of will over knowledge that has come to characterize the contemporary late modern era, as Strauss's thinking was always more occupied with the crisis of the West. This crisis emerged from the well-spring of Western thought, the search for truth, and as the Enlightenment version of this theme began to dissolve the Christian doctrinal structure, and then Semitic cosmology, it eroded the myths that sustained that search. Without the defining beliefs of the West the personal beliefs concerning moral and political matters were dangerously exposed. Or as Strauss emphasized, borrowing from Nietzsche, Christian morals must eventually go the way of Christian metaphysics.

"The crisis of modernity," Strauss wrote, "reveals itself in the fact, or consists in the fact, that modern western man no longer knows what he wants—that he no longer believes that he can know what is good and bad, what is right and wrong."[1] The disorientation that characterizes the late nineteenth and the twentieth centuries is the "end" or the logical conclusion of modernity. This part or phase of modernity occupied much of Strauss's attention because his own experiences and his early philosophical commitments reinforced in his mind the danger of the morally empty space left by the failed project.[2] The danger was great because moderns had cleared the philosophical ground to construct their own edifice—once it crumbled, the newly homeless had no philosophical structure in which to seek shelter. They had razed a cathedral to build a rational, efficient highrise; now only rubble dotted the landscape.

Although one may, with some justification, write about the "end" of modernity, one cannot write about the path to this end in the singular. The unraveling of the project is an enormously complex subject with numerous and apparently unrelated assaults upon Enlightenment beliefs. We must isolate the more prominent themes in this process, but nonetheless, the focal point remains the crisis that Strauss articulated—a culture unable to defend its very principles or to articulate a clear moral center. "If you will not have God you should pay your respects to Hitler or Stalin."[3]

The fragility of human knowledge proved to be the Achilles' heel of the modern project, a point the great philosophers understood. The period from Descartes to Kant is marked by an obsession with certainty, by a continuous effort to delimit the area of the knowable as a means of securing an epistemological grounding. This concern crossed the great rationalist-empiricist divide. Whether it was Descartes working deductively back to some unquestionable epistemological ground or an empiricist putting together countless bits of evidence into larger and more comprehensive constructions, the Enlightenment philosopher worked toward the indubitable. And then came Hume. When the great Scottish skeptic challenged the knowability of causation he threatened to tumble the entire house of constructed knowledge. Most at risk was the epistemological darling of the age—science. The empirical methods that had evolved in the most successful areas of inquiry (the physical and natural sciences) largely rested upon some conception of causation. The ability of scientists to claim predictability as a reasonable goal of their work was especially vulnerable in this connection. Without predictability the findings of scientists could never serve as a sure means of transforming the world. Similarly, predictability in the world of human behavior was all but hopeless. The modern project, it appeared, had greater limitations than expected.

When Hume's logical puzzle awakened Kant from his dogmatic slumber, a new phase in the quest for certainty began. In many important respects Kant forever crushed the hope for an all-encompassing knowledge (even as a heuristic ideal) because of the inherent limitedness of the human perspective. Out of the complicated conversation that attended Kant's work, one can, with some abuse to the subject, discern two broad responses. For some people the search for objective and indubitable knowledge became a moral obligation and, perhaps, an existential imperative. This group included such diverse people as the liberal positivists of the John S. Mill variety (and their successors down to the logical positivists) and the more ideologically charged work of Comte and Marx (both of whom largely ignored Kant's claims). Others emphasized the historical nature of knowledge and thereby cast into doubt the very possibility of the enterprise occupying the first group. Consequently, the epistemological field of battle was occupied by two groups, one moving toward a hardening ideology and the other toward relativism. The former sought to maintain the dual goals of the Enlightenment, but to do so, they had to supply a non-Christian teleology. The others understood the foundationlessness of all knowledge, which could be either liberating or incapacitating.

Like Voegelin, Strauss detected in the ideological closure of the first group a danger, and perhaps some responsibility for the ideological wars of the twentieth century. Yet the danger posed by the nihilism of the historicists loomed much greater. Strauss considered historicism to be the logical modern response to the limitations of ideology, and as such the final, bankrupt conclusion to the dialectic of modernity. The real challenge to the West, he believed, sprang from historicism.

The focus of the present section is Leo Strauss's account of the final stage of modernity. The hard core of the modern project, articulated by Machiavelli, was the turning of moral and political problems, once considered part of the human condition, into technical problems. Or, to put the matter another way, Machiavelli rejected nature as a standard in favor of nature as conditions to overcome, the raw material for human creativity. The manipulative possibilities of a nature turned on its head became evident in the physical sciences (in the work of Francis Bacon, for instance) and political science, in which Hobbes drew out Machiavelli's logic.

But the rejection of the "ancients" (for Strauss moderns are those who reject Platonic-Aristotelian science) by moderns was not exhausted by Machiavelli and the people who followed him. A more radical rejection came with Rousseau's anthropology. Drawing on the social contract theorists, Rousseau radicalized the state of nature. A person in this state was not human, being prerational but full of unlimited potential. Humanness comes through history, or through the process of cultural development. Most important for Strauss was Rousseau's denial of human nature. Rousseau collapsed the good into the rational, and his general will was the expression of the process of rationality. The particular wills of individuals, who must live in societies for reasons of survival, slowly conform to the general will. The universalizing of particular wills through the experiences of social and political life becomes the standard of goodness. "Therefore," wrote Strauss, "the moral laws, as laws of freedom, are no longer understood as natural laws. Moral and political ideals are established without reference to man's nature: man is radically liberated from the tutelage of nature."[4] Human nature is nothing other than historical development up to that point, which is to say, the history of human choices.

The complications of Rousseau's thought make simple reduction impossible. His emphasis upon the freedom in nature, which he contrasted to history, society, morality, and reason, makes the subject treacherous. What is important here is that Strauss stressed Rousseau's effective removal of nature as a standard, even as Rousseau otherwise worked at cross-purposes to the thought of Machiavelli and Hobbes.

The development of a historical consciousness, which came at the expense of "nature," made all of the moral (and hence political) and epistemological bases of Western civilization problematic. In the short run, following the first great historicist, Hegel, the historicity of human thought did not trouble thinkers who retained a strong faith in rationality. Nonetheless, the very nature of historicism undercut this faith, and "Nietzsche was the first to face this situation."[5] This historicism is the "end" or logical conclusion of modernity. For Strauss, who took his bearings from nature as understood by the ancients, the transformation of nature begun by Machiavelli had finally ended, by the late nineteenth century, in making nature unbelievable to most sensitive thinkers. Strauss's understanding of this philosophical climate becomes clear as we follow his exploration of the thought of two men: Nietzsche and Heidegger.

Strauss used the work of those men to represent two responses to the historicist insight: theoretical or skeptical historicism and existentialism. The distinction is decisive. To understand the contours of Strauss's comparison we turn to the first chapter of *Natural Right and History*—or, more precisely, to the last several pages of that chapter. The majority of the chapter explores historicism in the broader context, but beginning with paragraph twenty-three, Strauss concentrated on the "radical historicists." No names or specific references clutter his analysis, and the historicism he described ends up being logically self-contradictory and, as such, not particularly threatening.[6] Radical historicists avoid this flaw, which presented Strauss with a formidable challenge. In his largely descriptive account of this nemesis one detects clues that point to Strauss's response.

In paragraph twenty-two, Strauss opened up the grand possibility presented by the historicist experience (historical consciousness). He wrote: "Thought that recognizes the relativity of all comprehensive views has a different character from thought which is under the spell of, or which adopts, a comprehensive view. The former is absolute and neutral; the latter is relative and committed. The former is a theoretical insight that transcends history; the latter is the outcome of a fateful dispensation.'"[7] The insight that all comprehensive views are relative does not demand an incapacitating fatalism—indeed, Strauss hinted at the liberating potential of this discovery—but one catches a whiff of something premodern here.

Strauss did not argue that the discovery was modern as such; in the next paragraph (the paragraph that opens the section on radical historicists), he even hints at the ancient character of the insight. Nietzsche is the crucial or pivotal character in the story—though Strauss only mentioned him once in this chapter. Nietzsche takes his place among the select few whom Strauss designated as true, or truly great, philosophers. Emerging at the end of Enlightenment optimism, with the naive progressive hopes of Hegelian historicists and positivists still largely intact, Nietzsche punctured the progressive conceits. Europe was not at or near the end of history, though perhaps the end of a civilization was near. No hope emerged from recent scientific progress because Nietzsche exposed science as only one among many competing ideologies constructed on foundations of sand. The rock of a normative order was simply not exposed to human view. Nietzsche understood this truth to have potentially dire consequences, leading to the destruction of "the protecting atmosphere within which life or culture or action is alone possible." Strauss told the reader that Nietzsche had two options. He could follow Plato and insist upon "the strictly esoteric character of the theoretical analysis of life," or he could "conceive of thought as essentially subservient to, or dependent on, life or fate." The reader learns, therefore, that Plato and Nietzsche possessed the same insight, exposing Strauss's argument that the historicist discovery is not modern but available to humans (or certain humans) at all times.[8]

Nietzsche's choice appears stark, but Strauss leaves room for some maneuvering. "If not Nietzsche himself, at any rate his successors adopted the second alternative." Heidegger, in other words, believed thought to be a function of, and bound to, a historical horizon—or to fate. The existential variation of historicism, which Nietzsche made possible but a renewed interest in Kierkegaard consummated,[9] emphasized the unavoidability of committed thought, i.e., thought connected with and dependent upon a comprehensive view given to each person as a function of one's place in a cultural and historical horizon. The epistemic context, in other words, provides the necessary but arbitrary ground of all thought.

The modern context provided the ground for the historicist's "fundamental experience which, by its nature, is incapable of adequate expression on the level of noncommitted or detached thought." Like all truths, it depends on fate. The historicist claim is exempt from its own verdict because it "claims merely to mirror the character of historical reality. . . . The self-contradictory character of the historicist thesis should be charged not to historicism but to reality." Fate may close the window to this truth in the future, making it unbelievable, but Strauss argued that the truth that all comprehensive views are relative does not necessitate that one—or a few—

cannot escape them or that this truth is accessible to moderns only. At the center of the section on radical historicism, Strauss explored the relationship between philosophy as classically construed and historicism. He emphasized that historicism rests upon two claims: one, the impossibility of "theoretical metaphysics and of philosophical ethics or natural rights" and two, the insolubility of "the fundamental riddles."[10] Philosophers, on the other hand, conceive of their task to be the understanding of fundamental riddles, and it is because these riddles or problems are fundamental that they represent a permanent or natural structure of human reality. The struggle to understand them requires that one transcend the particularist construction to a more theoretical and abstract level. The reader must assume or believe that these riddles are universal, however, because Strauss only asserts it.

The most formidable challenge historicists pose to philosophers is the claim that philosophy, as the quest for knowledge of the whole, presupposes a whole not in evidence. To the "being" of classical philosophy the historicist counters with "becoming." Strauss does not pursue the complicated issue in the first chapter of *Natural Right and History* except to suggest that the challenge requires an "unbiased reconsideration of the most elementary premises whose validity is presupposed by philosophy"—i.e., the aim of the book. Still, Strauss emphasized "those simple experiences of right and wrong which are at the bottom of the philosophical contention that there is a natural right." These experiences serve as the prephilosophical source for theoretical analysis, and they point to the universal problems of human existence concerning, especially, the social and political matter of justice. Wrote Strauss: "In grasping these problems as problems, the human mind liberates itself from its historical limitation. No more is needed to legitimize philosophy in its original, Socratic, sense: philosophy is knowledge that one does not know; that is to say, it is knowledge of what one does not know, or awareness of the fundamental alternatives regarding their solution that are coeval with human thought."[11] Thus, Strauss limited the necessary and sufficient condition for philosophy to there being fundamental problems exposed to philosophers as such.[12] One of the premises of historicism is the insolubility of the fundamental riddles, and the insight into this truth gained by the "historical experience" led radical historicists to add another "truth" not logically entailed by the first: the impossibility of grounding either theoretical metaphysics or philosophical ethics. Strauss rejected this dogmatism and chose to remain a skeptic on such matters.

A careful reader cannot come away from the brief text under examination with any clear understanding of Strauss's thinking. On the one hand, Strauss validates, if not exactly in the open, the core of the historicist experience, i.e., that all comprehensive views are relative. On the other hand, the reader detects his deep concern that historicism leads to (or has led to) a life-denying nihilism. What is most clear is Strauss's contention that radical historicism blinds people to the import of their own experiences of right and wrong, leaving no means to transcend the particular in search of the human and no political will to defend right. Consequently, both philosophy and political philosophy become problematic. What is unclear is how the truth that Strauss affirmed as being as old as philosophy itself becomes life-affirming.

Nietzsche, Strauss believed, both prepared the way for these dire, historicist consequences and pointed the way out. Nietzsche was a historicist who believed in nature, an atheist who sought to vindicate God. To make sense of this paradoxical quality of Nietzsche's thought one must keep in mind the political and social requirements for human (i.e., genuinely human) life. Strauss explained the problem Nietzsche faced.

History becomes a spectacle that for the superficial is exciting and for the serious is enervating. It teaches a truth that is deadly. It shows us that culture is possible only if men are fully dedicated to principles and thought and action which they do not and cannot question, which limit their horizon and thus enable them to have a character and style. It shows us at the same time that any principles of this kind can be questioned and even rejected.[13]

Civilization requires artificial or created metaphysical boundaries that operate like the glass walls of a greenhouse. Compromise the boundaries or walls and you jeopardize the delicate life inside. When the members of a society recognize that their principles rest upon a comprehensive order that cannot be established as right or true, they find themselves unable to defend their most cherished and defining beliefs. What becomes of justice? Without the promise or hope or idea of justice, what becomes of human civilization?

The apparent solution—life-giving delusion or myth—is hardly satisfactory, or so Strauss would have us believe. At the very least, such myth making is impossible for the philosopher (or for "men of intellectual probity"). The answer rests in the nature of human society. Nietzsche "transformed the deadly truth of relativism into the most life-giving truth. . . . he discovered that the life-giving comprehensive truth is subjective or transtheoretical in that it cannot be grasped detachedly and that it cannot be the same for all men or for all ages."[14] By so understanding nature—i.e., the nature of political life—Nietzsche had escaped or transcended the realm he studied, joining the other philosophers in a sort of timeless communion of mind. But all of these philosophers transcended only the beliefs necessary to the social and political order, they did not transcend the need for that order. Indeed, by exposing the nature of the political realm to which they were not intellectually or existentially attached, they recognized the requirement that they support it. Docs this situation not amount to advocating the unsatisfying solution of the noble lie?

We are well placed, now, to understand what Strauss meant when he wrote that Nietzsche's "doctrine of the will to power . . . is in a manner a vindication of God."[15] In Strauss's last book, the chapter on Nietzsche ("Notes on the Plan of Nietzsche's *Beyond Good and Evil*") catches one's attention because it is placed between a chapter on the tension between philosophy and religion and a series of chapters on Maimonides. Moreover, with the exception of a final chapter on Machiavelli, no other chapter in the book deals with a modern thinker.[16] Nietzsche seems a strange subject for a book that bears the title *Studies in Platonic Political Philosophy,* but no stranger than Strauss's claim that Nietzsche's will to power is a vindication of God. Still, these arresting details have their purpose.

One might be justified in looking for some clues to the chapter on *Beyond Good and Evil* in the chapter preceding it. In "Jerusalem and Athens," Strauss explored the creative tension between philosophy (or the life of reason) and biblical faith (the life of obedience). "Western man," he wrote, "became what he is and is what he is through the coming together of biblical faith and Greek thought." What should the reader make of this statement in light of Strauss's claims elsewhere that in the modern era philosophy has become the history of philosophy and biblical claims no longer operate as unquestioned assumptions? Nietzsche is the modern exemplar of a genuine philosopher who recognized and respected the sources of Western civilization. "Nietzsche has a deeper reverence than any other beholder [i.e., one who truly understands] for the sacred tablets of the Hebrews as well as of the other nations in question," but Nietzsche understood that these tablets contradicted the commandments of other cultures. His respect, therefore, did not extend to believing in or being bound by the culture. As a philosopher he sought "the oneness of truth," and he "sought therefore for a culture that would no longer be particular and hence in the last analysis arbitrary. The single goal of Mankind is conceived by him as in a sense super-human: he speaks of the super-man of the future. The super-man is meant to unite in himself Jerusalem and Athens at the highest level."[17]

Jews and Athenians—or the tension that exists between their ways of seeing—supply "Western man" with his peculiar character, his genius. Strauss's silence regarding Christianity is loud, and the meaning of his silence is not presently clear. What is evident is that Strauss understood Nietzsche in the light of the two traditions to which Strauss himself felt connected. The nature of Nietzsche's attitude toward these two ways of living is complicated, but Strauss placed Nietzsche as a respectful outsider concerning Jerusalem.

In the chapter concerning *Beyond Good and Evil*, the reader finds numerous comparisons between Plato and Nietzsche. One learns that *Beyond Good and Evil* is Nietzsche's most Platonic book in terms of its form, by which Strauss meant that unlike Nietzsche's other books—especially *Thus Spoke Zarathustra*—he wrote esoterically in this one, employing the "graceful subtlety as regards form, as regards intention, as regards the art of silence."[18] So in this book, if not in other Nietzsche texts, one must read between the lines. Like Plato and Aristotle, Nietzsche assumed a close relationship between philosophy and religion. Yet while Plato and Aristotle put the choice between the political or philosophic life, Nietzsche emphasized that either philosophy will rule religion or religion will rule philosophy. Since, as Strauss pointed out, Nietzsche "intimates that his precursor par excellence is not a statesman nor even a philosopher but the *homo religiosus* Pascal," one is led to conclude that religion should rule philosophy or that philosophy must serve the needs of religion.[19] But Strauss also wrote about one of Nietzsche's precursors, someone who represented an earlier time. The issues confronted by Nietzsche, who lived with the death of God, had been confronted earlier by that precursor, Pascal, within the Christian horizon. The conclusion to which one is drawn applies only to the past; to the ages when God lived. But Nietzsche lived in an age of transition from Christianity to something else, and he wrote *Beyond Good and Evil* as a precursor of the philosopher of the future. Although he was one of those precursors, Nietzsche was nonetheless an heir of Christianity. For Strauss, this was a decisive fact.

Because, as Strauss argued, Nietzsche replaced the Platonic eros and pure mind with the will to power, "philosophizing becomes a mode or modification of the will to power: it is the most spiritual *(der geistigste)* will to power; it consists in prescribing to nature what or how it ought to be . . . ; *it is not love of the true that is independent of the will or decision.*"[20] The life-giving creativity of the will to power supplies truths and gods. But to what god could Nietzsche bow? None. He discovered the one detached and deadly truth that the "world in itself . . . is wholly chaotic and meaningless." Gods and truths emerge out of human creativity (i.e., the will to power), and meaning and purpose—which ground human civilization—do not depend upon some truth that is independent of human will. As creations they are fictions insofar as they cannot reflect "the world in itself," but in circumstances in which the object is unknowable and all we have are interpretations, a fiction functions much like the truth.[21] The distinction between the world we live in and the world in itself becomes meaningless. Nietzsche rescued truth by defining it as life-giving belief, and life-giving belief issues from the will to power.

Strauss emphasized Nietzsche's praise for the Old Testament. Keeping in mind how Nietzsche had thoroughly oriented human life to interpretations of the world, Strauss's emphasis on Nietzsche's vindication of God comes into perspective. Strauss made the connection this way: "For Nietzsche 'the great style' of (certain parts of) the Old Testament shows forth the greatness, not of God, but of what man once was: the holy God no less than the holy man are creatures of the human will to power." The Jews had (or created) a proper god—the sort of god one could respect. The Jewish god was a rich resource for social and political order, to say nothing of his existential resources. Nietzsche the atheist could not believe in this god, but as a detached observer he could provide an atheistic vindication of God.[22]

If God were dead, the need for one like him was not. Strauss emphasized the religiosity that Nietzsche thought characterized an atheistic age (i.e., the age when god is dead). Strauss wrote that Nietzsche's "atheism is not unambiguous, for he had doubts whether there can be a world, any world whose center is not God." The paradox Strauss pointed to is important, though not especially clear. Nietzsche the atheist recognized the necessity of God, without whom no "world" is possible.[23] The search for the only important knowledge—self-knowledge—leads to a contradiction, or at least to an impenetrable barrier. Characterizing Nietzsche's position on the seeker of self-knowledge, Strauss wrote: "Precisely because he [i.e., the seeker of self-knowledge] is concerned with the freedom of his own mind he must imprison his heart (*Beyond Good and Evil*, aphorisms 87, 107). Freedom of one's mind is not possible without a dash of stupidity (9). Self-knowledge is not only very difficult but impossible to achieve; man cannot live with perfect self-knowledge (80–81, 231, 249)."[24] In the aphorisms Strauss cited one notes the relationship between freedom and restraint and between change and the unchangeable. "But at the bottom of our souls," Nietzsche wrote, "quite 'deep down,' there is certainly something unteachable, a granite of spiritual fate, or predetermined decisions and answers to predetermined chosen questions" (aphorism 231).

One begins to detect the reason Strauss argued that Nietzsche pointed the way back to nature. The burden of establishing this claim more firmly falls on the second half of Strauss's chapter (paragraphs seventeen to thirty-seven). Nietzsche's fifth (and central) chapter, "Toward the Natural History of Morality," serves as the point of departure. Strauss noted that the earlier chapter on religion was not titled "a natural history of religion." The reason, he emphasized, was that religious experiences are inaccessible to the one examining religious beliefs.[25] A taxonomy of morals is possible without recourse to the hidden world of private experience (much less numinous experience). Still, Strauss noted, Nietzsche argued that no such knowledge provides the means for a "philosophic ethics, a science of morals which teaches the only true morality." The problem plaguing such a science is the false belief that morals belong to the natural order, which human reason discovers. In sharp contrast to rational morality, Nietzsche affirmed that, in Strauss's words, "every morality is based on some tyranny against nature as well as against reason." The imposition of a moral order is, from the standpoint of reason, arbitrary, but not for that reason undesirable. The coercive conditions of a moral code provide the necessary condition for "everything of value, every freedom."[26] But if these desirable results emerge from a revolt against nature, how is it that Nietzsche pointed the way back to nature?

To understand Strauss's answer to this problem, we consider briefly one of Nietzsche's most important aphorisms (188). Strauss noted it, and pointed out that within the aphorism Nietzsche always used nature in quotes, except for his final reference to it. Nature, Strauss suggested, "has become a problem for Nietzsche and yet he cannot do without nature."[27] Nietzsche's aphorism turns on the paradox that freedom rests on coercion, greatness on stupidity; all great achievements owe their existence to the "tyranny of arbitrary laws." Nietzsche wrote: "The essential thing 'in heaven and earth' is, apparently . . . that there should be long obedience in the same direction; from this there results, and has always resulted in the long run, something that has made life worth living; for instance, virtue, art, music, dancing, reason, spirituality—anything whatever that is transfiguring, refined, foolish, or divine." A human, totally free and unencumbered, lacks the conditions, the restraints, the context, to be genuinely free and creative. The conclusion of aphorism 188 warrants a lengthy quotation:

It ["nature"] teaches the *narrowing of perspectives*, and thus, in a certain sense, stupidity as a condition of life and development. "Thou must obey some one, and for a long time; otherwise thou wilt come to grief, and lose all respect for thyself"—this seems to me to be the moral imperative of nature, which is certainly neither "categorical," as old Kant wished . . . nor does it address itself to the individual . . . but to nations, races, ages, and ranks, above all, however, to the animal "man" generally, to mankind.

Nietzsche found in nature a moral imperative not to live by "nature." One sees, I think, what Strauss meant when he wrote that nature "has become a problem for Nietzsche and yet he cannot do without nature."

Nietzsche, as Strauss understood him, believed he lived between two noble ages (though any future is unknown and unpredictable). The will to power had acted unconsciously in the past to create gods and moralities, and thus the tyranny and "slavery" that are the "indispensable means even of spiritual education and discipline" (aphorism 188). The awful truth of God's death, which springs from "the historical sense," is also the contemporary generation's greatest virtue. The philosopher of the future will be the "first man who consciously creates values on the basis of the understanding of the will to power as the fundamental phenomenon." In this sense the philosopher of the future will be supplied with the knowledge of nature lacking before, thus putting him in a position of giving humans what they have heretofore lacked—a nature ("for the nature of a being is its end, its completed state, its peak").[28]

The creation of "natural man"—which is the highest freedom and creativity and, as such, represents the conquest of nature—does not solve the problem of nature that, Strauss thought, plagued Nietzsche. Nature, not reason, made human achievement possible because "all thought depends on something 'deep down,' on a fundamental stupidity." The struggle against "non-sense and chance," against the chaotic and meaningless world, is the necessary condition for the creation of the natural man. The conquering of the natural world (of inequality, chance, and nonsense) destroys the very ground for the "moral imperative of nature," which requires a "narrowing of perspectives," and a recognition of "stupidity as a condition of life and development" (aphorism 188). The modern condition, when the natural conditions were being ameliorated and a herd morality was replacing older, more noble, and life-affirming moralities, required that heretofore natural conditions be henceforth willed. Strauss wrote: "Nature, the eternity of nature, owes its being to a postulation, to an act of the will to power on the part of the highest nature."[29]

Strauss's essay is ambiguous and, I think, evasive. Most significantly, Strauss left vague the confusing array of meanings he and Nietzsche gave to the word "nature." In some places it referred to the natural conditions, i.e., chance, nonsense, struggle, inequality (nature one), but he also used the word to mean the end or peak of a being (nature two). Also, nature refers to that unteachable deep down, that fundamental stupidity (nature three). In what sense, then, did Nietzsche point to nature? One must focus on Strauss's claim that for Nietzsche, nature became a problem but that he could not do without nature. "Nature . . . has become a problem owing to the fact that man is conquering nature and there are no assignable limits to that conquest. As a consequence, people have come to think of abolishing suffering and inequality. Yet suffering and inequality are the prerequisites of human greatness."[30] Nature two depends on nature one. Nature three, meanwhile, has a special character as the individual source of all thought—the authentic self. "Stupidity," Nietzsche wrote, is a "condition of life and development" (aphorism 188). This quotation comes in the context of nature teaching the "narrowing of perspectives." The will to power is this narrowing, the creation and affirmation of beliefs by a people (a tribe). It is particular and, in a sense, arbitrary—but life-affirming. The nature here is the deep down that seeks to create the world in its image; philosophy is "the most spiritual Will to Power" because philosophers seek to create a world out of their stupidity (aphorism 9).

In all these senses, then, Nietzsche affirmed nature as the condition for greatness and creativity. Nonetheless, he wrote *Beyond Good and Evil* for the philosophers of the future—as a prelude to the philosophy of the future—because Western civilization stood in need of a spiritual will to power. Modernity had killed God but had affirmed nothing life-giving to replace it. The terrible truth enervated moderns who had nothing in which to believe except a weak morality shorn of the God who issued it. Yet as Strauss suggested, Nietzsche transformed this truth into an affirmation of life because he detected the natural foundations, or conditions of nature, necessary for noble thought. Strauss ended this difficult chapter on Nietzsche with a sentence written in German, but not, so far as I can tell, a quotation: Die vornehme Natur ersetzt die göttliche Natur ("the noble nature replaces divine nature").[31] God, created by the will to power, had died, and any fresh expression of that will must take into account that death.

Nietzsche is a special case. Strauss associated Nietzsche with the third wave of modernity in the same way he associated Machiavelli and Rousseau with the first two waves. In this sense, Strauss considered Nietzsche modern. But for Strauss, Nietzsche also pointed the way out of modernity, i.e., he pointed in the direction of the ancients, and this ambiguity is perhaps the richest source for speculation in Strauss's thought. An attempt to resolve finally this tension would do a terrible injustice to his thinking, for the question as to whether Strauss was Nietzschean or not is, simply, the wrong question.[32]

The ambiguity of Strauss's interpretation rests primarily on the fact that Nietzsche was a historicist who pointed to nature as the answer to the modern problem. His historicism provided much of the intellectual groundwork for the development of the most radical form of historicism, what Strauss designated existentialism. Nietzsche saw the emptiness of modern rationality, and his withering critique "cannot be dismissed or forgotten." His critique cannot be dismissed because it was entirely correct, and for moderns (in this case, those blinded to the ancient alternative) who see his point, the moral and political landscape must appear as bleak as Hiroshima on 7 August 1945. The point, if we are not careful, can get lost. The danger Nietzsche poses is the naked truth about the core of modernity—"this is the deepest reason for the crisis of liberal democracy." One remembers that Strauss defined this crisis as the inability to believe in anything—at least in anything concerning the social and political good. To the degree that a society is committed to the modern project it is vulnerable to Nietzsche's critique.[33]

"Nietzsche," wrote Strauss, "is the philosopher of relativism: the first thinker who faced the problem of relativism in its full extent and pointed to the way in which relativism can be overcome."[34] The optimism that still pervaded post-Hegel historicism was the final gasp of a nonpositivist modernity. Nietzsche recognized that the truth of historicism—its radical relativism—destroyed a belief in progress, which was so much a part of nineteenth-century thought. Most important, knowledge, truths, and beliefs are all products of premises that themselves cannot be questioned. Humans (qua social beings) must be committed to some way of looking at reality, but the historicist recognizes that all such commitments are groundless. Strauss wrote: "History [i.e., historical consciousness] becomes a spectacle that for the superficial is exciting and for the serious is enervating. It teaches a truth that is deadly. It shows us that culture is possible only if men are fully dedicated to principles of thought and action which they do not and cannot question, which limit their horizon and thus enable them to have a character and a style. It shows us at the same time that any principles of this kind can be questioned and even rejected."[35]

The principles one may reject are those historically limited principles that historical consciousness has exposed as such. The multiplicity of values and truths, like those encountered by Socrates who found different gods giving different revelations, may send one into a nihilist despair, or it may spur one to transcend the multiplicity of truths. "What man did in the past unconsciously and under the delusion of submitting to what is independent of his creative act, he must now do consciously."[36] This transvaluation of values is made possible through an understanding of the nature of things, i.e., that values and truths are human creations. The truths built upon this foundation are sturdier for the recognition of the nature of things. As philosophers committed to knowledge but convicted by ignorance, Strauss and Nietzsche saw what people committed to other goals could not.[37] They had, as it were, a detached perspective with regard to the moral truths that ground others, but their commitment to knowledge is, in the Socratic sense, a mania that limits the perspective of the philosopher. The moral or religious truths are inaccessible to philosophers qua philosophers because those truths rest upon a different epistemological foundation. The contents of these beliefs are unbelievable to the philosopher, but not the fact and social necessity of them (in their many forms).

Strauss argued that Nietzsche had come to accept the superiority of nature over "history" and that in this way he had "transformed the deadly truth of relativism into the most life-giving truth."[38] What should one think about Strauss's remarks? More is here than first meets the eye. Notice what Strauss wrote immediately following the above quotation: "To state the case with all necessary vagueness, he discovered that the life-giving comprehensive truth is subjective or transtheoretical in that it cannot be grasped detachedly and that it cannot be the same for all men or for all ages." Strauss went on to suggest the problems inherent in Nietzsche's philosophy, most important whether the will to power is a "subjective project." The natural and universal quality of Nietzsche's doctrine first impressed Strauss with the importance of reason and nature. Here was the beginning of Strauss's journey back to the ancients.[39] Still,

Nietzsche failed to break free from modernity, and by exposing the utter failure of modern philosophy, he buried philosophy. Nietzsche had not challenged his philosophical tradition radically enough and thus found himself trapped by the tradition he tried to overcome. More specifically, Nietzsche's historical understanding of human nature (i.e., it "is essentially historical") meant that he and the overman must be heirs of Christianity.

> Not only was biblical morality as veracity or intellectual probity at work in the destruction of biblical theology and biblical morality; not only is it at work in the question of that very probity, of "*our* virtue, which alone has remained to us"; biblical morality will remain at work in the morality of the overman. The overman is inseparable from "the philosophy of the future." The philosophy of the future is distinguished from traditional philosophy, which pretended to be purely theoretical, by the fact that it is consciously the outcome of a will: the fundamental awareness is not theoretical, but theoretical and practical, inseparable from an act of the will or a decision. The fundamental awareness characteristic of the new thinking is a secularized version of the biblical faith as interpreted by Christian theology.[40]

Philosophy as understood by the ancients must be overcome by a commitment to faith, to the will to power. The Socratic commitment to theory, to searching for knowledge while remaining skeptical about all claims to knowledge, to the philosophical way of living, would have no place if all thought were committed thought.

Nietzsche's transformation of relativism into a life-giving truth was lost or rejected by the philosophers who followed. Strauss often spoke of Nietzsche's followers, but he meant Heidegger. The specter of Heidegger haunts nearly every page of Strauss's work. Sometimes Strauss acknowledged him in oblique ways, like a poke in the ribs of the initiated; on other occasions he tossed out Heidegger's name as being the greatest and most dangerous modern thinker, but never did Strauss publish an extended study of this greatest of modern philosophers.[41] The only work, excluding some relatively brief remarks, that we have on this subject is the transcript of a lecture with the title "An Introduction to Heideggerian Existentialism."[42] This difficult source, however, presents special problems for interpretation. The lecture moves between personal observations, including sweeping characterizations and oblique references, and a historical and descriptive account. The form makes the problem of voice especially difficult. In general, then, Strauss avoided a sustained analysis of Heidegger's work. One senses in all his brief feints a hidden and mammoth struggle to answer a nemesis.[43]

Strauss and Heidegger shared an intellectual heritage. Both men drew from Husserl a common critique of modernity. Husserl argued that scientists fail to understand that their understanding of the world (qua scientists) is derivative of "our natural understanding," and Husserl and Strauss sought to recover those prescientific experiences that make theorizing possible. Heidegger wanted a deeper level. He sought "not the object of perception but the full thing as experienced as *part of the individual human context, the individual world to which it belongs.*"[44] Heidegger wanted to deconstruct Western ontology dating back to Plato,[45] arguing, in Strauss's words, that "the merely sensibly perceived thing is itself derivative; there are not first sensibly perceived things and thereafter the same thing in a state of being valued or in a state of affecting us."[46] The creative freedom of humans replaced the eternal essences of Plato as the ontological ground: existence precedes essence. So one sees that the natural world of prerational experience that Plato, Husserl, and Strauss assumed (and which formed the "objective" basis for theoretical—scientific—investigation) became the personal, individual creation of the "thrown" person.

Heidegger's rejection of Platonism (and hence Christianity as vulgarized Platonism) was more thorough than Nietzsche's. The entire discourse of "nature" had decentered the individual or, rather, had cut the individual off from the ground of his being. Modern homelessness *(Bodenlösegkeit)* testifies to the way modern thought— with roots back to Plato—had abstracted human life. By replacing the ontological universality of forms (nature) privileged in the West with a contextualized ontology (historicism), Heidegger hoped to ground human society in existence. Such a reorientation to the lifeworld circumvents the old dead-end ontological and epistemological questions while securing the conditions for human greatness that emerges from fidelity toward one's "existence" (i.e., life as experienced as rooted in a particular society—*Bodensandigkeit*). Heidegger, Strauss argued, could dream of a universal world order once the nihilist ontology inherited from Plato and Christianity had lost all force. The danger of this era was coupled with great possibility. As Strauss put it, "A dialogue between the most profound thinkers of the Occident and the most profound thinkers of the Orient and in particular East Asia may lead to the consummation prepared, accompanied or followed by a return of the gods."[47] Thus Heidegger's creative ontology opened possibilities closed by Platonism.

We have touched now upon the primary theoretical differences between Strauss and Heidegger: Strauss accepted the Platonic ontology grounded upon nature while Heidegger denied nature in favor of the creative will of "existing" humans. Nonetheless, the penetration of his philosophy, the admirable and manly search for truth no matter its effect, made Heidegger a worthy opponent for Strauss. Other thinkers had circled around the serious issues raised by modernity, but only Heidegger did not flinch from the abyss that lay beneath. Even if others did not face the real problem as squarely, however, they did experience a growing anxiety and sense of alienation as the ground of objective knowledge crumbled beneath them. For this reason Heideggerian existentialism thrived. The conditions, created by the failure of modern rationalism, convinced Strauss that the West had a fateful choice to make: "The question Plato or existentialism [sic] is today the ontological question."[48] In other words, the choice is between the ancients and the moderns (nature or history).

This dualism reminds us that for Strauss, modernity took its bearings from Platonic-Aristotelian science. As the first modern, Machiavelli consciously rejected the ancients in order to create "new modes and orders," and the people who inherited the new thinking lost sight of what they were reacting against. Political philosophers, nonetheless, continued through much of the modern era to ask the question that designates one a political philosopher: What is the good? Words like "good" and "justice" have meaning as long as people believe in human nature, and even when moderns sought to control rather than to live by nature, the constitutive questions of political philosophy remained possible—that is, as long as people argued from an anthropology. Take away, however, people's faith in "reason" dedicated to discovering and articulating these goods, abstract facts from the valuative political reality from which they grew, doubt the truth of civilization's (one's own civilization, that is) most cherished goals and political philosophy ceases to be a possibility. According to Strauss, once moderns came to believe that human values and ideas emerge from the changing conditions, "justice" became nothing more than a belief made possible by the intellectual conditions of one's own time. The radical subjectivity of Heidegger's existentialism was simply the acceptance of one's fate. Creativity and will take the place of nature and science (philosophy), and the life of faith overwhelms the life of reason.

THE PROBLEM WITH LIBERALISM: LEO STRAUSS

Modernity leads to the blond beast. The traumatic experiences of Nazism and the terror of World War II shaped the work of both Strauss and Voegelin in ways easy to see but difficult to calculate. In such disordered times they struggled to understand and then to transcend. Much like Nietzsche, both sought to order his own soul in resistance to the times. They offered no grand designs, nor did they introduce systems of their own. Political and social order is a function of the orderliness of the souls of the citizens. They were good Platonists. But the ideological madness that had gripped Germany and Italy, and which still gripped the Soviet Union and its puppets, seemed not only dissimilar but even the polar opposite of the stable and prosperous democracy in the United States. If modernity leads to ideological madness, either because diseased souls seek certainty or because the loss of faith in reason leaves room for the free reign of the *libido dominandi*, the United States seemed free from either condition. The United States, according to conventional wisdom, had become postideological.

America, to whatever degree these assumptions were true, was not simply and unambiguously liberal. Voegelin and Strauss, as it turns out, had high regard for the United States and its citizens. The ideological fashions of Europe had struck, initially at least, glancing blows. The "premodern" characteristics retained a strong hold, and the citizens were sufficiently suffused with the commonsense tradition that the few people who did get passionate about political beliefs were powerless intellectuals. These characteristics were changing, however. Liberalism (the use of an "ism" here suggests an ideology) won impressive gains among the educated classes during the course of the twentieth century. The list of beliefs that became articles of faith among liberals are familiar: an affirmation of equality (in all its earthly manifestations), a belief in progress (both ineluctable and materially oriented), a faith in science and technology to solve human "problems," the instrumentalizing of reason toward the realization of goods understood in exclusively worldly terms, the belief that a social and political order is a matter of free consent (or should be), the centralization of power for purposes of efficiency (and the elevating of efficiency to a good), the privatization of morals, the affirmation of the sovereignty of the individual, and the sacralizing of rights to name only a few. It is not important that these tendencies have precise meaning (indeed, it is important for their social success that they do not), only that we recognize a broad trend that has resonance with the themes identified as modern. We may clarify some of these issues by looking at the attitude of Strauss and then Voegelin toward liberalism, especially as it infected the United States.

Strauss emphasized that the American founding emerged from the first wave of modernity, that is, from a strain of thought associated with Machiavelli, Hobbes, and Locke. He did not, however, understand the founding by reference to these thinkers alone. Strauss wrote that the United States was the only country "founded in explicit opposition to Machiavellian principles."[49] Thus the character of American liberal democracy is bound up in its partial appropriation of modern thought. One may understand that Strauss believed American liberal democracy was in some sense salvageable; that in the modern context it represented a superior regime worthy of support and admiration. Strauss supported the American regime by calling for an examination and a reaffirmation of the traditional ideals of liberal democracy, and he sought to contribute to American liberalism by reviving political philosophy.

If the American founding took its bearings from the tradition inaugurated by Machiavelli, but not from Machiavelli himself, the transformations wrought by Hobbes and Locke appear decisive. Machiavelli, we recall from Chapter 4, broke from classical political philosophy by offering a critique of religion and morality. Hidden though he was in pious and traditionalist intellectual garb, Machiavelli was irreligious and amoral. Strauss, however, was generally unconcerned, at least by all appearances, with Machiavelli's critique of religion, which was "not original"; more important for Strauss was Machiavelli's "critique of morality which is identical to his critique of classical political philosophy."[50] Strauss often equated morality with political matters. Thus, the chief political objective, as least insofar as the ancients were concerned, is justice. Or, to put the matter a different way, justice is the highest goal of a political order. One may say that a regime has perfected itself to the extent that its political system had achieved justice (i.e., satisfied the demands of justice as an idea). Machiavelli rejected justice as a proper political goal on the grounds that such an objective could never be realized. He agreed with Plato that a just political order requires luck. A just society is so unlikely as to present no reasonable hope for fulfillment.[51]

Machiavelli dropped the ideal of the just society—the political "ought"—from his calculations, which freed him to explore manipulative possibilities with society as it presented itself to him. Unlike the ancients, he would no longer be guided by the highest in humans, by human excellence. "Machiavelli's 'realistic' revolt against tradition [i.e., the classical tradition] led to the substitution of patriotism or merely political virtue for human excellence or, more particularly, for moral virtue and the contemplative life."[52] Strauss argued that Machiavelli's contraction of the political horizon (i.e., eliminating the perfectly just order) opened up a whole new universe of possibility. Insofar as Machiavelli no longer felt bound by a restrictive paradigm, he could conceive of new goals and objectives, of new men and new societies. The transformations he envisioned required "enlightenment." Strauss wrote:

Machiavelli is the first philosopher who attempted to force change, to control the future by embarking on a campaign, a campaign of propaganda. This propaganda is of the opposite pole of what is now called propaganda, high-pressure salesmanship and hold-up of captive audiences. Machiavelli desires to convince, not merely to persuade or to bully. He was the first of a long series of modern thinkers who hoped to bring about the establishment of new modes and orders by means of enlightenment."[53]

Two related alternatives in the tradition of political philosophy remained fundamentally unaltered from Machiavelli to the American founding: lowering the objective in order to lessen the role of chance in human affairs and the belief that enlightenment will bring about a better political order. What did not survive during this period was Machiavelli's rejection of justice as *the* proper political objective.

Thomas Hobbes, according to Strauss, reaffirmed natural right (i.e., justice) by emphasizing ubiquitous human drives and desires rather than the classically understood human end (which only a few people can achieve). Moreover, Hobbes rejected the construction of natural man as being social and, hence, political. He began, along with the Epicureans, with the individual human—unconnected, asocial. Using this understanding of human nature, Hobbes could no longer think in terms of social and political justice but conceived of natural right in terms of the primordial drives of autonomous man. Hobbes's political hedonism, as Strauss labeled it, "revolutionized human life everywhere on a scale never yet approached by other teachings."[54] The "good" moved from the lofty heights of forms to the visceral drives of individual humans. The consequences proved dramatic, the most obvious being that modern natural right disconnects rights from duty. Hobbes left nothing to which humans ought to aspire—nothing, that is, beyond their most basic drives and ambitions. Humans are beholden to their passions, nothing more. By contrast, the ancients lived within a paradigm that called them to human excellence and a social order attuned to the hierarchy of ends. After Hobbes this paradigm no longer had the same purchase; moderns lived disconnected from duties.

In truly modern fashion, Hobbes sought to ground political philosophy on apodictic knowledge, in contrast to the "utopian" dreams of the ancients. He found terra firma, following Descartes's lead, by applying the acid of radical skepticism to the soft rock of human knowledge. What remained had to be indubitable and solid, and upon this rock Hobbes built his political order. He found that human knowledge extends only to those things humans create or cause.[55] Thus, he had not only cast out the classical teleological cosmology but found a mechanistic notion of the universe unable to "satisfy the requirement of intelligibility." The greatest good emerged out of "the most compelling end posited by human desire." Once Hobbes brought the greatest good down to earth, the method of exploring the subject changed. Social science usurped philosophy as the highest and most needful knowledge.[56]

If proper human ends emerge from human desires, the greatest (most powerful) and most universal desire serves best to identify human nature, which is the only source for natural right. The most powerful desire, expressed negatively, is fear of violent death (i.e., desire for self-preservation). Society, or more particularly the political order, is a human construct designed to address this need—by lowering, insofar as is practical, incidences of violent death. Society and government serve this prepolitical right of self-preservation. Consequently, "the fundamental moral fact is not a duty but a right, all duties are derivative from the fundamental and inalienable right of self-preservation." In Hobbes's political philosophy Strauss discovered the direct source of modern liberalism insofar as the word liberalism means a focus on rights before duties, on the individual as antecedent to the state.[57]

The centrality of Hobbes to Strauss's understanding of the crisis of American liberalism is evident. First, Hobbes jettisoned the entire tradition of political philosophy oriented toward human excellence, thus freeing the state from any obligation other than safeguarding individual natural rights. As a consequence, he reduced justice to the protection of rights rooted in nature. Second, Hobbes transformed political philosophy from the search for the highest and best regime (i.e., creating regimes in speech) into a source for political action. Political philosophers in the Hobbesian mode claim indubitable knowledge, universally applicable, that will transform the world. Moreover, the sort of knowledge required in this new age changed, and social science became the science of liberalism to the extent that it exposed conditions as they are. Hobbes presented the vision of a political order, fashioned by enlightened humans, capable of actualization here and now: a just order, created out of mutual consent and dedicated to the protection of natural rights. Political philosophy had become political science—theory had degenerated into techne.

What the bold Hobbes began, the "cautious" Locke completed. Strauss's argument with regard to both philosophers is, in crucial respects, unorthodox. His characterization of Hobbes's religious heterodoxy is not unusual, though in some particulars Strauss's argument is unique. What is more extraordinary is that he found in Locke a similar attitude toward religion. We must note Strauss's heterodoxy here, not to referee between him and others, but to emphasize the crucial theoretical challenge that the philosophers of liberalism posed to classical and biblical models. Locke presented himself as the most orthodox defender of the faith in order to persuade his readers of unorthodox beliefs. By penetrating to the core of Locke's argument, Strauss hoped to expose the logic of liberalism.[58]

Locke used Richard Hooker as camouflage. According to Strauss, Locke wasted no opportunity to point to his agreement with Hooker (an undeniable defender of the faith) while remaining silent, with one exception, concerning their differences. Similarly, Locke paraded out the usual natural law doctrines and Christian teachings. After examining Locke's affirmations of orthodoxy, Strauss wrote:

> We thus arrive at the conclusion that Locke cannot have recognized any law of nature in the proper sense of the term. This conclusion stands in shocking contrast to what is generally thought to be his doctrine, and especially the doctrine of the *Second Treatise*. Before turning to an examination of the *Second Treatise*, we beg the reader to consider the following facts: the accepted interpretation of Locke's teaching leads to the consequence that "Locke is full of illogical flaws and inconsistencies," of inconsistencies, we add, which are so obvious that they cannot have escaped the notice of a man of his rank and his sobriety. Furthermore, the accepted interpretation is based on what amounts to a complete disregard of Locke's caution, of a kind of caution which is, to say the least, compatible with so involving one's sense that one cannot easily be understood and with going with the herd in one's outward professions. Above all, the accepted interpretation does not pay sufficient attention to the character of the *Treatise*; it somehow assumes that the *Treatise* contains the philosophical presentation of Locke's political doctrine, whereas it contains, in fact, only its "civil" presentation.[59]

Locke paid greater attention and homage to the philosophical and religious tradition he inherited than did Hobbes, but Locke followed the path Hobbes blazed.[60]

Like Hobbes, Locke found no natural law but rather universal human characteristics that establish natural rights but not duties. Natural law becomes "reason"—or the capacity to secure natural rights.[61] The right of self-preservation still serves as the most fundamental right, establishing the need for peace and security. But whereas Hobbes remained more or less stuck on this right—and was willing therefore to give sovereignty to a single leader—Locke emphasized the right to pursue happiness.[62] Moreover, he connected both rights with property, which helps secure peace and provide happiness.[63]

It was Locke's view of property that most clearly separated him from Hobbes. The right to property emerges in Locke as an adjunct to the primary right to life. "If everyone has the natural right to preserve himself," wrote Strauss, "he necessarily has the right to everything that is necessary for his self-preservation." The individual who wishes to sustain himself must secure goods. Thus, while civil society sanctions and protects property, the origin of property is the self-interest of the individual.[64] The existence of government alters the rights associated with property. In nature one has right only to the product of one's labor, to that part of nature improved by one's hand. With the introduction of money individuals are free to own much more than their labor can produce, without injury to others. Locke not only freed acquisitiveness from its traditional moral constraints but transformed it into a virtue. Great wealth is only possible in a society in which individuals are free to acquire as much as possible. Strauss summed up the relationship thus:

> If the end of government is nothing but "the peace, the safety, and public good of the people"; if peace and safety are the indispensable conditions of plenty, and the public good of the people is identical with plenty; if the end of government is therefore plenty; if plenty requires the emancipation of acquisitiveness; and if acquisitiveness necessarily withers away whenever its rewards do not securely belong to those who serve them—if all this is true, it follows that the end of civil society is "the preservation of property."[65]

Despite Locke's use of natural law as a cover, Strauss found his philosophy to be subversive to both strands of the natural law tradition—biblical religion (or the moral teachings of the Bible) and classical political philosophy. First, Locke defended unlimited acquisition of wealth on the grounds that such freedom is just.[66] Second, like Hobbes, Locke oriented his philosophy around the individual (the ego)—or, more precisely, around the individual understood in terms of his "natural" and most fundamental drives. "Man's end" played no part in Locke's thinking. Thus modern natural right had become exclusively occupied with rights, while denying duties. "Not resigned gratitude and consciously obeying or imitating nature," Strauss complained, "but hopeful self-reliance and creativity became henceforth the mark of human nobility."[67]

Effectively unhinged from a normative order, the fecund if banal human imagination seeks happiness by harnessing old vices. The common good stands for the freedom of individuals to pursue their selfish ends in peace and security. Because the objective of this political philosophy is to achieve the best possible regime in accordance with the most universal human drives and needs, philosophy as understood by the ancients becomes eclipsed by social science. Reason becomes instrument reason—a tool to help reshape society.

To return to the American founding and liberal democracy, Strauss found in the United States a rejection of Machiavelli's dismissal of justice. To clarify the point, let me return to the quotation with which I began this portion of the inquiry: "The United States of America may be said to be the only country in the world which was founded in explicit opposition to Machiavellian principles." If one reads the rest of the paragraph in which this quotation appears, one will understand the point.

> According to Machiavelli, the founder of the most renowned commonwealth of the world was a fratricide: the foundation of political greatness is necessarily laid in crime. If we can believe Thomas Paine, all governments of the Old World have an origin of this description; their origin was conquest and tyranny. But "the independence of America [was] accompanied by a Revolution in the principles and practice of Governments": the foundation of the United States was laid in freedom and justice. "Government founded on a moral theory, on a system of universal peace, on the indefeasible hereditary Rights of Man, is now revolving from west to east by a stronger impulse than the Government of the sword revolved from east to west." This judg-

ment is far from being obsolete. While freedom is no longer a preserve of the United States, the United States is now the bulwark of freedom. And contemporary tyranny has its roots in Machiavelli's thought, in the Machiavellian principle that the good end justifies the means. At least to the extent that the American reality is inseparable from the American aspiration, one cannot understand Americanism without understanding Machiavellianism which is its opposite.[68]

Justice and freedom (two closely related ideals in this context) inspired the American founding, not tyranny and injustice. Moreover, the ideals of the American founding were grounded, as the founders and citizens understood them, in nature understood as an end, so they presented an unchangeable model for a just regime. The American regime was founded upon natural right (albeit more or less modern natural right). Americans have, until recently at least, had such faith in their idea of the good society that even when in action they fell short, they reaffirmed their goal. This idea restricted (or harnessed) the creative freedom espoused by Machiavelli. All teleologies restrict. Nonetheless, the goals of modern natural right suffer from a tendency to self-destruct. In the United States this weakness was not readily apparent because the American regime was founded, not on this principle alone, but on modern natural right as modified (or buttressed) by strongly held beliefs in revelation (both traditional Christian morality and the cosmology that supported it) and republican virtues. These beliefs tended to qualify rights in practice—to emphasize a sort of model for the proper use of one's rights or liberty.

Beyond this point it is difficult to go because Strauss wrote so little about this subject. Nonetheless, with all the lacunae in his work, one detects some of the developments that stripped modern natural right of its countervailing constraints and left the United States to drift toward moral relativism, which looses a people's commitments to the ideals for which they, as a collective, stand.

Strauss began *Natural Right and History* by quoting from the Declaration of Independence. The question he raised deals not with the failure of the ideals bound up in the Declaration; rather, it reads, "Does this nation in its maturity still cherish the faith in which it was conceived and raised?"[69] It is safe to say, I think, that Strauss affirmed this "faith" and was, to that degree, a friend of liberal democracy, or at least of a modified or protected form. The Declaration of Independence refers not only to unalienable rights but also to their divine source. Thus, the liberalism of the United States—in the beginning—drew sustenance from modern natural right theory (life, liberty, and the pursuit of happiness) and also from premodern beliefs in the Christian God and classical republican notions of virtue.[70] The two faiths (modern and premodern) established a regime in liberty—freedom understood as a protected right—in the context of Christian teleology and morality (not to mention republican themes that were largely understood in Christian terms). Still on the first page of *Natural Right and History*, Strauss wrote: "About a generation ago, an American diplomat could still say that 'the natural and the divine foundation of the rights of man . . . is self-evident to all Americans.'" In other words, Americans understood natural rights from a Christian perspective, and so long as this protective atmosphere remained, modern natural rights posed no danger and actually supported a healthy social and political order. Unalienable rights were lodged in a larger moral framework that shaped the range of appropriate uses of these freedoms.

Nonetheless, in the first paragraph of *Natural Right and History*, Strauss offered a contrast between the United States and the Germany of a generation ago (from the vantage point of 1950), only to argue that the United States was moving toward a German type of relativism. "Whatever might be true of the American people, certainly American social science has adopted the very attitude toward natural right which, a generation ago, could still be described, with some plausibility, as characteristic of German thought."[71] The introduction of social science so early in the book is important, as the kind of knowledge a people most esteem shapes the kind of society they become. In Germany, with Max Weber and others, social science, with its characteristic fact/value distinction, became the dominant academic and intellectual form. Strauss thought the same transformation was taking place in contemporary America, and the practical effects of this change proved dramatic. Strauss wrote that social scientists in the United States are "dedicated to the proposition that all men are endowed by the evolutionary process or by a mysterious fate with many kinds of urges and aspirations, but certainly with no natural right."[72] Strauss argued, in short, that with the growth in the prestige of the social sciences even modern natural right cannot survive.[73] This is the crisis of liberal democracy—to be wedded to ideals that are no longer defensible as good. Modern natural right, shorn of religious support, paradoxically leads to relativism.[74]

To unpack the meanings behind the "crisis of liberalism" one must examine the role Strauss believed social science plays in liberal democracy. In Chapter 3, I examined his argument that social scientists (qua positivists) moved, rather like sheep to slaughter, from firm belief in certain values (i.e., liberal democratic values) to an inability to affirm any values. In the present context the politically incapacitating characteristics of social science are most important. Social science has its roots in the modern project of controlling nature, and to the degree that that statement is true, Strauss traced its origin to Machiavelli. Modern understanding of nature led naturally to the elevation of the sort of knowledge useful for controlling or manipulating nature (including human nature). The Platonic/Aristotelian philosophy/science presented too metaphysical an orientation for moderns who chose to separate philosophy and science into distinct forms of knowledge. The success of the nonmetaphysical science—especially in physics—inspired a further devaluation of philosophy. Science represented power, human power, but science could not address the question of how this power ought to be used. In the context of a liberal democratic society, one in which society and government serve to protect natural right (including providing the best possible environment for its unhampered exercise), the question of the wise use of power rests with the individual. Thus, science—including social science—came to occupy a privileged place in liberal democracies as the source of knowledge that individual citizens may use to pursue their personal goods.

By extension, then, political science replaced political philosophy as the source of political knowledge relevant to a liberal democracy. So long as a society retains a strong sense of the common good—despite its grounding in modern natural rights—the elevation of political science does not present an overly threatening prospect. On the other hand, the common good presupposes a whole that is more than the sum of its parts. It suggests obligations. The common good is a value. All of these presuppositions require support (through political philosophy or religious education), which political science and the other social sciences cannot provide.

Strauss, to my knowledge, never applied these general principles to the history of liberal democracy in the United States. That is, he never traced the history of these developments. What is important is that somehow the "premodern" elements in the American regime were, in the postwar period, losing their force, and to the degree that these trends continued, Strauss suggested, the United States would be left with modern natural right and a privileged form of knowledge—social science—that undermines all beliefs in natural right.

We can understand Strauss's point by reminding ourselves of what he saw as the key characteristics of social science. The social scientists most relevant to the political arena—political scientists—are utterly incapable of understanding their subject. The rich, valuative political and social world is terra incognita for the political scientist who transforms the world as experienced into discrete facts. These "facts" have the advantage of being easily grasped and manipulated; they have the disadvantage of possessing little relationship to the subject. Strauss, in this manner, accused political scientists of distorting the political realm by falsely laying claim to "empiricism." Although political scientists claim to deal with the world as it is (thus denouncing metaphysics), Strauss emphasized how the classical philosophers dealt more fairly, and more empirically, with the political realm. They did not abstract from the messy, evaluative phenomena a scientifically pure language that dealt with the component and abstracted parts (assuming that the parts were truly components) of the phenomena. Rather, they remained true to political experience, including the language of the political arena.[75]

Unable to understand the nature of society, political scientists cannot help liberal democracy. Their devotion to method (or techne) makes them morally obtuse—incapable of holding one goal higher than another. By reinforcing the individualism inherent in liberal democracy, political scientists depreciate the language of the common good. Moreover, the "dogmatic atheism" upon which modern social science rests erodes the religious beliefs that help make liberal democracy possible—or at least livable. Strauss's argument on the subject of the atheistic grounding of social science bears quoting.

For a few years, logical positivism tried with much noise and little thought to dispose of religion by asserting that religious assertions are "meaningless statements." This trick seems to have been abandoned without noise. Some adherents of the new political science might rejoin with some liveliness that their posture toward religion is imposed on them by intellectual honesty: not being able to believe, they cannot accept belief as the basis of their science. We gladly grant that, other things being equal, a frank atheist is a better man than an alleged theist who conceives of God as a symbol. But we must add that intellectual honesty is not enough. Intellectual honesty is not love of truth. Intellectual honesty, a kind of self-denial, has taken the place of love of truth because truth has come to be believed to be repulsive, and one cannot love the repulsive. Yet just as our opponents refuse respect to unreasoned belief, we on our part, with at least equal right, must refuse respect to unreasoned unbelief; honesty with oneself regarding one's unbelief is in itself not more than unreasoned unbelief, probably accompanied by a vague confidence that the issue of unbelief versus belief has long since been settled once and for all. It is hardly necessary to add that the dogmatic exclusion of religious awareness proper renders questionable all long-range predictions concerning the future of societies.[76]

Social scientists teach an equality of all ends while they deprecate virtue (i.e., duty) and religious beliefs. Their teaching has the further effect of denying modern natural right a grounding because they find themselves unable to affirm any "natural" right by virtue of their moral obtuseness (fostered by devotion to method). A passage quoted earlier now takes on a special significance: "Present-day American social science . . . is dedicated to the proposition that all men are endowed by the evolutionary process or by a mysterious fate with many kinds of urges and aspirations, but certainly with no natural right."[77] The points to remember are one, social science has become the privileged form of inquiry, and as such provides sanctioned knowledge; two, social science is an eminently "practical" discipline and thus provides direction to the social and political order; and three, a regime must have something in which to believe in order to survive. One should not, moreover, overlook the example of Germany. In his most autobiographical essay, "Preface to Spinoza's *Critique of Religion*," Strauss examined the weakness of Germany's liberal democracy, Weimar. "The Weimar Republic was weak. . . . On the whole it presented the sorry spectacle of justice without a sword or of justice unable to use the sword."[78] The crisis of liberal democracy is the failure of will.

Liberal democracy in America, Strauss seemed to suggest, was going the way of Weimar. This claim ought not be taken as a simple comparison between two very different regimes. Rather, Strauss emphasized that the weakness of the Weimar regime was the inability to identify and defend its highest principles. German thinking (a generation in advance of the United States) had so undercut the rational defense of any ideals that no will existed to defend a regime constructed on a "rational" belief in tolerance and individual right. In the United States, Strauss suggested, the same erosion of beliefs about the good threatened to move from social scientists to the American people.

Describing the crisis in this fashion puts one in mind of Walter Lippmann, who made his way from *Drift and Mastery* to *The Public Philosophy*. For both Lippmann and Strauss one of the key ingredients for a vigorous liberal democracy (in contrast to a pathological one—i.e., Weimar) is political philosophy. Thus Strauss sought to save American liberal democracy by reviving normative political philosophy—not as a direct support to the regime, but because political philosophy is necessarily edifying to a society. Strauss, one may say, defended liberal democracy, not as the best form of government simply, but as the best possible form of government here and now. He accepted the classical argument that the best regime is rule by the wise. Since the modern circumstances did not allow for such a regime, Strauss hoped to help provide a stronger foundation for liberal democracy. If freedom were to be the goal (as opposed to duty or virtue), it needed to be defensible. Of course, from the philosopher's point of view, a vibrant and healthy liberal democracy has many virtues, the greatest being a tolerance for the philosopher: "We cannot forget the obvious fact that by giving freedom to all, democracy also gives freedom to those who care about human excellence. No one prevents us from cultivating our garden or from setting up outposts which may come to be regarded by many citizens as salutary to the republic and as deserving of giving to it its tone."[79]

Even though Strauss defended liberal democracy, he was hardly a cheerleader. His reticence to discuss the subject should tell one something—but what? I am disposed to leave the matter for other people who might be more adept at listening to silence. I am sure, though I cannot point to many places in his published work to support my claim, that Strauss possessed not an iota of respect for American "popular culture"—or what he called "mass culture." One could use Allan Bloom's invective about music and other "cultural" forms in his *Closing of the American Mind* to express Strauss's own sentiments on the subject.[80] In an essay entitled "What Is Liberal Democracy?" Strauss offered an evasive (it "is said to be") description of mass culture in a modern democracy that reads much like Bloom's animadversions. Strauss ended the paragraph in which this description appears with a discussion of liberal education:

> Liberal education is the counterpoison to mass culture, to the corroding effects of mass culture, to its inherent tendency to produce nothing but "specialists without spirit or vision and voluptuaries without heart." Liberal education is the ladder by which we try to ascend from mass democracy to democracy as originally meant. Liberal education is the necessary endeavor to found an aristocracy within democratic mass society. Liberal education reminds those members of mass democracy who have ears to hear, of human greatness.[81]

Education, we learn, is a key to saving liberal democracy, but we would be mistaken if we assumed that Strauss considered liberal education to be *the* answer to the problem. "We must not expect," he wrote, "that liberal education can ever become universal education."[82] Not only does the nature of liberal education limit its appeal and power, but it alone cannot solve modern problems. He noted that both Marx and Nietzsche "were liberally educated on a level to which we cannot even hope to aspire" but that they were not supporters of liberal democracy. Strauss emphasized, in a typically oblique passage, the need for "moderation" to protect society from "visionary expectations from politics and unmanly contempt for politics," i.e., the examples of Marx and Nietzsche. Political responsibility should also be a part of education, though technically not part of a liberal education as such.

Liberal education is, for Strauss, the study of the great books. The question, Which great books? he answered partially by saying "the great books of the West." One person cannot possibly master all the great books, and Strauss found compelling reason to choose the great books of his and America's tradition. On principle, though, the great books of India would serve a similar purpose, i.e., to introduce one to culture. The word "culture" indicates the cultivation of mind, i.e., the products of a cultivated mind. Because the greatest minds seek to understand the human condition, they explore and define the proper human life, or at least they introduce the problems that attend human life. Collectively, these authors have indicated the range of alternatives available to humans. Thus, by reading the great books and by engaging in a dialogue with the authors, one comes into contact with the greatest minds dealing with the most important issues—issues unbounded by time or place. For some people it is enough to come into contact with these subjects. These students leave formal education aware of the problems and the range of alternatives open to them as humans. For others this sort of education is a prelude to becoming a philosopher—for becoming a full participant in the conversation of the West.

One may say, then, that a liberal education is the proper education for future leaders and for future philosophers. Of course the future leaders of a democracy will, by and large, come from the most prestigious universities, so it is there that a regime should help shape their affections for the regime. They should believe in justice, even if they are unsure of its precise meaning. In other words, they ought to believe that as leaders, they have a duty to something greater than themselves. A liberal education is the proper introduction to these issues, and it has had the effect of turning potential tyrants into republicans, just as Socrates turned Thrasymachus and Glaucon into proper citizens. In brief, through liberal education for the few and religious education for the many, citizens and leaders of a liberal democracy affirm a moral center. The common good has meaning for such citizens in spite of their attachment to rights. Philosophers, who remain outside of politics, nonetheless pay their respects to the society in which they live and have freedom by educating the leaders ("gentlemen" in the language of Plato and Aristotle).

Strauss's hope for liberal democracy rested with two related goals. The first was the resurrection of political philosophy as a bulwark against social science. The second goal required the right kind of education, one that would provide the society with liberally educated leaders who could speak to the needs and desires of a more religious-minded citizenry. Both of Strauss's goals aimed at restoring a viable understanding of the common good—one that transcends the collective goods of individuals. In his own way Leo Strauss worked very hard to save American liberal democracy—a democracy in which the citizens feel a strong attachment to a moral center anchored in a cosmic order.

THE PROBLEM WITH LIBERALISM: ERIC VOEGELIN

The conclusions above bear a striking resemblance to Eric Voegelin's thought concerning liberalism. Both Voegelin and Strauss began their careers in the new but largely disordered world of post-1914 Europe. Constitutional democracy, even before 1933, appeared fragile, and World War I had exposed the weakness of old truths (ideas) and symbols. The institutions of a democracy rely for their strength upon widely shared beliefs in the assumptions or goals of those institutions; a society must have a spiritual core. "The wars," wrote Voegelin, referring to both world wars, "are symptomatic not only insofar as they reveal a positive will to an orgiastic discharge but also insofar as they must be endorsed because actions that might prevent them have become impossible through the paralysis of the will to order, which can be active only where its meaning is secured in the community myth."[83] The long catalog of modern horrors, Voegelin never tired of emphasizing, required not only the will to perform them but also the failure of will to prevent them. Both responses relate to the loss of a spiritual core—i.e., a socially dominant conception of the individual and social relationship to the whole or divine that is made real or useful through myth or other symbolizations.

A spiritual pathology, which he too loosely called gnostic, slowly infected Western civilization by heightening people's ubiquitous sense of alienation and persuading them to seek release from or domination over this world. Visions of imminent transfiguration turned into dreams of Prometheus, of immanent transformation. The desire to control "being" channeled understandings of truth into narrow subjects over which humans seemed to have control. The human horizon, which naturally includes the apperception of the mysterious divine ground of existence, suffered an artificial constriction. This process created enormous human power at the expense of knowledge or wisdom concerning ends. In other words, humans have lost access to the ordering principles inherent in the reality of which they form a part. The resulting "second realities," or modern ideologies, provide an ersatz order that fails to supply the most fundamental human (spiritual) needs.

It follows that the greatest danger for a liberal democracy is the omnipresent danger that the citizens will withdraw into their private world or employ themselves publicly in the defense of the private good as the greatest good. The inherent liberal ambiguity about the most profound and important matters is both a symptom of and a further corrosive to the spiritual center of a society. Voegelin had his say on this subject here and there with the occasional and usually brief broadside against the spiritual bankruptcy of modern liberal society. But since he devoted his energies to exposing the history and, hence, the source of this state of affairs, and to the arduous task of reorienting modern thought, he more or less ignored his contemporary context. Nonetheless, in those occasional discussions of current conditions he exposed a great deal.

The most penetrating of these essays, "The German University and the Order of German Society: A Reconsideration of the Nazi Era," concerns the failure of constitutional democracy in Germany to prevent the Nazi regime. Much like Strauss, Voegelin considered Germany's past illuminating for Western civilization in general. The essay was originally written as a lecture for a conference on The German University and the Third Reich. Voegelin pointed out in the first paragraph that he considered the "underlying idea" of the conference flawed because a "historical description" of the events of this era could illuminate nothing of importance. He even hinted that the "idea" of the conference sprang from the same spiritual pathology that had tolerated or even engendered Nazism. Voegelin had his arrogant side.

"Life in the insane asylum of our time has become such a habit for many that they no longer react in a sensitive manner to the grotesque events on the public scene."[84] Such characterizations sprinkle Voegelin's later essays and point to a deepening sense of social disorder. The Nazi phenomenon can never be understood nor can its legacy be exorcised by "descriptive history." A full accounting of the horrible events of that or any era allow the historian and readers to denounce the evil, but it fails to penetrate to the deeper spiritual problem. Indeed, the guilt that inspires such an effort is "an expression of genuine pathology." "To be sure," wrote Voegelin, "the consciousness of guilt following the completed act is not the same thing as the sympathizing 'before it happened.' But sympathy and guilt are intimately related to one another as expressions of complicity in the desolation of the spirit."[85] Descriptive history allows one to deal with events at the level of "value judgments," which is to remain alienated from the spiritual dimension of human existence.

The proper response requires a penetration to the spiritual disorder that precipitated the events—what Voegelin called "critical history," which, of course, is both the result of and the process by which one undergoes an "alteration in one's being."[86] Voegelin, then, assumed the role of guide at this conference, which was otherwise filled with expressions of guilt. The balance of his speech exposed the spiritual disorder of the Nazi era and the role of the German university in fostering this spiritual disorder.[87] The merits of Voegelin's arguments are not important here, but certain themes applicable to American liberalism are.

The evolution of the modern German university served as the hinge for Voegelin's argument. To capture the spirit of that university Voegelin concentrated on the work of Wilhelm von Humboldt (1767–1835), a prominent figure in the restructuring of Prussian universities and gymnasiums. Humboldt's emphasis on "individual development" unhinged education from the social environment by deemphasizing the public role of education even as the public lost sight of the normative ground toward which education had once aimed. German education became "narcissistic." Wrote Voegelin:

With the rejection of the question concerning the ground beyond the chain of finite causes and ends, and more still, with the anesthesia against the question as the criterion of human perfection, Wilhelm von Humboldt has found the perfect formula for the estrangement from the spirit. In place of the divine ground of being man emerges as the ground of himself. The narcissistic closure has many consequences for language and thinking, which today in the socially dominant public of Germany are so evident that there hardly exists anymore a consciousness of their existence.[88]

The consequences of which Voegelin spoke are of special interest here because they point to the weaknesses—or potential weaknesses—of liberal democracies insofar as they tend to accept the individualistic ethics Voegelin described. The apotheosis of the individual, and the corresponding emphasis upon "development" (*Bildung*) of one's uniqueness, elevate the private character of one's existence. One tends to replace virtue, duty, or—more generally—citizenship with freedom and originality. Universities no longer play the role of guardian and dispenser of "knowledge needed for the rational discussion and transaction of public business." Nor does education function to build character or, more precisely, to orient people to being (or at least the nature of human reality as experienced by spiritually sensitive people). Once people lose contact with the spiritual core of their being they no longer have access to "the ordering center of man." The natural "community" of human existence is lost, which creates a vacuum into which men like Hitler and Stalin sweep. For the people who embrace these "ersatz realities" the world takes on an identifiable form, and they are comforted. Those who have lost sight of the divine ground but who cannot believe in these "second realities" are unable to respond.[89]

It appears that most people—or at any rate most intellectual leaders—in modern Germany (and the West more generally) are constitutionally incapable of understanding Voegelin's critique. If one grants his argument, then members of the socially dominant public suffer a spiritual alienation that blinds them to the spiritual dimension of their existence. Of course, no one today would question the empirical claims embedded in Voegelin's critique. Few of the most influential intellectuals of our day try to extend their analysis beyond the chain of finite causes and ends to the divine ground of being. Most either deny such a ground or deny any meaningful contact with that ground, and therein lies a problem. Voegelin must remain on the intellectual margins as long as his apperception of this larger context of human existence remains unbelievable to the larger intellectual community. If one assumes, for the moment, the truth of Voegelin's normative claims, he nonetheless is doomed to the task of showing something to the blind. It matters little how his subjects came to be blind. All that really matters is that they cannot see.

Yet Voegelin did not write without hope. The blindness around him was partial—the sort that sees everything except the most obvious. The obvious has lost its distinctiveness and, therefore, tends to merge into an undifferentiated background. A refocusing—or a change of perspective—allows the shape of the object to stand out. The spiritual equivalent of this operation requires a return to a spiritually differentiated language. Indeed, the deformation of language into idioms of estrangement provides the means of sustaining an artificial reality, and the language of estrangement eliminates or transmogrifies all symbols of transcendence. The most important estrangement symbols for Voegelin were "objective-subjective," which deal with humans as discrete objects. Moreover, the object/subject dichotomy suggests a severe limit to socially relevant knowledge "There is a loss of those insights into the nature of reality from which the material ramification of a science of man receives its meaning, and correspondingly, the enormous expansion of material data without control through criteria of relevance."[90] This statement clarifies Voegelin's resistance to the language of "values," "value-free science," and "ideas" that is so prevalent in modern political science (and other social sciences) because they symbolized for him the knowledge of immanent reality cut off from the transcendental context.

Voegelin was a prophet whose words can mean precious little to the sinners. For all the beauty and complexity of Voegelin's assessment, it boils down to a single point. Either one apperceives the divine ground and understands it to be the criteria for relevance of all things human, or one does not. For this reason Voegelin ended his lecture with the example of the watchman who speaks God's words even though few will respond (Ezek. 33:7-9). Yet a few will respond. But to reach them Voegelin had to create a new symbolic structure representing the noetic structure of existence while exposing the untrue structure and motivations of ideologies.[91]

Voegelin's task was made more difficult by the problems inherent in a liberal democracy—or at least in a pluralistic liberal democracy—for the tendency of liberals to regard all matters of grave importance as private concerns has the effect of undermining the spiritual foundation of true community. Liberal societies do not depend upon divine sanction for their legitimacy, much less their direction. They emerge in response to human consensus of the barest sort; in the most extreme case, the members of a liberal society would agree only on the greatest evil (as represented by Hobbes's *summum ma-*

lum). But while most liberal societies have a reasonably clear concept of justice, the tendency is to allow beliefs about goods to thin out as a society comes to embrace greater diversity. At any rate, it is very difficult to think that a liberal society—so wedded to the idea of individual autonomy and private goods—can have a clear conception of the greatest good.

Because liberalism does not foster public discussion about fundamentals—about ontology—the communication necessary for the healthy functioning of a society proves especially difficult. Yet constructing the matter in this form may create confusion. Liberalism, as a cluster of beliefs, is not simply the cause of the problem but more precisely a form or product of the problem. To believe, as Humboldt did, that education concerns the development of the individual—that is, one's distinctiveness—or to accept that society is the bare condition for the actualization of private happiness is to expose oneself as alienated from the divine nous that provides the means for true human community. In its place one has posited immanent reason, which Voegelin liked to call "ontological reduction." Where once societies existed under God—took their form and their meaning, as well as the meaning of their members, from the divine as symbolized in gods or God—modern, liberal societies understand their existence relative to the immanent goals of their members, which in turn are often understood as products of biological drives (to cite the most reductive example).

Ontological reduction entails a loss of faith, and without faith humans have no purposes except those humans provide. The emptiness created by this ontological reduction produces anxiety, which people relieve in a variety of ways—usually by seeking endless diversions. Voegelin loved to target television, which he likened to drunkenness—though being drunk might be favored. At any rate, the proliferation of the entertainment industry operated as a "quantitative gage of spiritual destruction."[92] The gadgets of modern society allure only as long as people remain alienated from the spiritual dimensions of their existence. Diversions provide escape from the dreadful silence that overwhelms people in their moments of contemplation, but it is the silence that threatens the health of a liberal democracy because the silence signifies ignorance concerning the essentials of existence—those most important questions, Who am I? What kind of world do I live in? and What is my relation in the order of being?

This alienation from the ground means that the common context in which meaningful communication can take place is absent. The pluralism of modern states, therefore, takes on special significance insofar as the absence of a common experiential core leads to such a variety of answers to the most important political questions—even to the questions concerning justice—that the consensus necessary to maintain the political order is precarious.

Voegelin illustrated the peculiarly modern pluralism by referring to the manner of argument employed by Thomas Aquinas. In his *Summa contra Gentiles*, Aquinas emphasized that in arguing before pagans he would have to employ "intellect," which is part of human existence as well as the means of interpreting human existence. Therefore, he could appeal to pagans from a shared perspective. That shared perspective no longer obtains—or at least this was Voegelin's point—and debate is impossible in an intellectually and spiritually balkanized society.[93]

Voegelin found plenty of signs of spiritual disease in American culture, for most of what now goes under the label "popular culture" stood, in Voegelin's thinking, for little more than mindless diversions from human responsibility. Intellectual trends at mid century, while not without rays of hope, indicated a general inability to deal rationally with issues. In education, Americans focused more than ever upon personal fulfillment, understood in a most private and narcissistic way. Liberal America operated without a metaphysic—or, more precisely, with a decapitated metaphysic. Since Voegelin understood that all social and political orders reflect a shared ontology, liberal America must be understood as an order in revolt against God. Moreover, because political existence requires constant discussion about moral matters, the United States suffers from a decisive flaw. As a society in revolt against the divine ground, and therefore not participating in divine nous, it (that is, society in the corporate sense) is incapable of moral action: "moral action without rational action is impossible." In a society made up of individuals who seek their private goods because they accept no greatest good for all, communication is difficult—and maybe in the long run impossible. In a democracy communication is essential.

6

The Philosopher

The affinities between Voegelin and Strauss are strongest in their diagnosis of the modern crisis. With few variations, each has rounded up the usual suspects and charged them with the same crimes. Despite differences in emphasis, the diagnoses of Strauss and Voegelin are very close. Their answers to the crisis—their more positive philosophies—point in different, but by no means opposite, directions. In this chapter I examine Strauss's philosophy and his solution to the problem of modernity; the next chapter deals with Voegelin's answer. If Strauss offered conservatives the most extensive and persuasive diagnosis of the maladies of modernity, Voegelin offered them the most useful cures.[1]

PLATO IN SEARCH OF JERUSALEM

''Then let me follow the intimations of the will of God.'' The final words uttered by Socrates in *Crito* point to the decisive political truth: a political order rests upon laws that, in turn, depend upon unprovable beliefs. Socrates, the familiar story goes, was brought to court on charges of impiety and corrupting Athenian youth. The second charge depended upon the first, so Socrates defended himself by making the singular claim that he philosophized on behalf of the gods—or more precisely, that he philosophized by divine command. Socrates' divine mission made him unpopular with the most powerful Athenians. By examining all claims to wisdom and knowledge, Socrates exposed the conceits of powerful men who took their opinions for knowledge. Socrates suffered no such delusion. He understood the distinction between opinion and knowledge and the condition that fated humans, or at least the vast majority of humans, to live in the dimly lit cave of opinions (conventional truths). Although

Socrates' examination of others' opinions made powerful enemies, he remained loyal to Athens and its gods only when he followed the divine command to examine himself and others. As a loyal son of Athens and its gods (and the laws), he would not abandon his post. At least this is the story Socrates told in his defense.

One understands more fully Socrates' attachment to Athenian conventions after reading *Crito*. While discussing with Crito the wisdom of fleeing the death sentence, Socrates answered for the laws. The laws, we should know, referred to the specific laws of the city and to the conventional beliefs that gave the city its cohesiveness. In this sense, the laws were divine—that is, they flowed from the most profound beliefs of the people, which were about the gods. In one revealing section Socrates answered for the laws:

> "Tell us what complaint you have to make against us which justifies you in attempting to destroy us and the state? In the first place did we not bring you into existence? Your father married your mother by our aid and beget you. Say whether you have any objection to urge against those of us who regulate marriage?" None, I should reply. "Or against those of us who regulate the system of nurture and education of children in which you were trained? Were not the laws, who have the charge of this, right in commanding your father to train you in music and gymnastics?"

Socrates not only agreed that he owed his being to the city and the laws—and in this sense owed allegiance in the same way one owes allegiance to one's father—but said that throughout his life he had taken full advantage of the city and its laws. Socrates had, in effect, made a contract with the laws since he never left the city. Even the philosopher, who by nature is less a creature of convention than others, was beholden to the city.[2] Since social order rests upon a foundation of opinion—especially opinion about the good—a philosopher is obligated to defer publicly to conventional beliefs and their divine support. The questioning, doubting, and searching that define the philosophical life depend upon laws, which restrict the range of questioning.

If the philosopher qua philosopher lives in a paradoxical (not to say precarious) relationship with the social order, that is, if the philosopher is necessarily something of an outsider, consider the condition of a Jewish philosopher in a Christian society. Beyond the obvious tensions arising from one's heritage, such a person is caught between the commands of the law and the philosophical quest to replace opinion with knowledge, i.e., between belief and unbelief. This tension, symbolized by Strauss as the quarrel between Jerusalem and Athens, dominated Strauss's philosophical enterprise. With this "problem" he began his career, and with it he ended.

Strauss's first book, written between 1925 and 1928, examined Spinoza's *Theologico-political Treatise.* "The author," Strauss wrote of himself, "was a young Jew born and raised in Germany who found himself in the grips of the theologico-political predicament."[3] The Jewish problem, as some people labeled it, took on particular urgency for Strauss during the Weimar Republic. The liberal Weimar regime should have solved the problem since liberalism, as Strauss understood its essence, rested upon public morality but not public religion.[4] In what sense would a Jew be an outsider in a society dedicated to tolerance and pluralism? "Prior to Hitler's rise to power," suggested Strauss, "German Jews believed that their problem had been solved in principle by liberalism: the German Jews were Germans of the Jewish faith, that is, they were no less German than the Germans of the Christian faith or of no faith." But if liberalism prevented the state from interfering with Judaism, it also prevented interference with anti-Judaism. Liberalism as manifested during the Weimar regime proved too weak to solve the Jewish problem.[5]

In this context, then, Strauss began his long struggle to understand what it meant to be a Jew—or more specifically, to be a Jew in the modern, Christian world. Although his contemporary conditions pointed up these tensions, the modern era was not unique in this respect. The problems were universal. Strauss wrote: "Finite, relative problems can be solved; infinite, absolute problems cannot be solved. In other words, human beings will never create a society which is free from contradictions. From every point of view it looks as if the Jewish people were the chosen people, at least in the sense that the Jewish problem is the most manifest symbol of the human problem insofar as it is a social or political problem."[6] Despite the universality of the problem, we must not let Strauss deflect us from the very personal, difficult, and therefore nonuniversal questions of his own Jewish identity—that is, of his attitude toward his culture and, above all, his religious heritage. Strauss belonged to Jerusalem in the same way Socrates—or at least the old Socrates—belonged to Athens. In his own way Strauss called for repentance and a return to the God of Moses. More precisely, Strauss became a new Moses—a prophet and founder.

The subtleties of Strauss's discussion of subjects related to this problem necessitate a scrupulous devotion to the key texts. The lines of his argument crisscross, leaving the careful reader dazed but invigorated and the sloppy reader lost and helpless—which is exactly what Strauss intended. The "Preface to Spinoza's *Critique of Religion*" is Strauss's most self-revealing work and is, I think, the proper beginning and ending place for a study of Strauss's thought. To begin at the end: Strauss wrote the Preface in the 1960s, some forty years after he began his investigation of Spinoza. Looking back at the beginning he pointed to the problems that drove the study and obliquely pointed to Nietzsche as the source or origin of these problems.

> The hierarchy of moralities and wills to which the final atheism referred could not but be claimed to be intrinsically true, theoretically true: "the will to power" of the strong or of the weak may be the ground of every other doctrine; it is not the ground of the doctrine of the will to power: the will to power was said to be a fact. Other observations and experiences confirmed the suspicion that it would be unwise to say farewell to reason.[7]

If Nietzsche, the heir of a Christian tradition, served as the chief symbol of the modern dilemma, Strauss sought to begin his exploration of the problem by reference to Spinoza. Spinoza stands in relation to European Judaism as Machiavelli does to European Christianity. Thus the Jewish problem, "the most manifest symbol of the human problem insofar as it is a social or political problem," traces its modern roots back to Spinoza. In the late nineteenth and early twentieth centuries Jewish thinkers had two options: assimilation or Zionism.

In what sense were these Jewish options? What does a Jew risk with either option? Their souls? Strauss wondered. Liberals chose assimilation and embraced the minimalist state dedicated to protecting rights. Such a state is neutral about religious beliefs but rests upon a common morality. Weimar rested upon a Judeo-Christian moral foundation, but there was little or no concern about the substructure of beliefs that grounded the foundation. But for German Jews assimilation meant more than freedom from state-sanctioned persecution, it meant an active involvement in German cultural life. German Jews became Germans who were Jewish. Wrote Strauss: "The political dependence [of Jews] was also spiritual dependence. This was the core of the predicament of German Jewry."[8] Such dependence did not spare Jews from—and indeed may have fostered—their hideous fate. The Jewish problem represented more than a political problem, or rather, such a problem can be addressed successfully only as a socioreligious matter. Any regime that ignores the religious roots of conventional morality is vulnerable, i.e., is spiritually weak. Strauss understood this fact in terms of Nietzsche's dictum that Christian morality must eventually go the way of Christian cosmology, for the latter spawned and sustained the former. Not only was Weimar so constituted on the separation of religion and morals, but so also the members of the Jewish community who devalued their religious roots and beliefs by subordinating them to their German cultural aspirations.

The Jewishness of German Jews still mattered, even for the most acculturated. In response to the failure of assimilation to solve the problem, many Jews turned to Zionism. Strauss emphasized that they, too, cast the matter in human and political terms. Although the Zionists in some measure sought to tether their movement to traditional images of restoration, the goals were different and the traditional motif of God's chosen people had given way to a secular struggle over land and power. Zionism suffered from being a non-Jewish response to the Jewish problem, a state of affairs that was not, moreover, appreciably changed by the overlay of cultural Zionism. Strauss emphasized that the construction of a Jewish culture that was considered worth celebrating went forward without the central or defining cultural belief; that is, cultural Zionists approached the Jewish religion as a product of a nation or a people. By contrast, orthodox Jews understood that the Torah made the nation, and by thinking of the Torah as a cultural relic, cultural Zionists emptied it of its defining content.[9] Thus, both political and cultural Zionists attempted to solve the Jewish problem—the problem of being a Jew in a Christian society—in a way that violated the most basic Jewish inheritance.

The Jewish problem, Strauss maintained, is insoluble, but "there is a Jewish problem that is humanly soluble: the problem of the western Jewish individual who or whose parents severed his connection with the Jewish community in the expectation that he would thus become a normal member of a purely liberal or of a universal human society and who is naturally perplexed when he finds no such society." The Jewish problem is insoluble, Strauss seemed to argue, because one necessarily belongs to a particular society. Moreover, a Jewish problem is solved by embracing one's community. For the individual cut off from his society, "the solution to his problem is return to the Jewish community, the community established by the Jewish faith and the Jewish way of life."[10] The reader is bound to wonder how Strauss applied this solution to his own situation. He clearly connected the solution to orthodox faith—the community springs from faith—but because Strauss was a philosopher, which made him a skeptic about all beliefs, we must understand that Strauss's own relationship to his Jewishness was ambiguous. Nonetheless, as I will show later, Strauss did call for repentance, a return to the ancient faith.

Strauss's ensuing discussion of orthodoxy advances in a most perplexing manner. In the space of eight pages (pp. 231–239), the reader encounters Hegel, Franz Rosenzweig, Heidegger, Martin Buber, Nietzsche, Moses Mendelssohn, Maimonides, and Spinoza. The primary question concerns the defensibility of orthodox faith before philosophy (both modern and ancient). In the paragraph in which Strauss set out the solution to a Jewish problem he noted the difficulty facing Jewish intellectuals: "While admitting that their deepest problems would be solved by that return, they assert that intellectual probity forbids them to bring the sacrifice of the intellect for the sake of satisfying even the most vital need. Yet they can hardly deny that a vital need legitimately induces a man to probe whether what seems to be an impossibility is in fact only a very great difficulty."[11]

At least as early as his second book, *Philosophy and Law*, Strauss emphasized the moral posture that prevents modern intellectuals from seeing clearly. The term for this posture is "intellectual probity," and in the above quote one notices how Strauss thought this moral posture kept intellectuals from satisfying "the most vital need." Intellectual probity served to close intellectuals to religious beliefs, which they understood as irrational, superstitious, and backward. Thus, the agnosticism of modern intellectuals took the form of a mocking that served as part of a larger project of enlightening people. All careful thinkers had to grant the impossibility of disproving revelation, but Enlightenment intellectuals embraced their own epistemology with such tenacity that they eliminated all room for revelation. In short, these thinkers failed to understand revelation as believers understood it.[12] They placed their faith—and, it is a crucial point that Strauss considered it faith—in modern scientific epistemological conventions. By presenting the image of Enlightenment rationality as a faith that undermines religious beliefs through mockery, Strauss held up orthodoxy as an intellectually defensible alternative—one that, moreover, serves a vital need.

Having thus established a proper role for orthodoxy, and having defended its intellectual if not philosophical integrity, Strauss warned of one formidable challenge. "Vague difficulties," he wrote, "remained like some far away clouds on a beautiful summer sky. They soon took the shape of Spinoza—the greatest man of Jewish origin who openly denied the truth of Judaism and had ceased to belong to the Jewish people without becoming a Christian. It is not the 'God-intoxicated' philosopher, but the hardheaded, not to say hardhearted, pupil of Machiavelli and philologic-historical critic of the Bible. *Orthodoxy could be returned to only if Spinoza was wrong in every respect.*"[13] A bold claim. The reader, now nearly midway through the chapter (paragraph twenty-four out of fifty), must determine whether Spinoza was wrong in every respect. Strauss did not make the task easy, and he never answered the question directly.

In this chapter, Strauss approached Spinoza by way of Hermann Cohen. The reader is thus distanced from the primary subject, but also brought more squarely into the intellectual debate in which Strauss participated. The issues emerge with greater clarity, but Strauss's own position remains ambiguous, or perhaps just sheltered. Strauss stressed that Cohen and others misunderstood Spinoza in decisive ways. First, as heirs they could not properly understand Spinoza. His most scandalous claims appeared truistic to nineteenth-century Jewish philosophers, and thus the spirit of his philosophy, as well as the goals his arguments served, get lost in the commonplaceness of his argument. Second, Cohen never understood the role persecution played in shaping Spinoza's writing.[14]

According to Strauss, Spinoza was "the first philosopher who was both a democrat and a liberal." Whatever differences separate Spinoza from later liberal democrats, his philosophical enterprise contained the articulation and defense of a regime grounded on natural rights and dedicated to freedom. Like other modern philosophers, Spinoza jettisoned the notion of natural human ends: "man's end is not natural, but rational."[15] A liberal society dedicated to rational ends requires the subsuming of religious and cultural particularities. A liberal political society requires a good that cuts across these boundaries and bonds a nation together. A society dedicated to rational ends leads, in principle, to "the universal and homogenous state."

There are two questions to ask Strauss: Why did Spinoza advocate a liberal democracy? and What means did he employ or advocate to achieve this society? To the first question the simple answer is that Spinoza considered a liberal, democratic state the best possible order for philosophers.[16] Such a state transcends religious differences and provides the freedom for theorizing *(theoria)*. In this sense Spinoza reflected premodern philosophical predilections, and moreover, to this degree one can see interesting parallels between what Spinoza tried to accomplish and what Strauss advocated (in contrast to other modern thinkers who rejected theory). With regard to the purpose of Spinoza's *Treatise*—that is, to the means of achieving the liberal state—Strauss emphasized the need to read Spinoza esoterically. Whereas Cohen was disturbed by Spinoza's one-sided attack on Moses (one-sided insofar as Christian doctrines were equally vulnerable) and his flagrant contradictions, Strauss detected a deeper message. Living as a Jew in a Christian society, Spinoza had to fight "Christian prejudice by appealing to Christian prejudice . . . against Judaism." Spinoza constructed a foundation for a liberal order by means of seven biblical dogmas (i.e., beliefs common to both testaments) accepted universally. For more than political reasons—though these figured prominently—Spinoza found reason to favor the Christian faith. Strauss wrote: "The establishment of such a society required . . . the abrogation of the Mosaic law insofar as it is a particularistic and political law and especially of the ceremonial laws: since Moses' religion is a political law, to adhere to his religion as he proclaimed it is incompatible with being the citizen of any other state, whereas Jesus was not a legislator, but only a teacher."[17] A liberal society requires the dampening or elimination of tribalism, and Jewish law as law would always contend for the hearts of Jewish citizens. They would suffer as perpetual outsiders. Meanwhile, Christianity offered a more universalistic dogma that need not threaten a liberal society. Spinoza answered the Jewish problem by advocating the destruction of Judaism. Of course the creation of a rational society will require the sundering of Christianity as well. In short, a liberal society is a necessary stage in a history leading to the rational society.

The great Jewish philosopher held certain charms for Strauss. Spinoza brilliantly navigated treacherous philosophical waters. He wrote with such devious indirection as to change, like Machiavelli, the thinking of those who followed him without his followers' understanding fully how he had changed them. For Jewish thinkers, Spinoza's textual critiques became commonplace in due course. He more or less settled the matter of the revelatory authority of the Torah, and he also established the compelling logic for Jews to assimilate into the larger Christian culture. Strauss possessed great respect for Spinoza but found his answer to the Jewish problem—and by extension, the human problem—unacceptable.

Strauss rejected the liberal cum rational society—recall the passage quoted earlier in which Strauss noted the difficulty faced by a young Jew set loose from the Jewish community to "become a normal member of a purely liberal or of a universal human society and who is naturally perplexed when he finds no such society." Strauss understood the need to belong to a particular society, to be part of an identifiable community. Such community rests upon some faith— belief in a common good more or less rooted in divine or natural law—and the proper response to the Jewish problem is a return to the ancient faith. Spinoza presented a daunting challenge to such a return because he seemed to have "proved" that the ancient faith was superstition. But this idea, too, Strauss denied. Even the people who were critical of Spinoza, like Franz Rosenzweig, did not challenge thoroughly enough the beliefs handed them by Spinoza. Those attempts at "return" that Strauss witnessed in his own time struck him as too dependent upon modern (in contrast to Jewish) faith. "Rosenzweig," Strauss pointed out, "never believed that his return to the biblical faith could be a return to the form in which that faith had expressed or understood itself in the past.''[18] For Strauss, return meant return to the form of the ancient faith, and this form, or way, of belief offered the best sociopolitical alternative to the Enlightenment. In other words, classical philosophy requires the assistance of traditional religion to supplant the Enlightenment. Spinoza employed esotericism to erode faith; Strauss and Plato used it to buttress faith.

Spinoza begins to take on the sly, demonic, noble characteristics of Strauss's Machiavelli. Like his mentor, Spinoza used the Bible to undermine its authority; he played ''a most dangerous game.''[19] Unlike other moderns—though perhaps much like Machiavelli—Spinoza understood religion from the inside. He did not appeal to believers by reference to Enlightenment or modern assumptions—or at least he did not expose those assumptions. In the *Theologico-political Treatise*, Spinoza worked from the inside by beginning with those things granted to him by believers. Strauss interpreted this text as Spinoza's attempt to ''liberate'' believers from their ''prejudices'' so that they might be fit for philosophy: ''The *Treatise* is Spinoza's introduction to philosophy.'' The seductive way he used scripture to undermine belief in scripture accounts for Spinoza's long-term success, and the authority granted to the Bible made it impossible for those keen minds who took the Bible seriously enough to challenge it to doubt Spinoza's critique—or at least it would take a mind equal to Spinoza's to doubt it. Because Strauss understood this role of the *Treatise*, he could explain Spinoza's *Ethics* as beginning from assumptions already established in the *Treatise*. The *Ethics* presupposes ''the absurdity of orthodoxy'' whereas the *Treatise* does not. Spinoza wrote the *Ethics* to give ''a clear and distinct account of everything,'' and that book would serve as the philosophical answer to the question raised by the death of orthodoxy.[20]

Was the *Treatise* successful? Despite Spinoza's brilliance, Strauss contended that a philosophical refutation of the Bible is impossible. Spinoza's use of the Bible against itself—no matter how slyly performed—turned on assumptions alien to orthodoxy. Insofar as orthodoxy rests upon belief and does not claim ''to possess the binding power peculiar to the known,'' it is unassailable. Such cannot be said for Spinoza's philosophy. Notice how Strauss characterized orthodoxy: ''All assertions of orthodoxy rest on the irrefutable premise that the omnipotent God, whose will is unfathomable, whose ways are not our ways, who has decided to dwell in the thick darkness, may exist. Given this premise, miracles and revelations in general, and hence all biblical miracles and revelations in particular, are possible." Strauss emphasized that Spinoza could not refute the Bible except by positing alternative assumptions (e.g., accounting for the age of the solar system based upon the assumption that the solar system is natural, not created)—or, more to the point, by reference to beliefs and not to knowledge. Strauss argued that Spinoza, unable to find proofs, fought orthodoxy "by means of mockery."[21] Strauss's claim puts the great Spinoza in the same camp as lesser Enlightenment figures, but because Spinoza argued so well, and thus camouflaged the nature of his critique, he proved more successful than any others.

In the final analysis, however, Spinoza offered no philosophical answer to the questions raised by religion. What is more, Spinoza's attempt to supplant orthodoxy by a clear and distinct account of everything (in the *Ethics*) failed on the grounds that his account could not go beyond the hypothetical—that is, it remained in the same epistemological position as orthodoxy, though claiming much more. Strauss wrote that "philosophy, the quest for evident and necessary knowledge, rests itself on an unevident decision, on an act of the will, just as faith. Hence the antagonism between Spinoza and Judaism, between unbelief and belief, is ultimately not theoretical, but moral."[22]

As modern philosophy began to challenge for moral authority, the political and social order became the prize, and slowly, the philosophical alternative was eclipsed by the furor of the battle between two faiths, or acts of will. One can understand the issues better if one examines the end of Strauss's chapter on Spinoza. Strauss noted how modern philosophy altered an old antagonism, one characterized broadly as orthodoxy and Epicureanism. The term Epicureanism came from the old Jewish designation for the critique of religion generally. It was "cautious" and "retiring." The old atheism sought to relieve people of their religious delusions so that they might more fully enjoy life. Somehow, a new, more virulent and evangelical atheism, suffused with moral fervor, emerged. The genealogy of this atheism Strauss left unclear, and the reader is left perplexed even about the role Spinoza played, if any, in its evolution. Nonetheless, Strauss described a new atheism that displayed a hostility toward all religion, not on the ground that religion prevents the enjoyment of life, but because it shields people from the awful truth. The new atheism called for an honest, unblinking examination of existence, yet it was an understanding of existence created by the war against religion. These atheists sought to deny a transcendent realm that gave humans their dignity (e.g., made in the image of God) and to project in its place a world ripe for human control. Human creativity—the highest objective of modern rationalism—could be released fully only when all transcendent models or standards lost their persuasive power. Such an agenda required a fervent evangelicalism, complete with a moral attitude.[23]

The connection between these important themes is best illustrated by the following quotation from the penultimate paragraph in the chapter. Few paragraphs present as interesting a puzzle.

> This new fortitude, being the willingness to look man's forsakenness in its face, being the courage to welcome the most terrible truth, is "probity," "intellectual probity." This final atheism with a good conscience, or with a bad conscience, is distinguished from the atheism at which the past shuddered by its conscientiousness. Compared not only with Epicureanism but with the unbelief of the age of Spinoza, it reveals itself as a descendant of biblical morality. This atheism, the heir and the judge of the belief in revelation, of the secular struggle between belief and unbelief, and finally of the short-lived but by no means therefore inconsequential romantic longing for the lost belief, confronting orthodoxy in complex sophistication formed out of gratitude, rebellion, longing, and indifference, and in simple probity, is according to its claim as capable of an original understanding of the human roots of the belief in God as no earlier, no less complex-simple philosophy ever was. The last word and the ultimate justification of Spinoza's critique is the atheism from intellectual probity which overcomes orthodoxy radically by understanding it radically, that is, without the polemical bitterness of the Enlightenment and the equivocal reverence of romanticism. Yet this claim, however eloquently raised, cannot deceive one about the fact that its basis is an act of will, of belief, and that being based on belief is fatal to any philosophy.[24]

Take a deep breath. This terrible and exciting passage tells us much. We must come to a fuller understanding of "intellectual probity," since Strauss considered it the defining or at least most dangerous characteristic of modern unbelief. One notes that "the ultimate justification of Spinoza's critique is the atheism from intellectual probity." Whatever that phrase means, one can detect a relationship between probity, biblical morality, and the "final atheism"—a term Strauss used in the next paragraph to suggest Nietzsche and the end or logical conclusion to the Enlightenment. A reexamination of the chapter exposes internal clues near its center. Concerning Nietzsche, Strauss wrote that "biblical morality as veracity or intellectual probity [was] at work in the destruction of biblical theology and biblical morality."[25] Whatever probity means in this context, Strauss understood it to be a product of biblical morality; atheists inherited this morality and used it against their own religious heritage.

Strauss essentially lifted the material discussed above from his own book, *Philosophy and Law*, in which one finds an extended discussion of intellectual probity.[26] It is a posture—"a new form of bravery"—that examines human fate unblinkingly. More important, Strauss connected it with dogmatism, with an unshakeable attachment to beliefs not provable (the absence of a transcendent standard). The contrast with the older atheism (Epicureanism) is important. The old atheism did not demand an answer; it did not create a dramatic either/or. The intellectual probity of the new atheism presents just such a dichotomy—one must believe in God or believe there is no God. In a footnote Strauss explained the salient distinction between the two forms of atheism.

The opposition between probity and love of truth can be understood in the sense of this objection. The open confession that one is an atheist and the determined intention to draw all the consequences therefrom—especially the rejection, with all its implications, such as the belief in progress, of that half-atheism that was the dogmatic and dishonest presupposition of the post-Enlightenment synthesis—is doubtless more honest than all reconciliations and syntheses. But if one makes an admittedly unprovable atheism into a positive, dogmatic presupposition, then the probity that is thereby expressed is obviously something other than the love of truth.[27]

Epicureanism was skeptical, not dogmatic; withdrawn, not evangelistic. It emerged out of the philosophical culture of Greece. Modern atheism, on the other hand, "is a descendant of the tradition grounded in the Bible; it concedes the thesis, the negation of the Enlightenment, on the grounds of an attitude the Bible alone made possible." What is this biblical attitude? How does it relate to probity? The new atheism developed as a moral contender to orthodoxy. Recall that the "antagonism between Spinoza and Judaism . . . is ultimately not theoretical, but moral." That statement, however, does not hold true of the antagonism between Jerusalem and Athens. Philosophy proper offers no moral alternative to religion, as philosophers (qua philosophers) are unconcerned with moral matters except insofar as they become political philosophers—i.e., concerned with the nature of the polis. The Enlightenment, as a perversion of philosophy, sought to overthrow orthodoxy on moral grounds. Consequently, the Enlightenment could not accept an accommodation with orthodoxy—the two were intimately connected as combatants. That is what Strauss meant when he argued that the Enlightenment was a descendent of the tradition grounded in the Bible. "Just because of its conscientiousness and morality," Strauss wrote, "this atheism with a good, or even a bad, conscience must be distinguished from the conscienceless atheism at which the past shuddered."[28] Strauss considered Enlightenment philosophy an act of will, or a belief. Enlightenment thinkers proceeded from unevident assumptions, championed a moral objective, and sought to restructure Western civilization in accordance with their moral vision. Orthodoxy and the new enlightenment fought over a common territory;[29] only enlighteners dreamed of utopias.

Strauss lived after the demise of the Enlightenment, and it was only from this perspective—as he fully understood—that he could he make claims about its meaning. One begins to understand, perhaps, his more categorical claims in light of the end of modernity. If one takes Strauss's ubiquitous reifications of the Enlightenment to suggest an inherent logic (not always visible to the participants who accepted the modern project), one can account for his odd (often in quotes) use of the word "atheism." By atheism Strauss meant, variously, modern unbelief and the culmination of this form of unbelief in a final either/or. One comprehends his point better by glancing at his most simplified—and earliest—schema of modernity and the problem it (modernity) leaves for the philosopher.

The relationship between orthodox believers and Enlightenment philosophers turns out to be more complicated than Strauss let on. He differentiated between the radical Enlightenment (Hobbes, Spinoza, Bayle, Voltaire, and Reimanus—and later, of course, he included Machiavelli) and the moderate Enlightenment. The philosophers of the radical Enlightenment had the literal inspiration of the Bible—and the doctrines associated with this belief—as a prominent target. Thinkers of the moderate Enlightenment sought to bridge the two positions, but the utter failure of this project (doomed from the start) meant that any compromise between the two would be accomplished on Enlightenment ground (one thinks of the "return" of Rosenzweig and of Cohen).[30] More to the point, the apparent pluralities of options (especially those offered by the thinkers of the moderate Enlightenment) reduced to the either/or of the radical Enlightenment once the dust had settled. That is, the only live options in the late nineteenth and early twentieth centuries—well after the death of the Enlightenment—were modern unbelief (atheism) and orthodoxy. Because of the way conflict had developed between the two, the option for thinkers was hardly an option at all. How then did the quarrel between the Enlightenment and orthodoxy develop? This history exposes, Strauss believed, the nature of his contemporary intellectual environment.

In *Philosophy and Law*, Strauss emphasized the impregnability of orthodoxy on the familiar grounds that believers rest their faith on irrefutable presuppositions. Philosophers of the radical Enlightenment thus argued upon grounds that a priori rejected these presuppositions. In short, they did not disprove orthodoxy but laughed it out of bounds. Perhaps more important, Enlightenment philosophers successfully defended their assumptions from orthodox counterattacks. The significance of this success rests with how this part of the struggle exposed more clearly the faith foundations of orthodoxy. The orthodox could not claim the authority that comes from knowledge, but what went unnoticed was that Enlightenment thinkers suffered the same fate. Still more important, whereas "pre-Enlightenment science was in a certain harmony with the teachings of faith, the new science [the weapon of the Enlightenment], which had proved itself in the fight against orthodoxy . . . stood in an opposition to belief that was often concealed, always basically effective, and therefore always re-erupting.''[31] This disjunction, which developed slowly, created a problem that required attention. Science could no longer affirm the claims of orthodoxy, but neither could it satisfy human needs—spiritual needs. The common ground, what Strauss called "natural knowledge," no longer existed whereby "a meaningful quarrel between belief and unbelief is possible.''[32]

To redress the problem (i.e., the inability of science cum Enlightenment to satisfy human needs) Enlightenment thinkers were "compelled to reconstruct a world." They had to account for the whole in a manner similar to the old partnership between orthodoxy and Aristotelian science. Strauss addressed the issue with surprising clarity. "If one wished to refute Orthodoxy, no other way remained but to attempt a complete understanding of the world and life without the assumption of an unfathomable God. This means that the refutation of Orthodoxy depended on the success of a system.''[33] The need for a system forced those thinkers into a confrontational mode with the moral and political foundations of Western civilization as the stakes. Thus the quarrel between the Enlightenment and Orthodoxy, as Strauss liked to call it, was decidedly confrontational—a matter of hegemonic control. By contrast the quarrel between Jerusalem and Athens, of which the former quarrel was a perversion, supplied a mutually beneficial tension. One understands, then, why Strauss emphasized the attempt by Enlightenment philosophers to "overcome" orthodoxy. They had to explode the old myths about nature and God in order to create a new civilization and a new type of human, and this project—or rather its failure—established the moral horizon for the young Strauss.

The new comprehensive understanding (system) incorporated the new science that, Strauss suggested, the moderate Enlightenment made acceptable. Understood in this fashion, the project began with an ideal and employed (or created) modern science as a tool, which was the Enlightenment's undoing. "Modern natural science could be the foundation or the means of the victory of the Enlightenment over Orthodoxy only so long as the old concept of truth, which the Enlightenment had already destroyed, still ruled the dispositions of men." Modern science, while not useful for the support of the old metaphysics (as the thinkers of the modern Enlightenment hoped), operates in cold silence about ends, about the ought. Strauss concluded:

> If, therefore, modern natural science cannot justify the modern ideal, and if, correspondingly, the connection between the modern ideal and modern natural science is unmistakable, then the question must be posed whether, on the contrary, the modern ideal is in truth not the ground of modern natural science, and whether it is not also precisely a new belief rather than a new knowledge that justifies the Enlightenment.[34]

If this modern project kindled a flame by which humans might guide their steps, the source of illumination was the human ego—or the will to power. Thus the flame and the path it illumined proved delusory. If the ideal of the Enlightenment stood exposed as naked and foundationless in the end, the thinkers who shaped the ideal did so unaware of their vulnerability. They used tactics that exposed the fragile supports to orthodoxy, and more precisely, they argued that orthodoxy fails to sustain because it rests upon beliefs. In their attempt to fill the vacuum thus created, the philosophers of the Enlightenment "scarcely noticed the failure of [their] attack on orthodoxy"[35] or their own vulnerability. Nonetheless, quickened by an image of a better world, these thinkers put on the moral urgency appropriate for a revolutionary, and this urgency took the shape of intellectual probity—the imperative to look upon things as they are, not as one dreams them to be.[36] When the ideal self-destructed, the moral urgency remained as a fixture of the modern condition.

With this early construction of the modern dilemma, we are prepared to look again at the lengthy and difficult quote from Strauss's "Preface to Spinoza's *Critique of Religion*." The new atheism of which Strauss wrote referred to post-Enlightenment thought—especially Nietzsche and Heidegger—and post-Enlightenment thinkers retained the intellectual probity of the Enlightenment, which forced them into an atheism. This understanding helps us make sense of part of the quote: "The last word and the ultimate justification of Spinoza's critique is the atheism from intellectual probity which overcomes orthodoxy radically by understanding it radically, that is, without the polemical bitterness of the Enlightenment and the equivocal reverence of romanticism." To restate the point, Spinoza's critique and the moral posture that generated it culminated in Nietzsche's new atheism: no more romantic ideal or bitterness toward the enemy, only a painfully clear understanding of the old gods and their human roots. The failure of the new system to replace the old superstition left all the foundations useless. The sole remnant of the modern project was a moral integrity that, given these conditions, forced the unblinking eye of the philosopher to look at the dark abyss.

This new atheism did not allow for philosophy in the classical sense. Its peculiar understanding of the groundlessness of all fundamental claims forces—or appears to force—a choice between an acceptance of God or a rejection of God. This modern problem confronted the young Strauss. Yet hope appeared in the form of Nietzsche, whose will to power "was said to be a fact"[37] rather than another belief. Strauss sought to escape the modern prison by opening up the dusty old books and entering the premodern world. In an amazing footnote in *Philosophy and Law,* Strauss exposed more about the problem and his search for an answer than any published source of which I am aware.

That natural foundation that was intended by the Enlightenment but that precisely the Enlightenment itself buried can only be made accessible in the Enlightenment's battle against "prejudices"—a battle that has been prosecuted above all by empiricism and by the modern discipline of history—is carried appropriately to the end. The enlightened critique of the tradition must be radicalized, as it was by Nietzsche, into a critique of the principles of the tradition (the Greek as well as the biblical); thereby the original understanding of these principles may again become possible. The "historicization" of philosophy is therefore, and only therefore, justified and necessary. Only the history of philosophy makes possible the ascent out of the second, "unnatural" cave (into which we have fallen, less through the tradition than through the tradition of the polemic against the tradition), into the first, "natural" cave that Plato's image depicts, and the ascent from which, to the light, is the original meaning of philosophizing.[38]

Strauss became a part of a historical process that he hoped would culminate in the uncovering of philosophy—or rather, the necessary conditions for philosophy. First the "enlightened critique of the tradition must be radicalized." Nietzsche's radicalization made possible the "original understanding" of Enlightenment principles—that is, the principles perverted by Enlightenment thinkers—and a full recovery of this original understanding required a history of philosophy. Nietzsche cleared away the clutter, but he did not see clearly the object. A historian of philosophy, Strauss's role was to recover philosophy. In this sense he was a philosopher, but one who suffered the handicap of having to recover something lost.[39] He was like Socrates. Socrates discovered philosophy; Strauss rediscovered it. Still, in one important respect Socrates had the easier task. Notice Strauss's cave imagery. He occupied initially, by virtue of being a modern, a cave beneath Plato's cave, and this sub-cave was the "unnatural" cave designed by Machiavelli and Spinoza and built by Hobbes and Locke. The original or natural cave represents the conventional world—the world as constituted by faith in the law, i.e., divine law. Strauss largely dedicated himself to the ascent to this cave. True, the philosopher seeks to ascend to the light but remains, in important and decisive respects, tethered to the cave. At any rate, the unnatural cave does not allow ascent to the light. One must first recover the understanding essential for the philosophical ascent. Those are natural assumptions found in the poorly lit cave—the very cave to which Plato, in the *Republic*, claimed that the philosopher must return.

The distinction between the two caves remains ambiguous. To clarify, somewhat, I turn to the fuller but still evasive discussion found in *Persecution and the Art of Writing*. In an essay about Spinoza's *Theologico-political Treatise*, Strauss interrupted his examination to justify his historical methods. "Reading of old books," he wrote, "becomes extremely important to us for the very reason for which it was utterly unimportant to Spinoza." This elusive statement makes some sense in the context of the following claim: "We remain in perfect accord with Spinoza's way of thinking as long as we look at the devising of a more refined historical method as a desperate remedy for a desperate situation, rather than as a symptom of a healthy and thriving 'culture.'" The apparent riddle of Strauss the historian of philosophy attacking "history" and modern historical consciousness is solved by reference to the "desperate situation." Spinoza lived in the natural cave where the obstacles to philosophy stood clearly visible to the philosopher. The "natural" enemy of philosophy—superstition—did not engage in a systematic attempt to suppress or annihilate philosophy (at this point in our investigation the word "philosophy" has not been fully explicated). Who, then, created the "artificial obstacles" that obscure the philosophical life—and why? Strauss hid behind the most vacuous reifications. He wrote that "superstition, the natural enemy of philosophy, may arm itself with the weapons of philosophy and thus transform itself into pseudo-philosophy"—suggesting that somehow, someone used philosophy, or ideas philosophical, to bolster the enemies of philosophy. With the actors hidden behind the reified "superstition," the reader cannot hope to understand how, why, or who constructed the unnatural cave that damned late and postmoderns to a life cut off from the philosophical life, i.e., from the highest form of life. Moreover, so "long as that pseudo-philosophy rules, elaborate historical studies may be needed which would have been superfluous and therefore harmful in more fortunate times."[40] History, in Strauss's nonhistoricist sense, is the ladder from the pit to the natural cave. Only the pit dwellers really need the ladder.[41]

The "who question" Strauss answered only indirectly, yet the reader learns something about the kind of person hiding behind Strauss's use of the word "superstition." "People may become so frightened of the ascent to the light of the sun, and so desirous of making the ascent utterly impossible to any of their descendants, that they dig a deep pit beneath the cave in which they have been, and withdraw into that pit."[42] Modern thinkers suffer from the anxiety of life created by philosophical doubt and seek refuge in ideologies. They deny the worth of the philosophical life of questioning. Strauss, in other words, considered these people spiritually deficient, to borrow one of Voegelin's favorite terms. Life in the natural cave, with its dimly lit interior, includes for some the nagging question about the reality outside. The tension of existence supplies the desire to create a new world (the deep pit or unnatural cave) in which all things are known because human hands made them and the outside reality is so far removed as to present no tangible attraction.

We remain in the dark, so to speak, concerning the precise meaning of "natural" and "artificial," but Strauss embedded a few clues in several paragraphs. In the natural cave most people are "naturally" hostile toward philosophy but not systematically or obsessively so. This natural hostility takes the form of "superstition." Moreover, the "artificial" obstruction to philosophy emerges as a fortified or virulent superstition, or to put the matter more clearly, a class of thinkers developed who sought to control or manipulate the world. They could accomplish this task only by eliminating philosophers, who live in chronic awareness of problems that have no final solutions. To this end these modern thinkers transformed superstition into a "pseudo-philosophy," thereby obscuring the truths expressed by true philosophers. In sum, these thinkers won the battle and created an intellectual atmosphere so opaque as to eliminate all evidence of nature. The collapse of the modern project did not create a new natural environment, and it left future generations of potential philosophers in a dark intellectual and spiritual cave, completely cut off from natural light. The only illumination in such circumstances came from old books.

Even with this interpretive overlay, the careful reader still yearns for sharp definitions and some concrete details, but oddly, one gets precious few of either from this historian and philosopher. Whether the fault rests with the reader or the author is a matter of perspective. For Strauss, to attempt to understand and fail is an indictment of the reader. The author of important books cannot or ought not help the lost reader. Still, we readers have not exhausted the clues Strauss left behind. We have reason to hope. Spinoza, we learn, lived in the natural cave, and he understood the philosopher's natural obstacle to be "man's imaginative and passionate life." This kind of life produces superstition as a security against the chaos of the experienced reality. Thus, Spinoza understood the production of superstition to have the same spiritual source that Strauss considered pseudo-philosophy to have. The difference, one must assume, is that the former emerged from the many while the latter emerged from the few (potential philosophers).

The immediate question concerns the inability of philosophers to withstand or rebut pseudo-philosophy. The relationship of the three—superstition, philosophy, and pseudo-philosophy—emerges with reasonable clarity in one paragraph. "The alternative that confronts man by nature," Strauss wrote, "is . . . that of a superstitious account of the whole on the one hand, and of the philosophical account on the other." The reader cannot be certain that Strauss really agreed with this statement, since it forms part of his interpretation of Spinoza, and one should keep in mind that Strauss often wrote of philosophy being the quest for a knowledge of the whole rather than an "account of the whole." Nonetheless, he emphasized that philosophy and superstition have in common the assumption that life must be lived in light of some account of the whole. He wrote that "philosophy finds itself in its natural situation as long as its account of the whole is challenged only by superstitious accounts."[43] Pseudo-philosophy, whatever "it" is, hides this ground—"the one plane of truth"—which is common to the old antagonists.

One gets the sense that the new antagonist is something other than the Enlightenment. It is the intellectual residue left from the collapse of the modern project, or to put it another way, it is a modern form of sophistry. Sophists refuse to play by the rules; the old rules and goals have become "meaningless or absurd." Two reifications, examined in some detail earlier, provide the contemporary alternatives to the old antagonists: science and history. Both reject the quest for the whole, but history proves more damaging to philosophy because it overcomes or subsumes philosophy.[44] Philosophy—that is, the life of philosophy (as an erotic search) associated with Socrates— becomes the flower of a particular historical soil, and one understands it in relation to the context that gave it life. Understood this way, the historicist must reject the Socratic ideal on the ground that Socrates erred with regard to the nature of reality.[45] The point that was most significant for Strauss was that "once [historicism] has become a settled conviction constantly reinforced by an ever-increasing number of new observations, the idea of a final account of the whole [not historically conditioned] . . . appears untenable. . . . *Thereafter, there no longer exists direct access to the original meaning of philosophy, as quest for the true and final ground of the whole.*"[46] Like Husserl and Heidegger, Strauss sought to dig deeply enough to recover the original meaning—in this case of philosophy—which has been lost through the years.[47] He had to escape the provincialism of modern assumptions, and the fresh view for which he yearned was found between the lines of the old, great books. His contemporaries saw nothing in those spaces. How could they?[48]

Strauss's ascent to the natural cave (the only cave that can sustain philosophic life), which he sought to accomplish through history,[49] began with Maimonides. To escape modern provincialism Strauss examined "the medieval Enlightenment." He wrote at the end of his fascinating introduction to *Philosophy and Law:* "We will attempt to direct attention to the guiding idea of the Medieval Enlightenment that the modern Enlightenment and its heirs have lost. Through an understanding of that idea, many modern convictions and considerations lose their power: *It is the idea of Law.*"[50] In Maimonides, Strauss found a Jewish model of a philosopher and a man who lived the tension of the West (Jerusalem and Athens).

Strauss's return to the law reminds the reader of his Jewish context, but it is more than that; it is a critique of Christianity. Strauss devoted little space to an examination of Christianity. He often employed a most expansive language designed to suggest to the uninitiated reader a broad Judeo-Christian tradition when he meant the Jewish heritage simply. Nonetheless, near the center of his understanding of the nature of modernity and the modern limitations imposed on the would-be philosopher rests his harsh critique of Christianity. The great quarrel between Jerusalem and Athens—not Rome and Athens—is the root of Western civilization. Rome undermined the law, and the effects of this action on the many people who depend on the law to direct their actions are complicated and beyond the range of Strauss's analysis. More important, without the law philosophers could not as easily ground their own intellectual freedom in a secure epistemological-social foundation. Moreover, and this is speculative, Christian universalism and the emphasis upon individual faith might have seduced philosophers like Spinoza into dreaming of a new sort of society in which philosophers might live in complete freedom—that is, with no need to justify their lives to society.[51] The Christian society, theoretically, can be the tolerant society.

The contrasts Strauss drew between Judaism (and Islam) and Christianity concerned the sociopolitical role performed by the law. For the Jews, the Torah regulated their actions and thoughts; Christians operated by faith, which oriented them as *individuals* to a personal savior. The Christian orientation had two effects: it demolished Jewish tribalism and replaced it with a universalism (the God of all humans—all humans have access to saving grace), and it devalued the sociopolitical power of the law by a peculiar form of individualism and by chiliasm.[52] Yet with respect to the fate of philosophy, the influence of Christianity is not without some paradoxes.

Here, we are touching on what, from the point of view of the sociology of philosophy, is the most important difference between Christianity on the one hand, and Islam as well as Judaism on the other. For the Christian, the sacred doctrine is revealed theology; for the Jew and the Muslim, the sacred doctrine is, at least primarily, the legal interpretation of the Divine Law (talmud or fiqh). The sacred doctrine in the latter sense has, to say the least, much less in common with philosophy than the sacred doctrine in the former sense. It is ultimately for this reason that the status of philosophy was, as a matter of principle, much more precarious in Judaism and in Islam than in Christianity: in Christianity philosophy became an integral part of the officially recognized and even required training of the student of the sacred doctrine. This difference explains partly the eventual collapse of philosophic inquiry in the Islamic and in the Jewish world, a collapse which has no parallel in the Western Christian world.[53]

The attempt by Christians to incorporate philosophy into the Christian account of the whole ruptured the integrity of both religion and philosophy. The life of faith is utterly alien to the life of reason (skepticism).

In *Philosophy and Law*, Strauss addressed the subject of Christianity three times—twice directly and once indirectly. The first reference takes the form of a faithful report on the argument made by Julius Guttmann in his book *Die Philosophie des Judentums*: "The biblical conceptions could be more successfully defended in the element of philosophy only after medieval metaphysics, stemming from pagan antiquity, was replaced by the metaphysics of the Enlightenment, stemming directly from Christianity and indirectly from the Bible."[54] If this statement represents Strauss's belief—and I believe it does—then we must note that he connects the Enlightenment to Christianity, which we are expected to contrast with medieval Enlightenment (i.e., the Jewish Enlightenment).

The second reference is unambiguously in Strauss's voice: "The Islamic and Jewish philosophers of the Middle Ages are 'more primitive' than the modern philosophers because they are not, like the latter, guided by the derived idea of natural right but rather by the *original, ancient* idea of the *Law* as a unitary, total order of human life—in other words, because they are the disciples of Plato and not the disciples of Christians."[55] Third, in a footnote Strauss wrote that the remarks in the text following the note "about the 'medieval Enlightenment' orient themselves to the representative Islamic and Jewish *philosophers*."[56] The cumulative effect of these passages is to emphasize the difference between the Jewish Enlightenment and the (Christian) Enlightenment, the former drawing its inspiration from Plato, the latter from Christianity. We are left with the following paradox: philosophers—incorrigible free thinkers—thrive in a tribal society grounded on a socioreligious law that controls both the actions and the thoughts of its people.

A corollary to that paradox is the claim that freedom of thought is "being menaced in our time more than for several centuries."[57] By contrast, Maimonides, who submitted to the law, lived in a society that tolerated freedom of thought. If the law, however, controlled not only people's actions but their thought, then one must assume that the condition of freedom is an adjunct of firm belief. Thus understood, the law is prior to philosophizing. The confusions created by such claims do not disappear easily (nonetheless, the point is crucial for Strauss), but paying attention to the various meanings of key words helps. One does not, for instance, associate philosophy with Judaism. Indeed, Strauss never tired of posing the Jerusalem/Athens dualism. In the context of his study of medieval Jewish philosophy (though the philosophers did not so define themselves), Strauss explicated the complicated relationship between philosophy and the Mosaic law in the thought of Maimonides. Still, the truths Strauss found in the writings of the great Jewish thinker extended beyond the specific context. Strauss usually meant the Torah when he used the word "law," but the application went well beyond that meaning, and he told his readers as much when he suggested that in a decisive respect Maimonides was a Platonic thinker.[58]

The larger "human" meaning of law is the divine law. At least from Maimonides' perspective, not just the Jewish people but all people live with some understanding of divine law, yet the gods of Athens (or any pagan gods) were no match for Yahweh. For both Strauss and Strauss's Maimonides the superiority was important for philosophers as well as for believers. The significant differences between the Torah and the laws of the other gods meant that Maimonides lived in a socioreligious context toward which Plato had pointed but did not occupy.[59] Because Strauss believed that Maimonides operated with Platonic assumptions (but not presuppositions)[60] and that he lived in a political order outlined by Plato (in the *Laws* and the *Republic*), Strauss's interest in Maimonides takes on a special significance.

Strauss liked to emphasize that the "fact" of revelation preceded Maimonides' attempt to understand it. By "fact," I take Strauss to mean that the Torah effectively regulated the social, political, and spiritual lives of Jews. Revelation created an inhabitable world by effecting a moral code that oriented a people toward some transcendent object, but what is more important is that revelation encouraged a transcending of self. The object of that transcendence may not be important except that different objects produce different degrees of fidelity. Most important—i.e., most important for humans—is that revelation operates as a law which regulates the sociopolitical lives of the people. The reason Strauss tended to equate morality with political matters becomes clear. Moreover, his concern about two modern phenomena—the separation of morality from religion and the increasingly egoistic quality of modern morality—becomes important in light of Strauss's belief that a stable politicosocial order depends upon a transcendentally anchored morality. We understand now why Strauss considered the Torah the foundation of an inhabitable world.

Born into a world created by the law, Maimonides began his philosophical journey by finding justification for philosophy in the law. The law commanded him to philosophize. This was no universal command but related to specially gifted people. In the realm of "human things" (this world rather than the heavens), philosophers search for knowledge, but the law did not free them entirely. The philosopher must not teach publicly. The prohibition required that philosophers teach verbally so as to judge the worthiness of the pupil and be able to adjust to the abilities and preparedness of the listener. Maimonides, in deference to the demands of the law, could only write a book that incorporated the ways associated with verbal teaching. He therefore wrote a book that exposed the truth to some and hid it from the many; he wrote esoterically.

Although the law precedes and authorizes philosophy, philosophers do not exclude the law from their examination. The philosopher's charge is to examine all human things, and since the law came from a human prophet (Moses), it is the divine law as understandable and applicable to humans. To this degree, the law is a part of human things.[61] But unlike Plato, Maimonides did not consider the law to be the center of his inquiry. The reality of the law meant that Maimonides experienced no great desire to understand the political questions and instead devoted himself to the theoretical life primarily and to "practical" or political philosophy only secondarily. In this sense, the medieval Jewish philosophers were more Aristotelian than Platonic. They devoted themselves, more or less, to theory. Plato demanded that the philosopher descend back to the cave (i.e., engage in political matters); Maimonides could deemphasize Plato's requirement only because Moses had already met it. Strauss, on the other hand, sought a new "cosmos" after the death of God, and unlike Maimonides, he felt compelled to create, which means that his esotericism played a different role than Maimonides' did.

Strauss's examination of Maimonides' prophetology led him to conclude that Moses functioned in a capacity similar to Plato's philosopher-kings. Moses had—whatever sense one can make of this image—seen the reality beyond the cave. Or, in a more appropriate metaphor, he had been to the mountain top. Maimonides, as Strauss presented him, established that only Moses was a true prophet. Moreover, while the so-called prophets relied upon "imagination" to prophesy, Moses did not. He was both philosopher and prophet—one who saw the general (theory) and the partial (practical or political). The matter is confused. Strauss's emphasis upon Moses' prophecy as "natural," along with the claim that Maimonides' book was a critique of the power of imagination, leads one to the assumption that, in Strauss's characterization of Maimonides, Moses was not a prophet as traditionally understood but an especially gifted philosopher (a philosopher plus leader). Humans need prophets because "man is by nature a political being and, in distinction to the rest of the living beings, he needs association with others by nature." But humans are also individuals, and they think of their individual needs ahead of the needs of the whole or the many. Consequently, humans require a lawgiver, and the law must be of a sort that directs fractious human natures toward communal harmony. "The Law intends to make living together possible. Therefore, the prophet is the founder of a society that is directed to the proper perfection of man.''[62] This perfection is philosophy. Philosophers do not exist outside of societies, and in this sense the divine law, which is the ground for sociability and political order, is directed toward the same end as philosophy. Moses provided the divine law, and thus addressed the practical philosophical needs. Because Plato lived in a society that had no equivalent law, he pointed to the need for a lawgiver who was more than philosopher—a philosopher-king.[63] All subsequent philosophers must defer to the lawgiver.

What should one make of the ambiguity concerning Moses' divine law? If he was a philosopher who possessed the gift of leadership, then the divine origin of the Torah is no longer self-evident. As a great philosopher Moses recognized that a social order requires a normative order that supersedes individual conceptions of right and wrong and that binds a people together in a common goal or purpose. To supply a law to create this order he had to employ his imagination. Only in this way could he reach the many. His law thus orients an entire people, demanding obedience from the many and apparent obedience from the few. The mystery of Moses' God requires that the few instruct the many about proper beliefs in heavenly matters. The talmudic tradition allows for nearly infinite teachings since once the philosopher had established the legal foundation for his search he is free (indeed, by the law, commanded) to reinterpret the literal meaning of a text to accord with his theoretical insights. The Torah is thus enormously flexible, and the philosopher lives bound to the law, but entirely free.

The freedom made possible by the law stands in sharp contrast to the freedom presented by the Enlightenment. Strauss emphasized that for the Jewish and Islamic philosophers of the Middle Ages, the superiority of theory over practice meant they did not try to reshape the world radically.[64] They did not seek to "enlighten"; they lived and taught privately. But during the Enlightenment, thinkers reversed the priority and sought to reconstruct the world. Their hope for such a transformation rested on the astonishing advances in knowledge. The distinctions of the few and the many imposed by fate on an earlier people no longer need apply since through modern methods the mysteries of the universe were unraveling in such a way as to be understandable to all.[65] Knowledge and reason could replace superstition and faith as the compass of human action. No imperative remained in this environment to teach esoterically.[66] Freedom for the many then became the object of modern thinkers. What, from Strauss's point of view, the moderns did not realize was that the human race is divided into the vast majority and the very few and that freedom of thought is impossible for the many. By disabusing them of their beliefs, the enlighteners cut the many off from their moral roots. They became, not enlightened thinkers, but alienated and egoistic creatures. Some gravitated to mass movements, others to crass consumerism, but whichever way they went, the normative center fell apart. Not reason but passion ruled.

We can now understand Strauss's oblique calls for return. The differences in context help explain why he could not more openly call for repentance. The law was no more. God had died. Strauss found himself in that sub-cave, and all he could do was to recover the natural horizon that had been lost to the modern world. We are compelled, then, to amend the earlier comparison between Socrates and Strauss. Socrates belonged to Athens, surely enough, but Strauss could not belong to Jerusalem. He was not limited because he was a philosopher but because the world created by the Torah had ceased to exist.[67] Without the law morality is groundless, and as a transcendent morality fades, the prospect of a stable political order fades as well. Strauss the political philosopher displayed grave concern about moral questions even though Strauss the philosopher was unable to champion a specific transcendent morality. But, then, his objective was, not to provide a new moral foundation, but to secure a rationale for other people to reconstruct an old one. Who could tell what the remodeled universe would look like?

NATURE AND NATURAL RIGHT: OR HOW THE PHILOSOPHER LEARNED TO DISSEMBLE

Nothing stands out quite so clearly from a reading of Strauss's book on Maimonides than the extent to which Strauss avoided metaphysical questions. Overriding the matter of Maimonides' philosophical-theological beliefs was Strauss's concern for practical or moral-political matters. What should we think about Maimonides' personal beliefs? The effect of Strauss's book is that Maimonides must have had no opinion on the divine source of the law. As a philosopher—in this case, a philosopher in deed but not in name—Maimonides could

not have believed. So runs the logic springing from Strauss's definition of philosopher. At any rate, one realizes that the source of the
law is unimportant for the philosopher. As a commentator on
Maimonides' work, Strauss refused to take seriously the metaphysical matters about which Maimonides wrote. And so it went with
nearly everything Strauss wrote. He might have been honest when
he claimed he was no philosopher; he certainly seemed unable or
unwilling to explain the philosopher. So, while philosophy preceded
political philosophy, Strauss remained fixated on the latter. The reason is obvious. Political philosophy concerns the conditions that
make philosophy possible. Socrates came to political philosophy because his philosophical life so alienated him from the city that the
conditions could only be secured by attending to the needs of the
many. Maimonides, by contrast, lived in such a stable political order
that he did not need to question radically the political arrangements.
But Strauss lived in the pit beneath the cave. Philosophy in the modern era could not emerge until natural conditions returned, so
Strauss found himself in the odd position of making claims for the
philosopher that he could not know from personal experience.
Strauss knew enough about the life of the philosopher to recognize
the need for political philosophy.

One can begin to understand his philosophical assumptions by
glancing, one last time, at the debates in European phenomenology
during Strauss's formative years. He began his last book with an essay that rehearsed these debates because for him, they were the central questions. By beginning with these debates, Strauss established
the problems his philosophy addressed. Political philosophy, he
claimed, is all but dead. Killed in the cross fire of the positivists and
historicists, Strauss sought to resurrect it by disarming the latter
(the positivists had long since faded away as a philosophical challenge). The historicists posed a serious threat because they were
family; they and Strauss shared many of the same assumptions.

Husserl, Heidegger, and Strauss oriented their philosophical inquiries to the world of commonsense or phenomena. The world as
experienced forms the primordial ground of all understanding. The
scientific spirit rejects this prescientific ground, and the people who
are captured by this spirit distort the phenomena, but more important, they are blind to their utter dependence on understandings belonging to this ground and reducible to nothing else.[68] By returning

to the prephilosophic understanding, Husserl thought that he had located the objective (i.e., experience common to all) core of human reality.[69] "Scientific" knowledge, as Husserl understood it, could rest upon this foundation. Strauss explained it this way:

> The adequate theory of knowledge must be based on scientific knowledge of the consciousness as such, for which nature and being are correlates or intended objects that constitute themselves in and through consciousness alone, in pure "immanence"; "nature" or "being" must be made "completely intelligible." Such a radical clarification of every possible object of consciousness can be the task only of a phenomenology of the consciousness in contradistinction to the naturalistic science of psychic phenomena. Only phenomenology can supply that fundamental clarification of the consciousness and its acts the lack of which makes so-called exact psychology radically unscientific, for the latter constantly makes use of concepts which stem from every-day experience without having examined them as to their adequacy.[70]

Strauss remained close to Husserl in his hope of understanding, as Lawrence Berns called it, "the true, or intelligible, world underlying the world of ordinary experience."[71] Perhaps this desire amounts to little more than ontological realism, but at any rate, "the intelligible world underlying ordinary experience" suggests a universal ground or context or experience: "nature"—to use Strauss's but not Husserl's language. Moreover, the task begun by Husserl, and continued by Strauss, presupposes human access to this ground. In the language of Plato, this search is "science," and the knowledge Husserl sought through science would provide a sturdy ontological foundation for all philosophical knowledge.[72]

The ontological enterprise, as Strauss understood it, begins with a thorough and critical examination of all givens. The failure of scientists to acknowledge or even understand their dependence upon the givens of human experience leads them and the whole modern gaggle to accept uncritically (unscientifically) the truth of their claims. Even after Nietzsche exposed the groundlessness of modern reason, the "true" science of ontology remained obscure. Husserl reinitiated the search for the ground, and following Husserl's lead,

Strauss understood philosophy to be the rigorous examination of "our common understanding of the world, [of] our understanding of the world as sensibly perceived prior to all theorizing."[73] Husserl understood that this science proceeds slowly with the hope that eons hence it will produce pure rational norms. Strauss never expressed a similar hope about the cumulative enterprise. Indeed, his emphasis upon the discovery of the perennial problems suggests the severe limits of his optimism.

Therein rests the largest problem with Husserl's philosophy, as Strauss understood it. The inability of science to produce norms here and now force the scientist (i.e., philosopher) to accept the norms that emerge from the particular social and political order (Weltanschauung).[74] "Hence the temptation to forsake [philosophy as rigorous science] in favor of weltanschauungsphilosophie is very great."[75] Heidegger abandoned philosophy as science, as the search for supratemporal truths; Husserl, for his part, failed to grasp fully the limitations on philosophy as rigorous science imposed—or potentially imposed—by society. Consequently, Husserl did not understand either the philosopher's precarious status in society or the larger danger created by the withdrawal of philosophers from political concerns. Strauss reconnected ontology, which defines philosophy simply, with political philosophy. In short, the rigorous science of philosophy must proceed with the protection of, and in the form of, the changing Weltanschauung without capitulating to it. Although a private affair, philosophy must have a public face.[76]

The identification of philosophy with ontology is a reminder that philosophy is very different from political philosophy. Yet the close connection Strauss found between the two suggests that a philosopher who is willing to give up on ontology has no need of political philosophy. If philosophy emerges from the cultural soil of a given society its rootedness limits its goal as it makes political philosophy unnecessary. Perhaps that is what Strauss meant when he wrote, concerning Heidegger, that "he leaves no place whatever for political philosophy."[77] One comes to learn that the radically transcendental or unrooted nature of philosophy requires that the philosopher seek temporal or social accommodations. Since all good ontological exercises bring to doubt conventional or common sense constructions of being, a philosopher necessarily threatens a social order. Failure to understand this relationship dooms one to a misreading of Strauss.

The bringing to doubt, rather than the claim to knowledge, moved Strauss to advocate political philosophy as an important response to modernity. In this way Strauss could remain faithful to the beliefs of the American regime and to the doubts of the philosopher.

To speak of philosophy forces one back to philosophers, to individuals who live philosophically. In spite of Strauss's obsessive use of abstractions and reifications (e.g., "philosophy," "Jerusalem," "Athens"), he understood philosophy to refer to the existential condition of individual philosophers. Philosophy is a way of life rather than a set of beliefs or even a deeply reflective attitude toward the fundamental issues.[78] Philosophers form a distinct class whose interests become luminous with reference to the object or goal of their lives. Philosophers are erotic. Driven by a passionate desire to have what is missing, they live in apperceptive awareness of an object of their desire. Of course not all erotic people become philosophers. Many—probably the vast majority—look to inadequate objects for their satisfaction, and a sense of incompleteness sends many in search of power or other vulgar pursuits. But for the philosopher, knowledge is the object of satisfaction—knowledge of the "whole." The philosopher seeks to be a god. Naturally he lives in full awareness of the limitedness of his perspective, and this attraction to the unattainable or to the hidden engenders a curious piety.[79] The philosopher's peculiar piety and his wisdom amount to the same thing, a silence concerning the unknown.[80] Socrates was wise because he lived in full awareness of his ignorance; he was happy because he accepted the conditions of life.

If philosophy is dedicated to the life of reason—because only reason supplies self-evident knowledge—it is not itself self-evidently the best life.[81] Strauss took seriously the genuine and irresolvable tension between Jerusalem and Athens. In a revealing part of a lecture before an audience in Jerusalem, he said that "while being compelled, or compelling myself, to wander far away from our sacred heritage, or to be silent about it, I shall not for a moment forget what Jerusalem stands for."[82] The question of compulsion, with its shades of that Platonic cave, leaves some doubt as to whether Strauss's stance toward religion sprang from an act of will. The problem for Strauss, insofar as he sought to undermine modern "existentialism," was that his analysis of religion in the form of Christianity and Judaism (even in their most orthodox presentations) established the impregnability of faith. I have already noted his argument concerning Spinoza's attack. In the present context, one realizes that such a claim reduces both religion and philosophy to the status of faith or, more precisely, the will to believe. If they are both acts of the will, how could Strauss defend the philosophical life against the claims of Heidegger?

Here we find ourselves at the very heart of Strauss's philosophical life. All of his monographs on philosophers ancient and modern have as their genesis the resolution of this problem—the "theological-political" problem. In the end neither "faith" can argue away the other. The genius of the West, Strauss told us, is the tension between Jerusalem and Athens, and modernity is the name given to the progress of philosophers seeking to resolve this tension in favor of philosophy. Modernity is deicide. The attempt to enlighten the cave and to make its inhabitants philosophers—or at least practitioners of enlightened self-interest—not only failed to create a rational society (an unwalled city) but it exposed the ground of faith or will upon which reason rests. With Nietzsche the light was extinguished, or nearly so. Strauss emphasized Nietzsche's own reliance upon nature—which points to some transhistorical reality. Nonetheless, God was dead and knowledge, as such, appeared mortally wounded. Even "science" rested upon historically conditioned assumptions. Neither philosophy nor religion emitted much light, and in this dim twilight, where even the shadows flicker, Heidegger clutched to the one thing remaining—faith. But in what does one believe? Heidegger left no room for philosophers because they sought to escape faith—to transcend the cave. In silence he sat in this darkness, waiting.

Yet Strauss sought to recapture the Platonic concept of philosophy in spite of, or because of, its existential origins. The example of Socrates thus provides the starting place for understanding Strauss on this point. Socrates could not reject any claims to divine wisdom on the same ground that he could not accept them—they are neither evident to unaided reason nor open to falsification. But can one avoid taking a position on a matter as urgent as belief in revelation? Is not avoidance tantamount to rejection? To reject something without sufficient grounds violates the "idea of philosophy." Strauss's answer exposes much.

The philosophic reply can be stated as follows: the question of utmost urgency, the question which does not permit suspense,

is the question of how one should live. Now this question is settled for Socrates by the fact that he is a philosopher. As a philosopher, he knows that we are ignorant of the most important
things. The ignorance, the evident fact of this ignorance, evidently proves that quest for knowledge of the most important
things is the most important thing for us. Philosophy is then evidently the right way of life. This is in addition, according to
him confirmed by the fact that he finds his happiness in acquiring the highest possible degree of clarity which he can acquire.
He sees no necessity whatever to assent to something which is
not evident to him.[83]

Strauss argued from Socrates' existential position, i.e., Strauss argued that he was a philosopher. His failure to believe in revelation
sprang from his faith that the philosophical life is "the right way of
life." This life rested upon a rejection of revelation since philosophy
can only be the right way of life when one comes to understand one's
ignorance. To attest to one's ignorance in the context of a society oriented toward revelation is tantamount to claiming knowledge that
disproves the truths of revelation. Philosophers understand revelation from the point of view of the philosopher and judge divine
claims by the canons of human reason.[84] "In other words, the quest
for evident knowledge rests itself on an unevident premise."[85]

Thus we return to the question of the philosophical life after understanding that neither the skeptical nor the pious life appears self-
evidently good. Or, rather, neither may be understood as universally
good. Yet one cannot live without choosing one or the other; no synthesis is possible. For Socrates and Strauss the philosophical life was
preferable because it made them happy. Each made his choice, and it
was easy.

Strauss's insistence that philosophy is a way of life rather than a
rigid set of doctrines makes the subject slippery, which in no way indicates an evasiveness. The many and often thoughtless animadversions hurled at Strauss for his crude elitism, his perverse construction of a high priesthood of philosophers, too often miss the point
entirely. Great is the temptation to laugh at Strauss's pretensions
and to dismiss his esoteric readings—which is to dismiss Strauss. At
the very least he has good company in the gallery of comical and
misunderstood philosophers. However much abuse Strauss's philo-

sophical and hermeneutical claims warrant, they ought not be dismissed because Strauss was "antidemocratic" (whatever that means) or because he wrote in a manner as not to make himself immediately clear.

By entertaining, however briefly, the claim that philosophers experience different desires, or seek after different objects, than other people, then the difficulty of describing their way of life appears plausible if not self-evident. The same limitations face someone who endeavors to describe a deeply religious way of life. To draw in an unforgivably loose fashion from William James, the once-born and the twice-born experience life differently. A satisfactory rendering of the experience of one to a member of the other group is surely challenging. If we accept Strauss's contention that genuine philosophers live with a "mania" or an existential imperative, then the frame of reference would be too small to make the way of life fully intelligible to most readers. Indeed, Strauss surely considered himself to be an observer who sought to present a faithful rendering of the experiences he observed.

Nonetheless, the duty to describe Strauss's philosophy is not discharged in this manner. I established earlier the Husserlian foundation of Strauss's philosophy; the ontological enterprise requires that one begin with the presumption of a whole that is, in principle at any rate, intelligible. But, is this presumption warranted? Perhaps not. Strauss responded by reference to Socrates, "who knew that he knew nothing, who therewith admitted that the whole is not intelligible." The quotation does not end there. Strauss moved from an all too easy acquiescence to an assertion of something very near a rebuttal—"[Socrates] merely wondered whether by saying that the whole is not intelligible we do not admit to have some understanding of the whole, for of something of which we know absolutely nothing, we could of course not say anything, and that is the meaning, it seems to me, of what is so erroneously translated by the intelligible, that man necessarily has an awareness of the whole."[86]

The philosopher's life depends upon this awareness of the whole, and at the very least he must adopt it as a necessary fiction. The question of the source or manner of this awareness can only be answered—so far as I can tell—by a throwing up of one's hands. It is too primordial to uncover and may as well be described as a recollection or a remembering. Whatever the source, the whole may be rendered in many ways. Most people inhabit a cosmos thick with gods or otherwise attached to a divine source. In an enchanted universe, human obligations turn on the highest duty—to obey the gods. Consequently, the "philosophical" questions are resolved by reference to divine authority and, more prosaically, to the conventions and laws that emerge in a society dedicated to the gods. But appeals to the authority of an unseen and unheard divinity do not satisfy philosophers. They do not, in the first place, know which gods—or which claims about the God—to believe. Moreover, without direct access to the divine, philosophers have only human reports to test. Philosophers turn to "nature" as a means to understand the whole without appeal to authority. Strauss described the dialectical "ascent" in this manner.

> The philosophers transcend the dimension of divine codes altogether, the whole dimension of piety and of pious obedience to a pregiven code. Instead they embark on a free quest for beginnings, for the first things, for the principles. And they assume that on the basis of the knowledge of first principles, of the first principles, of the beginnings, it will be possible to determine what is by nature good, as distinguished from what is good merely by convention. This quest for the beginnings proceeds through sense perception, reasoning, and what they called *noesis*, which is literally translated by "understanding" or "intellect," and which we can perhaps translate a little bit more cautiously by "awareness," an awareness with the mind's eye as distinguished from sensible awareness. But while this awareness has certainly its biblical equivalent and even its mystical equivalent, this equivalent in the philosophical context is never divorced from sense perception and reasoning based on sense perception. In other words, philosophy never becomes oblivious of its kinship with the arts and crafts, with the knowledge used by the artisan and with this humble but solid kind of knowledge.[87]

The complaint that modern scientific tendencies abstract and thus distort human experiences is implied in this passage. By contrast, the philosopher must begin from experiences of the whole that emerge from everyday life—from commonsense. The oft employed "commonsense" must be taken literally—those things humans sense in common. From this universal frame of reference philosophers examine and test the various opinions about some part of the whole (e.g., What is justice?) to ascend from the partial to the universal. By examining these opinions dialectically, the conventional dross separates from the universal or commonly apperceived core. The participants in this process have made some progress from opinions to knowledge. At the very least they have come to understand how much their views partake in the spirit of their time and culture. They have become skeptics. Because the first step toward philosophical knowledge is recognition of opinion as opinion, the newfound ignorance is a transcendence of one's culture and the spur to fill the void left by exposing opinion as such.

Philosophy is derivative of convention because the philosopher must begin with opinions—or how the whole appears to a particular society. Only with this understanding can we make clear the meaning of Strauss's adaptation of Plato's cave. If the cave represents the "natural" state of society—before scientific or philosophic abstraction—then the conventions or mythical representations of the cosmos and all its parts provide the only proper starting place for philosophical investigation. Strauss's image of a sub-cave suggests a society deformed by modern, scientific abstraction. Modern society needs the historian of philosophy (Strauss) to recapture the natural conditions of social and political life. It was at the beginning of philosophical investigation, then, that the issues emerged with greatest clarity.[88]

However dependent on conventions, philosophers strive to transcend them. "The opinions," wrote Strauss, "are thus seen to be fragments of the truth, soiled fragments of the pure truth. In other words, the opinions prove to be solicited by the self-subsisting truth, the ascent to the truth proves to be guided by the self-subsistent truth which all men always divine."[89] One faces conflicting opinions about some truth, which points to an answer beyond the particular answers. From this concrete starting point the philosopher seeks the universal characteristic of the object under investigation. The answer to this question is the "nature" of the thing. Nature refers to the defining characteristic, or the appropriate end of the object. Phenomena may be conventional or natural. Philosophy is the search for the crucial or defining way or custom of a thing—that which makes it what it is. By isolating the class character, or nature, of a phenomenon one also identifies or points to its proper goal or purpose.

We must never stray far from the knowledge that for Strauss nature had to be presupposed—an apprehension of a transhistorical order in which the parts have a defining "way." However, Strauss's seemingly idealist ontology was not idealist nor even, in a formal sense, an ontology. When discussing Strauss's relation to Husserl's ontology, Stanley Rosen correctly noted that "the Straussian desedimentation is intended to take us back to nature as a discovery by the individual philosopher qua historical human being, not by the transcendental ego."[90] Strauss emphasized that humans have no justifiable reason for doubting the reality of common experience,[91] but he was clearly referring to a human reality—any larger reality has no bearing on human life and therefore remains beyond the scope of philosophical examination. In this sense Strauss remained always in the human realm, with all attempts at "transcendence" referring to transcending the historical or the partial. Like Socrates, Strauss left to others the examination of divine things (though he examined divine claims).[92] Theologians pursue their questions upon the basis of experience, and since philosophers do not share this experiential frame of reference (otherwise, how could they be philosophers), theological questions cannot be part of their examination of human things. On no other point is the contrast with Voegelin more instructive (as I will show in the next chapter).

How was Strauss's thought "Platonic" if most people associate Plato with the doctrine of ideas—self-subsisting forms? A purer example of idealist ontology one could not hope to find. Strauss understood "ideas" to refer to classification—the nature of something. The "idea" of something is the answer to the "what is" question. By asking, What is man? one points to some nature that defines humans in the abstract. Yet in a few passages Strauss equated "ideas" with permanent problems,[93] and still more curious is a section on ideas in which Strauss admitted to not making full sense of them.

The doctrine of ideas which Socrates expounds to his interlocutors [in the *Republic*] is very hard to understand; to begin with, it is utterly incredible, not to say that it appears to be fantastic. Hitherto we have been given to understand that justice is fundamentally a certain character of the human soul or of the city, i.e., something which is not self-subsisting. Now we are asked to believe that it is self-subsisting, being at home as it were in an entirely different place from human beings and everything else participating in justice. No one has ever succeeded in giving a satisfactory or clear account of this doctrine of ideas. It is possible however to define rather precisely the central difficulty. "Idea" means primarily the look or shape of a thing; it means then a kind or class of things which are united by the fact that they all possess the same looks, the same character or power, or the same "nature"; therewith it means the class-character or the nature of the things belonging to the class in question: the idea of a thing is that which we seek when we try to find out the "What" or the "nature" of a thing or a class of things. . . . This does not explain however why the ideas are presented as "separated" from the things which are what they are by participating in an idea.[94]

This quotation comes from a discussion of a section in the *Republic* in which Socrates is discussing justice with Glaucon and Adeimantus. For Strauss the nature of the participants in a discussion is crucial to uncovering Socrates' real intention. In this case, Strauss noted that "those who have come to accept . . . theology are best prepared for accepting the doctrine of ideas."[95] In other words, in this section Socrates gave "ideas" a meaning that would satisfy his listeners and help make them better citizens by establishing the idea of justice. Although Strauss dismissed this understanding of idea as mythical or theological, he did not reject Platonic ideas in the two forms noted earlier. Thomas Pangle has supplied the best explanation of Strauss's beliefs: "Strauss does take the doctrine [of ideas] seriously insofar as it appears to provide a sound way of conceiving our experience of the nature of things."[96] Pangle argues that ideas can be understood as both class character and permanent problems since one can never comprehend the nature of something outside of its relation to the whole. The whole comes into full view only after comprehending all the parts—the whole being the totality of heterogeneous parts.[97]

Now we are in a position to put the parts of Strauss's Platonic philosophy together. It begins in wonder and doubt. Competing cosmologies point to a commonly experienced whole but present the cosmos through conflicting myths. The philosopher, refusing to accept hearsay or any authority, begins his own investigation with existing opinions about the parts of the whole. The conflict of opinions leads, at least when led by a philosopher, to a synthesis that partly purifies the opinions of their conventional or historical properties. But this ascent does not lead to complete knowledge, even of one or more of the parts, because the whole remains beyond the scope of human ken—if not theoretically, then practically. The philosopher can, however, discover the permanent problems and the range of answers available to humans. By understanding the problems as such the philosopher transcends the particular answer of his society even as he learns the basis or ground of this answer.

Philosophers annoy. Doubting and questioning the most obvious truths, they feel no attachment to the things valued by the regime. Strauss highlighted the strange or alien character of the philosopher and noted that Socrates appeared comic or perhaps mad to many of his fellow Athenians. But, of course, we have more than one Socrates—those presented by Aristophanes, Xenophon, and Plato. Strauss found only one. Although all the reports about Socrates are artful and in some cases idealized, the different images presented by Aristophanes, on the one hand, and Plato and Xenophon, on the other, merely expose the difference between the young and the mature Socrates. The differences, Strauss would have us believe, are more cosmetic or political than substantive. Accordingly, Strauss found the different accounts of the Socratic life very revealing of how the philosopher learned to become the political philosopher. Or, to put the subject in a different light, Plato presented the philosopher who learned from the poet.

Aristophanes presented a Socrates lacking in prudence *(phronesis),* knowledge of souls and hence the needs of those souls, and knowledge of political, moral, and conventional matters. Plato and Xenophon defended Socrates by describing the philosopher as having acquired all these things he lacked. Strauss left unclear the degree to which this transformation constituted a change in life as opposed to a superior esotericism. Because a philosopher concerns himself with the whole as understood through the totality of the parts, Socrates must have moved to a greater concern for, and awareness of, souls and their natures. Such an awareness necessarily implicates the political realm since the conventional city appears as a necessary and, in that sense, natural part of human perfection. By turning his attention from the physical to the human realm, Socrates necessarily complicated the search for nature. Nonetheless, to whatever degree Plato created a Socrates whose philosophical life had changed substantively because of his confrontation with the poet, Socrates most clearly learned to accommodate himself better to the city.[98] Socratic political philosophy emerges as both a politically astute presentation of philosophy and a philosophy of politics. Separating out the parts—there is the trick.

Strauss's classic work of political philosophy is *Natural Right and History*. With a grand scope Strauss traced the history of natural right from its classical origins to the modern (or postmodern) rejection of all claims to nature. For our purposes, the more focused analysis of Plato's *Republic* found in *City and Man* better exposes Strauss's understanding of the Socratic political philosophy. This book's three chapters concern, in order, Aristotle's *Politics*, Plato's *Republic*, and Thucydides' *Peloponnesian War*. Strauss arranged the subjects so that the more recent appears first and the more ancient last, with Plato occupying the central position. Strauss often, even in his histories, arranged his material in such a way as to upset chronology, but in this case his reason for doing so is unclear. Strauss's only obvious clue, if indeed it is a clue, is expressed thus: "The quest for that 'common sense' understanding of political things which led us first to Aristotle's *Politics*, leads us eventually to Thucydides' *War of the Peloponnesians and the Athenians*." Socrates, who occupies the center of this book, is here conspicuous by his absence. Aristotle and Thucydides had in common a desire to express as clearly as possible political life as it emerges in real political situations. But Aristotle was a philosopher—a follower, in some respect, of Plato—so his understanding of politics was much influenced by political philosophy. Thucydides, who lived prior to philosophy, described the political realm in its original or prephilosophical state. Strauss wrote: "For what is 'first for us' is not the philosophic understanding of the city but that understanding which is inherent in the city as such, in the pre-philosophical city, according to which the city sees itself as subject and subservient to the divine in the ordinary understanding of the divine or looks up to it. Only by beginning at this point will we be open to the full impact of the all-important question which is coeval with philosophy although the philosophers do not frequently pronounce it—the question *quid sit deus.*''[99] By going back to Thucydides the historian, we see more clearly the pre-philosophical world—or the world as it appears to commonsense. Moreover, Strauss emphasized that by returning to this nonabstracted vision we come into contact with the reason for philosophy—the search for God.

In the central chapter Strauss discussed political philosophy. The centrality of Platonic thought is evident on the first page of the first chapter where instead of Aristotle, Socrates is the subject. Toward the end of that early examination of Socrates, Strauss pointed out that ''not Socrates or Plato but Aristotle is truly the founder of political science: as one discipline, and by no means the most fundamental or the highest discipline, among a number of disciplines.'' Aristotle, Strauss emphasized, did not approach political questions from a philosophical perspective. ''Aristotle's cosmology, as distinguished from Plato's, is unqualifiedly separable from the quest for the best political order. Aristotelian philosophizing has no longer to the same degree and in the same way as Socratic philosophizing the character of ascent.''[100] Aristotle's political writings differ from Plato's in that the latter sought a more thoroughgoing investigation of political matters with an eye toward philosophy, i.e., toward philosophical matters. In this sense, then, Plato (or Socrates) founded political philosophy in its two meanings.

Strauss insisted that the context or setting of the *Republic* supplies the first, and in some sense decisive, clue as to its purpose. Most important in this respect is the fact that Socrates engaged in this conversation about justice unwillingly. Being forced to answer questions put him in a position similar to his defense before the city in the *Apology.* In both cases the circumstances—a forced public presentation of belief—required that Socrates express himself with great evasion and with numerous pregnant silences. Above all, Strauss insisted that Socrates often expressed himself ironically.[101] He spoke differently to different people, in each case attempting to move them in one or another salutary direction. In other words Socrates spoke justly insofar as justice means to give to each person what he needs. Thus Socrates considered it necessary to provide Glaucon with a view of justice that would induce him to believe that justice is worth pursuing without regard to the consequences. Soc-

rates helped make Glaucon a good citizen while making himself appear equally virtuous. Of course the definition or nature of justice
remains maddeningly elusive in this rather "poetic" presentation of
philosophy.

Because justice cannot be found in any existing city, Socrates created a just city in speech in order to understand better the nature of
justice. In the middle paragraph of the decisive section of this essay,[102] Strauss insisted that according to Socrates, "the just city is
. . . impossible." Throughout the essay Strauss emphasized the
need for Socrates to "abstract" from real life, ignoring the very important differences between men and women and the very important
human attachment to family. Only philosophers can ignore these
things because they live in constant attraction toward universals—
toward the whole. The just city presented in speech "holds no attraction for anyone except for such lovers of justice as are willing to
destroy the family as something essentially conventional and to exchange it for a society in which no one knows of parents, children,
and brothers and sisters. . . . the Republic conveys the broadest and
deepest analysis of political idealism ever made."[103]

In Strauss's interpretation, Socrates argued against a city ruled by
philosophers—that is, against the possibility of a city ruled by philosophers. Moreover, the idea of justice emerges from this study as a
rather ambiguous object. Socrates created the just city with a definition of justice that fit the life of the philosopher. Justice is every person minding his own business, i.e., doing that which he ought to do
according to his nature and talents. This definition of justice requires an understanding of different natures (the guiding task of philosophers) and an understanding of the hierarchy of natures in accordance with the good. The philosopher lives erotically toward the
good, subordinating all parts of his life to contemplation in an effort
to understand the good. In short, the philosopher naturally lives
justly, which we know because he orders the parts of his soul in
proper relationship and because he acts toward others in a way that
is best for them—including the use of noble lies for souls like
Glaucon. But the justice found in a philosopher's soul cannot be extended to a city without violating the nature of a city (with all its attachments to conventions).

Justice, though, necessarily remains a primary object or goal of the
city. All cities must order themselves around some higher principle

that allows them to form laws that govern the citizens. These laws run along the conventional understanding of justice. Consequently, Socrates identified a second meaning for justice—obedience to the laws. It goes without saying that, unlike the first definition, this second is not "natural" as it issues from the opinions that dominate the city. The philosopher has great interest in the justice of the city, an interest that springs from his concern for the good, or the good life. Philosophers represent the highest form of human life because they fulfill human nature. Thought or contemplation is the defining human characteristic, and since no person can live a contemplative life in the absence of political society,[104] the city is a necessary condition for the perfection of human nature. As a consequence, the philosopher must concern himself with the health of the city, which is coeval with the health of philosophy.

The reason for Strauss's great concern for political philosophy should by now be clear. Although all political regimes are conventional, they are the necessary condition for a natural life. Cities cannot promote the skeptical life and long survive; laws emerge out of authoritative opinion about good and evil, right and wrong, which in turn depends upon some myth about the nature of reality. In this sense, then, political questions are always moral and religious. If liberal democracy—at least in its twentieth-century manifestations—leads to doubt about once-sacred truths, or even worse to dogmatic assertions about the impossibility of metaphysical truths, and to a dissociated society in which individuals pursue their own brand of happiness without regard to a social myth, then society will slowly lose the means of protecting itself. By introducing political philosophy to such an environment, Strauss hoped to reinvigorate the search for knowledge of transhistorical truths in order to secure a political and moral center.

The political philosophy of Leo Strauss moved along two parallel tracks. First—and this is where his book *Natural Right and History* succeeded so brilliantly—he wanted to breathe new life into the quest for natural right (i.e., justice). It is unnecessary and undesirable to secure a final answer to this permanent problem. One hopes only to point to the goal as worthy and thereby engage social leaders in the healthy task of discovering the truth to which the problem points. A political and social leader must believe that justice (however understood in its particulars) is worth pursuing without regard to personal consequences. I do not mean that natural right is altogether nonsense to the philosopher. The philosopher understands the problem of natural right as secondary to his private pursuits, but nonetheless necessary. A philosopher of necessity must be a political philosopher.

Strauss aimed also at reviving the second part of that great tension of the West—religion. As indicated earlier, he focused his rehabilitative efforts at Judaism, and whether doing so meant that he found Christianity too weak a religion to serve the purpose is uncertain, but likely. In a more general way he recognized the need for a defensible religious faith because political societies depend, in the end, upon some metaphysical construction. Philosophers, as such, cannot provide for this need. Yet, lest this claim be read cynically, Strauss, I think, displayed a genuine respect for religious faith—or for the people who possess such faith. To him the natural or commonsense experience of the world is bound up in a religious/mythical expression of reality. To recapture the experiences of the cave Strauss had not only to attack the atheistic dogmatism as expressed in historicism and positivism but also to repair the damage done to the cause of faith in the interest of enlightenment.

Strauss deserves the label conservative. He lived a largely private life in search of the truths locked away in great books. That was his reaction to modernity. But he emerged in public on numerous occasions, especially with his most influential book, *Natural Right and History.* Strauss was forced to speak to his society because Heidegger could not. Strauss felt compelled to answer Heidegger's silence. To the degree that his work influenced politicians and their advisers to respect and seek to recover the founding generation's mixture of classical assumptions and religious beliefs, he was happy. It is not a simple matter of Strauss's having fooled some people—though there is a good bit of that—but rather that he had a deep concern that the United States, and the West more generally, return to the guiding principles and problems that gave them vitality.

7
The Mystic

Serious encounters with Strauss's work will always require a re-thinking of Platonic philosophy. One may, of course, reasonably argue that Strauss hid his "modern" philosophy behind a hedgerow of ancients. I do not think so. Nonetheless, his highly unorthodox reading of Plato, for instance (as the source of Western philosophical orthodoxy), has the effect of making Strauss an intriguing voice in a contemporary philosophical conversation in which almost all the participants have given up entirely upon ontology and the Platonic project as traditionally construed. Strauss's Plato (i.e., Strauss), in short, presents tantalizing possibilities for contemporary thinkers without requiring that they leave their most cherished assumptions behind. Despite the splenetics about historicism and relativism, there is much in Strauss's work to engage contemporary historicists. The same is not true in the case of Eric Voegelin.

Despite a devoted and growing coterie of followers ("Voegelin-ians"), Voegelin is all but unknown in philosophical circles, which is as it should be. He was an ontologist who wrote of history as a story told by God. He devoted his greatest energies to understanding consciousness, which has the individual person as an index but otherwise may not be understood as an "I." At the very least, Voegelin wrote about unfashionable subjects, and it is likely that he violated the most fundamental assumptions of the philosophical zeitgeist.

Yet he was hardly a philosophical hack. The unfashionable nature of his work does not spring from an antiquated philosophical analysis. Voegelin was not a throwback to some other century. His work emerged from the same problems and conditions that drive more fashionable philosophers—in this sense he was quite literally a postmodern. Voegelin's works were acts of resistance to the philosophical and spiritual poverty of his age—or he so understood his enterprise.[1] His inquiry, therefore, was heavily freighted with moral significance, and that is the aspect that attracts admirers. Voegelin's response to modern dilemmas neither rested upon traditional and unpersuasive answers nor bowed to contemporary antifoundationalism. For a hardy band of antimoderns who refuse to become postmodern, Voegelin is the philosopher of choice. For traditionalist conservatives, Voegelin's early work was easily appropriated into a political agenda that Voegelin never endorsed but likely supported. (As a philosopher he considered it inappropriate to endorse any political agenda.)

Admirers usually try to persuade outsiders that Voegelin's philosophy follows lines established by more famous predecessors. Most such treatments identify very valuable affinities and influences, and in some important ways Voegelin's analysis does share much with the insights of Martin Heidegger, Edmund Husserl, Paul Ricoeur, Bernard Lonegan, Thomas Mann, Fyodor Dostoyevsky, and many others. The startlingly unpopular nature of his assumptions and arguments, nonetheless, identifies what is much more historically significant. The foundation of Voegelin's philosophy is the claim that the world is intelligible—not transparent to its structure and meaning, but intelligible.[2] Bound up in this claim are objectives long since abandoned by most twentieth-century philosophers. For most postmodern thinkers Voegelin's preoccupation with being is, at best, a quaint and harmless activity or, at worst, a dangerous psychological disorder. It is ironic that for many contemporary philosophers the sorts of claims Voegelin made lead to the very disorder against which Voegelin rebelled. After all, at a quick glance, Voegelin appears to be looking for *the* answer. One wonders how much the prejudice against ontology, philosophical anthropology, and epistemology blinds some people to Voegelin's claims. For now it is important only that one understands that Voegelin was out of step with the most powerful and persuasive strains of twentieth-century philosophical inquiry, the rich web of influence notwithstanding.

THE DISCOVERY OF CONSCIOUSNESS

Voegelin's concerns were social and political, but his philosophical investigation began and ended with the individual soul. One cannot engineer social transformations at the level of ideas or doctrines, Voegelin insisted. Change requires that individuals break through the accumulation of cherished beliefs to the most basic primordial experiences accessible to humans as such (what Voegelin called the primary experience of existence). In his *New Science of Politics*, Voegelin first emphasized the need to break through the nominalistic understanding that political science is composed of facts (things) and values (nonthings). A truly empirical science of politics necessitates an understanding and explication of the symbols of self-interpretation that form the foundation of social and political order. As his focus became more cosmic, Voegelin found the aperture to the great mysteries in consciousness, which in turn has as its portal the individual human existing in bodily form in the context of a specific time and place. The mysteries of humans, society, history, and God rest in the depths of the individual soul. How did so much get in that small bottle? The individual human is a limiting factor, a bottleneck through which the infinite must pass. For all the limitations such a spatiotemporal being suffers, the mysteries of existence nonetheless press in on the soul, and the meaningful truths that one seeks in response to the disordered world rest in the depths of consciousness. The soul, as the location of human participation in consciousness, serves as the omnipresent source of resistance to the modern world. Order and disorder are nothing more than attunement to, or alienation from, the truths apperceived in the soul. Social and political disorder are products of individual alienation; a society is disordered only if its citizens are disordered.

The journey home, therefore, must take place in the individual consciousness of the philosopher.[3] Through his historical analysis, Voegelin sought to recapture the experience that created the symbols of order that, for him, constituted history. Plato's experiences could make sense only if his symbols engendered a "responsive experience" in Voegelin.[4] Consequently, despite the historicity of human thought, Voegelin's analysis depended upon an ahistorical "reality" that allowed communication across huge cultural divides. The confusions are numerous. Voegelin often wrote of a consciousness as if it were a thing, and yet he warned his readers against falling into this trap. Moreover, how should one understand Voegelin's construction of a history of order that rests on an unchanging reality?

Voegelin often wrote of "tensions," which probably, on occasion, served as an escape from troublesome contradictions. Nonetheless, at the very heart of Voegelin's enterprise is an experience of mystery, which challenges one to accept contradictions as inherent in experience. One better understands experience by symbolizing the tension than by seeking a resolution. Indeed, Voegelin identified the desire to escape the tension as the source of modern deformations of reality (which necessarily implies a deformation of the language describing reality).

Voegelin's talk about consciousness reveals an inherent limitation in his language. He sought to dissolve all modern reifications and to confront process, tension, and rich but inherently ambiguous metaphors or myths. Yet no one reified more than Voegelin. The reason is simple but unsatisfying. Because he dissolved the objects of modern understanding into a rich and complex series of processes or tensional fields, Voegelin tended to discuss process as if "it" were something with a will. Although Voegelin would insist that consciousness is not an it—i.e., a thing—he could write about consciousness becoming luminous to itself. Since there is no-thing there, this construct leaves one, at best, with a mystery.[5]

In many respects the mystery of human existence is precisely the "object" Voegelin sought to recapture. The articulation of the mystery and its meaning requires an exegesis of experience, and in one form or another, all of Voegelin's major works were exegetical exercises. The most concrete things at his disposal were the language symbols of thinkers like Plato, which operate like windows to the experiences that created the stories or myths or analyses. That wording is important because for Voegelin, the great mythical stories and philosophical analyses emerged from experiences. Plato, for instance, did not have a self-contained experience but participated in an experience, and the dynamics of that experience produced a story or a novel philosophical distinction. Plato contributed to the experience—first of all by his openness to the whole—and symbolized his participation, and the truths that the experience illuminated, in his writings. I do not mean that Plato might have selected from a variety of symbols to express the truths of the experience. On the contrary, the experience was only had by Plato as he symbolized it, or, to fall back on the more precise but confusing Voegelinian terminology, symbols make the experience luminous to itself. That is what

Voegelin meant when he emphasized the ontological status of language as belonging to the experience.[6]

Symbols can only be transparent to the people who have experienced the same truth,[7] which does not mean that understanding precedes the reading of the great myths and philosophers. Rather, Voegelin could interpret these symbols of numinous experience only after working and puzzling over their meanings with a spirit of openness. While meditating on the spiritual struggles of Moses or Plato, the stories became incantations that helped Voegelin re-vision the experience. Voegelin worked exhaustively to understand the context for the story in order to uncover the universal experience resting beneath the historically conditioned veneer.

This makes Voegelin a mystical realist, but such labels tend to confuse the issue, if for no other reason than the fact that Voegelin used familiar philosophical terms in unfamiliar ways. Even Voegelin's exploration of being becomes something other than an ontology,[8] so one must begin an exegesis of Voegelin's work by taking his claims about modern "hypostatizations" seriously. What happens if one dissolves all of the reifications Voegelin attributed to modern myopia? Reading Voegelin remains a chore.

One has always to remind oneself that the spatial and temporal symbols Voegelin employed so often and with such care are never descriptive but exegetical. And so there one is, surrounded by reality, being, consciousness, and numerous other "things" that are not really things. Voegelin might retort that no better symbols have emerged from human experience and that, moreover, to the sufficiently supple mind the ambiguity inherent in such a language expresses the ambiguity of the articulated experience. There is a sense that for Voegelin, a fully satisfying expression of these experiences is unacceptable. The unquestionable truth of human experiences of reality is that they must remain dim images, as though looking in a glass darkly. To have penetrated that darkness is to have transcended the human condition. For this reason Voegelin targeted the "systems" of modernity (e.g., those of Hegel and Marx) as products of libidinous hearts. These systems help the authors hide the mysterious elements of reality in order to create (the hope of) a world without alienation. Still, the Voegelin reader remains mired in a confusing babble of linguistic indices, most borrowed from ancient Greece, looking for conceptual terra firma. It is best to start with the experiences of the single person (qua person). Yet even here one starts in the middle since the person turns out to be an index of reality. But then Voegelin argued that all human stories begin in the middle.[9]

As humans, "we are thrown into and out of existence without knowing the Why or the How, but while in it we know that we are of the being to which we return."[10] To be thrown into reality is to find oneself in the middle, confused but with some clues as to the meaning of one's existence. Those clues do not come to one as objects that might surrender their secrets to an inquiring physicist; rather, one comes to some understanding from inside the process. One participates in the very process under investigation. The "object" one seeks to understand includes one's self in relation to the rest of reality—the whole is hidden from view but understood as a necessary condition for one's search for personal meaning. The primordial character of the experience of participation binds one together with the other partners so forcibly that the "consubstantiality of the partners will [initially] override the separateness of substances."[11]

Nonetheless, the totality one apprehends displays structural elements that expose the partners as resting in hierarchical order. The experiences of life and death, of coming to be and expiring, of a fertile world, of the durability of the heavens, of the rise and fall of societies (at least in collective memory), and of the nothingness that collects all objects in the fullness of time display a hierarchy of being ranked according to duration. According to Voegelin, the partners in this community emerge as God and man, world and society. The individual participates in all four areas of being and through this participation comes to recognize a hierarchy descending from God to world to society to the fleeting individual. The discovery of these structures creates a struggle to find one's place in being, and this struggle for attunement finds expression through symbols of reality that help one—or a society—to find a place. Symbols of order maintain their legitimacy so long as conditions do not challenge them. But disorder befalls all societies. When experienced at the personal level, the disorder of an age spurs a search for new and more adequate symbols. But no matter how these symbols change, they must account for the basic structure found in experience. "Every society," Voegelin emphasized, "is burdened with the task, under its concrete conditions, of creating an order that will endow the fact of its existence of meaning in terms of ends divine and human."[12]

The search for more adequate symbols must not falsify the primary experience of being, argued Voegelin. People who kill off God as a partner in being merely transfer divinity from the "beyond" to the immanent. As new gods themselves, these ideologues will stop at nothing to re-create reality in their image. More satisfying symbols of order account for all the partners, but these new symbols provide a keener insight into experience, exposing hitherto unrecognized distinctions. Voegelin's philosophy of consciousness begins here, with the struggle to articulate a sufficiently differentiated structure of experience that does not violate the primary experience of the cosmos. Voegelin lived in a postcosmological age as philosophers and prophets had irreparably damaged the older cosmologies.[13] Moderns, however, had been unable to maintain the tension of existence and had thereby lost sight of the primary experience of reality. Thus Voegelin's task was to recover the differentiated insights of Plato and Aristotle, Moses and Jesus, and to translate them to a world whose understandings have been shaped by modern physics. He sought, not simply to recapture, but to recast these understandings in a way compatible with his perspective in being, which obviously differed from Plato's.

An overview of Voegelin's history of order is given in Chapter 4, but a brief description, with a slightly altered emphasis, is necessary here to clarify the issues. Cosmological symbols dealt with the problem of how existence proceeds from nonexistence. The gods, who inhabit the cosmos with humans, serve as the divine, but they do not resolve the matter of the ground or origin of the cosmos. The tension between existence and nonexistence is "absorbed into the wholeness of the intermediate reality that we call cosmic."[14] This tightly ordered cosmos, in which the parts interpenetrate, works according to a rather tenuous economy. That is, the in-betweenness of the cosmological order requires constant renewal. Life comes with numerous disasters that threaten to unbalance the system. Thus, in a society ordered in accordance with cosmological truth—in which the society understands itself to be an analogue of the cosmos—constant efforts at renewal (ritual or propitiatory) help maintain the delicate economy of being.

Societies so ordered (which Voegelin learned, to his surprise, created histories extending from divine origins to their present) face severe challenges in times of empire building. Multi-ethnic orders no longer reflect the order of the cosmos; political and spiritual order dissociate. During the age of empires (the ecumenic age), Voegelin argued, the great philosophical and prophetic achievements emerged out of resistance to the disorder experienced as a result of the spiritual dislocation attending conquest. For the Israelites, the articulation of the Moses "I AM" experience discerned a God beyond the cosmos (thereby differentiating the more compact experience of the cosmos). The myth of Genesis that followed symbolized the fundamental question of "beginnings"[15] even as it created history as a form of Jewish self-interpretation. The Jews were the people of *the* God whose will directs the course of human events. They had broken free of the closed cosmos and provided sturdy symbols for the "beginning" *(creatio ex nihilo)* and for the "beyond" (Yahweh). Human life would, thereby, take on meaning as part of an eschatologically oriented course rather than as part of a more static (or cyclical) cosmos. Attunement to reality now requires an orientation to the divine beyond the cosmos, which is its source and sustainer.

The discoveries (as Voegelin understood them) that constitute Hellenistic philosophy as well as Christianity further weakened the hold of the cosmological form of truth. "Consciousness" is the shorthand expression for these discoveries, and the rest of this section is devoted to this complicated subject, but it is important here to note that the discovery of consciousness placed the burden of truth on the individual who, by virtue of one's soul, participates directly in the four-part community of being. To the degree that the symbols created by the experiences of Plato, Aristotle, Jesus, and Paul create a social field of meaning, the burden of attunement rests with the soul of each person. The social implications are dramatic. Instead of the political and social order functioning as an analogue to the cosmic order, the locus of order rests with the individual who must attune his life to the order detected in his soul. Consequently, the social order becomes a reflection of the order attained by the individual. Society is "man written large" rather than the cosmos written small. The burden of this new, personal responsibility helped create numerous evasions from the immediacy of consciousness, so Voegelin looked back to the sources of differentiation—to Plato and Paul—to begin anew the meditation moderns had rejected.

Consciousness is the modern equivalent of the classical symbol "human nature." Voegelin preferred the modern term because the older phrase, with the language of a static "nature," had become encrusted with too many meanings, technical and otherwise. Consciousness, while usually employed as a reified object, is less susceptible to the subject-object fallacy. Still, as Glenn Hughes noted in his excellent monograph, *Mystery and Myth in the Philosophy of Eric Voegelin*, Voegelin appropriated the word but not the meanings normally associated with it. Hughes persuasively argues that in the contemporary philosophical context, Voegelin's use of consciousness most nearly parallels Heidegger's *Dasein* as the place in being where being becomes aware of itself (a process Voegelin called "luminosity").[16]

The apparent origins of Voegelin's serious investigation of consciousness date back to his reading of Husserl's *Krisis* in the early 1940s (English title, *The Crisis of European Sciences and Transcendental Phenomenology: An Introduction to Phenomenological Philosophy*).[17] He saw dangers in the Husserl of the *Krisis:* the exclusion of the historicity of consciousness from Husserl's investigation and the restriction of consciousness to its intentionality.[18] In a broader sense Voegelin argued against all the stream-of-consciousness theories, including Husserl's effort to make the ego into an agent that structures the stream into an intelligible unit. Moreover, Voegelin sought a way around the hopelessly confused idealist/materialist dichotomy. He began his work on consciousness in 1943 in some correspondence with Alfred Schuetz concerning Husserl's theory and printed the letters in *Anamnesis.*

In the key letter of this correspondence, bearing the title "On the Theory of Consciousness," the broad themes of Voegelin's understanding emerge, if in rather elliptical form (it was, after all, a personal letter). First, to understand consciousness as a stream is to mistake a process in consciousness for its character. The mistake issues from the misguided focus on the senses. Voegelin noted that "the limit experience of 'flowing' as demonstrated through the model of the perception of a tone is possible only in a specific act of turning attention to that limit. It is not consciousness of time that is constituted by the flow but rather the experience of the flow is constituted by consciousness, which itself is not flowing." Not only does consciousness not flow, it constitutes "the spaceless and timeless world of meaning, sense, and the soul's order," and the association of consciousness with flow requires a severe delimiting of experience, including sensual perceptions. The problem springs from the attempt to place a physiological limit on consciousness. Voegelin no doubt considered this construction of consciousness to be part of the larger process of restricting knowledge to the facts that emerge from the objectivizing sciences. At any rate, Voegelin insisted that "in experience, consciousness with its structures, whatever they may be, is an antecedent given."[19]

It follows, then, that consciousness does not take the form of "I"; indeed, the I is not a "given at all but rather a highly complex symbol for certain perspectives in consciousness."[20] The disappearing I formed an important part of Voegelin's understanding of consciousness from an early date. However he might have understood this issue, his constructions put one in mind of the German idealist tradition. Voegelin's work draws mightily from important idealists, including his great philosophical bogey, Hegel,[21] but nonetheless, Voegelin insisted that consciousness is always human consciousness, situated in an individual who lives in the physical world, bound by time and space. Voegelin could not make sense of a disembodied consciousness, much less something like a collective consciousness. Not only does one come away from these assertions asking the question, What is consciousness? but one must wonder about the meanings Voegelin invested in such key words as "society," "mankind," and "history."

To return to the initial problem, Voegelin recognized that consciousness has a "paradoxical structure," and his clearest articulation of this structure is in his last book, *In Search of Order.*

On the one hand, we speak of consciousness as something located in human beings in their bodily existence. In relation to this concretely embodied consciousness, reality assumes the position of an object intended. Moreover, by its position as an object intended by a consciousness that is bodily located, reality itself acquires a metaphorical touch of external thingness. We use this metaphor in such phrases as "being conscious of something," "remembering or imagining something," "thinking about something." I shall, therefore, call this structure of consciousness its intentionality, and the corresponding structure of reality its thingness. On the other hand, we know the bodily located consciousness to be also real; and this concretely located consciousness does not belong to another genus of reality, but is part of the same reality that has moved, in its relation to man's consciousness, into the position of a thing-reality. In this second sense, then, reality is not an object of consciousness but the something in which consciousness occurs as an event of participation between partners in the community of being.

In the complex of experience, presently in process of articulation, reality moves from the position of an intended object to that of a subject, while the consciousness of the human subject intending objects moves to the position of a predicative event in the subject "reality" as it becomes luminous for its truth. Consciousness, thus, has the structural aspect not only of intentionality but also of luminosity. Moreover, when consciousness is experienced as an event of participatory illumination in the reality that comprehends the partners to the event, it has to be located, not in one of the partners, but in the comprehending reality; consciousness has a structural dimension by which it belongs, not to man in his bodily existence, but to the reality in which man, the other partners to the community of being, and the participatory relations among them occur. If the spatial metaphor be still permitted, the luminosity of consciousness is located somewhere "between" human consciousness in bodily existence and reality intended in its mode of thingness.[22]

The two structural dimensions of consciousness must retain their proper relationship in one's thinking to prevent "deformations" common in the modern era. Voegelin thought that he escaped the limited horizon created by Husserl by differentiating the intentionalist function of consciousness—with its discrete objects apprehended by a subject—and the participatory quality of consciousness as an event in a comprehensive reality. By limiting consciousness to its intentionality, Husserl and others reified it. Once one becomes conscious of the participatory nature of existence, consciousness becomes "consciousness-reality," a complex that more accurately locates consciousness in a whole. As a complex, consciousness-reality may be understood, not as a relationship (which suggests a sense of separateness), but as a participation (event) that constitutes consciousness as it appears to the individual human. Humans learn about the story in which they discover themselves only from the perspective of participants. They seek to understand the story and their part in it.

The exploration of the world of things (what Voegelin called "thing-reality") in the form of intentionality produces a conceptual language appropriate to the experience of a subject apprehending objects—it names and groups things. But when one discovers that one's consciousness and its intentional acts participate in a comprehensive reality (which Voegelin called "it-reality"), the language of things no longer suffices. The matter is further confused because one cannot identify one's self as the subject of knowledge received. The subject, in this case, is the reality. Yet, this construction might lead to another reification—reality. Because there is no object or subject of knowledge, Voegelin talked of "luminosity," of the structure of consciousness-reality becoming luminous to "itself." The luminosity of consciousness creates a symbolic expression belonging, ontologically, to the experience. Because symbols relating the event of consciousness becoming luminous to itself have no object to which they refer, they must be understood as exegetical rather than descriptive in nature. The reality illumined includes the historical/cultural context in which the event takes place—at the immanent pole of the experience. Consequently, the symbols that emerge from the event are forged by the constituent parts of the complex, including humans drawing on their historical store of symbols and meanings. If consciousness-reality produces symbols articulating the luminous experience, those symbols reflect the historical conditions of their time but also share in the timelessness of the reality in which consciousness participates.

One wonders how satisfying this construction is for most people. By employing "luminosity" Voegelin meant to express a form of cognition different from that concerning the physical world. There is no object of cognition in the usual sense of the word, making propositional language useless—or worse. The luminous discovery identifies a part of reality in which "the knower and the known move into the position of tensional poles in a consciousness that we call luminous as far as it engenders the symbols which express the experience of its own structure" (the emphasis should rest on the phrase "its own structure"). The point, so difficult to make, is that there is not only no object of knowledge but also no subject. At times the claims become even more mystical, such as the claim that one must have "faith" that "man participates representatively in the divine drama of truth becoming luminous." Luminous to whom? To Voegelin this is an illegitimate question because it demonstrates the desire to have possessive knowledge in the form of propositions about physical reality.[23]

If consciousness possesses this two-part structure (remember that it is a structure of an event or an experience), how does one come to recognize this structure, or why is the structure not recognized readily by everyone? According to Voegelin, Plato described the process of examining one's consciousness as *Anamnesis*—remembering. In the German edition of *Anamnesis*, Voegelin wrote:

> Remembering is the activity of consciousness by which what has been forgotten, i.e., the knowledge latent within consciousness, is raised up out of unconsciousness into a specific presence of consciousness. In the *Enneads* (IV 3 30), Plotinus described this activity as the transition from non-articulated to articulate, self-perceiving thought. The non-articulated knowledge *(noema)* becomes conscious knowledge by an act of perceptive attending *(antilepsis)*; and this antileptic knowledge is fixed again by language *(logos)*. Remembering, then, is the process in which non-articulated *(ameres)* knowledge is elevated into the realm of linguistic picturability *(Bildlichkeit) (to phantastikon)* and through expression, in the pregnant sense of taking external shape *(eis to exo)*, attains to linguistically articulated presence of consciousness.[24]

To this process of remembering Voegelin attached the label "reflective distance." Consciousness is capable of looking back on itself, as if the act of reflection were separate from the "object" of its investigation. One comes to recognize the paradox of intentionality and luminosity, and thereby produces symbols expressing this paradoxical nature. Through meditation, one (though I do not think this means just anyone) re-visions experiences heretofore latent and therefore mute. The very language of "reflective distance" suggests that the event (and Voegelin never suggests that it is anything other than an event) includes no new experience but an analysis of a "past experience." This construction suffers from several problems, however, and it is truer to Voegelin's meaning, I think, to emphasize that meditation calls up experiences that have a "pastness" to them but that in their recall have an immediacy and are transformed by a differentiating vision. The "vision" does not eliminate the primary experience but exposes a structure bound in the more compact symbolism.

Voegelin's emphasis, in his later works, on "vision" (borrowed from Plato's *opsis*) stresses the experiential nature of reflective distance. Through meditation one gains reflective distance from consciousness (though the process takes place in consciousness). This distance not only differentiates intentionality from luminosity but reawakens experiences of luminosity that may, in the clearer light of reflective distance, be expressed with more adequate symbols. In other words, one always participates in reality in its mode of luminosity. Humans participate in the larger story of being, but this participation may not be clear to the human whose experiences they are. To apperceive reality means little more than to examine the experiences of participation that had heretofore relinquished none of their meanings. The re-experiencing, however, amounts to a new experience—a vision that exposes embedded structures and meanings.

Still, Voegelin could not escape the tension between reflective distance as an act of cognition of the sort associated with rationalists like Descartes and a theophanic experience in which one participates in an event not entirely of one's own making. Voegelin understood reflective distance to refer to the philosophical inquiry in which experienced unrest sends one back to the symbols of order readily at hand (for Plato, a species of cosmological symbols) in order to penetrate to their experiences as a means of supplying more adequate or precise symbols. "While the original symbols," wrote Voegelin, referring to nonreflective symbols that emerge out of luminous consciousness, "contain a rational structure that can be further articulated through reflection, the reflective acts of cognition can be true only if they participate in the divine reality that participated in the emergence of the symbols. . . . Reflection is not an external act of cognition directed toward the process as its object, but part of a process that internally has cognitive structure."[25] Here, as in so many other places, Voegelin used the language of process to subvert the tendency to reify. Reflective distance participates in the process it seeks to explicate, and the symbols that emerge from that process expose a noetic structure to the experience, but those symbols cannot be understood to apply to objects. In this way Voegelin undermined the now-accepted way of discussing Plato's philosophy as a set of beliefs or ideas (propositions about reality). Of course, one may choose to accept or reject another person's "ideas," but how can one reject someone's symbolic expression of an experience?

Is it really "someone's" symbolic expression? Earlier in this chapter I touched upon Voegelin's claim that the language expressing an experience belongs to the experience "itself." Although the mystery of the linguistic eruption makes some sense in terms of the cosmological symbols that emerge from luminosity, does it make sense to claim the same concerning reflection directed toward a noetically structured event? In other words, is not it safe to assume that philosophers choose their own words to express the results of their inquiries? No. Plato, in the *Timaeus* and *Republic*, employed vision *(opsis)* to express "the experiential process in which the order of reality is seen, becomes reflectively known, and finds *its* appropriate language symbols" (emphasis added). Again, Voegelin has reality (not a thing) engendering symbols out of a participatory experience. He emphasized that "Plato [was] careful about precluding subjectivist misunderstandings. The 'vision' is not somebody's fancy but the imaginative power of response to the reality seen; and the reality seen is the cause *(aition)* of this power *(dynamis)*."[26] The vision is a revelation, but it is also an "imaginative response," and surely imagination belongs to the person responding rather than to the event. Voegelin wrote:

> Imagination, as a structure in the process of a reality that moves toward its truth, belongs both to human consciousness in its bodily location and to the reality that comprehends bodily located man as a partner in a community of being. There is no truth symbolized without man's imaginative power to find the symbols that will express his response to the appeal of reality: but there is not truth to be symbolized without the comprehending It-reality in which such structures as man with his participatory consciousness, experiences of appeal and response, language, and imagination occur. Through the imaginative power of man the It-reality moves imaginatively toward its truth.[27]

The emphasis necessarily falls upon the human in his capacity to respond. If not, how could philosophers deform reality (a la modernity)? Voegelin strained to emphasize that the vision—at least as Plato used it—emerged out of human participation with the comprehensive reality, and the imaginative response takes place during the remembrance Voegelin called reflective distance. As a response, imagination is a partner in the process it seeks to illuminate. The human, in his imaginative capacity, is creative,[28] and because humans are creative participants in this process, they have the power to pervert the experience by stressing their creative roles *(libido dominandi)*. "Imaginative remembrance of the process," Voegelin emphasized, "implies the potential of imaginative oblivion,"[29] by which he meant the capacity to ignore the comprehensive reality— or rather, the divine ground of that reality—and create a system that replaced the tensions experienced in the *metaxy*.[30] By limiting the horizon of reality, these ideologues can more easily gain knowledge (they have removed from their system the unknown god of Plato and the mysterious "I AM" of Moses), and with (apodictic) knowledge comes power and control. Thus, all systems that either eliminate God (Marx) or claim to know him (Hegel) are cases of imaginative oblivion.

The three dimensions of consciousness (intentionality, luminosity, and reflective distance) help explain Voegelin's understanding of the relationship between disorder and philosophy. So long as the symbols forged out of the experience of luminosity retain a basic believability, one feels no compulsion to explore the subject. When, however, the social and political conditions fracture the symbols of order (which emerge as products of a particular historical condition), the individual begins to feel the disorder in his soul. Once the existential need emerges, a particularly sensitive soul begins the exploration of his own experiences of reality in search of a more adequate understanding.[31] Why this person and not another? Why Voegelin and not Karl Jaspers? Voegelin emphasized that all examples of reflective distance have the character of a theophany. In short, the mysterious reason for the timing and place and person of new and more adequate symbols of order is lodged in God.

I will later explore Voegelin's argument that history is nothing but the story of consciousness as it emerges from confrontation with disorder in the form of symbols produced by a divine-human encounter, but here I want to note that Voegelin implicitly gave to his work, especially late in his life, the status of theophany. He lived in a disordered world where the transcendent no longer operated as an ordering presence. Voegelin's historical exploration of order—that for which he is most known—was most of all his own search for order. The title of his five-volume opus, *Order and History*, therefore takes on a new meaning. The search for order creates history, but the examination of history (so defined) becomes a mode of the search itself. Voegelin surely understood his project in this light, and as early as 1956 he wrote: "If today the state of science permits the critical analysis of such phenomena, it is clearly a scholar's duty to undertake it for his own sake as a man and to make the results accessible to his fellow man. *Order and History* should be read, not as an attempt to explore curiosities of a dead past, but as an inquiry into the structure of the order in which we live presently." In other words, Voegelin wrote his books as part of his philosophical and personal search for order—the results of which he offered to a disordered world. Moreover, he connected his work of philosophy (in both purpose and nature) with Plato, who understood philosophy to be the "love of divine Being." Voegelin wrote that the

> diagnostic and therapeutic functions are inseparable in philosophy as a form of existence. And ever since Plato, in the disorder of his time, discovered the connection, philosophical inquiry has been one of the means of establishing islands of order in the disorder of the age. *Order and History* is a philosophical inquiry concerning the order of human existence in society and history. Perhaps it will have its remedial effect—in the modest measure that, in the passionate course of events, is allowed to philosophy.[32]

Voegelin identified himself so closely with Plato because the ancient Greek discovered philosophy and Voegelin rediscovered it.[33] Plato served as the primary guide to the primordial philosophical awareness that centuries of doctrinalization had obscured. Only late in his life did Voegelin believe he had liberated himself sufficiently from modernity to continue the philosophical journey (the work of reflective distance) begun by Plato.

In sharp contrast to the direction of Strauss's work, Voegelin found a prophetic impulse in Plato and all legitimate philosophers. Although philosophers stress the structure of the human response in the complex consciousness-reality, prophets stress the source of the experience rather than its structure. Nonetheless, Voegelin made prophets out of philosophers. A prophet who too closely resembles his age, or whose words echo the reigning orthodoxy, is no prophet. A prophet must speak to people's needs, not their wants. He brings an unpopular message of return (or repentance) and a warning about the perils of apostasy. The truth of his message becomes clear only with the fulfillment of his predictions. Is obscurity a form of testimony?

THE STRUCTURE OF CONSCIOUSNESS

Reflective distance differentiates the structure of the luminous dimension of consciousness—of consciousness-reality. Of course the word "structure" tends to obscure Voegelin's emphasis upon the tensions, movements, and events that constitute this structure, as the analysis is again plagued by the propensity of the terms of analysis to ossify into things. Reification, however, has become a pandemic in the modern era. For this reason Voegelin returned to the philosophical journey as expressed in its original simplicity. Philosophy began with Plato and Aristotle. Because Voegelin thought it necessary to recover the existential origins of philosophy, his own analysis rests upon the language originated by his Greek predecessors.

Much of Voegelin's examination of ancient Greek philosophy focused upon recovering the experiences obscured by modern reifications. When moderns speak of Plato's beliefs, ideas, or even ideology the vision is destroyed. The historian, then, must strip away the modern conceptual apparatus in order to rediscover the experiences that rest beneath the increasingly transparent Platonic symbols. The objective that dominated Voegelin's enterprise bears a striking resemblance to Strauss's quest for the "natural cave." For both philosophers Plato stands at the beginning of a process "derailed" by modernity (to employ another reification). The philosophical journey may begin again only by returning to its origin. Consequently, Voegelin explored his philosophical themes with the terms of analysis that emerged from his historical investigation.

Plato, Voegelin's primary guide, began his philosophy in the experience of call-response. The emphasis may fall upon the mysterious, divine drawing—as with Moses or Paul—or upon the questioning, seeking unrest—as with Plato or Aristotle. Either way, the experience requires both parts to form an intelligible unit. From the human perspective the questioning arises from the recognition of the contingency of one's existence and the further observation that all existing things eventually cease to exist. The precariousness of all being things raises the question of the ultimate ground—"the question is inherent in the experience from which it arises."[34] Plato and Aristotle, however, discovered that this restlessness of known ignorance was the defining human characteristic. The Question (capitalized), as Voegelin called it, is a constant in history.[35] Of course, this questioning was part of prephilosophical experiences, but not previously discovered as definitively human—as a defining characteristic. Moreover, the philosopher is sensitive to this structure in his consciousness. For him, "the questioning is experienced with an index of urgency. It is not a game to be played or not. The philosopher feels himself moved (kinein) by some unknown force to ask the question, he feels himself drawn (helkein) into the search." The Question becomes an overwhelming concern, and the pull of the golden cord of reason, borrowing from more Platonic imagery, is identified as the source of restlessness. Therefore, one's ignorance is structured by an object of one's desire. As Voegelin put the matter in reference to Aristotle's analysis: "The search . . . is not blind; the questioning is knowing and the knowing is questioning. The desire to know what one knows to desire injects internal order into the search, for the questioning is directed toward an object of knowledge (neoton) that is recognizable as the object desired (orekton) once it is found."[36]

The centrality of the symbol "eros" for Plato becomes evident. Since Eros, as the myth goes, was the offspring of Plenty and Poverty, he partook of both natures but belonged to neither. His life was spent in tension toward the fullness detected in his soul, and the tension expressed in the myth applied to the human whose mortality was structured by an awareness of immortality in which he had a part. Voegelin preferred the Platonic word metaxy, meaning in-between, as the preferred symbol of the peculiar human condition. Humans participate in both immanent reality and transcendent reality (or, rather, reality in both modes). Of course the tension is structured by the attraction toward the divine, transcendent pole. Human life is invested with an eschatological index. The tension in the *metaxy* may be so great that some people seek to give up the transcendent in favor of a transformed world; others might choose to believe they are about to escape their mortal bonds.

Voegelin exaggerated the significance of the term *metaxy* in Platonic thought, as the term appears in only two dialogues: *Symposium* and *Philebus*. He might have maintained the tensional character by emphasizing the erotic search but with the added benefit of pushing back the spatial imagery. No matter how often Voegelin warned the reader not to make the in-between *(metaxy)* into a place, or to reify the "poles" of this tension, the language rather defeats the purpose. In the end, how is one to think of poles in a tensional field except as things?

Voegelin also emphasized the Aristotelian construction of human as the *zoon noun echon*—the living being that possesses nous. Humans participate in all the strata of being, including the divine nous and the "Apeiron depth," or the nothingness over which existence hangs. These strata provide the boundaries of human participation and the means of ordering their individual and social lives. By participating in the divine nous one recognizes and participates in the hierarchy of being, and it is by means of this hierarchy that one may order or attune one's life in harmony with being.[37]

At any rate, the philosopher discovers the restless search for the ground of existence as the quintessentially human activity. Plato and Aristotle "locate" this search in the psyche, which is a metaphor for the location or area where the questioning takes place and as the instrument (sensorium) of human reception of the divine attraction.[38] Voegelin described the experience in this manner:

> The man who asks questions, and the divine ground about which the questions are asked, will merge in the experience of questioning as a divine-human encounter and reemerge as the participants in the encounter that has the luminosity and structure of consciousness. . . . The ground is not a spatially distant thing but a divine presence that becomes manifest in the experience of unrest and the desire to know. The wondering and questioning is sensed as the beginning of a theophanic event that can become fully luminous to itself if it finds the proper responses

in the psyche of concrete human beings. . . . Hence, philosophy in the classic sense is not a body of "ideas" or "opinions" about the divine ground dispensed by a person who calls himself a "philosopher," but a man's responsive pursuit of his questioning unrest to the divine source that has aroused it.[39]

The structure of the experience, as Voegelin understood it, requires both partners. There is no experience of seeking without the divine pull. They form an intelligible unit. Moreover, the "vision" or experience is invested with a noetic structure,[40] so the structure, therefore, presents itself for noetic analysis by the being possessing nous. "By nous," wrote Voegelin, Aristotle "understands both the human capacity for questioning about the ground and also the ground of being itself, which is experienced as the directing mover of questions."[41] Glenn Hughes emphasizes, with relation to this and similar claims, that Voegelin accepted the ontological claims made for nous by Aristotle and Plato, writing that "the tension of consciousness is not drawn toward the ground as a mere object of possible, or hoped for, knowledge. The ground is consciousness' *own identity*; human consciousness *participates* in the ground; the ground is a Thinking or Intelligence that is the fullness of human thinking and intelligence."[42]

Human nous participates in divine nous—or more precisely, the human feels the attraction to the divine as the fulfillment of one's nature. This mutual participation forms consciousness, which may be understood as belonging to the ground but which reaches the human soul. In this latter sense, one may speak of "human consciousness," which is shaped by the limitations of perspective associated with an embodied being structured by time, space, and cultural memory. Because consciousness is an event of participation, Voegelin could emphasize that there is no consciousness outside the "concrete person." Similarly, there are no symbols of this participation that are free of culturally defined meanings, and the meanings that become clear in this process of participation belong to the experience and may not be extended beyond that limit. The failure to recognize this limitation leads to a doctrinalization of the symbols of experience—the symbols take on a propositional character as if they referred to things one might observe from an Archimedean point. One might, under these conditions, ask about Plato's "ideas" or "beliefs" without referring to the experiences that created the symbols. In short, one may look to the writings of Plato and accept the "propositions" or not because one considers them to be the product of Plato the subject examining reality the object. Voegelin began to emphasize Plato's "vision" as a technical term in order to recapture the theophanic character of his writings. Because symbols emerge mysteriously from an event or a vision, Voegelin considered that his historical uncovering was radically empirical. He had recaptured the experiences by liberating the symbols of those events from modern deformations (reifications), thus restoring their transparency to their sources.

New experiences transform one's relationship with reality by exposing once-unknown structures. For Voegelin, the experiences of Plato or Moses presented a "differentiated" view of the structure of reality so that parts or tensions once bound together in the tighter construction of cosmological symbols are exposed as identifiable if related parts. The most powerful differentiation concerned the distinction between the existent world and the nonexistent ground. Once one understood that the cosmos was not self-sufficient—or when one recognized that "things" of the cosmos are not self-created, nor do they contain their meanings within themselves—the question of the ground of reality made the anxiety of the Question more acute. Voegelin referred to this newly differentiated state as the "truth of existence." The "truth of the cosmos" retains its hold on one because the discovery of the nonexistent ground does not remove one from the "world."[43] Nonetheless, the new understanding heightens the mystery of existence and makes problematic the place one occupies in the whole.

The answers that emerge from the Question take one of two forms (or stress one and imply the other): the "beginning" or the "beyond." The Israelites discovered the divine and mysterious origin of existence in the myth of the beginning (Genesis 1). "The creation story," wrote Voegelin, "lets the cosmos, with its hierarchy of being from inorganic universe, through vegetable and animal life, to man, be spoken into existence by God. Reality is a story spoken in the creative language of God; and in one of its figures, in man who is created in the image of God, reality responds to the mystery of the creative word with the truth of the creation story."[44] The myth thus provides excellent (useful or meaningful) symbols for the differentiated truths experienced. The cosmos emerges from a divine source who shapes his creation according to a hierarchy with God as the apex. The why of the creation is answered only by oblique references to the creation being good. The purpose of the cosmos—much less the divine ground—is impenetrable. Nonetheless, this reality has "man" as a being who can participate in all strata of reality. Thus the mystery of human anxiety is understood by reference to one's participation in the divine beyond of existence. By establishing a beginning, with the human as the creative participant in the story, the Israelites created history as the process in which the logos of human participation plays out. Humans, in their historical participation in the divine story, possess an eschatological index. Genesis 1 is the most important story ever told.

The tale of divine beginnings highlights the human-divine interplay at the historical and social level. That is, the divine imprint on the individual human, while not absent, is nonetheless unaccented. The Israelites may have discovered history, but they did not know of the soul. Plato reversed the emphasis. By discovering the psyche Plato could emphasize the ordering presence of divinity (detected in the psyche) that is both the source of existence and the goal of human seeking. Thus, while humans remain tethered to their bodily existence, Plato discovered the capacity of consciousness to "transcend" the immanent in the direction of a mysterious and divine beyond. However, the language of "transcendence" and "beyond" gives rise to a conception of a completely de-divinized world (i.e., a world shorn of divine presence) and a divine reality beyond. There is only one reality. Therefore, the words must break out of the intentionalist paradigm so that one might understand that for Plato, "the Beyond symbolizes the goal of a meditative act that transcends the divinely permeated reality of the 'cosmos.'" Voegelin emphasized further that "there is no 'transcendent reality' other than the Beyond experienced in the 'rise.'"[45]

For Plato, the experience of the beyond creates problems for understanding being. Does this beyond have status as being? At first, Voegelin emphasized, Plato could deal with the matter only by thinking of the beyond as non-being or beyond-being. In the *Phaedrus*, Plato characterized the divine ground as "truly-being" because the cosmos depends upon the beyond for its existence and essence. More precisely, the cosmos "is" because of the divine presence (*pa-*

rousia). Yet Plato was left with an insoluble paradox: "The divine reality that reveals its presence in the meditative act is both within Being as its creative core and outside of Being in some Beyond of it." Plato's paradoxical construction makes it impossible to think of his works in terms of propositional metaphysics. As Voegelin put it, "There is no Beyond lying around somewhere," there is just the beyond as experienced. Plato's experience did not nullify the truth of being presented by his predecessor, Anaximander—of things emerging from the Apeiron and returning to it. The universe is still ruled by the law of becoming and perishing. However, Plato's experience of the divine presence "reveals itself [as] a Being that is neither the Apeiron nor one of the cosmic things but the immortally divine reality that will redeem its followers from their Apeironic fate. The Beyond is indeed beyond the cosmos because the participation in its *parousia* permits the soul of man to 'rise' from intracosmic mortality to transcosmic immortality."[46] For Plato—and Aristotle—salvation from the fate of mortality comes with participation in the immortal divine presence.

Of course, all of this—the claims of Plato and Voegelin—rested upon faith. Nothing is so important to Voegelin's philosophy, nor so overlooked, as faith. It is the existential trait that allows one to search for the truth, and its loss is the reason for the monstrous deformations of reality, for the obsessive search for certainty, and even for final solutions. Modernity is one colossal loss of faith.

For Voegelin, the classic expression of faith appears in Hebrews II:I: "Now faith is the substance of things hoped and the evidence of things unseen." Voegelin found in Christianity, as expressed in such texts, an essential uncertainty. "Ontologically," he wrote concerning the Hebrews passage, "the substance of things hoped for is nowhere to be found but in faith itself; and, epistemologically, there is no proof for things unseen but again this very faith." Unlike tribal gods, the Christian God places the burden of belief on the individual human soul. In this most spiritualized of religions, belief is a response to a "movement" in one's soul, and in the end, one cannot look to another for confirmation. One detects God's presence and sets out to discover the meaning of, or proper response to, that presence. More accurately, one sets out in search of the source of the divine attraction. The Question that rises from this experience has no ready answer, but it presupposes that there is an answer.[47] When

speaking to others about such matters one can only discuss one's experiences—no more. As Voegelin emphasized in one of his most elo-
quent passages:

> The bond is tenuous, indeed, and it may snap easily. The life of
> the soul in openness toward God, the waiting, the periods of
> aridity and dulness, guilt and despondency, contrition and re-
> pentance, forsakenness and hope against hope, the silent stir-
> rings of love and grace, trembling on the verge of a certainty
> which if gained is loss—the very lightness of this fabric may
> prove too heavy a burden for men who lust for massively posses-
> sive experience.[48]

Of course, for most people the desire for certainty overwhelms the
call. The best one can hope for is a Socratic ignorance. Although
Socrates could live happily with the quest for the unknown, others
quake at the uncertainty inherent in such a life. They create universalist answers, and they draw from any number of sources for these
answers. The scriptures present an easy and likely target. One can
wrench these books from their experiential sources and turn them
into doctrinal tracts that give the possessors greater assurance of the
truth of one's religion. By clutching to doctrines (of a Christian or
Marxist or other sort) one can ignore (hide from) the uncertainties
engendered in the experiences of the soul. Thus, while the experiences of the soul are as "real" as any experiences, their meaning and
purpose is unclear. It is easier to close off that part of one's consciousness and the uncertainties created there. For this reason
Voegelin referred repeatedly to the openness of the soul as the precondition for an escape from the second realities of the modern era.
Oddly enough, Voegelin clarified many of the issues involved in
his use of the term "faith" by referring to St. Anselm's so-called ontological proof. Like so much else, Voegelin insisted, the matter is
confused by intentionalist reductions. Anselm attempted no
"proof," and even the word "ontological" is anachronistic. Anselm
felt no need to prove the "existence" of God—he believed. His faith
served as the point of departure rather than as the goal of his famous
prayer (Proslogion), for one who has such a faith seeks to understand
his faith. The prayer is an appeal for greater understanding of the already "known" (or experienced) relationship. Anselm, Voegelin in-

sisted, understood the *metaxy* of human existence. His faith—rather than his reason—sought understanding. "The labor of the mind," Voegelin wrote, "will not arrive at the understanding of anything unless the something to be understood is already present, even though in the form of an intellectually less satisfying response to the divine appeal." Only in response to challenges by the "fool" Gaunilo did Anselm resort to the language of "proof." In this case Anselm dealt with someone who sought to answer matters of this sort outside the *metaxy*—someone who ignored the apperceived reality and had thereby lost all contact with the *metaxy*. As Voegelin insisted, "one cannot prove reality by a syllogism; one can only point to it and invite the doubter to look." The confusions, he asserts further, surrounding the dual meanings of the word "proof" have become "a standard trick employed by the negators in the contemporary ideological debates."[49]

Why did Anselm have a faith that sought understanding? Unlike Plato, who, faced with the foolish negation of the sophists, created philosophy, Anselm inherited a traditionally burdened philosophy and creedal apparatus.[50] These conditions shaped Anselm's question: Is the God experienced in the soul the same God found in the creed? The mode of his investigation was further dictated by these conditions. He would examine the noetic structure of his faith to test the creed against the God experienced, or, as Voegelin put it, "He wants to discover the structure in human reason that permits the questioning response to man to understand the *ratio* [reason] in the symbols of Faith." This search requires four factors in the life of the seeker:

1. a trust in the existence of the unknown structure
2. an awareness that its knowledge is missing
3. a state of the intellectual means that will permit the discovery, and
4. a pressure in the historical situation that arouses the awareness of the problem and makes the search impelling.[51]

Although Anselm remained tethered to the creedal understanding of God, and thus did not achieve sufficient "distance," he nonetheless pursued the same objectives found in Plato's *Phaedrus*, for instance, or Voegelin's essay in which this analysis takes place.

Voegelin's philosophy of consciousness, it now appears, depends upon a number of basic assumptions. Most important, one must assume an intelligibility to reality. "It" is a mystery, to be sure, but a mystery with clues. Moreover, insight into this reality applies to all humans, and one discovers a truth about human existence (i.e., human nature).[52] Furthermore, one accepts the divine ground of existence—a ground that is not in the physical universe but is the source of the universe and whose presence permeates and maintains it. Of course, Voegelin insisted that these and other insights emerge from experiences that provide symbols which are translucent to their sources. These experiences are enormously variegated, according to historical, cultural conditions and the whim of God, but they all rest upon a theophanic ground—they are gifts. In this sense, the experiences of Moses and Plato are "equivalent" even if they expose different dimensions of the common experienced reality. Consequently, in sharp contrast to Strauss, Voegelin did not juxtapose faith and reason, nor did he suggest that they were complementary faculties. Faith and reason belong together as parts of the same experience. Faith carries with it a rational (noetic) structure that human reason (nous) can explore and differentiate. Paul and Moses felt the overwhelming immediacy of theophany and thus emphasized the sublime and awful God who calls. Plato and Aristotle discovered the human soul as the site of God's call, and they further discovered that the soul can detect the call because it shares in its nature—i.e., the human soul has reason (nous) that yearns after the perfection of itself in God. Now we see darkly . . .

A STORY TOLD BY GOD

There is no history without God. Moreover, the meaning of history, the theme of God's story, remains locked in His inscrutable will. Humans participate as actors in this drama more or less unaware of its goal or purpose. As Eugene Webb noted, one of Voegelin's favorite novelists, Thomas Mann, supplied a most apt expression of Voegelin's point at the conclusion of *Joseph and His Brothers*. Joseph, speaking to his brothers, said: "When you talk to me about forgiveness it seems to me you have missed the meaning of the whole story we are in. . . . One can easily be in a story and not understand it." Mann concluded the book with, "And so ended the beautiful story

and God-inventions of JOSEPH AND HIS BROTHERS."[53] Yet Voegelin's references to God—found predominantly, even prominently, in
the books he published in the 1950s—should not be turned into an affirmation of the doctrinally circumscribed God of the Jews or Christians. For Voegelin, one senses, such treatment demystifies God.
The mystery of divine-human interaction, and hence of history, cannot be penetrated by a set of doctrines about the nature of God. But
the term "God" is rather more satisfying than the "divine ground of
being" or even "reality." Even though the personalized God of Jewish and Christian doctrine does not exhaust Voegelin's understanding of the divine, the personal God Yahweh nonetheless serves as an
especially rich symbol (when understood as a symbol) of human-divine interaction.

One is apt to hear oblique references to providence from certain
Jewish and Christian believers, but one does not expect a philosopher of history to involve God so intimately in human matters, so it
is little wonder that Voegelin is all but unknown among philosophers of history. His obscurity, in part, rests with the unfashionable
meaning he attached to "history," emphatically rejecting all conceptions of history as an "object" of reflection. Hegel, Marx, and
others treated history as though they could observe it in both its beginning and its end. This presumption that one has cracked the code
of history and thus participated in its Logos requires that one forget
the perspectival nature of one's observation. More than that, it requires that one accept the mantle of the storyteller, with its over-
tones of divinity. Voegelin was both awed by the erudition that could
sustain such acts of divinization and appalled at the hubris that
drove them.

The problem of the reification of history[54] remained a prime concern because to Voegelin, history was a philosophical activity and,
therefore, his work was already cast in the mold of Hegel, Marx,
Spengler, Jaspers, and Toynbee. In a sense, then, Voegelin never escaped the issue of the meaning of history. His warnings against such
reification merely suggested the horizon imposed on the inquiring
human and the cloud of mystery cloaking the truth so desired. He
yearned to know what Hegel claimed to know. Voegelin simply
learned to be at peace with the mystery. Thus his work much more
closely resembles Hegel's than Toynbee's. Toynbee—at least the
early Toynbee—identified patterns in history but pronounced that

the process as a whole was meaningless.[55] Although Voegelin assiduously avoided the language of "meaning," he had faith in the meaningful configuration of history.

What is this configuration? In an astonishingly clear and overlooked passage, Voegelin wrote:

> Configuration refers to more than the patterns that are observable in history, such as sequences of institutions. In various high civilizations we know that we begin with certain types of political organization, usually of a monarchical or an aristocratic type, and that democratic types always come rather late in the course of a civilization. Such sequences would be patterns that can be empirically observed. But this is not all, because conceptions of order in a civilization are always accompanied by the self-interpretation of that order as meaningful; that is, the persons living in an order have opinions about the particular meaning that order has. In this sense, self-interpretation is always part of the reality which we live.[56]

This, of course, was what Voegelin meant by history—the story of human self-interpretation. He established this objective on the first page of the first volume of *Order and History:*

> The order of history emerges from the history of order. Every society is burdened with the task, under its concrete conditions, of creating an order that will endow the fact of its existence with meaning in terms of ends divine and human. And the attempts to find symbolic forms that will adequately express the meaning, while imperfect, do not form a senseless series of failures.[57]

The struggle for order is the attempt to attune one's self to the most real, to the form behind the image, or, at the most elemental level, to that which is most lasting. People living under cosmological symbolism understood the cosmos to be that which is most lasting.[58] Their societies functioned as analogues to the cosmos and the structures experienced therein. In due course cosmological symbols lost their potency and, in the anxiety of this fall from being,[59] the struggle for new symbols resulted in "leaps in being" that exposed the transcendent, divine ground "beyond" the cosmos as well as the soul (psyche or pneuma) as the location of divine participation in human affairs. The horizon changed, and in this case, one does not step from one horizon into another, as though they were so many rooms. The new perspective that has uncovered structures creates an awareness of change—a before-and-after experience. The older, more restrictive horizon is no longer "true" in light of the more comprehensive vision. One can see much more clearly now, and this clarity allows one to tell a story of change—of dramatic and epochal change. One has stepped into history. History, then, is the story of differentiating consciousness as told by one who understands the differentiations.

But is history a story rather than several stories? This question vexed Voegelin, though he did not pose it in this fashion. No one doubts that history, conventionally understood, is really an infinite number of stories told in response to particular questions. One might tell the story of the fall of the Roman Empire, and through carefully stipulated definitions of key words like "fall," "Roman," and "empire" and a lifetime of hard work one could tell a story with reasonably fixed temporal boundaries. But one who is engaged in such an enterprise is always aware of the artificiality of the story, aware that the storyteller defines the object. Moreover, an unanswered question goes largely ignored: How does this story fit into "the story"—History?

Toynbee addressed this problem by dividing history into sequential "civilizations" that have a sort of internal logic or cycle. Putting aside the numerous difficulties with which Toynbee grappled, especially later in his career,[60] he concluded with what one might consider a denial of history—a potentially endless course of civilizations. Voegelin emphasized that Toynbee dealt with history at the level of phenomena. But what are the experiences of order—or of disorder—that create and shape these civilizations? Voegelin hoped to penetrate to these experiential roots in order to understand better human understanding of itself in its modes of individual, society, and history. Thus a history of human self-interpretation must account for the socially relevant symbols of reality. What is one's place in being? What role does one's society play in reality? What is the meaning of the course of events leading to one's present? An ordered society supplies satisfactory answers to these questions. These questions find answers in consciousness—in the consciousness that is located in the individual and that supplies symbols which become socially relevant by speaking to the needs of other humans (a sense of place and purpose). A history of order is a history of consciousness; a history of consciousness is a history of divine-human interaction as articulated by the symbols that emerge from this mutual participation. History is a story told by God.

With amazing erudition, Voegelin began to tell God's story in the first three volumes of *Order and History.* The project, charged with concern about a contemporary fall from being, was to follow the empirical evidence of ordering experiences through time, from cosmological societies to Israelite and Hellenic differentiations through Christian forms to the modern gnostic forms of order.[61] Of course, Voegelin understood that this development does not follow so simple a course, but however shrouded in mystery, Voegelin nonetheless believed that a generally sequential and progressive course leading to the most differentiated symbols of the Christian order—followed by the deformation of modernity—characterized the history of order. Voegelin's was a more or less Western history, and when he expanded his study of order to encompass Eastern civilizations during the 1960s and early 1970s, an astonishing array of differentiations overwhelmed his project. The consequences were numerous. First, he distanced himself from the traditional Christian story, or at least he rejected emphatically the singular truth of Christianity. He maintained, however, that the New Testament expressed the most differentiated understanding of reality presently available. This proviso was not enough for his Catholic admirers, who had been his most ardent followers. Many could never forgive Voegelin for interpreting Paul as having allowed his epiphany to unbalance his consciousness—to allow him, however briefly, to reject the immanent pole of existence in anticipation of imminent transfiguration. But more to the point, Voegelin rejected Catholic understandings of the nature of revelation and the church.[62]

Second, and more important here, Voegelin had to give up all claims to a universal history (and they had been muted all along). The fourth volume of *Order and History (The Ecumenic Age),* was his answer to the problem. The first three volumes constitute an intellectual history of order proceeding chronologically from the ancient civilizations of the Near East to the symbols of order articulated by Plato and Aristotle. The two fundamental leaps in being represented by Israel (faith) and Athens (reason) do not evolve one out of the other. Indeed, Voegelin was always sensitive to the problems of accounting for these "leaps." If they fit on a time-line that ends with one's own philosophical efforts, then one might expect to detect some genetic relationship between them. Voegelin never did, which is what salvaged his project. Although he admitted he had conceived of a more or less unilinear history that led to the present, he could not account for the spiritual eruptions by any of the standard methods (e.g., cultural diffusion). His own answer was that social disorder created a search for order which produced new and improved symbols. This structural element survived the break in his project.

In the end, this understanding of history, especially when the histories of the East are taken into account, simply does not fit a single history in which one development prepared the way for another. To make matters worse, Voegelin discovered that this effort to force historical events into a single meaningful course (what he called "historiogenesis") has a long history going back at least as far as the Sumerian king list.[63] Historiogenesis reached manic proportions in the nineteenth and early twentieth centuries as Hegel, Comte, Marx, and others had to deal with an enormous range of recalcitrant data from the East to make the story complete with them. Still, Voegelin sought a way to account for the exceptional number of "spiritual outbursts" in the thousand years leading to Jesus, but since Voegelin concerned himself with self-interpretations in history and these outbursts occurred independent of one another, they could not be considered meaningful elements in the history of order. Consequently, these "events, though they constitute structures of meaning in history, do not themselves fall readily into a pattern that could be understood as meaningful." Voegelin concluded from these observations that the "process of history, and such order as can be discerned in it, is not a story to be told from the beginning to its happy, or unhappy, end; it is a mystery in process of revelation."[64] Even in his later works, Voegelin trusted in the meaningfulness of the totality, but as a whole, history is beyond human ken. No perspective in history can make sense of the totality.[65]

Consequently, *The Ecumenic Age* is a markedly nonlinear history. Voegelin told stories, of a sort, in this book, but they do not build upon one another into a large narrative that is structured by a beginning and an end. The book is a mansion of middles, each room a historical *metaxy*. Voegelin had given up on a history of order in favor of historical consciousness and the perpetual human struggle for order. Indeed, the whole of *Order and History* was to be a chapter in this struggle, with not insignificant advances in the differentiation of consciousness.

In the Preface to volume one, *Israel and Revelation*, Voegelin emphasized that his massive enterprise represented a diagnostic and therapeutic effort to bring order out of modern malaise. By the fourth volume, Voegelin had sharpened his understanding of the nature of both the diagnosis and the therapy. The great advances in differentiating consciousness, he emphasized in the Introduction to volume four, had emerged during the period of conquest beginning with the rise of the Persian Empire and concluding with the fall of the Roman Empire. Out of the disruptions attending empire building came the great prophetic and philosophical insights that the modern world inherited. The tensions created by such differentiations spawned a long series of doctrinalizations whereby the insights contained in Plato's work or Christian scriptures, for instance, were transformed into objects outside the *metaxy* of human consciousness. Plato's symbols became propositions about which one might agree or not. This process eclipses the experience Plato sought to illuminate because symbols of experience became ''ideas'' or ''beliefs.'' ''The return from symbols which have lost their meaning to experiences which constitute meaning is so generally recognizable as the problem of the present that specific references are unnecessary.'' But the problems of return are numerous. Of special importance ''is the massive block of accumulated symbols, secondary and tertiary, which eclipses the reality of man's existence in the Metaxy. To raise this obstacle and its structure into consciousness, and by its removal to help in the return to the truth of reality as it reveals itself in history, has become the purpose of *Order and History*.''[66] A more antimodern sentiment could hardly be expressed.

The problem with modern civilization is that it has inherited the symbols of the differentiated consciousness that found its synthesis in Christianity and those symbols have lost their transparency to truth. A bastardized set of ideas, beliefs, and ideologies have issued from this decay, and these ideas neither rest upon an experiential base nor function to orient individuals or societies to being. Indeed, control replaced attunement. Humans who grow tired of living in-between will ignore the pole of reality beyond human control and thereby declare themselves masters of a niggardly reality. Masters they become but at the cost of their humanity. People choose their realities by selecting from the array of ideas and ideologies. One might become a Christian if one wants to believe in some powerful "being" called God. One might choose to believe in Marx if one can stomach a reality bound by immanent limits. Either way, one must close one's eyes to the nonexistent ground. The bogus certainty of intellectually possessing objects (what moderns like to call "knowledge" or, better yet, "scientific knowledge") pastes over the uncertainty detected in Leibniz's paradigmatic questions: Why is there something, why not nothing? and Why is the something as it is? By recapturing the truth of human existence in the *metaxy,* Voegelin hoped to introduce a healthy dose of uncertainty to a world bent upon fighting over competing certainties.

Since truths emerge in history, history is the "place" to begin the return. The two meanings of history just suggested might be called "historical consciousness" and "historical inquiry" (i.e., inquiry into historical consciousness). At no point in Voegelin's work is history understood as a catalog of events, civilizations, technologies, ideas, and such. Political, social, economic, and technological developments over time play important roles in "history,"[67] but they are not the stuff of history, which is the story of consciousness as it becomes aware of its structure. But history is also a structure in consciousness. "Through the differentiations of consciousness," wrote Voegelin, "history becomes visible as the process in which the differentiations occur." And further, "Since the differentiations advance man's insight into the constitution of his humanity, history becomes visible as a dimension of humanity beyond man's personal existence in society."[68] Thus one recognizes that the process of differentiation—which is orchestrated by the God who calls—is historical. Moreover, by acquiring this historical awareness one transcends or escapes one's provincialism and participates in "humanity." An analysis of this last claim must wait, but one recognizes that a historical inquiry concerns the rather large question of human nature—or man's insight into the constitution of his humanity, which extends beyond any subject or object "man" to the process of reality in which the man participates. Indeed, Voegelin understood "humanity'' to mean this participation. Human history is the story of participation that necessarily includes the various constituents in their respective roles—or, more precisely, the understanding of man's humanity granted by the experience of theophany.

Voegelin's history of historical consciousness constitutes an examination of a dimension of consciousness clarified in the era he examined—the ecumenic age. In that age Voegelin detected a triadic structure of ecumenic empire, spiritual outburst, and historiography. When multicivilizational empires undermined faith in societies as the carriers of transcendent meaning the existential disorder that resulted precipitated a spiritual outburst. The newly differentiated understanding of reality exposed the older symbols of order as false, though they had been true in their time. Voegelin called this a before-and-after experience, by which he meant that the discovery created a recognition in the carrier that some new era had dawned—that the old symbols could never again be meaningful after such a leap in being. In the ecumenic age humans came to recognize distinct eras. God had written a new chapter.

When Moses discovered the ''I AM'' beyond the cosmos as the source and sustainer of existence he was forced to ask questions about the beginnings and the purposes of existence. As a result, the Israelites stepped out of the cycle of the cosmos and into the immediacy of God's presence in history. They were His people, and they would participate in the story He told. Similarly, Plato discovered the soul as the means of participation in the divine will. Right order, as a consequence, became a matter of personal or individual attunement with reality as apperceived.[69] In both cases, the older cosmological order represented an outdated understanding of reality, and of ''man.'' Man's humanity became luminous in its tension toward the beyond (God), and moreover, the process of discovery exposed the historical structure of humanity—i.e., that consciousness differentiates. ''What happens 'in' history is the very process of differentiating consciousness that constitutes history.''[70]

Christianity, with its emphasis upon individual salvation, created the strongest sense of history as a story told by God in which individuals might open their souls to God's spirit and be thereby transfigured. The Christian salvation story thus heightened the eschatological structure of consciousness, and it replaced the tribe with the individual soul yearning for God. If not balanced by the recognition

of human earthliness, the tensional direction detected in consciousness might give way to expectations of imminent transfiguration—
as it did for Paul. Paul then came to believe that he not only lived in
God's story—history—but that he had come to understand it in its
entirety. Paul was the first person, Voegelin argued, to think of history as an "it." Paul allowed his theophanic vision to become the final answer; he thought he had gained a perspective beyond history.

Nonetheless, Christianity, more than any other symbolism of order, exposes the individual living in immediacy before God in a story
structured by theophanies. Like Plato earlier, but with greater emphasis, New Testament writers stressed man's humanity as participation with the divine presence. In the age of empires, then, Christianity emerged as the great religion of humanity. By differentiating
consciousness and exposing the character of human existence, the
before-and-after experience that created historical consciousness extended to all humanity. History is universal history. That is, the
truth that emerges from differentiating consciousness (and history is
the story of differentiating consciousness) applies to Everyman.[71] In
this regard, again, Christian writers repeated with emphasis an understanding found in Plato.

The history of the discovery of history, Voegelin believed, exposed
the historical structure of consciousness. "History," he emphasized
in connection with both Plato and Paul, "is the area of reality where
the directional movement of the cosmos achieves luminosity in consciousness."[72] As Voegelin explored the meaning of history (the symbol "history"), the similarities with his analysis of consciousness
come to mind. As he put it one place, "The reality of history is . . .
the In-Between where man responds to the divine presence and divine presence evokes the response of man." History is located in the
metaxy.[73] Paradoxically, then, history is not only about change but
about changelessness. Because consciousness participates in the
time of the physical world in which the person finds himself and in
what Voegelin called the flux of divine presence, the discovery of the
structure, which takes place in calendar time, exposes the unchanging presence of the divine ground. That is, differentiation is about
the structure of consciousness—and history is God's revelation of
this structure. Of course, we must remind ourselves that consciousness is, not a thing, but a process in tension toward the ground.

Thus, Voegelin tried to limit "history" to mean theophanic events that engender an experience of historical consciousness. He considered all attempts to superimpose a structure of historical meaning not available in the experiences themselves illegitimate, and his awareness of Eastern differentiations—he tried to incorporate this in one chapter of *The Ecumenic Age*—forced him to give up a single story line leading to his present. Instead, he focused upon the historical dimension of consciousness that appeared in the ecumenic age as a way of recovering an understanding of consciousness long since buried under a mountain of doctrines, ideas, ideologies, and other intentionalist fallacies. He believed that his own history penetrated to the experiences of the paradigmatic theophanies of the West, and he tried to dissolve all nonmetaphorical reifications so as to make clear the experiences he exposed. Along the way he created another historical moment—a before-and-after experience. Voegelin exposed the gnosticism of modernity and illuminated a structure of reality altogether obscured by a severely delimited horizon. The order of history really does emerge out of the history of order.

PHILOSOPHY OF POLITICS

Even as historian, Voegelin focused upon a philosophy of consciousness, and his quest to understand consciousness in turn issued from a concern about the political and social disorder of his time. In the Foreword to the German edition of *Anamnesis*, Voegelin noted that "the philosophy of consciousness is the centerpiece of a philosophy of politics."[74] In his 1952 book, *New Science of Politics*, Voegelin sketched the numerous problems plaguing modern political science, as well as a brief history of modern gnosticism as the existential disease that stunted modern understanding of political reality.

The modern science of politics rested upon an antimetaphysical bias springing from a lust for power or control. The problems of both positivism and historicism discussed in Chapter 3 spring to mind. In light of his philosophy of consciousness, one must understand that Voegelin pointed to the eclipse of the transcendent pole of reality and the concomitant reification of immanent reality as the foundations for the despiritualized political philosophy of the nineteenth and twentieth centuries. Because modern theorists lost access to the *metaxy*, they could not conceive of a right order. Instead, they talked of "values," which began to take on the look of phenomena or objects. Such reductionism was required if one was limited to the intentionality of consciousness. Participation in the process of reality is obscured by immanent constructions of reality; as human constructs they tend to compete. Cut off from participation in the *metaxy*, how can one adjudicate? One cannot.

Such an intellectual and spiritual environment supplies no resistance to the development of the most monstrous ideologies. In an age of disorder in which one's spiritual roots are cut, in which economic upheaval follows cultural and social disorder, one is apt to believe in a messiah promising participation in a world-historic event or in the establishment of a thousand-year Reich or promising the dawning of the communist age. Realities become intellectual and existential fashions that one may choose or not according to one's whim.

The verities of liberalism, with abstract notions of human dignity and rights, sustain so long as generalized rules of conduct do not make a mockery of those verities. I do not think Voegelin believed America and the West could long last with such a minimalist conception of the good. True order, in other words, emerges from an understanding of the good that rests in something larger than collective individual goods. For Voegelin, then, a new science of politics requires an understanding of consciousness that enlarges the realm of human participation to include the divine pole of reality. Indeed, the only true order is structured by the tension toward the divine ground experienced in consciousness. Of course, Voegelin did not call for any old god—as Strauss came close to advocating—but for the mysterious God beyond existence whose revelations are revelations of mystery. Politics is equally dangerous with reified gods or with no gods at all.

8

Strauss, Voegelin, and the Conservative Imagination

THE CHARMS OF STRAUSS AND VOEGELIN

The works of Voegelin and especially Strauss charm many of their readers. As portals into the ghostly netherworld resting beneath contemporary life, their books give access to the unseen machinery of our modern, liberal world. They expose assumptions, motivations, pathologies, and the reader may wander around studying first this fixture—say Machiavelli—and then another—say Hegel. Pretty soon the whole system, so mysterious to those without access to that underworld, becomes a coherent whole. Mystery, or at least one mystery, is no more.

The problems of the contemporary world are bound up in a very elaborate intellectual or even philosophical struggle. A follower of these two philosophers not only can come to understand the nature of the problem but also can trace the often minute (sometimes arcane) philosophical events that led down the slippery slope. Their works lend themselves to this sort of reductionist understanding of the world and its history. The whole modern constellation of conundrums may be understood, for instance, as a gnostic revolt against reality. Although the actual histories provided by both Strauss and Voegelin are not so reductionist, their accounts are genetic in character, for the family of modern ideologies all trace back to the same ancestors.

The chronicling of the genealogy of modernity was a relatively simple task. Strauss's and Voegelin's efforts expose a few examples of strained logic and coerced interpretation, but the story was not terribly difficult to write. Yet far more interesting are their struggles to articulate an answer or response to the modern world. They failed insofar as their struggles did not produce easy or fully coherent answers. The dimensions of the problems became clear as they took up the search. If the relatively easy blame they assigned to a few ancestors provide some readers with a surer grasp of the problems, the real appeal of these two men (for people of independent mind) is their struggle to provide meaningful responses to the crisis they encountered.

Voegelin was much more interesting when engaged in a deadly serious investigation of Anselm or Plato than when he was attacking some faceless group of "positivists." Once one gets accustomed to Strauss, his engagement with Plato actually takes one away from the here and now, and his ubiquitous search for answers leads, not to answers, but to more interesting questions. The evasions, or qualifications, or even contradictions of the answers of both men to modern problems result, not from their limitations, but from their abilities. Of course, the answers do not satisfy. Why should one expect that they would? The search goes on, and in no small measure, that was their point. So long as the search continues the goal—even when understood as a heuristic goal—shapes the people who search. The loss of philosophy as the search for a normative order necessarily has, they believed, devastating effects. The thing most needed is the inspiration of the quest. By saving philosophy one saves society.

The struggle to understand two such complex thinkers is complicated by the way different audiences received them, for in the case of both Strauss and Voegelin, the question of intended audience creates numerous problems. Of course, in most of their works they wished to speak to other "specialists," and of all their audiences, other philosophers understood them best. Nonetheless, their works were almost always charged with a sense of significance that transcended the small orbit of philosophers. However odd it appears, these two abstruse writers functioned as public philosophers and communicated a strong sense of purpose. The world was in danger—in a crisis—and they sought to understand the nature of that danger. What could be more important? As a result, other people who had come to believe, for reasons very different, perhaps, from Strauss's and Voegelin's, that American or Western civilization was in peril naturally found reason to be curious about the work of these two philosophers. Consequently, Voegelin and Strauss became (perhaps unwilling) participants in more mundane political matters.

A group of politically oriented conservatives, few if any of whom had read Voegelin's work seriously, put the phrase "Don't Let Them Immanentize the Eschaton" on shirts and buttons. This example and numerous others just like it tell us that Voegelin and Strauss were appropriated, however inaccurately, by conservatives. Nearly every anthology of "conservative" works includes selections from both philosophers. They were adopted. But even as adopted sons they became targets for opponents who sought to discredit "conservatism"—whatever that is. As a result, conservatives and liberals alike have dealt with little more than caricature's of these philosophers and their works. In part, I have struggled to understand Strauss and Voegelin as reactionaries without forcing them into the conservative mold; I have tried to understand their response to their world almost in isolation from any intended audience. However, because their influence has so profoundly shaped some segments of the American conservative movement, it is worth returning to my earlier analysis of traditionalist conservatives to test the "conservatism" of Strauss and Voegelin. It might be helpful to expand the ideal type of conservative developed in Chapter 1 as the best means of establishing a comparison. Perhaps then we can find some hints of the larger role Voegelin and Strauss played in American life.[1]

THE CONSERVATIVE IMAGINATION

Conservatives seek to conserve something, real or imagined. To talk about them in the context of dissent to the dominant intellectual, social, and political trends of their day is to encounter a paradox. If one broadens the frame of reference from twentieth-century America to the past several centuries in the West, then the paradoxical quality of the conservative label disappears, at least in terms of self-designation. Conservatives think of themselves as defenders of Western civilization against an assault launched from any number of modern thinkers: liberals, socialists, Marxists, positivists, relativists, nihilists—philistines all.

Conservatives emerged as such in reaction to changes that threatened to undermine the moral, religious, social, political, and intellectual traditions and principles to which they were devoted. The great Whig reformer Edmund Burke did not think of himself as a conservative—the label did not exist then—but sought nonetheless to conserve the Western tradition against the threats posed by the French Revolution. Burke fought against the ideas or beliefs that gave impetus to the revolution, as it was the ideas, more than the actual revolution, that threatened the fragile fabric of European civilization, an artifice created from thousands of years of human experience guided by right reason and divine providence. The revolutionaries sought to rend this fabric and to construct a social and political order based upon abstract reasoning alone.

The French Revolution did not inaugurate the modern world; indeed, as far as I can tell, the modern world, a most porous conceptual vessel, has no beginning. But at least since Descartes split the subject from the object people here and there have fought a mostly losing battle against the emerging way moderns define knowledge, the political and social order, freedom, the individual, and of course reality. Over the years since Burke's *Reflections on the Revolution in France*, persons with a conservative turn of mind have emerged in every generation to defend the principles of Western civilization, as they construed them, against the most recent innovation. The list is long and includes John Adams, Alexis de Tocqueville, Cardinal Newman, Jakob Burckhardt, Henry Adams, the New Humanists, the Southern Agrarians, and the so-called new conservatives. Some affinities link these people and groups together as part of an ongoing tradition.

Conservative principles are bound up with an aesthetic sensibility. The search for a normative social order, for instance, is in part a quest for beauty, so it should come as no surprise that conservatives see a great deal of ugliness in the modern world. All around them they see a homogenization of American culture. Individuals get lost in the bureaucratized society, adrift without moorings or bearings. Rootless people in constant motion seek diversions to replace purpose. Industrialism and capitalism subvert craftsmanship and community while replacing these values with atomized individualism and crass materialism. The conservatives see huge tracts of land transformed into monotonous rows of look-alike houses occupied by think-alike people while grand, distinctive old homes and buildings succumb to the wrecking ball—testimony to the passion for the new and untried and disregard for the old and established. The United States has become, conservatives fear, a society bent on consumption and sensual gratification, a society possessing an utter disregard for ancestors, posterity, and creation.

In 1900, a particularly pessimistic conservative, Henry Adams, visited the Paris Exposition and ruminated about the contrasting symbols of social order that dominated the Middle Ages and modernity: the Virgin and the dynamo. The Virgin, which represented not only the Catholic church but also the compelling, charismatic figure of Mary, helped orient and inspire the people of the fourteenth century. The Virgin functioned as an organizing ideal so compelling that it inspired great cathedrals. The people living within this paradigm knew the comfort of unquestioned verities and established purposes that gave their existence meaning in this life and the life to come. Moderns, by contrast, are dedicated to the human ability to create, to transform nature and to turn it toward human ends. The dynamo, most perfectly represented in 1900 by the steam engine, could occupy the imagination of moderns obsessed with change and power, but, quoting Henry Adams, "All the steam in the world could not, like the Virgin, build Chartres."[2] An imagination so yoked to the material world, so stunted as to see only human ingenuity and power, could never see or understand the realm of beauty and order transcending the purely physical world. Conservative hope for restoration rests, therefore, upon the cultivation of a higher imagination. Like Aristophanes, conservatives fear that "Whirl is king, having driven out Zeus."

But what will a properly cultivated higher imagination apprehend? Basic to conservative thought is a belief in a normative structure transcending purely human existence. Conservatives appeal to an authoritative standard not created by humans but to which humans are responsible. The issue takes a variety of forms. From a natural law tradition and with it "right reason," to an appeal to revelation or to more clearly Platonic concepts of essences or forms, all conservatives rely upon a transhuman standard that makes appeals to truth, justice, and beauty, meaningful. Of necessity, conservatives must rest their social beliefs in an idealist philosophy, and perhaps this is where, more than anywhere else, conservative principles sound hollow to modern ears. Embedded in this issue are a number of related questions, the most important being, What constitutes knowledge? If conservatives wish to appeal to some normative structure, humans must have some knowledge of it, and this knowledge must be intersubjectively communicable.

During most of the nineteenth century, when normative theory appealed to virtually every intellectual, the issue separating conservatives from their rivals involved the substance, not the existence, of a normative order. By the late nineteenth century, conservatives found themselves in an intellectual environment that was hostile toward any constructions of reality that possessed a static nature. Certain historicists and pragmatists, especially, emphasized the ever-shifting character of existence. With the fall from fashion of conceptual ontologies, the emphasis shifted from understanding and articulating a timeless standard by which humans ought to be judged to the experimental methods of science as being the most efficient means of finding ways of living congruent with human desires. Humans, in the modern world, must create their own standards, and by these alone will they be judged.

Conservatives found themselves without a useful vocabulary in the new climate even as they grounded their entire body of beliefs upon a subject about which no claims to knowledge could gain a hearing. The conversation had shifted, and knowledge had been reconfigured to exclude those realms of human experience not amenable to the scientific method. To conservatives, the restriction of knowledge claims to evidence found only in the flux of human affairs was evidence of a nominalistic spirit and an atrophied imagination. Through imagination one might transcend the moment to capture a glimpse of the timeless. Moderns, conservatives suggest, have decided simply to live out their lives in Plato's cave, creating meaning out of those fleeting images on the wall. To people who are skeptical about anything beyond the cave, the claims of those who have made their way out of the cave cannot make sense because those claims rest on experiences that have engendered a vocabulary that is opaque to the cave dwellers.

Shifting from the metaphysical to the more prosaic, conservative commentary on the social and political order is very complicated and nuanced, and this social and political commentary presents important problems to people who wish to engage seriously in a dialogue with conservatives. First, critics very often present deformed caricatures of conservative thought that have more or less dominated popular perception. In other words, conservatives are misunderstood, which means that one must chop through the crude stereotypes. Moreover, while conservative critiques of the modern world touch perspicaciously on the numerous problems presented by liberalism and other isms, conservatives cannot present sweeping solutions because sweeping plans to remedy problems are the problem. The matter is complicated, and since neither conservatives nor their critics concern themselves with careful qualifications in these matters, they too often talk past one another. Emphasizing principles rather than an ideal type leaves conservatives without an ideological model simple enough to plaster on the bumper of a car or in some other way reach large numbers of people. Their critique of the modern evolution of state power puts them in an ambiguous position with regard to the significant improvements made possible by that evolution. Conservatives acknowledge that a number of injustices have been partially remedied as a result of this development. On the other hand they find the means for achieving these advances profoundly dangerous, as is the underlying belief in progress toward some equalitarian utopia. All that conservatives have achieved, in this regard, is an articulation of principles, for a clear and precise call to reform would require that they cease being conservatives.

The principles, conservatives argue, upon which a society ought to order its institutions emerge from an understanding of the normative order and of human nature, the two constants of human reality that ground the otherwise ever-changing political and social order. The specific contexts for emulating the principles of the normative order vary greatly, so no paradigmatic human political and social structure exists, only flexible and general principles learned through centuries of human experience, reason, and to a far lesser degree, revelation.

So much of the difference between liberals and conservatives with regard to political and social institutions and goals spring from contrasting anthropologies. Whereas liberals have typically considered humans as autonomous individuals and, consequently, social and political institutions as creations of those individuals, conservatives acknowledge no such thing as an individual outside of the social context. Consequently, they consider it a gross distortion of the nature of things to think of social and political institutions as being created by individuals. Individual humans are participants in several institutions in which they find their place. One is a member of a family, the local church, a guild or profession as well as a citizen of a city or village and a state. In the interstices of these institutions, along with the traditions and prejudices inherited from one's ancestors, one understands one's place in relation to the whole as well as one's duties and liberties. Both humans and rights are creations of society, and they cannot be understood in an anterior relationship to society.

More than the social nature of humans, conservatives argue that humans have a fundamental need to be a part of a community, including a community of purpose. If the balance of authority dissolves by virtue of the decay of one or more important social institutions, as has been the case with the growth of the modern state at the expense of competing institutions like family, church, voluntary organizations, and local government, humans look to the ascending power to fulfill the various community needs that a network of institutions once satisfied. (If the citizens feel especially rootless and alienated, then the state will provide them with a sense of national purpose in which they play a part and find their meaning.) The state apparatus expands to meet the new social demands, which means the state becomes increasingly centralized, bureaucratic, and popular. Indeed, the most conspicuous danger conservatives identify is, not the failure of centralized power to supply the needs of the citizens, but its relative success. By accumulating more functions, the state necessarily destroys those institutions that once performed those functions. The individuals served by the state then find themselves alienated from local and personal sources of identity and meaning, and the relationships that once constituted local institutions are replaced by a distant and impersonal relationship between equal, atomized, and homogenized individuals and the state.

Two additional problems issue from that state of affairs. Because conditions require a centralized and bureaucratized system that is inflexible with regard to individual cases or even local conditions— or so conservatives assume—the goods or ends of a society become the sole property of the political power. In an almost Rousseauean sense, the will of the majority not only decides that freedom is good but defines freedom. In such a system recalcitrant members—those "individualists"—must be forced to be free—i.e., conform. Under these conditions the individual possesses no defense. In a society with a very healthy church, a vigorous extended family, or similar institutions, the individual finds protection from arbitrary power because those institutions have authority in a wider field of competing nodes of authority. In their absence, the individual is defenseless against the power of the state.[3]

A conservative principle related to this affirmation of the social character of the individual is the belief that a proper social and political order requires a hierarchy that is roughly commensurate with abilities and effort. Here conservatives swim upstream against a rather vigorous current of equalitarianism. Conservatives recognize two forms of equality: equality before God and equality before the law. (They do not even embrace equality of opportunity because they cannot separate that formally from equality of condition.) Otherwise, they see an enormous variety of talents that deserve distinct places. Here they stand upon the Platonic definition of justice in which each person receives his or her due.

Hierarchy extends well beyond a simple concern for social justice, and it must do so, I think, because conservatives who are given to a justification of class distinctions based upon natural talent fail to explain how this just distribution of privileges might work, except to say that no human system can achieve justice fully. Perhaps more important to the conservative defense of hierarchy is an abhorrence for its opposite, "mass society." Any society that seeks to achieve equality of condition betrays the diversity that is so dear to the conservative heart. This sort of equality is maintained at enormous cost to the personal development of a society's citizens, even as the society robs itself of a just ordering of talents best suited for the common good. On this point, as in most others, conservative arguments contain an integral aesthetic critique. The argument for justice, though not without its merits, is almost ancillary to the conservative reaction to the blandness, the dullness of mass society. The real moral problem is that people display a boredom with life as evidenced in narcotic use, meaningless violence, and the endless search for new diversions.

Closely connected to the defense of hierarchy is the faith conservatives place in the role of tradition in maintaining order. There is a tension between the conservative emphasis upon tradition and the conservative emphasis upon normative principles. On the one hand, conservatives affirm a timeless standard for justice and truth while, on the other hand, they affirm the authoritative quality of the prevailing human traditions, which are historical and not timeless. Indeed, conservatives often warn against trying to transplant American institutions to nations with very different cultures. Those nations must find their own ways to approximate the normative standards, ways congruent with their cultural inheritance. The timeless principles humans wish to emulate are rather loose, and human understanding of them is weak. Therefore, a great deal of diversity in institutions does not war against an affirmation of the normative order. Moreover, tradition serves humans very well, conservatives insist, in bridging the gap between the conditions of the moment and the more permanent qualities of human social and political life. As Russell Kirk so aptly put it, tradition

> confers upon change the element of continuity, keeping the alteration of society in a regular train. Everything which the living possess has roots in the spiritual and intellectual achievements of the past. Everything man has—his body, his mind, his social order—is in large part an inheritance from people long dead. The passage of time brings new acquisitions; but unless men know the past, they are unable to understand distinctions between what is permanent and what is transient in their lives. Man always is beset by questions, of which the largest is the question of his own existence. He cannot even begin to think about his existence, and lesser questions, until he has acquired the command of means that come to him from the past, such as the names that people customarily use with reference to modes of being and acting.[4]

One can make sense of Kirk and other conservatives only if one understands that the fundamental constituents of reality possess a permanent nature, which is true not only of the transcendent normative order but also of humans. A great many things change about humans, and these changes over time constitute history. The task is to distinguish the temporary from the permanent. Conservatives chastise moderns for emphasizing the ever-shifting patterns of human life, for declaring human nature a fiction. Conservatives recognize in the chronicle of human history an intelligible structure that helps expose human nature. Humans are sinful, given congenitally to lusting for things immoral, especially power and control. Also, humans have a part of them that is unsatisfied with purely material things; they have a spirit or a soul that longs for order and beauty. This part of the human, often atrophied by degradations, requires the artifice of civilization, especially as expressed in the arts, to find fulfillment—or partial fulfillment. These cultural creations hint to the divine that one cannot apprehend directly, or grasp firmly. They require a highly developed imagination to make the symbols of these cultural creations transparent to the deeper truths they represent.

STRAUSS, VOEGELIN, AND THE CONSERVATIVES

In "liberal" America, where most people have possessed a strong belief in "truth"—even in the Christian truth—conservatives nonetheless have felt beleaguered because Americans were slowly accepting a rational or planned society over some supposed "traditional" society. Meanwhile, many intellectuals advocated these organizational trends because they believed that the sciences provided the means to achieve more fulfilling ways of living. Moreover, the "quest for certainty," as John Dewey put it, only hindered the collective human effort to build more satisfying societies. In short, tradition and particularity were under attack from different sides. Although conservatives expressed dismay at the path taken by most citizens, their real foes, they thought, were the godless intellectuals who cut American society from its moorings. Adrift, but in search of a more felicitous future, most Americans would recognize too late that they had not only thrown off tradition but God also.

During the 1950s, as conservatives began finding one another and forming institutions, the books by Leo Strauss and Eric Voegelin served as primary philosophical bulwarks against many challenges to the Western philosophical tradition. Although most self-proclaimed conservative intellectuals were not philosophers, nor particularly interested in engaging in debates about technical points, they generally recognized that their religious and philosophical inclinations required some systematic defense. In the authors of *The New Science of Politics* and *Natural Right and History* they found, or thought they found, able defenders of the citadel. Voegelin and Strauss exposed the modern philosophical fraud, and moreover, their enterprise—to reawaken the philosophical quest (though not the quest for certainty)—was a necessary part of the larger conservative agenda.

Traditionalist conservatives had use for the works of Strauss and Voegelin, but did these two philosophers have any use for conservatives? This difficult question deserves yet another book, but some observations are necessary here. Although traditionalist conservatives clearly favored Voegelin to Strauss, they found *Natural Right and History* very useful for resurrecting the natural rights tradition, and this point was so important they were able to overlook Strauss's "misreading" of Burke. The relationship became more strained, however, when they found in Strauss's other books an emphasis upon a necessary tension or even contradiction between a religious and a philosophical way of life. Nonetheless, Strauss himself sought to reinvigorate religious belief in the United States, and for all his attacks upon "conventions," he fought hard to reawaken allegiance to "traditional" moral codes. Strauss's political legacy has developed through the so-called neoconservatives who seek simultaneously to expand liberty and to create communal codes sturdy enough to check many kinds of social behavior. The neoconservatives can uphold capitalism as an outgrowth of freedom and emphasize the need for a society to cultivate traditional virtues. For Strauss, the justification for these two thrusts rested upon the beliefs that a social order depends upon clearly understood and widespread opinions about right and wrong and that if these restrictive beliefs are absent, the measure of freedom so adored by the philosopher will be more restricted. In brief, Strauss wanted a society that was reasonably bound by conventions so that the philosopher can live free to think and teach, so long as he teaches responsibly.

Voegelin, on the other hand, took seriously and participated in both the philosophical and the theological traditions of the West. That he did so by emphasizing that theology, properly understood, is an adjunct to philosophy, proved a minor annoyance to his admirers. Indeed, when in the 1950s Voegelin emphasized the "equivalence" between the symbols of Moses and Plato—with the Christian symbolism the most articulate expression of the underlying experience—Christians could accept alien traditions while recognizing a single normative order under which all people live. Voegelin provided no real comfort, much less ammunition, for the emerging neoconservatives, but for the traditionalists, his early and middle works seemed the best philosophical response to the liberal society in which they lived. Although the later Voegelin embarrassed his Catholic followers, his earlier works continue to gird them for battle.

For their parts, Strauss and Voegelin avoided labeling themselves or associating with any overtly political groups. Voegelin wandered in and out of conservative institutional circles, writing for the *Intercollegiate Review* and accepting a position at the Hoover Institution. He appears to have cultivated friendships with a few well-placed conservatives, but he largely remained independent of those circles as well. Strauss was more aloof—but not his students.

Strauss and Voegelin were two European emigrés who never felt entirely at home in the United States. Although their relationships among Americans were numerous, their most important intellectual partners were Europeans or other emigrés. They were more embroiled with debates about Husserl or Heidegger than about James or Dewey. Both men wrote as German thinkers, which means that one should explore their relationships with Hans-Georg Gadamer, Paul Ricoeuer, Alfred Schutz, Alexander Kojeve, and Hannah Arendt, to name a few. Yet it is their adopted home in which they are destined, I think, to have the greatest impact. They helped bring Continental thought to America—to the American right—and as a consequence, they changed the shape of conservatism in America. Another European emigré, Friedrich von Hayek, helped recast the conservative reaction to "the liberal state" by connecting the New Deal with totalitarianism. Similarly, Strauss and Voegelin provided conservatives with a frightening backdrop against which to view Anglo-American trends. The problems did not concern this or that policy, or even tradition, but emerged from the growing allegiance people were paying to instrumental reason. The belief that humans could control their world and their destiny, Strauss and Voegelin suggested, rested hidden beneath the enormous technical successes of the modern age, and conservatives who believed them could no longer consider technological advances as unqualified improvements. In short, Strauss and Voegelin helped give a historical sweep to the conservative struggle even as they more clearly identified the enemy.

THE CONSERVATIVE PREDICAMENT

If the enemy they identified was the Enlightenment and with it a faith in human-directed progress, there is some question today as to whether conservatives have abandoned the Enlightenment tradition that Voegelin and Strauss connected with liberalism. As the political fortunes of the right rose, beginning as early as 1968 but especially 1980, the debate within the right escalated. Increasingly it appears that the main fissure (though there are hundreds of others) in the right, at least at the level of ideas or principles, has developed between those who thoroughly reject modern liberalism and those who seek to restrain it by one means or another. The two sides of the growing divide might even be designated conservative (those who seek to conserve the American liberal tradition by saving it from its own excesses) and reactionary (those who reject root and branch liberal ideas as products of modern, Enlightenment principles). My purpose in undermining my own (earlier) definition is twofold. First, to make sense of the ideological and political topography of our times we must be aware of the various meanings attached to everyday words, and we must insist upon asking for definitions of any who use them. Second, I wish to make a point in this concluding section: conservatives whom I have described as possessing a conservative imagination have no choice in the present age but to become thorough reactionaries. Indeed, to maintain the integrity of their principles they may need to seek practical or political alliances with groups on the left. With many members of the left they share a critique of key characteristics of a consumerist society, but their varying prescriptions would prevent conservatives from losing their identity and thereby being enervated by success—as they are today.

A brief and selective look at the recent past may help expose the intellectual and political dynamic of the right generally and of conservatives more specifically. I hope, in the process, to shed some light on the recent rise of the right and what that means for conservatives—especially for the conservative intellectual movement.

The heart of the "respectable right" that emerged in the 1950s was a constellation of thinkers who advocated either traditionalism— usually Catholic devotees of natural law—or a 1950s' version of libertarianism, usually emphasizing the baneful effects of government intervention in economic affairs. For all their differences, these two groups shared a fear of what James Burnham called the managerial revolution, the attempt of certain elites to construct a "new man" and a new age by managing most aspects of human life. Outside of the sweeping historical and philosophical arguments about the nature of the modern age, members of this coalition could point to the European drift toward wholesale restructuring and to the growth of centripetal forces in the United States inaugurated by the New Deal and which accelerated during the war. For these thinkers, recent events (going back to 1933) marked a dramatic shift in the equilibrium of American political, economic, and social life, and it was to these events that they were reacting.

It took William F. Buckley, Jr., to "fuse" these two elements of resistance into a conservative front with the *National Review* articulating the view of the responsible right. Traditionalist conservatives participated—sometimes reluctantly—in this common front, but they also worked in their own institutions and through their own journals to advance a conservative response to larger and somewhat more esoteric modern trends. They tended to emphasize cultural matters more than governmental issues, and in the context of their own journals said almost nothing about the nostrum of the other half of the movement, "free enterprise." The economic question is the most difficult for the traditionalists to deal with effectively. In the late 1940s Richard Weaver, a southern traditionalist, emphasized that property rights (what he called a metaphysical right) concerned the property of a farmer or small businessman but not the "abstract" property of stock, bonds, and corporations. Traditionalists feared a growing, centralizing, and bureaucratizing federal government, but they never forgot that "capitalism" tends to undermine the traditions, customs, and reverence for the past that they so cherish. On this subject they have remained reticent if not entirely silent.

Nonetheless, the coalition worked temporarily for several reasons, of which two strike me as especially significant. First, its members had a common enemy, however abstract. Insofar as they focused upon the encroachment of centralizing forces their differences could even strengthen their bond. The traditionalist could assent to the most important statements by libertarians (and various other groups like Taft Republicans) who devoted their energy to fighting the enemy while at the same time traditionalists could concentrate in their more academic journals on the cultural questions that did not much concern the libertarians. Second, the conservative movement had to fight against more radical and populist right-wing groups, most famously the John Birch Society. Buckley effectively defined the "respectable right" during the late 1950s and early 1960s to exclude the most populist movements. This exclusion had the effect of binding together the other elements of the right (in their own minds and in the minds of liberals) into a conservative movement and at the same time created an elitist movement dominated by northeastern, Ivy-league educated, cosmopolitan, and wealthy conservatives.

The raucous years of the late 1960s and early 1970s brought new elements into the conservative movement, giving it more political power at the expense of a clear identity. Richard Nixon's 1968 presidential campaign, aimed at the "silent majority," indicated the growing political importance of frustrated and even alienated Americans. The growth of two groups changed the dynamics of the conservative movement. The first might be called the populist right. These are the people who had long felt that the federal government was working against their interest and that the nation was increasingly controlled by a class of intellectuals who sought to reshape America in their image. These "middle Americans" were upset not only by the antiwar ferment but by the way the federal government (especially the unelected Supreme Court) was forcing changes on them. They resented the elitist intrusion into their local affairs. Many of these people were Christian fundamentalists who had come to feel that the changes in the United States, both in policy matters and in social and cultural matters, reflected an anti-Christian bias. To the chagrin of a great many liberals who had thought that Christian fundamentalism had died in the 1920s, fundamentalists proved to be very numerous indeed, making them the largest untapped source of political power in the 1970s.

The neoconservatives, whose leaders had begun as intellectuals on the left but who had become disillusioned with the radicalism of the 1960s and early 1970s, also joined the conservative movement. They brought a more pragmatic perspective. Although they usually emphasized the great virtues of the Western tradition they were generally less interested in that heritage than in finding practical, political means of curbing liberalism. They sought to roll back many of the government programs of the Great Society on the grounds that they did not work. Indeed, many of the neoconservatives advocated alternative programs (some governmental, others private) that they argued would better deal with the problems. In short, then, they accepted more of the liberal assumptions than did either of the original groups that composed the conservative movement. Furthermore, the neoconservatives shared with their liberal counterparts a passion for politics and political action. As these intellectuals moved into conservative institutions (which they came to dominate by 1980) they turned them into think tanks designed to provide policy analysis and advice. It is not surprising, then, that when a "conservative" president came to office he drew upon these policy specialists to implement his conservative revolution. As one might expect, the conservative revolution amounted, in part, to an ideological takeover of the instruments of power (bureaucracy) rather than a fundamental change in the nature and extent of government.

The current era of the conservative movement (beginning in 1980) is astonishingly complex, but the major elements were already in place by 1980—traditionalists, free-market advocates, populists, neoconservatives. The introduction of the snake oil of supply-side economics would complicate matters by providing a common political cause that hid but also aggravated internal divisions. The movement stayed together partly because Ronald Reagan was capable of being all things to all people, but in the struggle to get control over the levers of power, the neoconservatives and their free market allies won.

Their victory was indeed meaningful—the center of the political debate had shifted to the right. Democratic candidates avoid the taint of the "liberal" label, and hardly anyone advocates a return to the Great Society, at least directly. But was the victory translated into a revolution? Nothing could be further from the truth. By any indicator one wishes to consult, the fifteen years after the election of Ronald Reagan were characterized more by continuity than by change. Even the rhetoric of the president himself was charged with the electricity of progress, not return. Reagan promised to bring about peace and widespread prosperity by new means. He reminded his listeners time and again of the power of the American people to chart their own course, to create a future of their own making. He would facilitate this great awakening by unleashing the power of the market—which had been transformed by supply-siders into a system of benevolence that could translate individual self-interest into public altruism—to create full employment and rising wages.

The political success of the broader conservative movement meant the defeat of the traditionalist conservatives. The neoconservatives and their allies became the new "respectable" right, but while the political center moved to the right, the right end of the spectrum was truncated. The "Reagan revolution" effectively eliminated socialists and conservatives—all those who challenge the value of large-scale capitalist enterprises and consumerism—from the acceptable political spectrum.

The conservative imagination now seems further removed from American experience—or at least political experience—than ever before. The social order is no longer shaped by a dedication to tradition, governed by a clearly articulated concept of natural law, or organized into variegated and largely local institutions. All forms of localism, it seems to conservatives, are imperiled or dead as a result of the growing integration of the world economy, with increased political and military internationalism, and with judicial nationalism. Hierarchy is more or less tied to wealth, which in turn is connected to the complex and international corporate economy, making old notions of noblesse oblige (which entails obligations to one's own people) archaic. Even traditional virtues—so cherished by conservatives as necessary for a democratic order—are undermined by the institutions they helped create. If capitalism depended, originally, upon the virtues of hard work, extensive savings, and deferred gratification, today the dynamics of the consumer culture encourage consumption over production; immediate gratification; a preference for the new over the old; and, in general, a hostility toward all restrictions (internal or external) on behavior.

The conservative predicament, then, is that the American people are no longer guided by the internal principles of restraint and motivation that once made them conservative just as the social and political order no longer has the essential means of buttressing the virtues necessary for a successful conservative renascence. The realistic options for conservatives are few. Many conservatives (especially neoconservatives) choose to draw upon Strauss's conclusion that the United States represents a salutary balance of modern and premodern beliefs and that the resulting society of freedom and opportunity can be sustained by working to keep premodern beliefs (especially notions of a transcendental moral order) as restraining influences. Yet for them there must be a sense in which the balance is out of kilter, which would send them back to the founding fathers as venerable exemplars for our troubled times. Unfortunately, for many of this group, their goal will be undermined by the fact that they do not truly believe in what they call others to believe.

Traditionalist conservatives find themselves without much to conserve. Their only real option in these times is to seek recovery rather than conservation. Even though many of them might devote a good deal of energy to the political realm, their own understanding of the world dictates that they must seek social restructuring by calling upon individuals and small groups to resist the charms of the modern world in favor of the truths represented by the Christian natural law tradition. They might call people back to an older notion of responsibility to family and community, they might try to educate people into living lives of virtue, and they might remind people of the larger reality (transcending the physical world) in which they play a part and to which they have a responsibility. They might do all of these things, but as they very well know, a society ordered around these virtues and beliefs requires institutions that shape citizens. They know as well that people must feel an affection or love for their family, community, and other social units for them to participate as virtuous citizens. Finally, these conservatives know that faith of the sort they require is not a matter of simple choice but part of the great patrimony one inherits from a society one cherishes.

A favorite aphorism of traditionalist conservatives comes from Edmund Burke: "To make us love our country, our country ought to be lovely." Burke penned these words as part of a lament about the direction of his own time. "All the decent drapery of life," he wrote, "is to be rudely torn off. All the superadded ideas, furnished from the wardrobe of a moral imagination, which the heart owns, and the understanding ratifies, as necessary to cover the defects of our naked, shivering nature, and to raise it to dignity in our own estimation, are to be exploded as ridiculous, absurd, and antiquated fashion."[5] Perhaps not since Burke wrote those words have conservatives had as much reason to feel so utterly besieged. What is different, however, is that contemporary conservatives are operating in a more thoroughly modern, secularized age. They find themselves, then, like Voegelin, in a disordered age seeking the roots of order. They no longer have the luxury of conservation, but of necessity they must become reactionaries who call for a return to Christian faith and to political philosophy as a normative enterprise.

In some ways, then, Strauss and Voegelin become more important to conservatives in the 1990s than they were in the 1950s, not because the two philosophers became conservatives but because conservatives must become reactionaries. Now more than ever conservatives require, for their own survival, a clear understanding (in practical terms it does not matter that their understanding be historically accurate) of the origins and nature of their situation as well as some sense of that to which they are calling their nation back. Strauss and Voegelin provide them with versions of the causes of the present problem, but conservatives will have to look elsewhere, I suspect, for a clear articulation of their plea.

I have not attempted in this book to describe the precise influence of these two philosophers on the thinking of specific conservatives. Rather, I found Strauss and Voegelin to be two compelling figures who sought to make sense of their world. They believed that they lived in an age of crisis. As political philosophers, they devoted their lives to understanding the nature of that crisis and to finding answers (or to rearticulating the problems as the only acceptable solutions). This is the story I have tried to tell—two men in reaction to their times. Whether they were correct about the nature of our world or not, their struggles tell us something of the anxiety that accompanies life in a universe adrift.

NOTES

CHAPTER I. LABELS, DEFINITIONS, AND OTHER FORMS OF
COERCION

1. T. S. Eliot, *The Idea of Christian Society* (New York: Harcourt, Brace, and Company, 1940), 64–65.

2. Several letters from Voegelin testify to his rejection of the label. The most interesting letters were directed to John East and George Nash. Consult the Voegelin Papers, Hoover Institution Archives, Box 10, file 23, and Box 26, file 13, which are also the sources of the quotations.

3. James Kloppenberg, *Uncertain Victory* (New York: Oxford University Press, 1986).

4. Eric Voegelin, *Order and History,* vol. 1, *Israel and Revelation* (Baton Rouge: Louisiana State University Press, 1956), ix, 1 (hereafter cited as OH 1). Others of the 5-volume work are vol. 2, *The World of the Polis* (1957, hereafter cited as OH 2); *Plato and Aristotle* (1957, OH 3); *The Ecumenic Age* (1974, OH 4); and *In Search of Order* (1978, OH 5).

5. Eric Voegelin, *Autobiographical Reflections* (Baton Rouge: Louisiana State University Press, 1989), 18 (hereafter cited as AR).

6. Ibid., 9–10.

7. Gregor Sebba, "Prelude and Variations on the Theme of Eric Voegelin," *Southern Review* 13 (Autumn 1977): 649.

8. AR, 21.

9. Ibid., 11.

10. Ibid., 28.

11. From this work Voegelin grew to appreciate the way traditions can incorporate philosophical wisdom without the "technical apparatus." Germany, he later realized, did not have "political institutions rooted in an intact common sense tradition" (see AR, 29).

12. He never published this work, though a small portion came out later in a volume edited by John H. Hallowell, *From Enlightenment to Revolution* (Durham: Duke University Press, 1975); hereafter cited as FER. Louisiana State University Press will publish the entire work in a *Complete Works of Eric Voegelin* series.

13. AR, 63.

14. There is good reason to be suspicious of Voegelin's memory concerning this project. He set out to write a textbook, but the book ballooned into many

thousands of pages, making the original project impractical, and he was unsuccessful in his attempts to publish the work. Moreover, he incorporated much of this material into volumes 2 and 3 of *Order and History.* Voegelin overstated the break he made, but the shift from reified ideas to experience is real enough.

15. *The New Science of Politics* (Chicago: University of Chicago Press, 1952), III (hereafter cited as NSP).

16. Ibid., 167.

17. Ibid., 162–63.

18. Ibid., 130–31.

19. Allan Bloom's brief retrospective on Strauss's work is excellent, though a bit hagiographic. Bloom's essay examines many of the same issues that I explore in this section. See "Leo Strauss: September 20, 1899–October 18, 1973," *Political Theory* 2 (November 1974): 379.

20. Strauss borrowed this phrase from Spinoza's book. For Strauss it is a very rich phrase, without a clear definition. It stands for a number of issues about the nature of politics and the role of religious beliefs in society.

21. A proper discussion of Strauss necessarily entails textual analysis. Therefore much of my discussion in later sections dealing with Strauss will revolve around key texts.

22. *On Tyranny: An Interpretation of Xenophon's Hiero,* rev. and expanded ed., including the Strauss-Kojeve correspondence, ed. Victor Gourevitch and Michael Roth (New York: Free Press, 1991), 27 (hereafter cited as OT). It strikes one as odd that Strauss would use "Socratic rhetoric" as an example of language strategies designed to meet the needs of the philosopher while protecting both the society and him from society. Socrates, of course, was killed by the city of Athens for corrupting the youth. Although Strauss does not discuss this matter here, he argued on other occasions that the young and unwise Socrates—the Socrates of Aristophanes—presented himself unvarnished to his fellow Athenians and that he learned too late the need to protect himself and the city with rhetorical strategies designed to buttress the religious beliefs of the city.

23. Ibid., 28.

24. In 1952 Strauss published *Persecution and the Art of Writing* (Chicago: University of Chicago Press, 1988, hereafter cited as PAW) in which he developed more fully his theory of esoteric writing. The book also includes an essay representing Strauss's revised reading of Spinoza—his esoteric reading.

25. Strauss's desire to return to the dawn of philosophy has striking parallels with Heidegger.

26. "The Three Waves of Modernity," in *Political Philosophy: Six Essays by Leo Strauss,* ed. Hilail Gildin (Indianapolis: Pegasus, 1975), 91.

CHAPTER 2. LIBERAL AMERICA AND ITS DISCONTENTS

1. Several scholars have written useful books on this subject. See H. Stuart Hughes, *The Sea Change* (New York: Harper and Row, 1975), and Martin

Jay has written an excellent book on the logical positivists, *The Dialectical Imagination* (New York: Little, Brown, 1973). See also Laura Fermi's *Illustrious Immigrants* (Chicago: University of Chicago Press, 1968) and Donald Fleming and Bernard Bailyn, eds., *The Intellectual Migration* (Cambridge, Mass.: Belknap Press, 1968).

2. Alfred Kazin described watching the scenes in theaters: "It was unbearable. People coughed in embarrassment, and in embarrassment many laughed." The quote comes from Kazin's book *Starting Out in the Thirties* (Boston: Little, Brown, 1965), 166, but I first ran across it in Richard Pells's excellent book on this period, *The Liberal Mind in a Conservative Age* (New York: Harper and Row, 1985), 47. Of the profusion of recent books on the fifties, Pells's book stands out. Pells has shaped my opinion of this period in numerous ways, but certainly his discussion of Arendt forced me to reassess her work. I also found John Diggins's book, *The Proud Decades* (New York: W. W. Norton, 1988), very useful. See also William O'Neil, *American High: The Years of Confidence, 1945-1960* (New York: Free Press, 1986).

3. Many people believed—and still believe—that the concentration camps were secret and therefore largely unknown among the general population. Such a belief makes it much easier to blame their existence on Hitler, Himmler, and company. The question of the complicity, or even knowledge, of the general population with regard to "the final solution" is very much debated and debatable. A more fruitful discussion about the complicity of the German population requires examining the role the population played in the larger context of legalized anti-Semitism, and the literature on this subject is overwhelming. A good starting point is Hans Mommsen, "The Reaction of the German Population to the Anti-Jewish Persecution and the Holocaust," in *Lessons and Legacies: The Meaning of the Holocaust in a Changing World*, ed. Peter Hayes (Evanston: Northwestern Illinois Press, 1991). A very provocative examination of the Holocaust is Richard Rubenstein, *The Cunning of History* (New York: Harper and Row, 1975).

4. The nature and objectives of war had changed slowly, but in World War II the issues appeared especially stark. The distinction between combatant and noncombatant almost disappeared, and new weapons provided new and fearsome means of terrorizing. It was a war between whole nations rather than between armies. Neither side of the war remained innocent with regard to violating traditional limits governing warfare.

5. Consult John Diggins's excellent book, *Up from Communism* (New York: Harper and Row, 1975).

6. James Burnham, *The Machiavellians: Defenders of Freedom* (New York: John Day, 1943). The subtitle reveals much about the book: "A Defense of Political Truth Against Wishful Thinking."

7. James Burnham, "Lenin's Heir," *Partisan Review* 12 (Winter 1945): 66.

8. Many scholars have chipped away at Arendt's theses. With regard to the Nazi regime, Arendt probably overstates her case, especially with regard to the economic institutions.

9. This is a complicated subject. Even among early so-called liberal phi-

losophers like Hobbes and Locke the state-of-nature construct served heuristic purposes. By the nineteenth and twentieth centuries, this fiction had clearly lost its usefulness. John Dewey, for instance, argued forcefully that society provides the context for individual human development. Nonetheless, liberalism, as a coherent body of thought, depends upon this fiction, which creates a great deal of tension for liberal intellectuals.

10. A powerful strain of liberalism has attempted to escape this language. Max Weber was the most articulate spokesman of this view, which emphasizes a procedural liberalism whereby government and other social institutions serve as means to adjudicate differences among competing social groups in a pluralistic society. The goal of such a liberalism is accommodation of as many views (and behaviors) as possible through the procedures of government. Critics of this view argue that it further separates liberalism from the necessary moral questions concerning the proper ends of government. Moreover, although this view influenced the development of liberal governments in Europe and the United States and found expression in powerful thinkers like John Dewey, liberals have never completely escaped from their rights-oriented tradition. Some intellectuals, in light of the fate of Weimar, even suggest that these trends contributed to the horrific experiences of this century.

11. The claim here is that government exists to protect individuals from harm (crime, national defense, etc.) and to foster an environment in which individuals have as much freedom to pursue their goals as possible. One need take only a small leap to find in this definition a role for government to help those people who find themselves at a disadvantage in getting a fair shot to accomplish their goals. Here begins the long-standing tension among liberals between the incompatible goals of liberty and equality. Liberals remain true to their heritage by seeking a balance between the two.

12. Since rights can be created or eliminated with relative ease in an intellectual environment that does not depend heavily upon tradition and does not have a reasonably strong theological or metaphysical base for rights, the focus of government can change to secure the changing conceptions of rights.

13. I offer here the emphases of twentieth-century liberals. These goals are compatible with earlier goals. Tolerance is little more than a dedication to pluralism just as social justice emphasizes the fairness for which constitutions were written.

14. Lionel Trilling, *The Liberal Imagination* (New York: Viking Press, 1950), x.

15. See Lionel Trilling's essay (untitled) in *Partisan Review* 15 (August 1948): 389.

16. *The Liberal Imagination*, xi.

17. Ibid., xiii-xiv.

18. Louis Hartz, *The Liberal Tradition in America* (New York: Harcourt, Brace, and Company, 1955), 32, 309.

19. Reinhold Niebuhr, *The Irony of American History* (New York: Charles Scribner's Sons, 1952), 22.

20. Ibid., 16.

21. Arthur Schlesinger, *The Vital Center* (Boston: Houghton Mifflin Company, 1949), x, ix.

22. From the perspective of the late twentieth century the word "democracy" appears problematic. Widely differing regimes argue that they act according to democratic principles, each type of regime defining the concept differently. In the years before 1917, democracy referred to relatively generous suffrage laws and an active electorate with regard to policy issues.

23. Walter Lippmann, *Drift and Mastery* (Englewood Cliffs, N.J.: Prentice-Hall, 1961), 14, 18.

24. David Hollinger, "Science and Anarchy: Walter Lippmann's *Drift and Mastery,*" *American Quarterly* 29 (1977): 467.

25. Walter Lippmann, *An Inquiry into the Principles of the Good Society* (Boston: Little, Brown, 1937), 3.

26. Ibid., 373–74.

27. Walter Lippmann, *Essays in the Public Philosophy* (Boston: Little, Brown, 1955), 5.

CHAPTER 3. FROM PHILOSOPHY TO POSITIVISM

1. One is almost reduced to reifying modernity when discussing Strauss and Voegelin. The complicated meanings of the word will become clear later, but it is important to note that the term referred to a cluster of beliefs, expectations, and aspirations that had become socially effective. Because they were so widely accepted in intellectual circles Strauss and Voegelin felt justified in giving these beliefs a life that developed and adapted to the changing times through the thoughts of concrete individuals.

2. Leo Strauss, *The Rebirth of Classical Political Rationalism*, ed. Thomas L. Pangle (Chicago: University of Chicago Press, 1989), 28; italics in original (hereafter cited as RCPR).

3. Ibid.

4. OT, 250; emphasis added.

5. Ibid., 27–28. The essay from which this quote comes was not originally published by Strauss. Thomas Pangle brought together typescript notes of a lecture, and it has a disarmed quality that one rarely finds in Strauss's works.

6. NSP, 11.

7. The most common complaint, on the occasion of a severe disagreement concerning a substantive question, is that one's opponent wrongly framed the question, that he or she chose a language or concept ill-suited to the problem. Perhaps the common ground is the assertion of an intimate connection between language and problem. The fight takes place, then, over the proper language. Whose conceptualizations will rule?

8. This is a very long and detailed letter dealing with nearly every page of Voegelin's book. Voegelin made passing references to the "letter," but as far as I know he never responded in any detail to Kelsen (Hoover Institution, Voegelin Papers, Box 63, folder 13).

9. The question, What does statement X mean? when posed by a positivist has the effect of forcing one to play according to her rules. By meaningfulness she wants to relate a statement to phenomena, which requires, in matters of greatest importance, the reduction of a symbol to a concept.

10. Several points emerge in this paragraph that we cannot unpack in this context. In a very illuminating letter to Leo Strauss (22 April 1951), Voegelin addressed the issue of pregivens in the context of revelation: "Revealed knowledge is, in the building of human knowledge, that knowledge of the pregivens of perception. . . . To these pregivens belongs the experience of man of himself as *esse, nosse, velle*, the inseparable primal experience: I am as knowing and willing being; I know myself as being and willing; I will myself as a being and a knowing human. . . . the human being is not a consciousness . . . that neither the 'I' nor the 'Thou' can be 'constituted' out of consciousness . . . that one cannot construct self-consciousness as the act of perception after the model of a sensuous perception . . . instead what is involved here is the pregivens of perception." This letter is found in *Faith and Political Philosophy: The Correspondence Between Leo Strauss and Eric Voegelin, 1934–1964*, ed. Peter Emberley and Barry Cooper (University Park: Pennsylvania State University Press, 1993), 83 (hereafter cited as FPP).

11. "The Origins of Scientism," *Social Research* 15 (1948): 462–94.

12. He would always emphasize the events of that century as crucial, but he pushed the roots of modernity back to the thirteenth century in NSP and then back to Jesus and Paul in OH 4.

13. Voegelin could write about the ideational structure of a society because certain ideas become socially relevant and powerful at the expense of others. This process exposes much about the spiritual health of a society, i.e., the people who compose the society.

14. "The Origins of Scientism," 473.

15. Ibid., 481–82, 484.

16. Ibid., 485, 487.

17. Ibid., 490–91.

18. Voegelin, "The Theory of Legal Science," *Louisiana Law Review* 4 (1942): 564.

19. "The Origins of Scientism," 494.

20. See for example Strauss's *What Is Political Philosophy?* (Chicago: University of Chicago Press, 1988), 18–20 (hereafter cited as WPP).

21. RCPR, 3.

22. Ibid., 4. See also Leo Strauss, *Natural Right and History* (Chicago: University of Chicago Press, 1950), 76–80 (hereafter cited as NRH). Here Strauss compared the world created by scientists and the world experienced prescientifically. The context was Max Weber's use of ideal types and other artificial constructs as well as his fact/value distinction. Strauss wrote,

"The natural world, the world in which we live and act is not the object or the product of a theoretical attitude, it is a world not of mere objects at which we detachedly look but of 'things' and 'affairs' which we handle."

23. Ibid., 5.

24. WPP, 18–19.

25. Ibid., 20.

26. RCPR, 6. Note also his "Restatement on Xenophon's Hiero," in which he wrote: "A social science that cannot speak of tyranny with the same confidence with which medicine speaks, for example, of cancer, cannot understand social phenomena as what they are. It is therefore not scientific" (OT, 177). Because social science concerns fundamentally value-laden and moral issues, a value-free social science makes only a little more sense than a value-free moral science.

27. Ibid.

28. Ibid., 8.

29. Ibid.

30. Strauss's emphasis upon positivism in some measure cloaks his much greater concern about the danger of "historicism." He wrote about both because he considered them to be intimately related. One might expect that the failure of dogmatism (that search for certain and irrefutable knowledge) to provide answers to political and social problems would lead to a cynical reaction or a radical skepticism (historicism). When the effort to find the final answer fails, one might be prone to deny all claims to knowledge or truth. If we pursue this simplified schema of modernity a bit, we might say that Strauss pitched a battle against the cynics while Voegelin opened a front against the dogmatists. This comparison is meant to suggest matters of emphasis, but it also suggests some ways of understanding the evident differences that separate Strauss and Voegelin. Admiral Nimitz and General Eisenhower employed very different methods in their respective fronts, but the foe was still, in a meaningful way, common.

CHAPTER 4. THE NATURE OF MODERNITY

1. Leo Strauss, *Thoughts on Machiavelli* (Chicago: University of Chicago Press, 1958), 13 (hereafter cited as TM).

2. In a letter to Voegelin (29 April 1953), Strauss wrote about Machiavelli, "I can't help loving him—in spite of his errors" (see FPP, 98). Strauss's analyses of many moderns display a deep respect for the thinker—and not a little love. In the case of those like Locke or Burke who did not earn Strauss's respect, he treats their work almost cavalierly—in the case of Burke, Strauss was downright dishonest in his analysis. See Steven J. Lenzner's helpful essay, "Strauss's Three Burkes: The Problem of Edmund Burke in *Natural Right and History*," *Political Theory* 19 (August 1991): 364–90.

3. Strauss argued that the real message of a philosophic book is not directed to either nonphilosophers or mature philosophers. "All books of that

kind owe their existence to the love of the mature philosopher for the puppies of his race'' (PAW, 36). Strauss always referred to the ''teaching'' of a philosopher, indicating a relationship between student and teacher.

4. Ibid., 14.

5. TM, 14.

6. Ibid., 13.

7. The standard Strauss has established is an extremely difficult one. Problems abound in texts great and small; for those found in great texts, providing an explanation regarding the author's intention requires not only great rigor but perhaps a good bit of creativity. Nonetheless, Strauss was adamant on this point: ''Reading between the lines is strictly prohibited in all cases where it would be less exact than not doing so. Only such reading between the lines as starts from an exact consideration of the explicit statements of the author is legitimate. The context in which a statement occurs, and the literary character of the whole work as well as its plan, must be perfectly understood before an interpretation of the statement can reasonably claim to be adequate or even correct. One is not entitled to delete a passage, nor to emend its text, before one has fully considered all reasonable possibilities of understanding the passage as it stands—one of the possibilities being that the passage may be ironic'' (PAW, 30).

8. Ibid., 35.

9. For examples see TM, 400-441, and PAW, 68-74.

10. PAW, 70-71.

11. TM, 43. Strauss quoted Machiavelli to support his case: ''For some time I never say what I believe and I never believe what I say; and if it sometimes occurs to me that I say the truth, I conceal it among so many lies that it is hard to find it out'' (TM, 36).

12. Ibid., 30.

13. Ibid., 30-31.

14. Ibid., 45, 47.

15. For example, see PAW, 24-25.

16. *History of Political Philosophy*, ed. Leo Strauss and Joseph Cropsey (Chicago: University of Chicago Press, 1987), 311. See also TM, 48, 52.

17. The lengthy quote cited earlier concerning the argument from silence is found in the nineteenth paragraph in a chapter containing thirty-seven paragraphs—that is, it is at the very center of the chapter.

18. TM, 12.

19. Ibid., 10, 13.

20. For a sharply contrasting interpretation see Shadia Drury's misguided chapter on Machiavelli, ''Machiavelli's Subversion of Esotericism,'' in *The Political Ideas of Leo Strauss*, 114-32 (New York: St. Martin's Press, 1988).

21. The key to this interpretation is Machiavelli's shift in personal pronouns. He used ''thou'' when addressing the prince and ''you'' ''when addressing those whose interest is primarily theoretical''—the young (TM, 77).

22. Ibid., 67.

23. Ibid., 82.

24. Ibid., 80, 56–60.

25. Ibid., 139.

26. Ibid., 116.

27. Ibid., 133.

28. See ibid., 132, for his method.

29. Ibid., 126–27.

30. Ibid., 153–54.

31. Ibid., 168. Machiavelli politicized philosophy, destroying the older separateness of theory and action. The real problem of Machiavelli was that he sought to eliminate theory in favor of "techne," or instrumental reason for reason—the better to transform the world. Later thinkers, of course, sought to realize their ideal cities on earth. Marx stands out as the supreme example, but Heidegger's involvement in the Nazi regime was, for Strauss, the most telling.

32. Ibid., 173.

33. Ibid., 12.

34. Strauss never labeled Machiavelli's religious beliefs. He wrote that "it is not misleading to count Machiavelli among 'the wise of the world,'" whom he later identified as "*falasifa* or Averroists" (ibid., 175).

35. Ibid., 179.

36. Apparently Machiavelli's skills, great though they were, proved inadequate in this connection, as Machiavelli was placed on the Index. Strauss never mentioned this fact.

37. Note as examples TM, 176, 200, 202, 208. The first of these references provides a good example of Strauss's argument from Machiavelli's silence. The issue involves the fratricide committed at the founding of Rome and Machiavelli's silence concerning "what the Bible says about the fratricide committed by the first founder of any city." Machiavelli, Strauss insisted, needed to buttress his argument with reference to biblical teaching. "The fact that he failed to do so and at the same time spoke so rarely about revelation cannot be explained by blindness or ignorance but only by a peculiar mixture of boldness and caution: he silently makes superficial readers oblivious of the Biblical teaching."

38. Ibid., 183.

39. Ibid., 204. This is a particularly rich discussion by Strauss. He examined the use Machiavelli made of Moses—who was God's direct representative and so acted only in his capacity as a lieutenant—and King David, Jesus's direct ancestor. By accepting the traditional view that Moses acted as God's representative and David was a godly king, Machiavelli made the case that God is a tyrant. This claim follows from the argument Machiavelli made that all founders are tyrants and that no substantial differences separate Moses and David from those historical characters normally considered tyrants. Of course, the objective of this line of argument is to dissolve the distinction between prince and tyrant. See also ibid., 49.

40. Ibid., 185–86, 198–200.

41. Ibid., 218, 222, 223.

42. One of Strauss's characteristic arguments was that a creative tension obtains between religion and philosophy and that this tension is the genius of Western civilization. Machiavelli sought to tumble both as Strauss understood them.

43. TM, 132–33.

44. Ibid., 241.

45. Ibid., 279–80.

46. Ibid., 296, 297.

47. Ibid., 120.

48. Ibid., 231.

49. Consider two examples from TM: "Time and again we have become bewildered by the fact that the man who is more responsible than any other man for the break with the Great Tradition should in the very act of breaking prove to be the heir, the by no means unworthy heir, to that supreme art of writing which that tradition manifested at its peaks" (120); "Machiavelli did know pre-modern thought: it was before him. He could not have know the thought of the present time, which emerged as it were behind his back" (12).

50. Ibid., 231.

51. Ibid., 299.

52. I am grateful to Larry Peterman's insightful essay "Approaching Leo Strauss: Some Comments on *Thoughts on Machiavelli*," *Political Science Reviewer* 16 (Fall 1986): 317–51 for pointing out this reference that I otherwise would have overlooked. His essay clarified my thinking concerning the problem of problems in this text.

53. TM, 13–14.

54. These tensions are resolved by removing one of the poles. Hence, Machiavelli eliminated theory as understood by Plato in favor of techne (instrumental reason). He would not be bound by the ideal regime, which even Plato emphasized could only exist in speech. Machiavelli liberated moderns from the paradigm, thus elevating action over theory, and the technical approach to human life replaced the theoretical conception. Moreover, by eliminating the theoretical constructions of ideal regimes, Machiavelli lowered the dependence on chance by lowering the threshold of acceptability. The philosopher is liberated from the "ought."

55. From an unpublished manuscript "Political Science and the Intellectuals" found in the Voegelin Collection, Hoover Institution, Box 64, folder 13. This quote comes from p. 4.

56. Ibid., 5.

57. Ibid., 5–6.

58. It is important to emphasize that the divine-mundane symbolism of the cosmological societies was not disproved in some doctrinal sense but the experience was differentiated. The "beyond" symbol establishes a divine structure to reality that is outside of, and the ground of, historical existence.

59. The two chapters of OH 4 that deal with this subject (chapters 4 and

5) are the most controversial. Voegelin's Catholic followers especially find his characterization of Paul misleading. Nonetheless, few sections of his work are as brilliant as these two chapters.

60. NSP, 122.

61. Because history is a symbol for the teleological process directed by God, Joachim could speak of history rather than histories. There is only one history. Much like Paul before him, this hardened understanding of a singular and linear historical process became characteristic of ideologues like Marx. Of course such a single history was much simpler in the twelfth century than in the eighteenth or nineteenth centuries when knowledge of other civilizations (especially in the Orient) posed problems for any construction of history in the singular. It required the greatest intellectual talents of ideologues to work around this problem.

62. "Political Scientists and the Intellectuals," 15.

63. FPP, 73. The letter is dated 4 December 1950.

64. NSP, 144.

65. Doctrinalization formed part of a larger deformation of language. The mythical imagery of Plato or the Bible became opaque because the richness of the language got flattened into a catalogue of "ideas." In place of truth symbolized by myth or revelation, moderns live in a realm of competing *doxai* (opinions). Consider the way even respected scholars employ the word "ideology." Everyone, they would have us believe, must have an ideology. Clearly one's experiences will delimit the live options, but still one only gets opinions or "ideas." A person whose life is ordered by an openness to reality in its mundane and transcendent modes is literally unbelievable to the intellectual and gets turned into another ideologue. Voegelin's work on the deformation of language (nonsense to a deconstructionist—but what is not?) is understudied. A good place to start is OH 4, 36–43.

66. NSP, 155

67. "Political Science and the Intellectuals," 7.

68. See Hallowell's introduction to FER, ix.

69. Ibid., 25.

70. Voegelin substantiated this claim by reference to Voltaire's categories of meaning, which Voegelin claimed were Christian analogues (ibid., 11).

71. Ibid., 26.

72. Ibid., 27; quote from Voltaire.

73. Voegelin defined the term in an unpublished essay, "The Necessary Moral Bases for Communication in a Democracy" (Hoover Institution, Box 66, file 7): "the transformation of our conceptions of society by moving the substance of society from the Mystical Body of Christ through the scale of the ontological hierarchy down to organic substances and drives" (11).

74. FER, 28–29.

75. Ibid., 32.

76. One especially splenetic case is in a letter to Leo Strauss in which Voegelin suggested that Locke wrote esoterically, hiding the real nihilist

message from himself. In FPP, 92–93 (20 April 1953). See also the lengthy footnote on Locke in FER, 37–38.

77. FER, 69–70.

78. Ibid., 246.

79. Voegelin emphasized the swindle perpetrated by Marx and outlined Marx's intellectual dishonesty in *Science, Politics, and Gnosticism* (Chicago: Henry Regnery Company, 1968), 27–28 (hereafter cited as SPG), and FER, 259.

80. Voegelin discussed his use of magical imagery for Hegel in a response to Thomas J. J. Altizer's review essay of the essay under investigation. Voegelin wrote that he found "Hegel's self-declaration of the *Phanomenologie* as a work of magic. . . . I had read the passages on the 'magic words' and the 'magic force' in the *Phanomenologie* many a time without becoming aware of their implications." Later in the same essay he wrote, "In the contemporary world, alchemist magic is primarily to be found among the ideologists who infest the social sciences with their efforts to transform man, society, and history." Eric Voegelin, *Published Essays, 1966–1985,* ed. Ellis Sandoz, vol. 12 of *The Collected Works of Eric Voegelin* (Baton Rouge: Louisiana State University Press, 1990), 298 (hereafter cited as CW 12).

81. Ibid., 216–17.

82. Ibid., 218.

83. Ibid., 219–20.

84. Voegelin does suggest this point. He emphasized how the French Revolution and Napoleon's glorious battles disturbed Hegel: "He was worried in these days by the question how a philosopher could participate in the meaning of the bloody events which to him were the only meaningful reality in the world" (CW 12, 220).

85. The source for this quote is *Dokumente zu Hegels Entwicklung* (Stuttgart, 1936), 324.

86. CW 12, 221.

87. OH 4, 264.

88. Ibid., 266.

CHAPTER 5. THE CRISIS OF MODERNITY

1. Leo Strauss, *Political Philosophy: Six Essays by Leo Strauss,* ed., Hilail Gildin (Indianapolis: Pegasus, 1975), 81 (hereafter cited as PP).

2. See, for instance, Leo Strauss, *Studies in Platonic Political Philosophy,* Introduction and Bibliography by Thomas L. Pangle (Chicago: University of Chicago Press, 1983), 168 (hereafter cited as SPPP). The section reads in part: "Catastrophes and horrors of a magnitude hitherto unknown, which we have seen and through which we have lived, were better provided for, or made intelligible, by both Plato and the prophets than by the modern belief in progress."

3. T. S. Eliot, *The Idea of a Christian Society* (London: Faber and Faber, 1939), 63.

4. PP, 92.

5. Ibid., 95.

6. "Historicism asserts that all human thoughts or beliefs are historical, and hence deservedly destined to perish; but historicism itself is a human thought; hence historicism can be of only temporary validity, or it cannot be simply true. To assert the historicist thesis means to doubt it and thus to transcend it" (NRH, 25).

7. Ibid., 25.

8. Ibid., 26.

9. See RCPR, 25.

10. NRH, 27, 29.

11. Ibid., 31–32.

12. Thus philosophers do not have a comprehensive view. They are skeptics.

13. RCPR, 25.

14. Ibid., 26.

15. SPPP, 178.

16. The book also includes three book reviews, bringing the total number of "chapters" to fifteen. The chapter on Nietzsche is number eight.

17. Ibid., 147, 148, 149.

18. Ibid., 175.

19. Ibid., 176.

20. Ibid.; emphasis added.

21. Ibid., 177.

22. Ibid., 179.

23. Nietzsche's *Beyond Good and Evil*, aphorism 150. "Around the hero everything becomes a tragedy; around the demigod everything becomes a satyr-play; and around God everything becomes—what? perhaps a 'world'?" Strauss pointed to this aphorism as "Nietzsche's own theology" (SPPP, 181).

24. SPPP, 181, 182.

25. "He led us to suspect that the true science of religion, i.e. the empirical psychology of religion, is for all practical purposes impossible, for the psychologist would have to be familiar with the religious experience of the most profound homines religiosi and at the same time to be able to look down, from above, on these experiences" (ibid., 182).

26. Ibid., 182.

27. Ibid., 183.

28. Ibid., 188–89.

29. Ibid., 190.

30. Ibid.

31. Ibid., 191.

32. The most infamous attempt to answer this question is Shadia Drury's book, *The Political Ideas of Leo Strauss* (New York: St. Martin's Press, 1988). In her chapter on Nietzsche, Drury draws from very slim evidence to suggest

that Strauss's greatest intellectual debt was to Nietzsche (which Nietzsche is unclear) but that, unlike his intellectual father, he had learned to hide his real teaching. In the hands of Drury this conclusion takes on an almost sinister character. It is worth quoting the conclusion to her chapter on Nietzsche: "It is no use protesting that Strauss's real intellectual debt is to Plato and the ancients. For as we have seen, the ancients to whom Strauss appeals have been transfigured by Nietzsche. That Strauss insists on appealing to Plato rather than Nietzsche should not surprise us. He has learnt a lesson in political prudence from Machiavelli. He has learnt to use the 'prejudice in favor of antiquity' to establish 'new modes and orders'" (181). The problem—or the biggest problem—with Drury's conclusion is that one is left thinking of Strauss as a closet modern, a wiser Machiavelli. Strauss did see important connections between Nietzsche and Plato, but he did not see a Plato transfigured by Nietzsche. He saw a Nietzsche who in one important respect pointed back to Plato, but Nietzsche also pointed forward to Heidegger.

33. PP, 98.

34. RCPR, 24; emphasis in original.

35. Ibid., 25.

36. Ibid., 25–26.

37. Because all people are committed to some way of looking at the world, the difference between philosopher and nonphilosopher must be fate.

38. RCPR, 26.

39. See Leo Strauss, *Liberalism Ancient and Modern* (Ithaca: Cornell University Press, 1989), 256–57 (hereafter cited as LAM).

40. Ibid., 236–37.

41. See, for example, RCPR, 29.

42. One exception is Strauss's very important but very short essay "Philosophy as Rigorous Science and Political Philosophy" (republished in SPPP), in which he discussed Heidegger and Husserl.

43. "The more I understand what Heidegger is aiming at, the more I see how much still escapes me. The most stupid thing I could do would be to close my eyes or to reject his work" (RCPP, 30).

44. SPPP, 31; emphasis added.

45. Plato, Strauss, and Heidegger agreed on one thing: ontology is the heart of the philosophical pursuit.

46. RCPR, 29.

47. SPPP, 33.

48. Letter to Voegelin dated 17 December 1949, found in FPP, 63.

49. TM, 13.

50. WPP, 41.

51. A just order requires rule by the wise. But only the most favorable and fantastic conditions would allow the wisest to rule.

52. NRH, 178.

53. WPP, 46.

54. NRH, 169.

55. See ibid., 171, 173.

56. Ibid., 176, 177. "What Hobbes attempted to do on the basis of Machiavelli's fundamental objection to the utopian teaching of the tradition, although in opposition to Machiavelli's own solution, was to maintain the idea of natural law but to divorce it from the idea of man's perfection; only if natural law can be deduced from how men actually live, from the most powerful force that actually determines all men, or most men most of the time, can it be effectual or of practical value. The complete basis of natural law must be sought, not in the end of man, but in his beginnings, in the prima naturae or, rather, in the primum naturae. What is most powerful in most men most of the time is not reason but passion. Natural law will not be effectual if its principles are distrusted by passion or are not agreeable to passion. Natural law must be deduced from the most powerful of all passions" (180).

57. Ibid., 181–82.

58. The emphasis Strauss placed on the destruction to Christian beliefs caused by thinkers like Locke makes one reassess Strauss's claims about Machiavelli. Clearly, Strauss considered Machiavelli's attack on religion very important. Indeed, as I show later in this book, Strauss understood morality to be a function of religious beliefs.

59. NRH, 220.

60. Ibid., 221. Voegelin agreed with Strauss concerning Locke's Hobbesian trajectory. See Voegelin's letters to Strauss, 20 April 1953 and 15 April 1953, and Strauss's reply on 29 April 1953 in FPP, 92–98.

61. Strauss's reading of Locke was very selective. On this point concerning natural law, and when Strauss interpreted Locke to advocate the unlimited acquisition of wealth, Strauss focused upon a few key passages while ignoring the large number of contradictory passages. Because Strauss assumed that Locke, as a philosopher, could not be contradictory without the contradictions suggesting some esoteric meaning, Strauss was forced into an interpretation that took the minor note to really be the major note. But with Locke the method is strikingly unpersuasive. John Dunn examined Strauss's argument in an excellent article, "Justice and the Interpretation of Locke's Political Theory," *Political Studies* 16 (1968): 68–87. Dunn understands the contradictions in Locke's work as evidence of a genuine dilemma, or an ambiguity Locke was unable to clarify. But for Dunn, Locke remained faithful to the natural law tradition and to the Christian beliefs he professed. On the other hand, Dunn never took seriously Strauss's beliefs about philosophers and the manner in which they write. Concerning Locke and natural rights and natural law see NRH, 226–28, as well as the discussion of natural law in "The Law of Reason in the Kuzari" in PAW, 95–141, esp. 126–41.

62. "It is on the basis of Hobbes's view of the law of nature that Locke opposes Hobbes's conclusions. He tries to show that Hobbes's principle—the right of self-preservation—far from favoring absolute government, requires limited government. Freedom, 'freedom from arbitrary, absolute power,' is 'the fence' to self-preservation. Slavery is therefore against natural law ex-

cept as a substitute for capital punishment. Nothing which is incompatible with the basic right of self-preservation, and hence nothing to which a rational creature cannot suppose to have given free consent, can be just; hence civil society or government cannot be established lawfully by force or conquest: consent alone 'did or could give beginning to any lawful government of the world' " (NRH, 231). Moreover, with regard to Locke's view of happiness Strauss wrote: "Since there are therefore no pure pleasures, there is no necessary tension between civil society as the mighty leviathan or coercive society, on the one hand, and the good life, on the other: hedonism becomes utilitarianism or political hedonism. The painful relief of pain [i.e., the work that brings one out of the state of nature] culminates not so much in the greatest pleasures as 'in the having those things which produce the greatest pleasures.' Life is the joyless quest for joy" (NRH, 251).

63. Thus Locke did not consider property to be an absolute right but, rather, the means to secure natural rights. One may say that the right of property is dictated by natural law but not natural right. See NRH, 242.

64. Ibid., 235, 236.

65. Ibid., 244–45.

66. See ibid., 246–47.

67. Ibid., 248.

68. TM, 13–14.

69. NRH, 1.

70. Still, Strauss did not display great optimism. When commenting on the "Jewish problem" and the American experience he wrote: "I do not believe that the American experience forces us to qualify this statement. It is very far from me to minimize the difference between a nation conceived in liberty and dedicated to the proposition that all men are created equal, and the nations of the old world, which certainly were not conceived in liberty. I share the hope in America and the faith in America, but I am compelled to add that that faith and that hope cannot be of the same character as that faith and that hope which a Jew has in regard to Judaism and which the Christian has in regard to Christianity. No one claims that the faith in America and the hope in America are based on explicit divine promises" (RCPR, 233).

71. NRH, 2.

72. Ibid.

73. Strauss's argument suggests that the rise of social science as a privileged form of knowledge eventually undermined religious faith. On the other hand, Strauss does not suggest, so far as I can tell, that social science emerges as religion fades.

74. "Liberal relativism has its roots in the natural right tradition of tolerance or in the notion that everyone has a natural right to the pursuit of happiness as he understands happiness; but in itself it is a seminary of intolerance" (NRH, 6).

75. Political scientists begin with theories that they apply to real experiences. Political philosophers begin with real experiences as experienced by

political actors. Political philosophers believe that a much wider gap separates theory from praxis and thus do not seek to inform directly political actions. Nonetheless, political philosophy is edifying, without meaning to be so. See LAM, 8, 203–23.

76. Ibid., 218–19.

77. NRH, 2.

78. LAM, 224.

79. Ibid., 24.

80. Allan Bloom, *The Closing of the American Mind* (New York: Simon and Schuster, 1987). This is a crazy and wonderful book in desperate need of a good esoteric read. How is it possible that a book about America could leave almost all of America's heritage out and replace it with the German heritage? How could such a book become a best-seller? The chapter about rock music is the best expression of Bloom's attitude toward American popular culture.

81. LAM, 5.

82. Ibid., 24.

83. AN, 26.

84. CW 12, 34.

85. Ibid., 6.

86. Ibid., 5.

87. The essay also includes a section on the literary response to this disorder. The lack of public influence of these spiritually sensitive writers suggested to Voegelin that the people had lost contact with spiritual reality. The German university was "the iron curtain" that separated the spiritually sensitive literary figures from the larger educated public.

88. Ibid., 21.

89. Ibid., see especially 18–28.

90. Ibid., 25.

91. See ibid., 51.

92. All quotes from here to the end of this chapter, except where otherwise noted, come from a transcript of one of Voegelin's speeches, "The Necessary Moral Bases for Communication in a Democracy," found in the Voegelin Collection at the Hoover Institution, Box 66, folder 7.

93. See CW 12, 37–42.

CHAPTER 6. THE PHILOSOPHER

1. Speaking generally, Strauss's philosophy may have had a more direct impact on political conservatism. The coalition that, at least by the late 1970s, marched together as conservatives included a very influential group who were directly or indirectly Straussian. Voegelin, on the other hand, directly influenced few conservative thinkers, and they were largely Catholic, traditional conservatives—the core of what I am calling conservatism.

2. Strauss emphasized that for Socrates a contract was conventional, not natural. His admission to a contractual obligation to the city points out the ambiguous relationship between the philosopher (a person who lives according to nature) and the conventional city. No contract was necessary in the Republic since it represented the natural city. See NRH, 119.

3. LAM, 224.

4. "According to liberal democracy, the bond of society is universal human morality, whereas religion (positive religion) is a private affair. . . . The German Jews owed their emancipation to the French Revolution or its effects. They were given full political rights for the first time by the Weimar Republic. The Weimar Republic was succeeded by the only German regime—by the only regime that ever was anywhere—which had no other clear principle except murderous hatred of Jews, for 'Aryan' had no clear meaning other than 'non-Jewish.' One must keep in mind the fact that Hitler did not come from Prussia, nor even from Bismarck's Reich" (LAM, 226).

5. See ibid., 228, 230, 224.

6. Ibid., 230.

7. Ibid., 256.

8. Ibid., 227.

9. "I experience a tree; in doing so, I am not necessarily aware of my 'Ego' which is the condition of possibility of my experiencing anything." Strauss related this example to understanding Judaism. "Accordingly, when speaking of the Jewish experience, one must start from what is primary or authoritative for the Jewish consciousness, and not from what is the primary condition of possibility of Jewish experience: one must start from God's Law, the Torah, and not from the Jewish nation" (ibid., 237–38).

10. Ibid., 213.

11. Ibid., 231.

12. Strauss wrote in numerous places about the internal logic of orthodox faith. One example: The attacks by cultural Zionists on orthodoxy "and similar denials and interpretations lost all their force by the simple observation that they contradict not merely inherited opinion but present experience. . . . God's revealing Himself to man, His addressing man, is not merely known through tradition going back to the remote past and is therefore now 'merely believed' but is genuinely known through present experience which every human being can have if he does not refuse himself to it. This experience is not a kind of self-experience . . . [but] something undesired, coming from the outside, going against man's grain; it is the only awareness of something absolute which cannot be relativized in any way as everything else, rational or nonrational, can; it is the experience of God as the Thou, the father and king of all men" (LAM, 232).

13. Ibid., 239; emphasis added.

14. Ibid., 253.

15. Ibid., 241.

16. See ibid., 246.

17. Ibid., 245.

18. Ibid., 238.

19. Ibid., 246.

20. Ibid., 254.

21. See also Leo Strauss, *Philosophy and Law*, trans. Fred Baumann, foreword by Ralph Lerner (Philadelphia: Jewish Publication Society, 1987), 11 (hereafter cited as PL). Kenneth Hart Green identified Strauss's dependence on Gottfried Lessing for Strauss's understanding of the use of mockery by Enlightenment philosophers in their war against orthodoxy. See his essay " 'In the Grip of the Theological-Political Predicament:' The Turn to Maimonides in the Jewish Thought of Leo Strauss," in *Leo Strauss's Thought*, ed. Alan Udoff (Boulder, Colo.: Lynne Rienner Publishers, 1991), 41–74. See especially pp. 55–56.

22. LAM, 255.

23. When the greatest good becomes creativity (or the freedom to create) then the moral standard becomes self-control. No "transcendent" standard like God or nature creates an end to govern human behavior. Humans control ends and means.

24. LAM, 256.

25. Ibid., 236.

26. See Eve Adler's essay, "Leo Strauss's *Philosophie and Gersetz*," in *Leo Strauss's Thought*, 183–226, for problems concerning translation of this passage.

27. PL, 113–14.

28. Ibid., 18–19.

29. One of the several places in which Strauss mentioned the unevident foundations (i.e., grounded on belief) of modern philosophy is RCPR, 269–70. Consult also NRH, 173–76.

30. See PL, 5.

31. Ibid., 12.

32. The term "natural" is ambiguous. Earlier in the paragraph he mentioned the destruction of "natural theology and natural law." Strauss probably meant to suggest a holistic knowledge that emerges from a people's spiritual beliefs. Because, as I show later, Strauss used "natural" to refer to the conventional world—Plato's cave—(although at other times Strauss contrasted natural to conventional) which was governed by assumptions about the whole, natural knowledge should refer to the knowledge that springs from that cosmological myth. Because Strauss believed the Enlightenment philosophers also operated according to a myth (belief), we must consider that "natural" refers to something more. Perhaps the best way of understanding this issue is Strauss's belief that the Enlightenment was a revolt against nature—an attempt to overcome or master nature. Consequently those philosophers rejected the natural understanding and sought abstract (and the more empirical the more distanced from the experienced whole, and thus more abstract) ideals and tools. Thus, while they stepped out of the natural realm, they did not transcend it. More important, as I show later,

"natural" probably meant the assumption common to believers and philosophers that there is a whole about which we can know something meaningful. Also, this whole contains a transcendent standard for human life. Consult Kenneth Hart Green's essay, " 'In the Grip of the Theological-Political Predicament:' The Turn to Maimonides in the Jewish Thought of Leo Strauss," 47, 66–67.

33. PL, 12–13.

34. Ibid., 15.

35. Ibid., 13.

36. Note the attacks on all utopias. NRH, 178–97, 200–201; see also Strauss, *Spinoza's Critique of Religion* (New York: Schocken Books, 1965), 226–29.

37. LAM, 257.

38. PL, 112.

39. "There is no investigation into the history of philosophy that is not at the same time a *philosophical* investigation" (ibid., 23).

40. PAW, 154–55.

41. See Strauss's "On Collingwood's Philosophy of History," *Review of Metaphysics* 5 (June 1952): 559–86. Note especially on pp. 585–86: "History takes on philosophical significance for men living in an age of intellectual decline. Studying the thinkers of the past becomes essential for men living in an age of intellectual decline because it is the only practicable way in which they can recover a proper understanding of the fundamental problems."

42. PAW, 155.

43. Ibid., 156.

44. As for science, Strauss wrote: "Science, rejecting the idea of a final account of the whole, essentially conceives of itself as progressive, as being the outcome of progress of human thought beyond the thought of all earlier periods, and of being capable of still further progress in the future" (ibid., 15).

45. See "On Collingwood's Philosophy of History" for an examination of the blindness of modern historians to the ancient world.

46. PAW, 157; emphasis added.

47. In light of the preceding quote the original meaning of philosophy must be made in reference to an unprovable assumption that there is a whole or "a being." Such an assumption rested upon "commonsense"—or on the necessary posits of everyday life.

48. To make another stab at the meaning of "natural" in this context, Strauss equated natural with the assumptions that (a) there exists a whole about which humans can know something and (b) the account of the whole is important to human life. Thus, to live in Plato's cave is to live in primordial awareness of a whole of which one forms a part.

49. Only people seeking the natural cave have need of history.

50. PL, 20; emphasis added.

51. Strauss understood that the Jewish philosophers took their inspiration

from Plato (despite the apparent Aristotelianism of their thought) while Christian thought was obviously more influenced by Aristotle. The differences in Plato's and Aristotle's conceptions of natural right discussed in NRH may be important with regard to the appropriation of these doctrines by Jews and Christians.

52. See PAW, 9–10.

53. Ibid., 18–19.

54. PL, 25.

55. Ibid., 53; emphasis in original. See also note 88 on p. 121.

56. Ibid., 126; emphasis in original.

57. PAW, 56.

58. PL, 55–58. See also NRH, 91.

59. See PL, 106–10.

60. By presuppositions Strauss meant the given of the social world into which one is born.

61. See PL, 83.

62. Ibid., 84, 99.

63. See NRH, 141, for Strauss's discussion of the need to establish a code that is persuasive to the unwise, thus giving the wise consent to rule.

64. See RCPR, 236.

65. See Ibid., 236–37.

66. See PAW, 31–32.

67. Of course when old worlds die, new ones may be created. An unmistakable sense of expectation and excitement creeps into Strauss's work. After all, if Strauss considered the Christian religion a poor foundation for political order, then the process of modernity, or rather the final collapse of the modern project, produces a terrifying chaos waiting for a new creator to give it form. Strauss wrote about how these conditions made an understanding of the classics possible again (traditions had obscured them). Thus the principles of classical political philosophy could be applied to novel circumstances. Great danger and great opportunity go together in the postmodern age. We are left with the conclusion—however paradoxical—that Strauss's return to the ancients was part of his attempt to create "new modes and orders." Consult *The City and Man* (Chicago: University of Chicago Press, 1964), 9, 11 (hereafter cited as CM). See also Strauss's comments concerning Heidegger in SPPP, 33.

68. Strauss wrote, concerning Husserl's views: "As theory of knowledge naturalism must give an account of natural science, of its truth or validity. But every natural science accepts nature in the sense in which nature is intended by natural science, as given, as 'being in itself.' . . . Hence naturalism is completely blind to the riddles inherent in the 'givenness' of nature. It is constitutionally incapable of a radical critique of experience as such. The scientific positing or taking for granted of nature is preceded by and based upon the prescientific one, and the latter is as much in need of radical clarification as the first. Hence an adequate theory of knowledge cannot be

based on the naive acceptance of nature in any sense of nature" (SPPP, 35). See also CM, 11–12.

69. See SPPP, 31.

70. Ibid., 35.

71. Berns's essay, "The Prescientific World and Historicism: Some Reflections on Strauss, Heidegger, and Husserl," is in *Leo Strauss's Thought*, 169–82. See pp. 169–70.

72. SPPP, 31.

73. Ibid.

74. This acceptance is tantamount to a rejection of nature, as Plato understood it. Nature, applied to the social and political realm, resupposes something common to all humans. Thus Strauss understood this move to parallel, essentially, the claims by the sophists that all norms are conventional and thus political science is part of rhetoric. See CM, 16–17.

75. SPPP, 36.

76. Strauss emphasized that for Socrates political philosophy was not distinct from philosophy because "each part of the whole, and hence in particular the political sphere, is in a sense open to the whole." Aristotle, on the other hand, created political science "as one discipline . . . among a number of disciplines" (CM, 20–21).

77. SPPP, 34.

78. See WPP, 91.

79. CM, 20.

80. This observation must not be construed to mean that philosophers do not seek to know divine things. On the contrary, their attraction, which Strauss called a madness or mania, was precisely to the hidden origins of the whole. So while their lives are oriented to the divine, they gain only knowledge of their ignorance on this most important of subjects. See CM, 20–21, 241.

81. See, for example, CM, 29.

82. WPP, 10.

83. FPP, 222.

84. Ibid., 229.

85. Ibid., 233. See also NRH, 74–76.

86. Ibid., 225. See also WPP, 11.

87. Ibid., 219.

88. See WPP, 27, and Stanley Rosen's excellent book, *Hermeneutics as Politics* (New York: Oxford University Press, 1987), 127–28.

89. NRH, 124.

90. Rosen, *Hermeneutics as Politics*, 131.

91. Thomas Pangle noted this point in his introduction to SPPP, 4. See also his references.

92. See CM, 13–14, for a counterexample.

93. WPP, 38–39.

94. CM, 119–20.

95. Ibid., 121.

96. SPPP, 3.

97. Ibid., 3–5.

98. See Strauss, *Socrates and Aristophanes* (Chicago: University of Chicago Press, 1966), esp. 311–14.

99. CM, 240, 241.

100. Ibid., 21.

101. Ibid., 51.

102. At the end of paragraph fifty-nine Strauss noted the need for a new beginning, so paragraphs sixty through seventy-seven form a section. The discussion in the text concerns paragraph sixty-nine.

103. CM, 127.

104. The philosopher produces nothing useful for everyday life. He has no art or craft that brings him money or provides the city with anything. Consequently, the philosopher needs the city to produce all the things necessary for bodily life. The philosopher needs the city, but the city has no need for the philosopher. He must make himself acceptable to the city or else be exposed as a danger—or at the very least as useless. Aristophanes exposed Socrates, Plato and Xenophon exhibited the changed philosopher who sought to assist the city. Socrates' concern for the health of the city was based, not upon personal concerns, but upon the fate of philosophy. If the world was to see future philosophers they would require cities—cities that were not pathologically frightened of philosophers. For this reason Socrates chose death rather than escape.

CHAPTER 7. THE MYSTIC

1. Something of a paradox shades Voegelin's understanding of philosophy as resistance to disorder. All philosophy, as Voegelin employed the word, emerges from a powerfully felt sense of disorder, which is as true of Anselm as of Plato—indeed of Hegel, Marx, and especially Nietzsche. The presence of widespread hunger, suffering, injustice, and the like might inspire one to seek some new order—to posit some felicitous future awaiting human creativity. So also might the destruction of the old gods send one in search of new symbols of order. Nonetheless, whether it is the creation of ideological dream worlds or the recovery, in a new and more differentiated form, of the spiritual source of human order, philosophy requires disorder—history requires the dyad, disorder and the search for order. The process has, at this most superficial level, a structure reminiscent of Hegel's system.

2. OH 4, 237.

3. When puzzling over several questions concerning consciousness, Voegelin emphasized that the "reasons [or answers to the problems] had to be sought, not in a theory of consciousness, but concretely in the constitutions of the responding and verifying consciousness. And that concrete consciousness was my own" (*Anamnesis*, ed. and trans. Gerhart Niemeyer [Notre Dame: University of Notre Dame Press, 1978], 12; hereafter cited as AN).

4. Ibid., 11.

5. Voegelin examined this problem with regard to his own use of a reified "reality." In the context of his analysis of Plato's use of the word "vision" to suggest "an event in the cognitive process of reality," Voegelin wrote that "the partners of the encounter [in the vision] must not be converted into the grammatical subjects of such statements of 'Plato thinks . . .' or 'God reveals . . .'; a Platonic *opsis* ["vision"] is neither a Cartesian *cogito* nor a revealed doctrine. Faced by this difficulty, one might then feel tempted to make 'reality' the grammatical subject and to predicate of it the process of becoming luminous in the vision. In fact, I have used this proposition more than once myself, in order to avoid hypostatizing the partners to the encounter. But its use would be a misuse if it were to suggest 'reality' as a something about which propositions can be advanced short of the experiences analyzed. For as soon as we ask further what this 'reality' that now has become the grammatical subject 'really' is, we can only say that it is as what it appears when it becomes luminous for itself in the visionary event. Again, the transformation of the term into the subject of a defining proposition leads only back to the insight of the vision itself." The quote is on pp. 230–31 of Voegelin's very suggestive essay, "The Beginning and the Beyond," in *What Is History? and Other Late Unpublished Writings*, ed. Thomas A. Hollweck and Paul Caringella, vol. 28 of *The Collected Works of Eric Voegelin* (Baton Rouge: Louisiana State University Press, 1990); hereafter cited as CW 28.

6. Voegelin wrote often on this subject, and I cite one example: "In the event of the *opsis* ["vision"] and its language we reach the limit at which language does not merely refer to reality but is reality emerging as the luminous 'word' from the divine-human encounter" (CW 28, 231; see also p. 184).

7. See, for instance, CW 12, 344.

8. For most of his career Voegelin freely associated the word with his work. Late in life he came to think the word too much a product of modern forms of dividing up philosophy. See, for instance, CW 12, 197–98.

9. See Chapter 1, "The Beginning of the Beginning," in OH 5. Because humans are thrown into a story—the story of reality—one's life begins in the middle. Only through exploration of the meaning of the story in which one participates does "the beginning" become clear. The classical expression of the beginning, as Voegelin pointed out, is in Genesis 1.

10. OH 1, 5.

11. Ibid., 3.

12. Ibid., ix.

13. More precisely, "pragmatic" events, as Voegelin called them, made cosmological symbols of order dubious. Philosophers and prophets destroyed the cosmological order by supplying more adequate symbols of reality, thus rendering older symbols unbelievable.

14. OH 4, 77.

15. The question of beginning emerges when one discovers the beyond. See, for instance, OH 4, 7–20.

16. Glenn Hughes, *Mystery and Myth in the Philosophy of Eric Voegelin* (Columbia: University of Missouri Press, 1993), 11–12. Hughes has written a book about Voegelin's philosophy of consciousness, myth, and history that is clear and largely disentangled, or at least distanced, from Voegelin's jargon. A noble achievement. His book helped clarify my thinking on a number of points, though differences in interpretation remain.

17. Voegelin pointed to his 1928 book, *Ueber die Form des amerikanischen Geistes* (Tübingen: J.C.B. Mohr, 1928), as his earliest effort to create "a new philosophy of consciousness." See his Foreword to the German edition of *Anamnesis* as translated in *The Beginning and the Beyond: Papers from the Gadamer and Voegelin Conferences*, ed. Frederick Lawrence (Chico, Calif.: Scholars Press, 1984), 35.

18. Voegelin never distinguished among different positions staked out by Husserl over his career.

19. AN, 16–18.

20. Ibid., 19.

21. It has become commonplace to recognize the influence of Schelling, Kant, and Hegel on Voegelin's thought. However, few people have worked to expose the nature of these influences. With regard to the influence of Hegel, two interesting sources deserve attention. Paul Gottfried wrote an overlooked book on the influence of Hegel on the American right, *The Search for Historical Meaning: Hegel and the Postwar American Right* (Dekalb: Northern Illinois University Press, 1986). His discussion of Voegelin is instructive. Also, Voegelin engaged in a published exchange with Thomas J. J. Altizer who, in a review essay of Voegelin's "On Hegel: A Study in Sorcery," found that Voegelin was engaged in patricide. See *Journal of American Academy of Religion* 43 (1975): 765–72. See also Voegelin's response in CW 12, 292–303.

22. OH 5, 15–16.

23. CW 12, 121, 133. See also p. 131.

24. Translation is found in *The Beginning and the Beyond*, 58.

25. CW 28, 189.

26. Ibid., 229.

27. OH 5, 38.

28. "By virtue of his imaginative responsiveness man is a creative partner in the movement of reality toward its truth" (ibid.).

29. Ibid., 41.

30. "The folly of responding to the divine appeal by denial or evasion is just as much a human possibility as the positive response" (CW 28, 199).

31. The conditions of the disorder dictate the nature of the search. For Plato the search could proceed rather directly because the cosmological symbols had retained their integrity, even if they were no longer sufficient. In the modern era, countless efforts to gain dominion over reality have so confused the issues as to make the symbols opaque. Voegelin, therefore, had first to escape the restrictive doctrines of his time—especially the various forms (recognized or not) of positivism.

32. OH 1, xiii–xiv.

33. See AN, 113.

34. Ibid., 92.

35. Ibid., 93.

36. AN, 93; OH 4, 190.

37. See AN, 114, for a graph of this structure.

38. Voegelin often identified the psyche as the site and the sensorium of human participation with the divine presence. He used the same description, nonetheless, for consciousness, and consciousness and psyche come very close to collapsing into one another.

39. AN, 95–96.

40. CW 28, 227.

41. AN, 149.

42. Hughes, *Mystery and Myth in the Philosophy of Eric Voegelin*, 27; emphasis in original.

43. See OH 4, 8–9, 71–73. See also Hughes, *Mystery and Myth in the Philosophy of Eric Voegelin*, 43–44.

44. CW 28, 185.

45. Ibid., 218. See also p. 185 for discussion of the exegetical nature of terms like "immanent" and "transcendent."

46. Ibid., 221–22.

47. In another context Voegelin wrote that "the experience of consciousness . . . is not phenomenal, but not noumenal, but even the *noumena* of *Vernunft* are not the *noumena* of being as a whole. That being which is the ground of all experienceable particular being is an ontological hypothesis without which the experienced reality of the ontic nexus in human existence remains incomprehensible, but it is nowhere a datum of human existence rather it is always strictly transcendence that we can approach only through meditation. It cannot be drawn from that Beyond of finiteness into finiteness itself. Our human finiteness is always within being" (AN, 32).

48. NSP, 122.

49. Voegelin explored the meanings of the root words for "fool" going back to Hebrew usage, especially in the Psalms, and Greek usage, especially by Plato. See the section "folly and theology" found in the essay "The Beginning and the Beyond" in CW 28, 198–203.

50. Voegelin argued further that the Christian order, at the beginning of Scholasticism, was experiencing numerous tensions—from emerging nations to new religious orders to more general questions concerning the relationship between secular and spiritual authority. Keen minds during periods of such change challenge traditional beliefs and call for answers based upon reason rather than biblical authority.

51. CW 28, 205.

52. See, for instance, CW 12, 127, 132–33. "The imaginative play has its hard core of reality as its is motivated by man's trust (*pistis*) in reality as intelligibly ordered, as a Cosmos. Our perspectival experiences of reality in process may render no more than fragments of insight, the fragmentary elements may be heterogeneous, and they may look even incommensurable,

but the trust in the underlying oneness of reality, its coherence, lastingness, constancy of structure, order, and intelligibility, will inspire the creation of images which express the ordered wholeness sensed in the depth." Surely, Voegelin and his critics would agree that in the late modern era there is little *pistis* to go around.

53. See Eugene Webb, *Eric Voegelin: Philosopher of History* (Seattle: University of Washington Press, 1981), 267. See also OH 5, 24.

54. The problem extends well beyond the few "speculative" philosophers of history. One is apt to hear or read phrases like "History tells us" nearly everywhere, even among historians. Voegelin would have considered this a problem extending well beyond naiveté and suggesting a profound and basic misunderstanding of the nature of human existence.

55. Voegelin thought that Toynbee (and Spengler) made a crucial mistake by considering ordering experiences and their symbols as products of civilizations rather than of their "constitutive forms." See OH 1, 126.

56. CW 12, 97.

57. OH 1, ix.

58. See Hughes, *Mystery and Myth in the Philosophy of Eric Voegelin*, 106–7, for a discussion of the distinction between universe and cosmos in Voegelin's work.

59. See OH 1, 21.

60. The problem of the place of Israel in these cycles of civilizations is an illustrative example. The Toynbee presented here is the earlier Toynbee. He later came to rethink much of his original enterprise.

61. See OH 4, 1.

62. See ibid., 7 and chap. 5.

63. This discovery surprised Voegelin because he had thought that a cosmological society could not conceive of history as a course rather than a cycle.

64. OH 4, 6.

65. See ibid., 1–7, for Voegelin's discussion of the foregoing problems.

66. Ibid., 58.

67. See ibid., 306.

68. Ibid., 304.

69. Plato's discovery also created a before-and-after experience. He became aware of history as the process of human-divine conversation.

70. OH 4, 332.

71. "The recognition of universal mankind as an eschatological index penetrates to the center of the problem presented by history as a dimension of humanity. Without universality, there would be no mankind other than the aggregate of members of a biological species; there would be no more a history of mankind than there is a history catkind or horsekind. If mankind is to have history, its members must be able to respond to the movement of divine presence in their souls. But if that is the condition, then the mankind who has history is constituted by the God to whom man responds. A scattering of societies, belonging to the same biological type, thus, is discovered to

be one mankind with one history, by virtue of participation in the same flux of divine presence'' (OH 4, 305).

72. Ibid., 242.

73. ''There is no history other than the history constituted in the metaxy of differentiating consciousness'' (ibid., 243).

74. Translation is found in *The Beginning and the Beyond*, 35.

CHAPTER 8. STRAUSS, VOEGELIN, AND THE CONSERVATIVE IMAGINATION

1. By emphasizing their role in conservative intellectual circles here, I do not suggest that this was their only role. One might wish to look at their influence among philosophers or political scientists or classicists. Of course, they fit into several stories of European life as well.

2. Henry Adams, *The Education of Henry Adams* (Boston: Houghton Mifflin Company, 1973), 388.

3. The purest expression of this view is found in the works of Robert Nisbet.

4. Russell Kirk, *Prospects for Conservatives* (Washington, D.C.: Regnery Gateway, 1989), 228–29.

5. Quoted in Russell Kirk's anthology, *The Portable Conservative Reader* (New York: Penguin Books, 1982), 22–23.

BIBLIOGRAPHY

MAJOR WORKS BY LEO STRAUSS

Consult the bibliography prepared by Thomas L. Pangle in Strauss's *Studies in Platonic Political Philosophy* (see below) for a more exhaustive list.

The Argument and the Action of Plato's Laws. Chicago: University of Chicago Press, 1975.

The City and Man. Chicago: University of Chicago Press, 1964.

"Correspondence Concerning Modernity." Exchange of letters with Karl Lowith. *Independent Journal of Philosophy* 4 (1983): 105–19.

History of Political Philosophy. Coedited with Joseph Cropsey. "Introduction," "Plato," and "Marsilius of Padua." Chicago: University of Chicago Press, 1987.

Liberalism Ancient and Modern. Ithaca: Cornell University Press, 1989.

"The Mutual Influence of Theology and Philosophy." *Independent Journal of Philosophy* 8 (1979): 111–18.

Natural Right and History. Chicago: University of Chicago Press, 1950.

"On Collingwood's Philosophy of History." *Review of Metaphysics* 5 (June 1952): 559–86.

On Tyranny: An Interpretation of Xenophon's Hiero. Revised and expanded edition, including the Strauss-Kojeve correspondence. Edited by Victor Gourevitch and Michael Roth. New York: Free Press, 1991.

Persecution and the Art of Writing. Chicago: University of Chicago Press, 1988.

Philosophy and Law. Translated by Fred Baumann, foreword by Ralph Lerner. Philadelphia: Jewish Publication Society, 1987.

"Philosophy as Rigorous Science and Political Philosophy." *Journal of Political Philosophy* 2 (Summer 1971): 1–9.

Political Philosophy: Six Essays by Leo Strauss. Edited by Hilail Gildin. Indianapolis: Pegasus, 1975.

"Political Philosophy and the Crisis of Our Time." In *The Post-Behavioral Era: Perspectives on Political Science,* edited by George J. Graham and George W. Carey, 217–42. New York: David McKay, 1972.

The Political Philosophy of Hobbes: Its Basis and Its Genesis. Translated by Elsa M. Sinclair. Chicago: University of Chicago Press, 1952.

The Rebirth of Classical Political Rationalism: An Introduction to the

Thought of Leo Strauss. Edited by Thomas L. Pangle. Chicago: University of Chicago Press, 1989.

Socrates and Aristophanes. Chicago: University of Chicago Press, 1966.

Spinoza's Critique of Religion. New York: Schocken Books, 1965.

Studies in Platonic Political Philosophy. Introduction and Bibliography by Thomas L. Pangle. Chicago: University of Chicago Press, 1983.

Thoughts on Machiavelli. Chicago: University of Chicago Press, 1958.

What Is Political Philosophy? Chicago: University of Chicago Press, 1988.

Xenophon's Socrates. Ithaca: Cornell University Press, 1972.

Xenophon's Socratic Discourse: An Interpretation of the "Oeconomicus." Ithaca: Cornell University Press, 1970.

MAJOR WORKS BY ERIC VOEGELIN

Consult Barry Cooper, *The Political Theory of Eric Voegelin* (see below) for an extensive bibliography of Voegelin's works.

Anamnesis. Translated and edited by Gerhart Niemeyer. Notre Dame: University of Notre Dame Press, 1978.

Anamnesis: Zur Theorie der Geschichte und Politik. Munich: R. Piper and Company, 1966.

Autobiographical Reflections. Edited by Ellis Sandoz. Baton Rouge: Louisiana State University Press, 1989.

Der autoritaere Staat. Vienna: Springer, 1936.

"Bakunin's Confession." *Journal of Politics* 8 (1946): 24–43.

The Collected Works of Eric Voegelin. 3 vols. to date. Vol. 12, *Published Essays, 1966–1985,* ed. Ellis Sandoz, 1990; vol. 27, *The Nature of the Law and Related Legal Writings,* ed. Robert Anthony Pascal, James Lee Babin, and John William Corrington, 1991; vol. 28, *What Is History? and Other Late Unpublished Writings,* ed. Thomas A. Hollweck and Paul Caringella, 1990. Baton Rouge: Louisiana State University Press.

Conversations with Eric Voegelin. Edited by R. Eric O'Connor. Thomas More Institute Papers, no. 76. Montreal: Perry Printing, 1980.

From Enlightenment to Revolution. Edited by John H. Hallowell. Durham: Duke University Press, 1975.

"The Growth of the Race Idea." *Review of Politics* 2 (1940): 283–317.

"Kelsen's Pure Theory of Law." *Political Science Quarterly* 17 (1927): 268–76.

"Liberalism and Its History." Translated by Mary and Keith Algozin. *Review of Politics* 36 (1972): 504–20.

"Machiavelli's Prince: Background and Formation." *Review of Politics* 13 (1951): 142–68.

The New Science of Politics. Chicago: University of Chicago Press, 1952.

"Nietzsche, the Crisis, and the War." *Journal of Politics* 6 (1944): 177–212.

Order and History. 5 vols. Vol. 1, *Israel and Revelation,* 1956; vol. 2, *The World of the Polis,* 1957; vol. 3, *Plato and Aristotle,* 1957; vol. 4, *The Ecu-*

menic Age, 1974; vol. 5, *In Search of Order,* 1987. Baton Rouge: Louisiana State University Press.

"The Origins of Scientism." *Social Research* 15 (1948): 462–94.

"The Origins of Totalitarianism." With a reply from Hannah Arendt. *Review of Politics* 15 (1953): 68–85.

"The Oxford Political Philosophers." *Philosophical Quarterly* 3 (April 1953): 97–114.

"The Philosophy of Existence: Plato's *Gorgias.*" *Review of Politics* 11 (1949): 477–98.

Political Religions. Translated by T. J. DiNapoli and E. S. Easterly III. Lewiston, N.Y.: Edwin Mellen Press, 1986.

Rasse und Staat. Tübingen: J.C.B. Mohr, 1933.

Science, Politics, and Gnosticism. Chicago: Henry Regnery Company, 1968.

"The Theory of Legal Science: A Review." *Louisiana Law Review* 4 (1942): 554–72.

"Toynbee's *History* as a Search for Truth." In *The Intent of Toynbee's History,* ed. Edward T. Gargan, 183–98. Chicago: Loyola University Press, 1961.

Ueber die Form des amerikanischen Geistes. Tübingen: J.C.B. Mohr, 1928.

The Voegelin Papers. Hoover Institution Archives, Stanford, California.

SECONDARY WORKS

Books

Adams, Henry. *The Education of Henry Adams.* Boston: Houghton Mifflin Company, 1973.

Arendt, Hannah. *The Origins of Totalitarianism.* New York: Harcourt, Brace, and Company, 1951.

Bloom, Allan. *The Closing of the American Mind.* New York: Simon and Schuster, 1987.

Boorstin, Daniel J. *The Genius of American Politics.* Chicago: University of Chicago Press, 1953.

_____. *The Image: A Guide to Pseudo-events in America.* New York: Harper and Row, 1964.

Boyer, Paul. *By the Bombs Early Light.* New York: Pantheon, 1985.

Buckley, William F., Jr. *Up From Liberalism: 25th Anniversary Edition.* Briarcliff Manor, N.Y.: Stein and Day, 1985.

Burnham, James. *The Machiavellians: Defenders of Freedom.* New York: John Day, 1943.

_____. *Suicide of the West.* Chicago: Regnery Gateway, 1985.

Cooper, Barry. *The Political Theory of Eric Voegelin.* Toronto Studies in Theology, vol. 27. Lewiston, N.Y.: Edwin Mellen Press, 1986.

Diggins, John Patrick. *The Proud Decades.* New York: W. W. Norton, 1988.

_____. *Up From Communism.* New York: Harper and Row, 1975.

Drury, Shadia B. *The Political Ideas of Leo Strauss.* New York: St. Martin's Press, 1988.

Dunn, John. *The Political Thought of John Locke.* Cambridge: Cambridge University Press, 1969.

Eliot, T. S. *The Idea of Christian Society.* New York: Harcourt, Brace, and Company, 1940.

Emberley, Peter, and Barry Cooper, eds. *Faith and Political Philosophy: The Correspondence Between Leo Strauss and Eric Voegelin, 1934–1964.* University Park: Pennsylvania State University Press, 1993.

Fermi, Laura. *Illustrious Immigrants.* Chicago: University of Chicago Press, 1968.

Ferry, Luc. *Rights: The New Quarrel Between the Ancients and the Moderns.* Chicago: University of Chicago Press, 1990.

Fleming, Donald, and Bernard Bailyn, eds. *The Intellectual Migration.* Cambridge, Mass.: Belknap Press, 1968.

Gadamer, Hans-Georg. *Truth and Method.* New York: Seabury Press, 1975.

Germino, Dante. *Beyond Ideology: The Revival of Political Theory.* Chicago: University of Chicago Press, 1967.

———. *Political Philosophy and the Open Society.* Baton Rouge: Louisiana State University Press, 1982.

Gottfried, Paul. *The Conservative Movement.* New York: Twayne Publishers, 1993.

———. *The Search for Historical Meaning: Hegel and the Postwar American Right.* Dekalb: Northern Illinois University Press, 1986.

Graham, George J., and George W. Carey, eds. *The Post-Behavioral Era: Perspectives on Political Science.* New York: David McKay, 1972.

Gunnell, John. *Between Philosophy and Politics: The Alienation of Political Theory.* Amherst: University of Massachusetts Press, 1986.

———. *Political Theory: Tradition and Interpretation.* Cambridge, Mass.: Winthrop Press, 1979.

Harbour, William R. *The Foundations of Conservative Thought: An Anglo-American Tradition in Perspective.* Notre Dame: University of Notre Dame Press, 1982.

Hartz, Louis. *The Liberal Tradition in America.* New York: Harcourt, Brace, and Company, 1955.

Hayek, Friedrich A. *The Road to Serfdom.* Chicago: University of Chicago Press, 1956.

Hays, Peter, ed. *Lessons and Legacies: The Meaning of the Holocaust in a Changing World.* Evanston: Northwestern Illinois Press, 1991.

Heidegger, Martin. *Being and Time.* Translated by John Macquarrie and Edward Robinson. New York: Harper and Row, 1962.

Hoeveler, J. David, Jr. *Watch on the Right: Conservative Intellectuals in the Reagan Era.* Madison: University of Wisconsin Press, 1991.

Hughes, Glenn. *Mystery and Myth in the Philosophy of Eric Voegelin.* Columbia: University of Missouri Press, 1993.

Hughes, H. Stuart. *The Sea Change.* New York: Harper and Row, 1975.

Husserl, Edmund. *The Crisis of European Sciences and Transcendental Phenomenology: An Introduction to Phenomenological Philosophy*. Translated with an introduction by David Carr. Evanston: Northwestern University Press, 1970.

Jaspers, Karl. *The Origin and Goal of History*. Translated by Michael Bullock. London: Routledge and Kegan Paul, 1953.

Jay, Martin. *The Dialectical Imagination*. New York: Little, Brown, 1973.

Jonas, Hans. *The Gnostic Religion*. Boston: Beacon Press, 1958.

Kazin, Alfred. *Starting Out in the Thirties*. Boston: Little, Brown, 1965.

Kendall, Willmoore. *The Conservative Affirmation*. Chicago: Henry Regnery, 1985.

Keulman, Kenneth. *The Balance of Consciousness: Eric Voegelin's Political Theory*. University Park: Pennsylvania State University Press, 1990.

Kirby, John, and William M. Thompson, eds. *Voegelin and the Theologian: Ten Studies in Interpretation*. Toronto Studies in Theology, vol. 10. Lewiston, N.Y.: Edwin Mellen Press, 1983.

Kirk, Russell. *The Conservative Mind*. Seventh ed. Chicago: Henry Regnery, 1986.

———. *A Program for Conservatives*. Chicago: Henry Regnery, 1954.

———. *Prospects for Conservatives*. Washington, D.C.: Regnery Gateway, 1989.

Kloppenberg, James. *Uncertain Victory*. New York: Oxford University Press, 1986.

Lawrence, Frederick, ed. *The Beginning and the Beyond: Papers from the Gadamer and Voegelin Conferences; Supplementary Issue of Lonergan Workshop, Volume 4*. Chico, Calif.: Scholars Press, 1984.

Lippmann, Walter. *Drift and Mastery*. New York: Mitchell Kennerley, 1914. Reprinted, Englewood Cliffs, N.J.: Prentice-Hall, 1961.

———. *Essays in the Public Philosophy*. Boston: Little, Brown, 1955.

———. *The Good Society*. Boston: Little, Brown, 1937.

———. *An Inquiry into the Principles of the Good Society*. Boston: Little, Brown, 1937.

———. *A Preface to Politics*. New York: Mitchell Kennerley, 1913.

———. *Public Opinion*. New York: Harcourt, Brace, 1922.

Lora, Ronald. *Conservative Minds in America*. Westport, Conn.: Greenwood Press, 1979.

Lowith, Karl. *Meaning in History*. Phoenix Book edition. Chicago: University of Chicago Press, 1964.

McKnight, Stephen A., ed. *Eric Voegelin's Search for Order in History*. Baton Rouge: Louisiana State University Press, 1978.

Nash, George H. *The Conservative Intellectual Movement in America Since 1945*. New York: Basic Books, 1976.

Niebuhr, Reinhold. *The Irony of American History*. New York: Charles Scribner's Sons, 1952.

Nietzsche, Friedrich. *Beyond God and Evil: Prelude to a Philosophy of the Future*. New York: Penguin Books, 1990.

_____. *Thus Spake Zarathustra*. New York: Tudor, 1936.

Nisbet, Robert. *Conservatism: Dream and Reality*. Minneapolis: University of Minnesota Press, 1986.

_____. *The Quest for Community*. San Francisco: Institute for Contemporary Studies Press, 1990.

O'Neil, William L. *American High: The Years of Confidence, 1945–1960*. New York: Free Press, 1986.

Opitz, Peter J., and Gregor Sebba, eds. *The Philosophy of Order: Essays on History, Consciousness, and Politics*. Stuttgart: Klett-Cotta, 1981.

Pells, Richard H. *The Liberal Mind in a Conservative Age: American Intellectuals in the 1940s and 1950s*. New York: Harper and Row, 1985.

Plato. *The Collected Dialogues of Plato*. Edited by Edith Hamilton and Huntington Cairns. New York: Pantheon Books, 1961.

Rosen, Stanley. *The Ancients and Moderns: Rethinking Modernity*. New Haven: Yale University Press, 1989.

_____. *Hermeneutics as Politics*. New York: Oxford University Press, 1987.

Rossiter, Clinton L. *Conservatism in America: The Thankless Persuasion*. Revised ed. New York: Alfred A. Knopf, 1962.

Rubenstein, Richard. *The Cunning of History*. New York: Harper and Row, 1975.

Sandoz, Ellis. *The Voegelinian Revolution: A Biographical Introduction*. Baton Rouge: Louisiana State University Press, 1981.

Sandoz, Ellis, ed. *Eric Voegelin's Significance for the Modern Mind*. Baton Rouge: Louisiana State University Press, 1991.

_____. *Eric Voegelin's Thought: A Critical Appraisal*. Durham: Duke University Press, 1982.

Schlesinger, Arthur. *The Vital Center*. Boston: Houghton Mifflin Company, 1949.

Steel, Ronald. *Walter Lippmann and the American Century*. New York: Vintage, 1981.

Trilling, Lionel. *The Liberal Imagination*. New York: Viking Press, 1950.

Udoff, Alan, ed. *Leo Strauss's Thought: Toward a Critical Engagement*. Boulder, Colo.: Lynne Rienner Publishers, 1991.

Walsh, David. *After Ideology: Recovering the Spiritual Foundations of Freedom*. San Francisco: HarperCollins, 1990.

Weaver, Richard. *Ideas Have Consequences*. Chicago: University of Chicago Press, 1984.

Webb, Eugene. *Eric Voegelin: Philosopher of History*. Seattle: University of Washington Press, 1981.

_____. *Philosophers of Consciousness: Polanyi, Lonergan, Voegelin, Ricoeur, Girard, Kierkegaard*. Seattle: University of Washington Press, 1988.

Articles

Anastaplo, George. "On How Eric Voegelin Has Read Plato and Aristotle." *Independent Journal of Philosophy* 5–6 (1988): 85–91.

Andrew, Edward. "Descent to the Cave." *Review of Politics* 45 (October 1983): 510–35.

Beiner, Ronald. "Hannah Arendt and Leo Strauss: The Uncommenced Dialogue." *Political Theory* 18 (May 1990): 238–54.

Benardete, Seth. "Leo Strauss's *The City and Man.*" *Political Science Reviewer* 8 (Fall 1978): 853–66.

Bloom, Allan. "Leo Strauss: September 20, 1899–October 18, 1973." *Political Theory* 2 (November 1974): 372–92.

Bruell, Christopher. "A Return to Classical Political Philosophy and the Understanding of the American Founding." *Review of Politics* 53 (Winter 1991): 173–86.

———. "Strauss on Xenophon's Socrates." *Political Science Reviewer* 14 (Fall 1984): 263–318.

Burnyeat, M. F. "Sphinx Without a Secret." *New York Review* 32 (30 May 1985): 30–36.

Caringella, Paul. "Eric Voegelin: Philosopher of Divine Presence." *Modern Age* 34 (Spring 1990): 7–22.

Cropsey, Joseph. "Leo Strauss: A Bibliography and Memorial, 1889–1973." *Interpretation* 5 (1975): 133–47.

Dallmayr, Fred. "Voegelin's Search for Order." *Journal of Politics* 51 (May 1989): 411–30.

Dannhauser, Werner J. "Leo Strauss: Becoming Naive Again." *American Scholar* 44 (1974–1975): 636–42.

Dunn, John. "Justice and the Interpretation of Locke's Political Theory." *Political Studies* 16 (1968): 68–87.

Fortin, Ernest L. "Gadamer on Strauss: An Interview." *Interpretation* 12 (January 1984): 1–13.

Fradkin, Hillel. "Philosophy and Law: Leo Strauss as a Student of Medieval Jewish Thought." *Review of Politics* 53 (Winter 1991): 40–52.

Germino, Dante. "Blasphemy and Leo Strauss's Machiavelli." *Review of Politics* 53 (Winter 1991): 146–56.

———. "The Revival of Political Theory." *Journal of Politics* 25 (August 1963): 437–60.

———. "Second Thoughts on Leo Strauss's Machiavelli." *Journal of Politics* 28 (1966): 794–817.

Gourevitch, Victor. "Philosophy and Politics: I" and "Philosophy and Politics: II." *Review of Metaphysics* 22 (September 1968): 58–84 and 22 (December 1968): 281–328.

Grant, George P. "Tyranny and Wisdom: A Comment on the Controversy Between Leo Strauss and Alexander Kojeve." *Social Research* 21 (1964): 45–72.

Gunnell, John. "The Myth of the Tradition." *American Political Science Review* 72 (1978): 122–34.

———. "Political Theory and Politics: The Case of Leo Strauss." *Political Theory* 13 (August 1985): 339–61.

_____. "Strauss Before Straussianism: Reason, Revelation, and Nature." *Review of Politics* 53 (Winter 1991): 53–74.

Himmelfarb, Milton. "On Leo Strauss." *Commentary* 58 (May 1974): 60–66.

Hollinger, David. "Science and Anarchy: Walter Lippmann's *Drift and Mastery.*" *American Quarterly* 29 (1977); 463–75.

Jaffa, Harry. "Crisis of the Strauss Divided: The Legacy Reconsidered." *Social Research* 54 (Autumn 1987): 579–603.

_____. "The Legacy of Leo Strauss." *Claremont Review* 3 (Fall 1984): 14–21.

_____. "The Legacy of Leo Strauss Defended." *Claremont Review* 4 (Spring 1985): 20–24.

Jung, Hwa Jol. "A Post-Polemic." *American Political Science Review* 58 (June 1964): 400–401.

_____. "Strauss's Conception of Political Philosophy: A Critique." *Review of Politics* 29 (October 1967): 492–517.

_____. "Two Critics of Scientism: Leo Strauss and Edmund Husserl." *Independent Journal of Philosophy* 3 (1978): 11–25.

Kennington, Richard. "Strauss's *Natural Right and History.*" *Review of Metaphysics* 35 (September 1981): 57–86.

Lampert, Laurence. "The Argument of Leo Strauss in *What Is Political Philosophy.*" *Modern Age* 22 (Winter 1978): 38–46.

Lenzner, Steven J. "Strauss's Three Burkes: The Problem of Edmund Burke in *Natural Right and History.*" *Political Theory* 19 (August 1991): 364–90.

Levine, David Lawrence. "Without Malice but with Forethought: A Response to Burnyeat." *Review of Politics* 53 (Winter 1991): 200–218.

Lowenthal, David. "Leo Strauss's *Studies in Platonic Political Philosophy.*" *Interpretation* 13 (September 1985): 297–320.

Mansfield, Harvey C. J. "Strauss's Machiavelli." *Political Theory* 3 (November 1975): 372–83.

Neumann, Harry. "Civic Piety and Socratic Atheism: An Interpretation of Strauss's *Socrates and Aristophanes.*" *Independent Journal of Philosophy* 2 (1978): 33–37.

Nicgorski, Walter. "Leo Strauss and Liberal Education." *Interpretation* 13 (1984): 233–50.

Nieli, Russell. "Eric Voegelin's Evolving Ideas on Gnosticism, Mysticism, and Modern Radical Politics." *Independent Journal of Philosophy* 5–6 (1988): 93–102.

Niemeyer, Gerhart. "The Depth and Height of Political Order." *Review of Politics* 21 (1959): 588–96.

_____. "Eric Voegelin's Achievement." *Modern Age* 9 (1965): 132–40.

_____. "Eric Voegelin's Philosophy and the Drama of Mankind." *Modern Age* 20 (1976): 28–39.

_____. "God and Man, World and Society: The Last Work of Eric Voegelin." *Review of Politics* 51 (1989): 107–23.

_____. "The Order of Consciousness." *Review of Politics* 30 (1968): 251–56.

_____. "The Order of History and the History of Order." *Review of Politics* 19 (1957): 403–9.

Pangle, Thomas L. "On the Epistolary Dialogue Between Leo Strauss and Eric Voegelin." *Review of Politics* 53 (Winter 1991): 100–125.

———. "The Platonism of Leo Strauss: A Reply to Harry Jaffa." *Claremont Review* 4 (Spring 1985): 18–20.

Parcel, A. J. "The Question of Machiavelli's Modernity." *Review of Politics* 53 (Spring 1991): 320–39.

Peterman, Larry. "Approaching Leo Strauss: Some Comments on *Thoughts on Machiavelli.*" *Political Science Reviewer* 16 (Fall 1986): 317–51.

Pocock, J. G. A. "Prophet and Inquisitor." *Political Theory* 3 (November 1975): 385–401.

Rhodes, James M. "Philosophy, Revelation, and Political Theory: Leo Strauss and Eric Voegelin." *Journal of Politics* 49 (1987): 1036–60.

Rosen, Stanley. "Order and History." *Review of Metaphysics* 12 (1958): 257–76.

Rothman, Stanley. "The Revival of Classical Political Philosophy: A Critique." *American Political Science Review* 56 (June 1962): 341–52.

Russell, Peter A. "Eric Voegelin: An Eschatological Direction to History?" *Fides et Historia* 22 (Fall 1990): 3–15.

Schaefer, David. "Leo Strauss and American Democracy: A Response to Wood and Holmes." *Review of Politics* 53 (Winter 1991): 187–99.

Schall, James V., S.J. "A Latitude for Statesmanship? Strauss and St. Thomas." *Review of Politics* 53 (Winter 1991): 126–45.

Sebba, Gregor. "Eric Voegelin: From Enlightenment to Universal Humanity." *Southern Review* 11 (1975): 918–25.

———. "Order and Disorders of the Soul: Eric Voegelin's Philosophy of History." *Southern Review* 3 (1967): 282–310.

———. "Prelude and Variations on the Theme of Eric Voegelin." *Southern Review* 13 (1977): 646–76.

Smith, Steven B. "Leo Strauss: Between Athens and Jerusalem." *Review of Politics* 53 (Winter 1991): 75–99.

Susser, Bernard. "Leo Strauss: The Ancient as Modern." *Political Studies* 36 (1988): 497–514.

Tarcov, Nathan. "On a Certain Critique of 'Straussianism.' " *Review of Politics* 53 (Winter 1991): 3–18.

———. "Philosophy and History: Tradition and Interpretation in the Work of Leo Strauss." *Polity* 16 (Fall 1983): 5–29.

Umphrey, Stewart. "Natural Right and Philosophy." *Review of Politics* 53 (Winter 1991): 19–39.

Walsh, David. "Voegelin's Response to the Disorder of the Age." *Review of Politics* 46 (1984): 266–87.

Ward, James F. "Experience and Political Philosophy: Notes on Reading Leo Straus." *Polity* 13 (Summer 1981): 668–87.

Webb, Eugene. "Politics and the Problem of a Philosophical Rhetoric in the Thought of Eric Voegelin." *Journal of Politics* 48 (1986): 260–73.

Weiss, Raymond L. "Voegelin's Biblical Hermeneutics." *Independent Journal of Philosophy* 5–6 (1988): 81–84.

West, Thomas G. "Leo Strauss and the American Founding." *Review of Politics* 53 (Winter 1991): 157–73.

Wiser, James L. "Philosophy and Human Order." *Political Science Reviewer* 2 (1972): 137–61.

———. "Voegelin's Concept of Gnosticism." *Review of Politics* 42 (1980): 92–104.

Yaffe, Martin D. "Leo Strauss as Judaic Thinker: Some First Notions." *Religious Studies Review* 17 (January 1991): 33–41.

INDEX